A PEWTER SPOON

An Architectural Odyssey

An autobiographical sketch
recalling highlights of one architect´s eclectic career

JAMES BAKER

Warning

*"...there is really not such a thing as a true memory. It is a record of
experience - but is (ones') experience a true record of reality?"*

Memory and the Law: British Psychological Society, 2008

A PEWTER SPOON

An Architectural Odyssey

Enquiries should be addressed to:

Morgan Baker

89 Fairweather

Cambridge, MA

02138 - USA

Front cover graphics:

Jane Page, Tavira, Portugal

Graphic Design by:

Quill & Apple

Publisher:

Quill & Apple

Mayfield, East Sussex

United Kingdom

Printed in the United Kingdom by:

Print2Demand

Westoning, Bedfordshire.

ISBN 978-0-9935775-4-3

ABOUT THE AUTHOR

James Baker was born in New York City in 1933 and spent his early childhood in Greenwich, Connecticut. The son of an architect, William Edgar Baker, Jr. and an artist, Violet Twachtman, the youngest daughter of the American Impressionist painter, John Henry Twachtman, Baker was subliminally tutored in the arts from an early age. Following his father's death in 1942 and his mother's consequent incapacity he spent the next few years in the care of aunts, uncles, cousins and obliging friends.

He was sent to Darrow School in 1944 to be under the avuncular care of Charles Lambert Heyniger, the brother of one of his father's Princeton classmates Sinclair Heyniger. From Darrow he went on to Princeton. Not altogether surprisingly, but against his mother's wishes he ultimately majored in architecture, graduating in 1954. Upon graduation he served as an artillery officer with the 11th Airborne Division, mostly in Munich. He went on to Yale in 1957, receiving his master's degree in architecture in 1960.

Like his father, his professional career has been eclectic. He has managed a conventional practice, worked as a developer-builder, entrepreneur, construction innovator and teacher. He has practiced his profession in twelve states and more than thirty countries/territories. After a professional life of fifty years, he is now retired, but still works on the occasional residential project and paints: for pleasure.

Baker has been married four times. He has four children and eight grandchildren. He now lives with his partner, Jill Jackson. They split their year between East Sussex, Devon and Sao Bras de Alportel, in Portugal's Algarve.

INTRODUCTION and APOLOGIES

A Pewter Spoon is an autobiographical sketch of one architect's professional odyssey, searching for an elusive and ill-defined architectural goal while enjoying, well, for the most part, the vicissitudes of the search. While personal and extra curricular events are woven into the text the main theme is always about a professional career and events pertaining to it.

Dates and events are based on a fallible memory, though, they are supported by a collection of some eighty contemporary journals, beginning in the nineteen sixties. It should be noted, (with appropriate apologies), that some journals, are partially incomplete with dates and/or events missing. On the whole, though, the journals have served as good 'aide memoires' of passed events, places and people.

An apology is required. I have called *A Pewter Spoon* an autobiographic 'sketch' as some events, meetings, persons etc. have been omitted in the story. The decision, 'for better or worse', is because the omitted, persons and events are not critical to the professional theme and story and would serve as unnecessary digressions, even though some digressions might be stories in themselves.

I thank my partner, Jill, for putting up with the boring bit of my writing this story but, more importantly, Jill has provided me with justified criticism and helpful comments. I also have been encouraged by volunteer readers including, Ronnie Brown, Karin Crooks and Brenda Niemand. My thanks to them for their editing and comments.

Crossways, 18 February 2019

Sharing a joke with my sister Marty: Porchuck Road ,1937

For

Morgan, Jamie, Trina, and Alden

Who may have wondered where I was and what I was doing those many years gone by:

and

Maggie, Ellie, Jamie, Noe, Grant, Rowen

Victoria, Molly, and Eleanor

Who may, sometime, wonder about what 'Gran'bear or 'Grandpa Jim' did:

and

Jill

Who may not wonder but is wonderful

CONTENTS

PREFACE

MAGGIE'S WEDDING

2017

Martha's Vineyard

On a sunny afternoon, the last day of August 2017, Nick Britten, owner of 'Mayfield Garage', drove Jill, my partner, and me to the Southampton docks to board the QM2 to New York. The QM2 would take us to Maggie's wedding. Nick is, perhaps, best described as our 'helpmeet'. We joke that we are his surrogate parents. He drives us to and from Gatwick Airport on our periodic visits to Sao Bras de Alportel in the Algarve where Jill has her holiday home, Monte do Cerrito. He looks after our mail when we are away and as an example of his general attention to us, Nick was the first to call when a young lady from Mayfield School, the boarding school, opposite 'Crossways' Jill's Mayfield home, demolished 'Crossway's' brick-arched gate.

Jill and I were on our way to my granddaughter Maggie's wedding. It would take place on Martha's Vineyard on the ninth of September. Maggie, was my eldest daughter Morgan's, eldest daughter, my eldest granddaughter. Morgan, a professional writer and professor (adjunct) at Emerson College and her husband Matt lived in Cambridge where Maggie and her sister, Ellie grew up. Maggie was engaged to Jay Farrell, a native of Montserrat. We didn't know Jay very well but certainly well enough to see him as a caring, cheerful and robust individual matching some of Maggie's own traits. Maggie, almost twenty-six, and Jay had been going together for some eight years and were living in LA where Maggie was an assistant to the president of Universal Pictures. Maggie and Jay got on well, were happy and in love. We thought it a good match and were pleased for them, enthusiastic about the wedding as well as the trip itself. Martha's Vineyard had been chosen as the site as it was, for all emotional purposes, Morgan's mother's (my first wife, Mary Brooks 'Molly' Griswold), ancestral home. Morgan and Matt were married there in 1988.

Jill and I had last been to the US two years earlier to attend my youngest daughter Trina's marriage (her second) to Curvin Huber. Trina, a successful professional equestrian since college, was now, after twenty-five years, happily, on the art faculty of Lesley University and Chair of the Animation Department. Having been injured on sufficient occasions as an equestrian Trina had finally chosen a less risky career: although to be accurate Trina still teaches riding to a selective clientele. Trina is both a Therapeutic Riding instructor and a certified Hunter Jumper Trainer. We had not seen my four children and six grandchildren, (two of my eight grandchildren are Jill's grandchildren) since Trina's wedding. Even then we didn't see Alden, my youngest son (from my marriage (second) to Catriona Shafer) or his wife Heidi and children Noe and Rowen. Alden, after a number of years as a paramedic, (amongst other work experiences), was settling into the professional medical career that my mother had wished for me. At the time Alden was finishing his medical studies at the University of Utah in Salt Lake City and was, as a result, unable to join in celebrating Trina's wedding. In his own words on entering medical school Alden told me, "Dad, I've tried every dead-end job I can find…this is what I need to do." Well done Alden: it would be good to see him.

Jamie, my eldest son would be conducting the ceremony under his aegis as a senior Article I federal judge. Jamie had recently retired as Chief Judge of the US Court of Appeals for the Armed Forces after serving as the National Security Council's Legal Advisor in the Clinton Administration. Jamie is currently writing a book about AI while a Wilhelm fellow at MIT's Centre for International Studies. Jamie is also looking for a new career in education: perhaps as a head of a school. He found the search tougher than expected (he is now Director of the Institute for National Security and Counter Terrorism at Syracuse University).

This would be the fifth or sixth joint US trip for Jill and me during our almost sixteen years together – a longer period than any of my four marriages. Jill and I had met while visiting an exhibition of Macartney-Snape drawings at the Sloane Club in London. The casual meeting, or whatever you would call it, led to a dinner on the 4th of December 2001 at the Bluebird restaurant (one of Conran's) on the second (US nomenclature) floor of a remodelled garage in Chelsea. The dinner almost didn't happen. Jill had a hard time finding a place to park her Range Rover and was seriously late. I was waiting for the elevator in order to leave when Jill, strikingly-dressed in one of her favourite (I was to learn) brown dresses adorned with a large plastic flower stepped off the elevator. (I quickly learned that Jill always dressed fashionably, usually in natural colours, her favourite.)

The meal was engaging (the food was good too) and we agreed to meet again. In contrast to my own formal education Jill announced that she had attended the "University of Life". I was to learn that she certainly had. I think it was the same school that my mother attended. Jill did have a number of recognizable Twachtman, my mother's family, traits: forthright, a broad sense of humour including a sense for good fun, outspoken and smart. Jill, as she, herself, was wont to say had "nous".

We met a few times before I left to spend a snowy Christmas with my long-standing friends, Anne and John Fraser, in their charming rustic farmhouse in the Jura foothills. It was obvious that I was quite smitten by Jill and I stayed in touch by phone over the holiday. In fact I cut the holiday a little short in order to get back to London and Jill.

Though, on most days, I commuted to London from Collyweston, my home with Rosemary, my late wife, it wasn't long before I had all but 'moved in' to Jill's large flat on the second floor of Macartney House, on the edge of Greenwich Park. Macartney House was once home to General Wolfe's family and had been remodelled by John Soane in the first decade of the nineteenth century. Jill's flat was unusual and quite handsome, if that is an appropriate word. It was only a convenient 'stone's throw' across the park to 'Chole', Jill's fashion boutique in Blackheath village.

Jill was a successful fashion retailer. She had opened her first shop when only twenty-three. Eventually, Jill owned, at one time or another, six shops in southeast London. Her commercial acumen was recognized when Jill was runner up to Anita Roddick as woman entrepreneur of the year. As I said, "Jill had 'nous' ". Despite coming from disparate backgrounds Jill and I got on well and, importantly too, I got on well with Jill's daughter Victoria. Jill, it would turn out would get on well with my own children and grandchildren and Jill is appreciated by them. Those good relationships, developed over sixteen years, added to our positive outlook for the wedding trip.

The QM2 trip was enjoyable: calm seas helped too. Jill and I had been on only one cruise before, in the Baltic. Though we found that cruise interesting we were less than enthralled by the Costa line and its clientele. I think we were mostly attracted to the QM2 by the idea of getting away from jet lag and the discomfort (Jill was awaiting a knee replacement operation) and complications of twenty-first century air travel. We were not disappointed. We found the crossing a pleasant option, making new friends, attending lectures, and enjoying (modest) entertainment: well, some of the entertainment was actually quite good. Getting the five-hour difference between the UK and East Coast US in small bites was amenable: we might do the crossing again.

We docked in New York harbour in the early morning of Thursday the 7th of September, some 364 years since, Jacobus Backer, a young merchant trader arrived from Amsterdam. Two years later, in 1655, Jacobus met and married Margaretha Stuyvesant (Peter Stuyvesant's half-sister) and together they started the branch of the Ba(c)ker family to which I belong. Looking across the harbour I could just make out 17 Battery Place, my office in the 1980s. While now living in the UK and a dual citizen an extra heartbeat signalled that I was 'home'.

We disembarked at the newish cruise terminal in Brooklyn and made our way by taxi to the Avis car rental on Atlantic Avenue. We struggled with our four suitcases, extra clothing for the ship and wedding fare, more baggage than the carry-on luggage we take to Portugal. With the help of the friendly Avis agent, we were able to stow everything into a modest compact car. Despite the fact that New York was my birthplace and principal residence for more than sixty years I am not that familiar with Brooklyn. Nevertheless, we made it across the Brooklyn Bridge to Manhattan and the East River Drive (aka FDR Drive) and headed north.

As we passed the various exits on the Drive, itself constructed by J. Rich Steers the father of my Springland partner, Dick Steers, nostalgia kicked in. Each entrance to the Drive evoked memories: 20th street, used when I lived in 8th street: 49th street, used when I was with Bill McDonough and earlier at Park Tower's first office: 63rd street used for nearly thirty years when living on that street, as well where Llewellyn Davies's offices were located: 96th street used when I lived uptown at 95th, 93rd, 89th and 86th streets. I thought I knew many of the potholes, (they seemed still there from years ago) and yes, there some new ones as well. We passed over the East River, joined the Bruckner expressway to take us to the Connecticut Turnpike.

Our first stop would be New Haven. I thought Jill might like to see a bit of Yale, Jill had certainly heard enough about it. As we were running a little ahead of schedule I asked Jill whether a windshield visit to Greenwich, my childhood hometown, would be of interest. Jill's enthusiastic "yes" was just in time to make the exit ramp. We turned right by the railroad station where Fitzsimmon's garage used to be. It was where I stashed my 1½ Litre Riley during my Princeton years. The traffic pattern had changed since my last Greenwich visit. We were unable to go up Putnam Avenue (the north-south main street), where Uncle Alden used to lead 4th of July parades. The parallel Mason Street was now the 'uptown' route. From Mason Street we turned left on Elm Street that led us back to Putnam Avenue. As we were crossing Putnam Avenue, past the old Greenwich Bank & Trust Company (where I had my first bank account, age seven) Jill declared, "I could live here, how much would a flat cost?" (my answer: "a lot"). Greenwich, it is true, was always appealing but now much more up-market than in the 1930s and 40s of my childhood. We went on, around a couple of corners and turned up the Old Post Road past the site of Grandfather Baker's house on the right next to where the Pickwick

Theatre stood and opposite what used to be the bowling alley where my friend Boris and I occasionally, and ineptly, bowled. The Pickwick Theatre was exciting. Its domed ceiling was painted midnight blue and contained small lights placed, I believe, to represent familiar constellations. Father had taught me to recognize the big dipper, North Star and Orion, my 'expertise' after that was thin. Westerns (black and white of course) were typical fare on rainy Saturday mornings or afternoons but, to be fair, I remember the domed ceiling more than the movies. Further up the Post Road we passed the location of the little shop where my sister Marty and I bought little glass figurines and other small items for Christmases or birthdays. We turned left on Lafayette (Greenwich does have revolutionary overtones) past my first dentist and the Greenwich Hospital, site of childhood Emergency Room events, my tonsillectomy and where Uncle Carl (Dr. Knapp) was once president. We turned right onto Lake Avenue past the turn off for Rosemary Hall, Marty's and mother's (and a number of cousins) Alma Mater and where Aunt Eugenia presided as Headmistress for many years. Further on we came, finally, to the left-hand turn onto Round Hill Road and almost immediately passed Grandfather Twachtman's and Uncle Alden's houses. From the outside they were hardly changed, well, Uncle Alden's seemed a bit straighter and in better repair than I remembered. About a mile on we rounded the corner where, in 1938 I fell out of our Ford Station Wagon (yes, that was one of the trips to the ER). Finally we came to Porchuck Road on the left, just after you cross over the Merritt Parkway. Our house was on the corner. We couldn't see much of it except I could tell it had been remodelled and enlarged. I think Jill was a little disappointed but for me it was a catalyst for a flood of childhood memories. That was the 'windshield' visit completed. We turned around a little further up Porchuck Road, came back and joined the Merritt Parkway: next stop, New Haven.

In a frustrating struggle to find our way from the parkway to downtown we saw more of outer New Haven than we planned. We did eventually find the Omni Hotel and made it to the reception on the second pass. Not much of a hotel but our room overlooked the green with its three historic churches and Yale buildings as a backdrop. After a quick dinner we ambled up to Kahn's Yale Art Gallery, the fourth floor of which in 'my day' was the site of the Architectural School's studios. The gallery had been updated and we enjoyed the art on exhibit and of course Kahn's building itself. Opened in 1953, the gallery was his first masterpiece and it is one of my all-time favourite buildings. Kahn had been commissioned to design the Gallery by my first father-in-law, Whitney Griswold, Yale's President.

On Friday, early, we visited the architecture school in Rudolph's iconic sixty's building. It was too early to see any students at work but we were impressed by their work on display and we had a pleasant chat with Peter Eisenman. We didn't stay long; we had to get to Woods Hole by three to get the ferry to Martha's Vineyard. While it was a nominal three-hour drive, on a Friday (it was Friday) it could be four hours plus another half hour for lunch.

The drive turned out to take less time than planned and even with a long lunch break at a bizarre grocery store cum fast food restaurant (only in America) we were early. We passed the time getting a coffee and boarded the crowded ferry: on time. As it was a bit breezy on deck there were only a few seats available inside. We found two seats at a table occupied by a comely lady (she could have been a Helen Hunt double) and her lively rescue dog (one look and it had to have been rescued) working on her MacBook Pro. She looked to be a Martha's 'Vineyarder' not a tourist: yes, you can tell. We all smiled at each other in that way when you are unsure of whether to say something banal, "nice weather" or whatever: or not. Perhaps it was Jill, probably was, Jill has a knack of encouraging discussions with strangers, we joke that she might have had a career with MI5. Anyway we fell into desultory conversation. Before long we learned that the lady was a 'Vineyarder' (Vineyard Haven), lived in Brooklyn and taught writing as an adjunct professor at Hunter College, which is just up Park Avenue at 68th street, my neck of the New York 'woods'. Hunter was a constituent college of City University, as was City College where I taught for 25 years. Further exploration of the Hunter connection revealed that her specialty was memoir writing! It was like bumping into a doctor at a party and wondering if you should ask him/her about that nagging ache you have been meaning to look into. Should I, shouldn't I? I couldn't resist. She (we had not introduced ourselves and in fact never did) must have thought, "oh, not again". Anyway we talked memoirs. Her main advice that I took away was, "do not do a memoir chronologically". Well, that was about fifteen years too late, BUT, it has led to this memoir's Preface and Postface.

The ferry docked, the conversation was over, I thanked her and we 'went our ways'. A little research confirmed that we had been talking to Alexandra Styron author of "Reading My Father" a memoir of her father William Styron.

We debarked and found our way to the 1720 house where we would stay three nights. We caught up with Morgan, Matt, Jamie, Trina, Maggie and Jay and rest of the wedding party at the rehearsal dinner in Chilmark. It was a large and cheerful crowd. After the lively dinner replete with the normal wedding banter and speeches we left to meet Alden on the night's last ferry. Alden had flown into Boston from Salt Lake City and came down to Woods Hole by bus. Trina, Jill and I greeted Alden. He was his normal bouncy, cheerful and chatty, self as he walked off the ferry. It was great to see him: it had been a few years. We caught up for an hour or so before Trina whisked him off, someplace, for the night.

On Saturday Jill and I met Jamie and Alden at the Scotch House for a leisurely lunch and a laugh or two. Later a bus took us and other guests to Lambert's cove for the wedding ceremony that took place in the field overlooking James's Pond. Jamie presided with his usual style. It was simple, elegant and appropriately moving. A massive tent had been erected for the reception dinner and dancing that followed the ceremony. Morgan and Matt had arranged it all including the dinner seating arrangements. My dinner companion to my right (Jill was to my left to be sure) was Sergio Modigliani. Sergio, an architect, was the son of Franco Modigliani, the MIT Nobel Laureate in Economics. His wife had been one of Molly's long-standing tennis partners. I couldn't resist asking the obvious, and yes, he said he was a distant relation to the artist. Though I had never heard of, or met him he certainly knew of me. I hesitate to imagine just what he might have been told. We fell into a friendly conversation. In due course he turned and said, rhetorically, "Jim, I've heard something about you but not much about your architectural career. What, exactly, did you do as an architect?"

Well, "he will probably regret that question", I thought, as I launched into a précis of what follows: here it is, of course, a bit longer, and, if you (and Alexandra) will forgive me, it is 'more or less' chronological.

PART 1

CHILDHOOD

1933 TO 1944

1

PORCHUCK ROAD

Greenwich, Connecticut

1933 – 1942

"We shape our buildings: thereafter they shape us."
Winston Churchill

"When every blessed thing you hold is made of silver or of gold you long
for simple pewter."
From The Gondoliers

"Saturday's child works hard for a living"
Anon

The late George Wilkie a New York psychiatrist, with whom I consulted for a time, used to say that I was born with a 'pewter spoon', a serious cut below silver, but still something. He was probably right.

According to mother I arrived on Saturday the eighteenth of February 1933 in New York City at the Harbour Hospital, on the corner of Madison Avenue and 61st street.[1] Most of my childhood, however, was spent in Greenwich, Connecticut, where my father[2] had designed and built a marvellous, perhaps eccentric, house on the corner of Porchuck and Round Hill roads. The house was constructed around a small eighteenth-century farmhouse at the time of my father and mother's marriage in 1928[3]. By the time I arrived in 1933, four years after my sister Marty[4] perhaps at the height of the depression, the house and its grounds had matured into a rich mixture of gardens and terraces, all on a small scale, appropriate to children[5].

Taking into consideration the timing of the construction of the Porchuck Road house and the general standard of living we enjoyed, the depression, apparently, did not have as much effect on our family as it had on others. Father did have to give up his New York architectural practice and abandon his much-loved yachting activities. He complained (a lot) about Roosevelt's taxes, but on the whole, from my point of view, at least, life was 'comfortable'.

It was nearly impossible to realize that the house was constructed around the 18th century farmhouse that had been built into this gently sloping Connecticut hillside. The ceiling heights of the house were effectively the only remaining reference to the original farmhouse, as they were, for the most part, not much more than seven feet. My uncle Jackie[6] well over six feet, had to remember to duck through the doorways. He often forgot and complained loudly to my mother, "Sissie" to him. It was part of Jackie's ritual when he visited which was frequently, at least up until he joined the French Army in 1939[7].

The house was three stories high. Its brick-paved, inset entrance with its two convenient green Windsor chairs was located on the uphill side at the middle floor. The front door was, in an effort to keep father's sometimes dozen Cairn Terriers out of the house, a Dutch door, solid on the bottom half and with the opening upper half glass with divided lights. This top part was often left open in warm weather to improve ventilation and only the nimblest of the dogs could jump the bottom half. By 1936, the dozen dogs were down to two quite sedate seniors, Bubbins and Zephyr, respectively black and white, male and female. Neither would, or more likely, could jump over the bottom half.

The front door opened into a small, but elegant hall with a gently curved staircase leading to the ground floor dining room and my father's study or "den", as he called it. A niche, about a third of the way down the stair held a terracotta bust of mother. One day this bust mysteriously disappeared. I was told that mother had 'accidentally' dropped it down the stairs. Another theory, supported by Marty, was that mother had thrown it down the stairs in a fit of pique or self-deprecation. A coatroom was reached through a door on the left of the entrance hall as were the "back" stairs connecting the 'help's' apartment on the attic floor above to the kitchen below. For some reason there was a radio kept in this coatroom and it was here that the family gathered to hear Roosevelt's "Day of Infamy" address on December 8th, 1941[8]. Two Hitchcock chairs, a Dutch marquetry desk and a portrait of Great Uncle William Edgar Baker[9] were the entrance hall's only furnishings.

Ahead of the hall, through an open archway was a small living room; three French doors with silk curtains hung from gilded pelmets led onto a colonnaded porch. The south end of the room was a floor to ceiling bookcase containing rather classic books, mostly from the Baker family –English literature, histories, a number of books on Napoleon, apparently a favourite subject of grandfather Baker, and the black, leather-bound eleventh edition of the Encyclopaedia Britannica. Marty and I were often referred to this when asking a question of our parents. We actually enjoyed this pursuit. I even took out volumes at random just to see what was in them – it was, so to speak, how we 'browsed the net' in the thirties.

An opening in the bookcase framed three steps leading to father and mother's bedroom. To the left of this opening stood a gilded round table, and on it, in a gilded cage a pair of yellow canaries chirped away. An elegant highly polished veneered table of Italian origin, was placed to the right in front of the bookcase and on it, almost always, there was an elegant vase containing flowers from the garden. The table was a little inconvenient in that we had to crawl under it to get to the encyclopaedia but it was a convenient surface for books.

The north wall of the living room consisted of painted wood panelling, a coved cupboard filled with ceramic objects, and a traditionally detailed 'colonial' fireplace; on its hearth were two white china doves with their tails spread out into fans. In this room as well as in the rest of the house, the furniture was scaled to fit the rather small rooms with their low ceilings – even to the point of shortening chair legs. I think the deceit worked very well.

My bedroom, quite small, was just off the living room to the right of the bookcase. It was decorated in a rather effeminate French manner with a green-grey painted Empire sleigh bed and matching bureau and table. Marty's room, also known as the north bedroom, was also off the living room, its door just to the right of the fireplace. (Actually, as an infant, until I was able to climb out of my crib it was 'my room'.) The room was also finished in a French style dominated by a Toile de Jouy curtained Empire canopy bed and French wallpaper depicting 18th century hunting scenes. In the fall of 1940 Marty left home to board at Rosemary Hall, in Greenwich, where, in 1938, my Aunt Eugenia[10], one of father's younger sisters had become Headmistress. Soon after Marty left, my father was taken ill through a combination of a heart attack and consequential diabetes. A stomach ulcer further compromised his health. Marty's bedroom then became father's 'sick-room' so that he could be more easily cared-for. When he recovered some six months later, father moved out and I moved in: the north bedroom became 'my room', again.

My parent's bedroom, as noted, was at the south end of the house. It was the largest of the three bedrooms. Its lofted ceiling made it seem even larger than it really was. The room had a fireplace and two pairs of French doors leading to a south-facing brick-paved patio. The room was generally filled with a warm light. My father's dressing room was off the west side of the room, next to the bathroom. It was a little room, containing, in addition to closets, a bureau and a single chair. On top of the bureau father placed various little boxes containing his shirt studs, tiepins, watches and other small items of male jewellery. When no one was around, I found these items made great playthings. I was careful not to lose anything. If my father knew I was playing with his things he didn't say anything. My mother's Empire desk sat against the bedroom's east wall between two casement windows. This too, with its little drawers full of drawing and writing instruments, letters, and bits and pieces, fascinated me. I believed it contained at least one secret drawer for which, even as an adult, I was always searching. As I rummaged through the desk one day, age about five, I became fascinated with the several inkbottles contained in the drawers. Out of curiosity and while my parents were out on a walk, I drank most of a bottle of blue-black ink. It was pretty foul but apart from getting a blue face and an admonishment on parental return there was no obvious harmful effect – however, I do not recommend ink as a drink.

The dining room was directly below the living room. This was an elegant, marble-floored room, with doors opening out into a formal courtyard with a dining table of Italian descent. I think the table originally belonged to Grandmother Baker[11] and was from her 'Roman period'[12] when she had a large and impressive penthouse apartment near the Spanish Steps. The table had two tall crystal vases, almost always filled with flowers. The room's walls were covered with a wrap-around, French inspired fantasy landscape mural, painted by mother[13]. Next to the fireplace at the north end was a partially open-shelved, corner cupboard. Inside there was a silver tea service. I found this fascinating as it had a rather complex urn with an alcohol-based heating device, great fun to play with in the absence of parental or governess supervision.

I recall only a few occasions when I ate in the dining room. I usually had my meals in the kitchen on the white enamel metal-topped kitchen table. Porchuck Road in the 1930s was still in a kind of Edwardian time warp, when children were seen, sometimes, and hopefully, never heard.

One occasion was Marty's tenth birthday party in 1939. To the dismay of her friends, Marty insisted that I attend the party. She was funny that way. On the one hand she was always 'on my case'[14] and the resulting fights this created could be violent. Several times we sent each other to the hospital for patching up. Once Marty needed a long operation to fix her wrist after putting it through the glass front door while chasing me for some long-forgotten offence: one, probably, only perceived. On another occasion I went to the hospital to have my eyelid put back together after Marty had, gleefully, pulled me down a set of brick steps in my red wagon. Marty loved to tease me and, if she felt like it, she would take out her anger, frustration or whatever on my Dinky toys, reducing my "air force" of iconic British warplanes (e.g. Bristol Blenheims, Wellingtons, Hurricanes and Spitfires) to wingless hunks of metal[15]. On the other hand, let any of Marty's friends deprecate her younger brother and she would carry the day in my favour. On the birthday in question, I was given the 'honor' of carrying in her heavily iced, candle-lit, birthday cake. With great pride I brought it from the kitchen through the pantry managing with great ease, to flip the cake upside down on one of the rush-seated Italian, dining room chairs – much to the sarcastic hoots and hollers of Marty's friends. Marty, however, to her friends' astonishment, was 'cool': I think she thought it was funny.

At the south end of the dining room was my father's study. This was his retreat and the place where he and mother, family and guests, would often gather for cocktails before dinner. The room's painted dark-red wood wainscot and trim and polished brick floor set the room's masculine tone. In one corner, next to the musty, burnt ash-smelling fireplace was father's red velvet wingback chair. Next to this was a corner cabinet with shelves to carry a collection of horse, dog, chicken, cattle and yachting trophies. Under the shelves was a sometimes-locked cabinet. This, I remember from personal examination, almost always contained a bottle of my father's favourite scotch, Cutty Sark, a bottle of Gilbey's Gin and one of vermouth. Martinis were the favourite cocktail for mother and most visitors, except for Aunt Marjorie, who was an 'Old Fashioned' aficionado. A collection of eight bird prints by the American artist Alexander Pope Jr., two Currier and Ives yacht pictures, photographs of father's boats, and his Chelsea brass ship's clock and Tiffany barometer from his boats were hung on the walls. Two tall, semi-concealed vertical cabinets held his collection of fly rods. I have no recollection of father's fishing events but there were lots of rods to play with. Grandfather Baker's cut glass humidor, that I still have, was placed on a table next to father's wing back chair ready for filling my father's pipes. I often lifted its silver handled glass stopper to draw in its moist aromatic smell. Following father's illness he had to give up smoking but could still be seen at least holding a pipe in his hand. A large fish tank burbled away in one of the two windows. A chintz-covered sofa, two Hitchcock chairs, another table and the good-sized aquarium completed the room's furnishings. Except for architectural representation, this room with its mementos of horses, birds, dogs, chickens, dairy cows, boats, fishing gear, and pipes was a condensed iconographic presentation of father's life interests.

I was allowed in the den only when my father was there, but I broke the rule, often. The 'den' was too intriguing a place not to take the risk and for the most part I got away with surreptitious visits. My 'official' visits were generally just before bedtime when I was invited to sit on father's lap: for a moment.

In addition to his 'den', father's other 'private' domain was his studio. This was outside the house under part of the garage. It had a large north facing floor to ceiling window and contained, in addition to father's large flat drawing table, a sofa and a rather grand Dutch marquetry cabinet[16] which was used to store father's drawings, pencils, paper and drawing tools and, as well, grandfather Baker's Keuffel and Esser transit and level used when he was surveying for the western railroads in the 1880s. The cabinet was big enough to conceal oneself (and I did) when playing hide and seek. Another of mother's murals was on the back wall of the studio. This large, twelve by five foot mural depicted our immediate family members, some Twachtman cousins, their dogs and horses in an imaginary Round Hill landscape with Long Island Sound in the distance.

Even during the depression, before he was taken ill, father managed to obtain sufficient residential commissions from family and friends to keep him relatively busy. Father occasionally took me with him to visit 'his' houses[17] while they were under construction. It was an outing I really enjoyed but doubt that the visits had anything to do with my becoming an architect. Mostly, I just enjoyed sitting at the drawing table, fiddling with father's drawing tools, playing architect, whatever. This was the time of tracing paper, thumbtacks, ink ruling pens and real blueprints[18]. Father was educated (civil engineering) at Princeton,[19] at Harvard (graduate school) and he had apprenticed with McKim, Mead and White[20]. Father was a good, classic architect, that is to say he was adept at colonial-style buildings. He was a superb draughtsman, his ink on paper drawings of actual or would-be buildings or yachts (probably his favourite occupation) are quite extraordinary, especially the boats.

The kitchen was at the opposite end of the house from father's study and it was here, that Marty and I generally ate, overseen by the cook. The kitchen opened onto a service court and had its own garden. Each appliance, refrigerator, sink and range were stand-alone items. Between the kitchen and dining room was a butler's pantry. A larder occupied an interior corner. I was fascinated to watch the cook make morning coffee by spooning coffee into a large, white, enamelled pot into which, at the right moment, she would throw eggshells; I was told this made for excellent coffee!

On Sunday nights, while dining on milk toast, Marty and I would listen to our favourite radio programs: Captain Midnight, Bulldog Drummond, The Shadow, Jack Armstrong and Uncle Don. I still recall Uncle Don's theme song:

"Hibbidy-Gits has-ha ring boree,
Sibonia Skividy, hi-lo-dee!
Honi-ko-doke with an ali-ka-zon,
Sing this song with your Uncle Don"

Marty even won a $25 War Bond in one of Uncle Don's many competitions for her drawing of the Liberty Bell.

The 'help's' area on the third floor consisted of a large bedroom, dressing room and bath. This was usually home for a married couple or perhaps just a cook who also often served, I think reluctantly, as a maid and child minder. When there was a 'couple' the husband looked after the 'grounds' and would act as a butler or chauffeur when required. I was not permitted upstairs and generally obeyed this fiat as I was rather fearful of the German cook who was the last occupant before the war. There was apparently some problem with her immigration status as she disappeared, rather suddenly, soon after December 7th 1941 – she wasn't much fun anyway.

The grounds around the house were organized into purpose-designed terraces with discrete functions. The entrance court was framed on one side by a two-car garage, on another by a tack room and one of the two horse stalls[21] (given over to the Cairns in my time), on the third side by a pump house and garden retaining wall. The main house enclosed the fourth side. Standing nearly in the middle of the court was a large and ancient ivy-covered apple tree. Though it had seen better days it was still important for the balance of the space. It remained protected while we lived there.

The little tack room was a great place to 'hang out'. Its walls were covered with framed ribbon collections won by dogs, chickens, horses and cattle. You could spend a lot of time just looking. It was here that the dogs were groomed. It was also where Uncle Alden's[22] cheeky pet monkey, Coco, was kept when Uncle Alden went on holiday to Maine. It was from the tack room that Coco escaped one night when Marty and I were feeding him soon after Uncle Alden left for his holiday! We couldn't find Coco and an embarrassed mother had to call Uncle Alden in Maine. Uncle Alden returned and in due course retrieved Coco from a neighbour's roof with the help, I recall, of some bananas. Uncle Alden was none too pleased: it was Coco's last visit.

The two car garage usually contained a Ford 'woodie' station wagon, and in the early thirties, mother's LaSalle coupe with rumble seat[23]. I spent hours sitting in the Ford pretending to drive. It was from one of these 'woodies' that I fell as we rounded a corner coming back from a shopping trip to Greenwich. My mother was driving and because of the general noise these cars made she was unaware of my exit for some minutes. I was only scraped a bit and by the time she returned I had already started running after the car. Though I was really none the worse for wear, just a little shook up, mother insisted on a check-up at Greenwich Hospital anyway. Another 'woodie' event was orchestrated by Marty who decided, on trip to downtown Greenwich, to experiment with the car's lighter. The resulting fire was exciting but fatal for the car. Marty got into some trouble and father had to buy a new 'woodie', though at the time we referred to the vehicles as 'station wagons'.

On the east side of the garage was my father's workbench[24]. Above and beyond the bench was an attic space that could be reached by climbing onto the workbench and crawling through the attic's access door. The attic was packed with unused furniture and artifacts from another generation. Marty and I used this room as a place to be "out-of-sight". I liked to be there because I could play Grandfather

Baker's large nineteenth century wind-up music box. The box was full of musical bits and pieces, drums, bells and chimes. Of the several large (and heavy) metal music rolls that drove the machine, my favourite was Handel's 'See The Conquering Hero Come': it still is. Marty liked to be there mostly, I think, because she could corner me and, with conviction, tell me that I was not my parent's child and that one day I would find out and be sent away. I didn't really believe her, but all the same, it was a little worrying. The garage was also where the gardener had lunch. I used to slip in to 'talk' to him and he would let me taste his delicious sweet tea and ham salad sandwich that he ate, ritually, each day.

One reached the principal garden by stone stairs that led up from the courtyard. The garden was framed on the east and west by trimmed beech hedges. At its south apex was a summerhouse made from latticed ironwork, covered by clematis. A small fishpond, fed by water spouting from a lead swan that, I was told, Uncle Jackie made, was in the garden's centre. Marty and I played in the little pond on hot summer days. The southwest side of the garden was given over to Marty and me to grow vegetables. From the time I could hold a trowel I was encouraged to garden - whether that meant growing vegetables or flowers. Presents were used for encouragement and these included a small wheelbarrow, spades, hoes, and rakes and one day United Parcel delivered, from Grandmother Baker, a miniature, working lawn mower! My favourite vegetable to grow was cucumber perhaps because cucumbers managed to grow very well on their own. Marty and I sold our gardening excess, mostly the cucumbers, from a little stand we made and placed at the Porchuck road entrance to the house. We actually managed to sell some for five cents each, mostly to sympathetic neighbours.

The ground floor of the house, essentially the dining room, opened out on to what could best be described as a parterre. Two symmetrically placed linden trees framed a gravelled rectangle that was also additionally framed by oleander trees in painted green wooden boxes. This space provided a pleasant area for outdoor dining – but as I recall it was used in good weather, mainly, as a place to enjoy a martini, or two. (an alternative to the 'den'). Having a cocktail 'hour' before dinner or hosting a cocktail party was a parental ritual. However, except for one or two exceptions I was never aware of any inebriation.

At the south end of the parterre father had constructed a small columned loggia that he flanked with two marble statues of Roman mythology, Bacchus and a goddess with a birdcage, I don't know who she was. The statues, like the furniture in the house were small scale giving the illusion that the Loggia was much bigger. The loggia was yet another fantasy space in which to play: as were the two linden trees.

Climbing the linden trees, particularly, for some reason the more northerly one, was fun especially the climbing part. Strangely coming down was more difficult and I sometimes got stuck and needed assistance. Tree climbing should have taught me a life lesson, which is that it is sometimes easier to go up than come down: it didn't. Beyond the linden tree was a large gate leading to the back lawn and kitchen garden.

Adjacent to the back lawn was a paddock ready for a horse that never arrived. Father had reclaimed the back lawn as a short running track with a high jump for Marty. Father was relatively short and in the thirties bordered on stocky. However, at The Hill and Princeton photographs show him as a thin, wiry, track athlete, looking much taller than he was. He had the cups and medals to prove his athletic prowess. Marty too was skilled as an athlete and was later to be a terror on the hockey field. Although I tried to compete with Marty I mostly ran through the bamboo bar over which Marty could easily jump.

Adjacent to the driveway was another small field dedicated to fruit trees, crab apples and pears. In an almost forgotten and hidden corner of this field father had placed a swing and sand box though given the other opportunities for play and exploration these structured playthings did not get that much use. In another corner of this mini-orchard was a large rock overhung by a witch hazel tree. I spent hours on this rock: I loved the smell of the witch hazel that could be induced by crushing the leaves in your fingers. More importantly, by standing on top of the rock I could look over the stone wall separating us from the rather large estate next door and watch the gardeners work the estate's large garden - I often watched them for what seemed like hours.

In the fall, the orchard's crab apples provided a source of ammunition for "feudal wars" between Marty and myself. Uncle Alden had made each of us "medieval" shields from plywood. He decorated these with marvellous heraldic symbols; mine was a red dragon. We cut sappers from the base of the apple trees, sharpened their ends and pushed the little apples into the sharpened ends. By whipping the sapper through the air the apple would come loose and be propelled at great force. If you were hit it hurt – the shield was your only defence!

Yet another small field, on the other side of the driveway, was given to growing sweet corn. Marty and I dutifully planted this each year under father's direction in what we were told was the "Indian way". This meant scooping out rows of little earth bowls and placing in each four corn kernels and a rotting fish head - a not so pleasant task, Indian or not, but the corn was very good.

Although the property was small in scale, its variety was delightful and it was, perhaps inadvertently, a purposed-designed playground. In addition we had the full run of several adjacent fields, woods, a little stream and small pond. I spent hours building dams in the stream, fishing for carp and sunfish, or building seriously sinkable coracles to navigate the pond. There were only a few neighbours with children, so for the most part Marty and I played, or fought, together. More often I played, happily, on my own. The one frequent playmate I had was Boris Said, and he was a mixed blessing.

Boris was the only son of a Syrian father who had done very well, after immigrating to the US, rising to near the top of Standard Oil of New Jersey. Boris's mother, Sonia had emigrated from Odessa. My parents liked the Saids, whom I believe they met because both Boris and I attended kindergarten at Rosemary Hall, normally an all-girls school. Although we were the only male members of our class we were oblivious of any differences and we played more or less happily, with our female classmates. The following year Boris and I were enrolled at Greenwich Country Day School. I commuted by bus, waiting daily at the junction of Porchuck

Road and Round Hill Road for the yellow, rather smelly bus to take me to Country Day. Country Day was certainly a good school but I didn't find it all that much fun. For me the three highlights of my Country Day years were winning (to everyone's surprise) the sixth grade Class race on 'Field Day', having an embarrassing digestive system "accident" on the football (American) field (I was a lousy footballer anyway) and having an unrequited crush on Nancy Green. That probably says it all.

But back to Boris: he was, by his parents' own description, a little "wild". They thought that by associating with me Boris might become calmer: no chance of that. After several visits to Porchuck Road, Boris was banned from ever setting foot on the property as a result of being caught trying to demolish, with a hammer, the brick paving at the front porch. The fact that he and Marty were always at loggerheads didn't help either. While Marty could hold her own in most encounters, boxing wasn't really her sport and her confrontations with Boris could be quite violent. So I went to play at Applecrest, the Said's house, on the corner of Sherwood Avenue and Riversville Road, near Glenville. I was either driven the several miles there by mother or father or picked up by the Said's chauffeur, sometimes in their classic open front Packard limousine.

Applecrest was a large Tudor pastiche of a house, with extensive grounds that included tennis courts, lakes, woods and a chicken farm. The entire property was quite impressive though not elegant. Boris's collection of toys was extensive. In addition to the usual trains, boats and airplane models that filled the large attic playroom, they even included a full size, battery-powered runabout. In anticipation of Boris's later Formula 1 and bobsled career, he tried, somehow, to 'soup up' the electric motor so that he could race down the steep driveway at breakneck speed. I chose, mostly, to watch this event from the sidelines.

Despite all these toys Boris managed, simply, to reduce almost any 'game' to a fight. We became masters at two-man American football, and 'fighter plane'. Both games were resolved by the result of who could wrestle whom to the ground first. Sometimes, when Boris was tired of his wrestling games we would get the chauffer to take us to the bowling alley in Greenwich. This wasn't such a great idea as we sometimes ended up being chased off the premises by the pin boys due to Boris's lack of protocol. Boris, for example, might decide to bowl when the pin boys were still setting up the pins. In fact, on more than one occasion the chauffeur had to rescue us. The close playmate relationship changed somewhat after Boris's father died, quite suddenly, in 1941, of a heart attack while driving his Lincoln Zephyr home from his office in New York. Soon after this event Sonia married a Russian named, if I recall correctly, Alexander Orloff (that sounds a little like the UK meercat advertisements for "The Market dot com", but I believe I am correct). Orloff was a little rough, if not unfriendly. Boris not only didn't like him, he thought he was some kind of a communist spy: and perhaps he was. Visits became uncomfortable and, partially, as a result, Boris and I didn't see that much of each other for a few years.

In addition to just 'mucking around' at Porchuck Road summer activities in the thirties were accented by daytrips: taking the little ferry to Island Beach, (Greenwich's public beach in Long Island Sound) occasional visits to Playland, an early prototype amusement park still in operation; and visits to other local attractions.

In 1939, Marty and I were sent off to summer camp in New Hampshire: she to Waukeela and me, in company with cousin John Baker, to Wonalancet[25] both in Eaton Centre, not far from North Conway the nearest train stop. The camps were both on Crystal Lake but at opposite ends. Wonalancet was what I imagine most summer camps were like at the time – not all that much fun. We hiked up Mount Washington, swam in the cold water, were bitten by mosquitoes, got rained on, were bullied by the older campers and played pretend Indians, Mohicans and Pennacooks, around campfires. We were awarded coloured feathers for minor camping achievements. In today's climate not very politically correct. Despite the proximity of the camps Marty and I saw very little of each other.

The following years, when I was old enough to qualify, Marty and I spent two summers at the Indian Harbour Yacht Club attending their junior sailing program.

We trained, daily, in old Pirate class, deep keel displacement sloops, about eighteen feet overall: probably designed by Herreshoff. It was quite an intensive program and by the end of the first summer we could sail a Pirate single-handedly.

We were nearly thrown out of the program when Marty absconded with a girlfriend and me in tow from a special day trip to see the ship models at the prestigious New York Yacht Club on 44th street just off Fifth Avenue. Marty, instead of looking at the ship models, took us to the movies at 86th street. Some eight hours later, after the police had been called, we arrived back, still on our own, at Porchuck Road where a rather irate father greeted us. We were not punished but I think Marty was persona non grata at the Yacht Club for some time. Actually, I don't know why we didn't get pitched out of Indian Harbour: I suspect there were some serious interventions. Anyway, by the time Marty was twelve and I nine, we were quite reasonable sailors, certainly for our ages.

In between the managed activities and camps we spent time visiting family friends and relatives around Greenwich – there were a lot of them. On the whole these were fun occasions particularly when we were taken to Grandfather Twachtman's house, then occupied by Aunt Marjorie, and to Uncle Alden's studio that was next door.

The house at Porchuck Road, however, was the physical centre of my early childhood and it would be hard to imagine a better or more interesting environment. I am certain that it shaped me in one way or another.[26]

Gardening' at Porchuck Road c. 1937

Marty and Zepher at Porchuck Road c. 1938

My First Bedroom

The entrance (west) side of the house

The dining room on the ground floor - the door leads to father's 'Den'. Murals by mother.

The 'parterre' outside the dining room

The north bedroom - Marty's room and later my room

Entrance courtyard: The tack room with stable door to right and the two car garage - cornfield is up the driveway on the right
From Architectural Record [26]

Grandmother Baker's fourteen grandchildren (John Baker missing): at the Field Club in Greenwich - December 24th, 1935 - four Generations, though the second generation, for some reason, was not in the photo. I am on Grandmother's left, Marty on her right

2

ROUND HILL ROAD

Grandfather's and Uncle Alden's Houses

1933 - 1944

If Marty and I were not involved in other activities such as sailing classes, visits to Island Beach, or to friends we were probably with Mother visiting Aunt Marjorie or Uncle Alden in their houses on Round Hill Road, just a few miles south of Porchuck Road. Aunt Marjorie with her two daughters, our cousins Peggy and Elizabeth, had moved into grandfather's house (or perhaps we should call it Grandmother's house) sometime after Grandmother's death in 1935. Uncle Alden still lived in his studio-house (or house-studio) since he built it, sometime after 1908, which was about the time he married Aunt Louise.

Although Grandfather Twachtman died in 1902, grandmother Twachtman[27] continued to live in what they referred to as a "Farm" for another thirty-three years. Uncle Alden continued in his home until he retired to a nursing home near his son Eric in Essex Connecticut. My recollections of both houses are mostly from the years between Grandmother's death until the late 1940s when the Grandfather's farm was sold though I did visit Uncle Alden's after that time.

Grandfather purchased his "Farm", depending upon conflicting records, either in 1888 or 1890. By the 1930s the "farm" consisted of four buildings; the main house and a horse barn now partly used as a garage. Uncle Alden's studio-house perched on a rocky hillock overlooking the entire property and included a two-story studio-like structure that now leaned threateningly towards the Round Hill Road and was all but abandoned. The siting of the several structures was determined principally by the rather rugged, rocky site. However, Grandfather, and perhaps Uncle Alden, had connected the several buildings into a related whole by paths, terraces and stonewalls.[28] The property, more or less triangular in plan, consisted of about fifteen acres bounded on the east side by Round Hill Road, near where it joins Lake Avenue, on the West by Horseneck brook, and to the South by William (Goodsell) Rockefeller's property[29]. Mother became a close friend of William Rockefeller's wife Elsie (Stillman) and there are many references to mother in Elsie's diary held in the Rockefeller archives[30].

Like the Porchuck Road house, Grandfather's house was modestly sized but, perhaps, had grander presumptions. This architectural feat was achieved in both houses by the careful design and interweaving of porches and terraces with the landscape adjacent to the houses so that they seemed to be part of the buildings' architecture. In spirit the two houses were very similar. Looking back, some seventy years on, I wondered if there was not some 'cross pollination', though, probably, the similarities were pure coincidence.

Both houses began their architectural life as small farmhouses. Both used colonial style detailing but they could not be considered 'colonial'. They were 'one-off', eclectic, designs. Though Grandfather's house was remodelled in the Victorian era it was not that 'Victorian' in the dark, brown, fussy and moody sense. Father's, constructed in 1928, in the robust beginning of the 'modern' era was certainly not 'modern', at least in the Bauhaus vernacular. Neither house was an historic pastiche. Father's house was mostly brick, painted white, with some clapboard, while Grandfather's was mostly white clapboard with a bit of local stone thrown in. Both had dormers. Both nestled into hills, and were surrounded by stonewalls that were part of the whole. Finally, both made ample use of 'French doors' and floor to ceiling windows.

The houses and properties were fun for children (and adults) to explore. Grandfather's house, may, perhaps, just have had the edge, mostly, I think, because of the property's larger size and configuration. As Susan Larkin said, "The setting offered surprising variety within a small area." In architecture terms there was a lot 'going on'.

'A lot going on' would also include the rather outspoken, lively, Twachtman family. It was not unusual to meet any of the Twachtman relatives, Uncle Alden, Uncle Jackie[31], Uncle Quentin, Aunt Marjorie, cousins Elizabeth, Peggy, Mary Charlotte, Phyllis, Johnny, Eric and David when visiting the Round Hill Road property. As Marty and I were, by far, the youngest cousins this friendly, humorous, bantering, wisecracking, and witty, Twachtman crowd were outgoing towards Marty and myself. Outside of Aunt Louise, Uncle Alden's wife, I do not have recall of any in-laws being present during these visits.

You could enter grandfather's house formally through the robust but elegant south-facing portico, designed with the assistance of grandfather's architect-friend, Stanford White. Mostly, however, we came in on the kitchen or garden side having parked the car, somewhat precariously, on Round Hill Road – there wasn't much parking room as the property was, of course, designed around horses.

The interior of the house was light and open with high ceilings. Big south-facing windows came down close to floor level on the south side and French doors were strategically placed for access to porches. A stone fireplace dominated the living room and a stair leading to the main bedroom wound up behind it. Another stair led to several second floor bedrooms all with large dormer windows. There were paintings and artefacts everywhere. I occasionally "worked" in the garden but spent more of my time exploring the house and property on my own.

Uncle Alden's green LaSalle Series 50 Coupe, a car that he was still driving in the 1960s, and Aunt Marjorie's Ford roadster with rumble seat occupied the horse barn. In addition, and rather bizarrely, a vintage glider hung from the ceiling. One might have thought, not unreasonably, that it was the Wright Brothers plane without the motor. I do not know when or where or even if Uncle Alden flew it. I assumed that he had since it fitted his adventurous 'character', but I cannot remember getting a straight answer from him upon my questions relating to the aircraft.

Uncle Alden's house, or house-studio, (it was uniquely both house and studio) was set some thirty feet above Round Hill road on a rocky outcrop. It overlooked the little gorge through which Horseneck brook flowed, as it cascaded down into the "Hemlock Pool"[32]. The house could be reached either from Grandfather's house by wandering up steps and paths or, as we did more often, from the north side, across a sloping, wobbly, rustic wooden bridge that Uncle Alden had constructed over a bit of the Horseneck brook.

After crossing the bridge one continued climbing up a number of wood and earth steps to arrive on a sandy terrace that ran the entire length of Uncle Alden's house. The terrace overlooked the Hemlock pool and a little stone swimming pool, surrounded by ivy and bamboo, that Uncle Alden had constructed in the stream just downstream of the "Hemlock Pool". Uncle Alden had diverted part of the brook to run through the swimming pool so that the water was always fresh and clear. The pool provided a cool, shaded respite from the sometimes-sultry Connecticut summers. We used it often trying not to bash ourselves on the great boulder in the centre or on the sharp rocks from which it was constructed. Uncle Alden told us that he swam in it every morning: at least in the summer. Halfway down the steep hill leading to the brook and pool was a large maple tree under which were the graves of Grandfather's two children, who would have been another aunt and uncle, Eric Christian and Elsie.[33] Both died in their childhood.

A few French park chairs, a pair of rustic wood benches and a table were the terrace's principal furnishings. In summer, potted flowers, mostly geraniums were casually placed about the terrace. Terracotta fish and other similar objects made by family or friends were scattered about. A flimsy wooden railing provided a gesture against a long tumble down to the brook. In good weather family and visitors would gather on the terrace to chat, have tea or a drink and enjoy the ambiance. I would sit quietly and listen to the conversation, or if bored, would wander off to explore the property or house and particularly the small cement castle that Uncle Alden had constructed for his sons, my cousins Eric (1909-1985) and David (1916-1975?). The castle was a cross between Norman and German castles, including slate roofs, battlements, a moat and keep. It was, more or less, to the scale of lead soldiers and was covered in places with moss and small-leafed ivy. I could spend what seemed like hours at the castle.

By the time I got to know my cousins Eric was already a doctor and David was working for Jo Mielziner as a theatrical set designer. Mother was close to David and stayed in touch with him during her lifetime. Both cousins joined the services before the United States had entered the War in 1941: Eric, a doctor served in the Navy first on the USS Borie, an old four-stacker, (he was not aboard when it was sunk after engaging and sinking a German submarine off the New England coast). David was a captain in the artillery, a battery commander (no surprise there) and served in the Pacific theatre.

Between the terrace and the house was a broad bed of ivy into which, near the centre, Uncle Alden had constructed a goldfish pond. One had to walk over the pond on stepping-stones to reach shallow steps that led up to the full-length veranda across the front of the house. The veranda was a study in artistic lethargy and personal history. Objects Uncle Alden no longer needed but were part of his past or perhaps, even a little of his present, were attached to the wall or hung from beams. The objects included; polo mallets and helmets, a pith helmet or two, saddlery, an occasional garden tool, hoe, rake or basket, and semi-abandoned jackets or raincoats. I found these artifacts fascinating; they provided additional fuel to my imagination that was already stimulated by the Twachtman surroundings.

Entering Uncle Alden's house through the central, large panelled door one found oneself in a large rectangular room, two-thirds the length of the house. This room was the living room, a spare bedroom, an animal catchment and probably most importantly Uncle Alden's studio. The main bedroom for Uncle Alden and Aunt Louise[34] was at the south end of the house making up a third of its length. The room's ceiling was gambrel shaped and many years before, had been, painted a deep blue - it showed its age. A Venetian glass chandelier hung at a slight angle from the ceiling, as did a large, wood and paper model airplane. Both were dusty and draped with cobwebs. Opposite the door was a large stone fireplace and chimney covered with objects from Uncle Alden's World War I period: German, American and French helmets, a German Mauser rifle[35], an American Springfield rifle, cartridge bandoliers and a couple of swords. On a small section of wall between the chimney and the door to the adjacent dining room were dusty photographs from this period including one of Uncle Alden, when regimental commander of the 103rd FA Regiment, receiving the Distinguished Service Medal from General Pershing. Below this was a typed copy of the citation[36]. The medal itself, and if I recall correctly, another, were in frames below the pictures. To the right of the fireplace was a large chest of drawers dominated by a vase of dried flowers that were reflected in a large mirror in a carved wooden frame. On the right hand side of the chest's top, my favourite object of all from this intriguing room, was a hand-made, bronze, scale model of a 155mm Schneider howitzer, the principal field piece of Uncle Alden's 103rd FA Regiment. Uncle Alden told me that it had been made and presented to him by a jeweller in his regiment. The model was fully operational; wheels and gears turned, boxes in its trails opened to reveal spare screws of the size one would find in eyeglasses. A remarkable interrupted screw-thread breach block permitted the little howitzer to fire a real 45-calibre bullet. It was certainly not a toy but I was permitted to play with it anyway and I did, for hours on end.

Perhaps because I was so enthralled by the model, Uncle Alden invented the game of "Howitzer" that he played with me on a carpet in front of the fireplace. The game was designed for only two, Uncle Alden and myself. Key to the game were the toy howitzers that he had made from mousetraps, modified by the addition of little copper cradles in which marbles could be fitted. A set number of marbles were then lobbed alternatively at the "enemy" that consisted of a given number of lead soldiers lined up creatively on our respective sides of the carpet. After all the marbles were fired the number of soldiers felled were counted and the winner declared.

Uncle Alden was, not surprisingly, an artillery enthusiast. He told me, often, that when (and not if) I went into the army I should be in the artillery. I think it was

Uncle Alden's theory of the biggest bang or that artillery was the "king of battle". As it turned out, I did. He was also quite adamant that the study of architecture was an excellent basis for a military career. [37]

A canopied Chinese daybed used for a nap or perhaps the odd overflow visitor occupied most of the south end of the room. On the west wall a large armoire filled the space between the entrance door and a window. This contained Uncle Alden's painting and drawing materials and a lot more besides. In front of the armoire was an easel on which was most always mounted an unfinished painting. Uncle Alden was a combination of soldier, artist, muralist, equestrian, sportsman and architect. I am not sure in what order these occupations should be put. He was a graduate of Yale Architecture School (1901) and the Ecole des Beaux Arts in Paris. As an architect he was responsible, in collaboration with Uncle Quentin, an engineer, for a number of large and distinguished houses in Greenwich. His murals that have only recently been rediscovered are impressive. The Frick Museum in New York where some of his work still exists on ceilings has reproductions of his work on bags and mugs. While Uncle Alden painted in grandfather's style and their paintings were sometimes exhibited together, he was not grandfather. Ira Spanierman[38], after looking at some of my own paintings declared that I was a better painter than Uncle Alden – I think Ira's comment was an attempt at humor, or perhaps, sarcasm.

Next to the easel was a classic T-shaped perch for Polly his parrot. Polly was noisy and had a typical parrot vocabulary; "Polly wants a cracker; hello; goodbye!" Polly was sometimes accompanied in the room by Uncle Alden's feisty, escapologist monkey, Coco. Both animals were a health and safety risk to young children and we were told to stay clear.

The north end of the room was Uncle Alden's architectural "office". A classic studio window more akin to a greenhouse made up most of the north wall. It was this window, more than anything else that gave this room the overall feeling that it was a studio not a living room. The sill of the window was cluttered with dusty bits and pieces that had found their resting place years before; soldiers, little objects, jars for pencils and brushes and anything else that would fit. In front of this window was Uncle Alden's flat draughting table supported by sawhorses. House plans, sketches and other drawings on which he might be working were attached to the board by large thumbtacks. I would often see him sitting on his stool, working away on something or other; I remember a little summerhouse[39], while chatting and smoking. He was almost a chain smoker and a cigarette was often hanging limply from his lip while the ash lengthened until it fell onto his drawing. He would brush it off with the back of his hand as if it were a moth.

Behind the living room, on the edge of the rock outcropping were the dining room, kitchen, a back hall entrance, single bathroom and two small bedrooms for Eric and David. In Eric's room was a footlocker within which were kept a collection of handguns: Uncle Alden's service 45, a colt 44 and various other revolvers from the First World War and before. Uncle Alden took the time to explain the pertinent details about each of them.

There was only one room upstairs, it was directly over Uncle Alden's bedroom and it was reached by a short, steep, stair. It served, technically, as a guest room, and I sometime slept there on an overnight visit. The room was really for Uncle Alden's extensive collection of World War One lead soldiers, toy tanks, toy guns and other militaria. I was allowed to play with the lead soldiers but was admonished to be VERY careful. I did once break a soldier and Uncle Alden was well displeased – he kept me out of the room for at least a week – the worst part of the 'punishment' was, however, Uncle Alden's displeasure and my, unfounded, fear that I would not be allowed to visit Uncle Alden's again.

Uncle Alden always told me, with a wry twinkle that I was his favourite nephew – although he only had one other, Johnny, Quentin's son. In any event Uncle Alden was certainly my favourite uncle and I had five[40]! My youngest son, Alden, born in 1972, was named after Uncle Alden out of respect but I do not recall if Uncle Alden, who died in 1974, knew that.

Grandfather's house - South facade - 1902
From 'An Artist's Unspoiled Country Homes' 1905 p. 626
Essentially unchanged in the 1930s

Uncle Alden's House/Studio overlooking
Horseneck Brook

Uncle Alden's eclectic and snowbound, 'castle'

Uncle Alden (front) with staff inspecting his
regimental positions - 1918

Uncles Alden and Jackie - 1918
Jackie in uniform of a French Lieutenant

Gardening at Grandmother's House c. 1940 (?)

Peggy Twachtman and Emery Katzenbach's wedding party 1937(?)
in Grandmother's living room - left to right:
unknown, Aunt Marjorie, Peggy, Marty, Emery, me, Elizabeth, Phyllis, Charlotte, unknown

3

CASEY AND SIESTA KEYS

SARASOTA
1933 – 1942

For reasons that were never altogether clear to me mother and father liked to 'winter', as they called it, at least for a few months, in Florida. Probably they just didn't like the worst of New England's cold weather. Florida's winter weather was not exactly hot but it was at least sunny and mild. I have only vague memories of the first trips that were to Bradenton. By the mid-thirties, however, we had moved further south to spend several winters on Casey Key. Sometimes at the time it was referred to as "Treasure Island" a name that was the product of a would-be developer of the 1920s. We called it, apparently incorrectly, "Casey's Key".

In the Bradenton years we had travelled south on the Seaboard Airline's[41] Orange Blossom Special or the Silver Meteor. Later, when we had moved to "Casey's Key" we drove the twelve hundred or so miles in our maroon 'woodie' Ford station wagon[42].

Father and mother shared the driving with the emphasis on father. Marty and I sat in the back watching for the next Burma Shave signs[43] or for anything equally interesting, or not, but most often we just squabbled over nothing much at all. On the way south (or north) we visited historic houses; Mount Vernon, Monticello: cities and towns; Philadelphia, Frederick, Williamsburg, Richmond, Charleston, Savannah, St. Augustine: Civil War battlefields; Gettysburg, Bull Run and others that I have forgotten. On rare occasions we also visited "natural wonders" such as the Luray Caverns. The "natural wonders" were not father's favourite attraction; not surprisingly he was more interested in buildings.

In Frederick, Maryland we were required to learn Whittier's Barbara Fritchie legend and poem. Much to everyone's amusement I usually got the poem backwards having Mrs. Fritchie request Jackson's troops to shoot the flag instead of her head. This story, I learned much, much later was made up so what or who was shot was irrelevant anyway.

The trip took us about ten days and was, as advertised by father, educational. The driving between stops could be fraught due to the competing interests of what to see, where to stay, where to eat and when and where to stop to "chase squirrels" or "bears", our code phrases for need to relieve ourselves, one way or the other, usually in some roadside wilderness. We stayed in modest family-run motels or cabins selected, by sight only, late each afternoon. At the time there were no national chains and the quality of accommodation ranged from modest, at best to pretty awful. In Williamsburg, however, we got to stay in a proper inn and I slept in a four-poster bed that required the use of a small stepladder to reach the mattress. I loved it. We ate at roadside cafes where the quality of the food matched the quality of accommodation.

The house we rented on "Casey's Key" was an H-shaped, one-story, brown-stained, wooden bungalow set on the bay side of the narrow, sandy road that ran the length of the key. The road was linked to the mainland, at more or less the halfway point, by a one-lane swing bridge over the costal waterway and bay. The road was barely wide enough for one car. Some years later, after the War, during my first and last driving lesson in a surplus WWII jeep, on "Casey's Key", I was able to confirm that two cars couldn't pass each other on the road. Rounding, probably the only curve in the entire road I was confronted by a behemoth four hole black Buick coming right at us. It wouldn't move over so I swerved to the right. When everything stopped, except the Buick, the jeep was hanging vertically half way up a palm tree and the instructor was in my lap. We were not hurt but it took a lot of effort to get the Jeep down. The instructor quit the business, pretty much on the spot: as for me I just started driving the station wagon and anything else with four wheels. The road, though not heavily trafficked, was, nevertheless, periodically reduced to "washboard status" requiring frequent servicing by the local convict chain gang. The convicts were dressed in the traditional black and white striped baggy uniforms, some were chained at the ankles; I do not recall if there were any iron balls. The gangs, consisting of maybe ten or twelve men were brought from the mainland by truck and were overseen by one or two shotgun-armed guards. The gangs shuffled along using shovels, pick axes and rakes and slowly beat the road into submission. The improvement would last not much more than a month or so before the process had to start all over again. Oddly, the convicts seemed quite friendly towards Marty and me and they and their guards did not mind if we watched them - as long as we kept our distance. Though our parents tolerated our watching the work I am not sure if they were very happy about it.

Our bungalow was one of several similar buildings built as investment properties in the 1930s. Father liked the simple but comfortable design. He even sketched a number of hypothetical house designs based on this simple bungalow and I still have one or two of them.

Between the road and the unspoiled white sand beach and the clear waters of the Gulf of Mexico was an irregular hundred yard wide stretch of grassy dunes, dotted with large clumps of sea grapes, occasional Spanish Bayonet plants and covered with all too ubiquitous sand spurs. The latter made visits to the beach without shoes, even on little sandy paths, an irritating if not painful experience. The east side of the road, slightly more protected from the Gulf's waters, was where the bungalows were built. It was essentially a flat sandy area, a few hundred yards wide and ended where it met the intercostal bay. The area was covered with a mixed and random collection of palmetto, cabbage and coconut palms with some scruffy Australian pines thrown into the mix. However, in some parts of the eight-mile long key the landscape was one of dense, subtropical, impassable undergrowth. Modest plantings of ornamental flora and rough spongy lawns of common Bermuda grass surrounded each bungalow. The whole landscape was rather scruffy though, in the 1930s, that could be said for a lot of the Florida Keys as well as the interior land.

We had a small dock on the bay side where we moored our skiff. Taking the little boat out to explore the mangrove-filled bay was a daily activity and a treat for my imagination. As later confirmed by Ratty in *Wind in the Willows*, "There is nothing-absolutely nothing - half so much worth doing as simply messing about in boats." That is what I did. Despite my age, or lack of it, I was permitted to "mess about" in our small boat. By the time I was seven, thanks to the summer sailing classes I could row, sail and operate an outboard motor and I knew my way around the local mangroves, bays and waterways of 'Casey's Key'. Though there were other children on the key my boating was mostly a solo activity it absorbed both my time and imagination.

I do not remember what father and mother did to pass the time every day. They did not participate in any sporting activities and anyway "Casey's Key" was not a sporting community. I only recall low-keyed socializing: perhaps that was enough. The principal family activity, which was frequent, was collecting seashells. We called it "shelling" as in, "let's go shelling!" While this sounds essentially passive, "shelling" was quite competitive. Sneaky early morning treks, trying to stake out one's own areas of beach and running to get ahead of family members and other "shellers" on the beach were all 'de rigueur'. The object in all this hoorah was to find the best specimen shells.

Mother and father did go off on rare occasions leaving me "home alone" a fact that confirms, at least in part, the generally peaceful and remote quality of life on "Casey's Key". (After Marty was enrolled in Rosemary Hall she only remained south for the proper school holidays). We did have friendly neighbours, a widow and her sister, to whom I could turn if needed. One night, "home alone", a scary, violent storm hit "Casey's Key. It was too much for me and I sought the willing support of our neighbours. Father didn't think much of what he thought was "unmanly" behaviour and I was chastised for 'escaping' to the neighbours. I didn't seek them out again. From time to time father and mother entertained family visitors and friends, Twachtman cousins mostly: that was fun.

We had a 'live-in' cook, Mary, I think that was her name. She was a seriously large, friendly but bossy black woman who all but lived on Coca-Cola. Each week, when she was there, the local Coca Cola truck delivered caseloads of the drink. What it must have done to her teeth and general health I hate to think. Marty and I were not permitted Mary's Coca Cola and we rarely broke that dictum.

I think we spent three or four winters at "Casey's Key". Outside of Christmas, Easter was probably the highpoint and it marked the approximate time when we would return north. We didn't attend church celebrations on the day. Instead mother and neighbours created an extensive Easter egg hunt for the twelve or so mixed-age children in our general neighbourhood. In an attempt to keep everyone happy there were a number of prizes. The best prize, something like a box of chocolates was for the winner, the child with the greatest number of eggs. However, perhaps Biblically, a second prize was given for the least number of eggs collected. It was almost as good as the first prize. Marty, true to her form and ambition was usually the winner. One Easter, however, I was giving her a run for her money or so I thought until, halfway through the event, I checked her almost full basket. I was convinced that I could not catch up so I decided to download. By discretely putting my eggs back in the bushes I easily garnered the "booby prize". Under the circumstances I didn't mind what it was called. I don't know if the parents twigged what happened. They may have, as that was the last of the Easter egg hunts.

When she was there Marty sometimes went boating with me but her chief activity was following after the neighbour's teenage son Teddy. Marty was already quite precocious in her interest in the opposite sex and Teddy was the best and quite possibly the only candidate for her attention and he didn't seem to mind. The good news from this activity was that Teddy was very helpful to me. Father was only really interested in sailing and he had encouraged that activity but it was Teddy who taught me how to operate outboard motors: he would even let me use his Johnson 'Seahorse' motor. Teddy's family, the Jacksons, were quite well off and friendly. Their rather elaborate house, at least compared to our bungalow, was only a few hundred yards down the road to the south. We occasionally went sailing on their handsome schooner that was moored not far from "my" dock.

At least once a week we went on an outing, mostly to shop for food but also to break-up what was the quite simple daily activities. Sometimes it was just to shop for groceries at the general store and gas station in Nokomis; sometimes it was to travel a few miles further south via the Tamiami Trail to Venice, which was the better choice.

Venice, dry and dusty was not much of a town in the late thirties. Its population was probably not more than 500. The town of Venice had been laid out during the enthusiastic boom of the 1920's and was replete with an ambitious road network, (eighteen miles of it going nowhere), with sidewalks (128,000 feet of them[43]) and lampposts. The sidewalks were covered with sand, sandspurs and drifting trash. The once aspiring San Marco hotel was now the winter quarters of the Kentucky Military Institute. A few small, sleepy shops managed, barely, to keep open. We frequented one little shop where Marty and I could buy little figures made from coquina shells for a nickel or a dime. We could also visit the handsome Seaboard Railway terminal. On occasion our visits might concur with the arrival of the West Coast Silver Meteor[44] or Orange Blossom Special with its snorting, hissing steam locomotive relaxing after its run. If we were having a lucky day the train's engineer, much to our screaming delight, would take us on board the engine and let us press the pedal that opened the locomotive's butterfly firehole doors. On other occasions, more rarely, mother or father or a friend would take us to Sarasota where we could spend a happy day at the winter quarters of the Ringling Brothers circus.

Still more rarely we would go on special "shelling" trips to Sanibel, Captiva or Marco Island further to the south. These islands were barely inhabited in the thirties. The inn on Captiva, (or it may have been Marco) where we stayed was without electricity, a bit reminiscent of the movie "Key Largo". The shelling, however, was terrific. You could count on bringing back rarities such as junonias, specimen angel wings, or perhaps even a lace murexe. One of mother's occupations was making a glass topped coffee table to display our best shells and these trips would provide mother with many specimens. The table showed up in odd places for a few years: ultimately, mother gave it away.

Though enrolled full time at Greenwich Country Day, there seemed to have been an arrangement that permitted me to spend considerable time Florida but only if I attended an alternate school. As there was no school on or near "Casey's Key" I was tutored: that was also acceptable. My tutor was the head of a boy's camp in New Hampshire and he "wintered" in the area. He was an adept teacher and friendly, in fact, on occasion he was a little too "friendly". As I never knew what to say to my parents about his "friendliness", I didn't say anything. In any event, he kept me up in my studies, and I was usually ahead of my class when we returned to Greenwich after Easter.

In the spring of 1940 father became ill with heart problems and (I believe) diabetes. By the fall, however, he was well enough to travel and his doctor thought it a good idea for father to be in the Florida sun. This time we travelled by train as driving that distance was not on. Without a car "Casey's Key" couldn't work and anyway it was thought that father should be nearer medical facilities. Consequently we moved one island up to Siesta Key, which was in effect a southern suburb of Sarasota and its good hospital. In addition to medical facilities Sarasota, as noted, had not only the Ringling Brothers Circus but also it was the Boston Red Sox's winter quarters and it had a great "5 and 10"[44] store that we frequently visited. The best part for me, however, was watching the Seaboard railway trains that ran right through the streets of the town, the big locomotives vying for the right of way with car traffic: exciting. However, despite all the facilities Sarasota and Siesta Key only partially compensated for my easy-going boating activities of Casey's Key.

Like Venice, Siesta Key still had the decaying artefacts of the Florida's land boom of the twenties. One could cycle off the main road, away from the beachfront, on overgrown roads yet to be finished. The beginnings of an infrastructure for future development were everywhere. Concrete curbs, sidewalks and unpowered light poles studded the palmetto scrub. It all fascinated me. I spent hours prowling round this imaginary world afoot or on my bicycle. The explorations were not without the excitement of scary encounters with rattlesnakes and even once with a dreaded coral snake. It would be decades before development materialized, though when it came, it materialized with a vengeance.

We stayed first at a posh hotel called "Whispering Sands". While rather lush and comfortable "Whispering Sands" did not (for one or another unknown reasons) appeal to mother and father and we soon moved a mile or so further down the key to the "Gulf View Inn", an apt name for it was right on the beach. The Inn was owned and run by the Whipples, a friendly couple, from Maine's, "… stern and rock-bound coast". They were of the same age as mother and father and we got on well. The Inn's clientele was mostly northern families of similar disposition to us: it was all very congenial.

The Inn, itself, consisted of a main building containing the principal lounge, the hotel's reception desk and bedrooms that opened off the lounge on two levels, a modest forerunner of latter-day atriums. The inside was visually attractive, lively in a rustic way: a Florida version of an Adirondack style hotel. The court had been constructed from rough-cut timber, lagged on to tall pine tree trunks on which the bark was still intact. Railings were made from smaller, interlaced branches stripped of their bark. A stream and pond, replete with goldfish, and designed so that one had to cross and re-cross it, meandered through the court[45] ending in a central pond and stone fountain. For inexplicable reasons the guests insisted on throwing coins into the fountain. Marty and I periodically tried to recover some of these but it was a dodgy business and we were not very successful. The stream's little waterfalls created a pleasant, natural, musical background to compete with the Gulf's breaking waves. During the day people were usually out and about and the court was mostly empty but at night when it was set up for bridge and poker, the principal evening entertainments, the court came alive, full of chattering guests. The dress code was unwritten but quite formal, women were well dressed and the men wore coats and ties. The atmosphere was upbeat and noisy. Two one-armed bandits were tucked away behind a palm tree in a dark corner. When they were played, the "cachungs" of these machines added tambourine-like musical accents. Marty and I were allowed to play the nickel machine but our success was modest.

A corridor connected the lounge area to a slightly newer two-story wing containing the dining room, kitchen and additional first[46] floor bedrooms. There were two annexes, a fairly large one, motel like, next to the Inn's entrance and the other, a newer, smaller, but singularly uninteresting building that contained only six or eight larger rooms. We stayed first in the main part of the Inn but soon moved to the smaller annexe. It was less busy, quieter, more private and comfortable.

The exterior of the Inn was finished with lapped wood siding, painted a rather sickly looking yellowish-cream accented with brown trim around doors and windows. The roof was flat. In all there was little to recommend the Inn - architecturally.

The Inn's surrounding landscape was scruffy, consisting (mostly) of tall Australian pines growing in musty, dirty sand covered with sandspurs, pine needles and cones. As we mostly went barefoot the latter were a serious hazard. We were constantly pulling the spurs from our bare, pained feet and stumbling over the pinecones.

We did not go south in the fall of 1941 either because of father's illness or the war, or both. When we returned the year after in late August, again by train, the Gulf View Inn had changed.

The Coast Guard had commandeered the Inn. A thirty man, more or less, detachment was ensconced in the annex near the entrance and in part of the main building. The Whipples were left with the balance, including our annex, in which to house their few guests. For me the change was exciting. It was the early days of the war and the security operations of the Coast Guard were, initially, something less than stringent. I was often taken in the detachment's jeep to help post the sentries and their dogs that patrolled the beaches at night. The morning and evening ceremonies of raising and lowering the colours provided opportunities to march, mostly out-of-step, behind the detachment. I learned, more or less, how to fieldstrip Thompson sub-machine gun and could, sort of, manage the manual of arms. It was all built-in entertainment for a nine year old. For Marty who came south with us, the Coast Guard entertainment was a little different. She saw the detachment as an opportunity to observe the male species and to find ways to tease them. This worked reasonably well for a while but ended the day the detachment's commander, Chief Petty Officer Boswell, was showing off new hand-cuffs. He demonstrated how they worked by locking them on his wrists and giving Marty the key to un-lock them. Marty took the key and promptly scurried into the crawl space under the Annex. By the time several Coastguardsmen collared her, Marty had lost the key in the sand. An unsuccessful search for the key resulted in CPO Boswell having to travel to the Coast Guard base in Tampa to have the new cuffs sawn off. He and the Coast Guard were not well pleased.

Three things resulted from the misadventure: first, Marty was banned from going anywhere near the Coast Guard, second, (which negated the first) realizing that this might not work, Marty was sent back to Rosemary Hall, hopefully under the control of Aunt Eugenia, "Auntiepuss", as we affectionately called her (behind her back), third, I became more or less tarred with the same brush and was now rather less welcome. That could have been either from Marty's shenanigans or perhaps from the deep "foxhole" I left on the beach – the one into which one of the sentries fell.

Every weekday I cycled the few miles from the Inn to the Out-of-door School[45], which we, more simply, called "the outdoor school" in which I was now officially enrolled. This kindergarten to eighth grade school, was, as the name describes, a school where the classes were held outdoors or alternatively, in poor weather, in modest, screened-in, wooden, open-air classroom structures, one for each class. Not surprisingly the atmosphere was quite relaxed. One day, and in an instant, this rather carefree spirit changed.

Early on in WWII, airfields for several types of warplanes were established at various locations in Florida, Fort Myers, Sarasota, Venice and Tampa were among the locations. The aircraft based at these training sites included, among others, the four-engine, B-24"Liberator" bombers and the Curtiss P40s, "Flying Tiger'" fighters. Siesta Key and the Gulf waters to its west were one of their gunnery training areas. From early morning to sundown the sounds of these aircraft with their powerful throaty engines and machine-gun firing exercises on towed targets, pervaded the environment. Tree-top flying was not unusual and, once, when I was standing on the breakwater in front of the Inn I could actually briefly watch at eyelevel one particularly low-flying P40 thunder past with its prop wash flattening the water's surface. Often the trainee pilots would show off doing acrobatics that under more normal, peacetime, circumstances, would get them grounded, if not arrested. The sounds and airborne activities were also not desperately conducive to our study at the Out-of-Door School.

On one warm and sunny October morning our teacher was trying to hold our attention on arithmetic exercises while we were distracted by the sounds from a P40 practicing dive bombing (or as some said later showing off to his girlfriend) nearby. The teacher eventually gave in to the distraction and permitted us to simply watch until the pilot's exercise was over. We watched the plane climb almost vertically to several thousand feet then roll over into another, almost vertical, dive. The plane briefly disappeared behind the nearby Australian pines; we heard a 'crack' and then a mighty roar from its Allison engine as the plane pulled out of the dive – only then could we see that it was missing half of its right wing. It rose to just above the tree line and started an uncontrolled barrel roll - straight at the school. We could just make out the pilot as the plane passed overhead - a second or two later it crashed. There was a thunderous explosion and a huge ball of fire erupted a few hundred yards from us. The plane was fully armed for target practice and moments after the crash its ammunition was exploding, sending bullets in all directions. We were all in shock. The teachers hurried us out of the school and we hastily returned to our homes on our bikes.

Later that same day the second-ranking coastguardsman found me at the Inn and quietly handed me a rather heavy sack suggesting that I might be interested in its contents. Apparently, I was not as much of a "persona non grata" as I had thought. In a rather, seriously inappropriate act, he had recovered the throttle controls from the crashed plane, possibly the last control the dead pilot touched. It was a macabre souvenir of the crash. There was always a strange metallic smell to the controls. I had them for years until they mysteriously disappeared – perhaps mother dumped them, she never liked me having them.

Not long after this event on a warm, late November day, we were enjoying a buffet lunch on the beach along with a handful of other guests. The lunch was nearly over when father said he felt "funny" and was almost immediately sick. Mother took him to their room in our Annex. I was told that it was, "probably something he ate" and that father would take a nap. Later in the afternoon I was told he wanted to see me. I went to his room. He had a flannel over his face and therefore he could only hear me come in. I joked with him, pretending to be someone else but was caught short by the urgent sound in his voice when he asked me not to joke. We talked for a little while, about what I cannot remember. After a while, my mother came into the room. She told me that his doctor had advised father to be taken the Sarasota Hospital, " just a precaution - he could be better looked after there". The ambulance had been called and it soon arrived. Father, accompanied by mother, was off to the hospital.

I ate dinner, went to my room, read a little and went to bed. Early the next morning November 25th, the Wednesday before Thanksgiving, I was woken, quite early, by Mrs. Whipple. She told me that my mother wanted to see me. I was taken to the little room that, even during the war, still served as the Inn's library. Mother was sitting there before a small fire, alone. I knew before she told me, that my father, whom I had yet to really know, had died. Mother said, "you are now the man of the family..."

A few days later in Sarasota, sitting in the Silver Meteor, I watched from a compartment window as two porters trundled my father's large, rectangular, wooden coffin to the baggage car for what was to be a long, silent, trip back to Greenwich.

We would not again return to Florida as a family. Mother returned alone in 1944, She did not return to the Gulf View Inn but spent most of the four following winters in a little cottage, further down Siesta Key in an area otherwise consisting of large single-family houses. One, I was told (correctly or not), belonged to the McLean's, owners of the Hope Diamond. I travelled south via the Silver Meteor from the old Pennsylvania Station in New York to join mother for most Christmas holidays but the 'real' Florida winters were over.

A 1938 "Woodie" Ford station wagon similar to father's in which we travelled to Florida.

Casey's Key: "Messing about in boats" with cousin Phylis (?) and her setter

Sitting on the breakwater at the Gulf View Inn 1942

Mother, Marty and me on Casey's Key c. 1939?

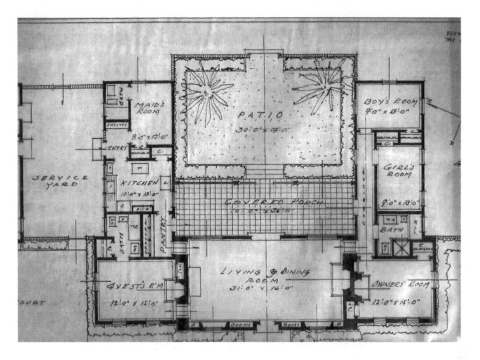

Father's design for a house based on the bungalow on Casey's Key.

The road on Casey Key - 1940?

4

DEER PARK

Greenwich
1942 - 1944

Father's funeral was held in a large chapel within Christ Church, on the Post Road in Greenwich. I have little recollection of the service other than the sense of being in a 'crowd' of relatives and friends: father was popular and respected. Burial was in the Putnam cemetery near the Twachtman plot. Afterwards there was a well-attended reception at Aunt Phoebe and Uncle Carl's house on Maple Avenue, not far from the church.

Christ Church was chosen for the funeral as it was considered, as I found out much later, the 'Baker family's church'. Though Christ Church was Episcopal, when Marty and I went to church, which was 'sometimes', we went to the Catholic Church on Greenwich Avenue and attended their catechism classes. Mother was a professed Catholic, probably because she had been sent to convent schools in France (St. Omer and Paris). She practiced her Catholicism, however, according to a personal credo that, I believe, was unfamiliar to the Pope. I learned later that mother was christened in the Swedenborgian Church in Cincinnati with which her mother's family was associated.

The Twachtman's religiosity is confusing, at best[46] and little effort was made to illuminate either Marty or me on this subject. We did know that Mother had her favourite saints: Francis and Anthony. The latter possibly of some help in finding her glasses. In any event the family, Bakers as well as Twachtmans seemed anything but 'churchy' in the formal, 'belonging' sense.

Mother was clearly distressed by father's death. The extent of this distress was evidenced by two events. Firstly, mother determined, probably in consultation with family, that she could not manage 'Porchuck Road', alone. With only the briefest of discussions with Marty and me, mother sold the house early in 1943. Secondly, mother withdrew, voluntarily, for several years to Silver Hill, a private, low-keyed, psychiatric centre in New Canaan. She was not 'restricted' and could come and go at will. I visited her there, several times, but, mostly, we saw each other during the Christmas and summer holidays.[47]

Under the circumstances Marty and I needed a place, or places, to live. Marty, for her part, returned to Rosemary Hall where she boarded. I went to stay with Aunt Marjorie and her daughter, cousin Elizabeth (Frazer), first in Wilton and then in their rented house on Strickland Road in Cos Cob, effectively a suburb of Greenwich. At first this was fine but there were difficulties between Elizabeth and her husband, Charlie. This and perhaps other matters, perhaps only habit, helped to bring about a high consumption of 'Old Fashioneds', as noted, Aunt Marjorie's favourite drink. Aunt Marjorie and Elizabeth were kind and supportive but the household atmosphere after five pm became a bit, let's say, argumentative. As a result mother thought it best to find an alternative 'home' for me. The MacRaes, friends of Grandfather's lived just down Strickland Road in the 'Holley House'[48].

I went there. The Holley House, built in 1728, was where Grandfather painted, taught and often stayed in the late 1890s. I do not know why, or under what conditions, the MacRaes agreed to look after me, but they did. Perhaps it was because Elmer MacRae had been a student of Grandfathers or, perhaps more pertinently, Grandfather and they had been good friends.

There was no electricity or central heating and little plumbing in the "Holley House". In the evening the MacRaes read by kerosene lamp in front of the large, central, living room fireplace that served to keep the house relatively warm, well, at least in the living room. My small room was in the southeast corner of the second floor, it was quite cold. In the mornings I would get dressed quickly and come down to the warm kitchen, around seven. Elmer would be there preparing oatmeal on the hot, coal-fired range. He would have been up for an hour or so, working around the house in his red felt slippers, tending the fires as well as making breakfast. He was a sprightly sixty-eight, obliging and friendly. When fortified with Elmer's stick-to-the-ribs oatmeal breakfast I would run down the drive and wait for the bus to take me to Greenwich Country Day. These arrangements lasted perfectly happily for some time (I cannot recall how long) but they were obviously temporary. Looking after even Twachtman's quiet grandson was probably a little much for the MacRaes: new sleeping arrangements had to be made. Going back to Aunt Marjorie's was not an option.

Aunt Eugenia already had Marty in tow, more or less, so it made some sense that I now went to live with Aunt Eugenia[49] and her son, cousin Henry. This had not been the original choice as in 1943 neither of them spent much time at home. Aunt Eugenia, headmistress of Rosemary Hall was off early and home late most days. Though Henry was medically unfit for military service, he had a high-security position throughout the war in the New York centre for the planning of North Atlantic Convoys. He was rarely home and his younger brother, cousin John was a lieutenant in the Navy.

Aunt Eugenia's house was located in Deer Park, a mature, private residential development of the 1920s. Located off Lake Avenue, it was almost midway between grandfather Twachtman's house and Rosemary Hall. The house was substantial but 'plain vanilla', a white-clapboard Colonial, with a central hall: large and comfortable. Set well back from a private road it was approached by a circular, gravel drive. I was given a small bedroom, on the second floor, opposite cousin Henry's room, overlooking the back lawn and communal woodland. Aunt Eugenia's house was more central to Greenwich Country Day than Cos Cob, to Marty and any potential after school activities. Though, as it turned out, with wartime gas rationing there were few to none of these. I rarely saw Marty. Boris was in my class but extracurricular visits with him were rare. After school and on weekends I managed on my own or occasionally spent time with Donald Grossett a classmate (and later Princeton classmate) and Deer Park neighbour. There were roads and woods to explore. Cousin Henry's pump action BB gun and antique Colt 44 provided substantial make-believe distractions. I also read every Life magazine and National Geographic printed since the 1920s, or even before. They had been assiduously collected and stacked, head high, in the closet of my room: very educational. Henry did come home from time to time. Though hardly a playmate, he was both friendly and amusing. He was an adept sailor and he sometimes took me sailing in his sloop the 'Julie'. One trip to Hamburg Cove and Essex on the Connecticut River, gave me a romantic taste of cruising that was to linger in my memory.

The only other person in Aunt Eugenia's household was James, part time gardener, butler and general all around handyman. James had also worked, part time, for father at Porchuck Road. He was a lovely, gentle, elderly man whose grandparents had been slaves. I looked forward to seeing his Hudson car pull into the drive (for some reason he was devoted to this rather eccentric make). He would look after the house and its rather simple grounds, patiently cleaning, raking the drive and picking up. It wasn't difficult because Henry and Aunt Eugenia were particularly neat and tidy. At lunchtime James would make us soup, boil some potatoes and sometimes, when available, cook a hamburger. When I was not at school, we would sit in the kitchen talk about the war, the family and sometimes, but seldom himself. He would leave by mid-afternoon.

Aunt Eugenia was rarely home during the day. Running Rosemary was a fulltime business. She was off to school well before eight and would not return until six-thirty or seven in the evening. Despite our familiar joking about Aunt Eugenia she was, in fact, about as good an aunt as one could have. She was firm, fair and caring in her relations with Marty and myself. Her longevity as headmistress of Rosemary attests to her qualities in that role. She was, perhaps understandably, not particularly interested in domestic life but nevertheless managed healthy meals consisting, typically, of lamb chops[50], peas (Birds Eye) and baked potatoes. Henry, when he was there, did his best to teach me how eat a lamb chop without using my fingers to pick it up and gnaw: he failed.

Greenwich Country Day was not a failure for me but not a great success either. 'Average' would be an apt description for both my academic and extracurricular and sports achievements. An example of an extracurricular activity was the sixth grade's production of the Mikado. Assigned to the chorus I was an enthusiastic participant in the first rehearsal. At the end of the first chorus, "If you want to know who we are", the music teacher suggested or rather requested that I "just mouth the words": even then I could not carry a tune. Baseball was a flop; I liked to bat but couldn't hit and throwing or catching eluded me. Football was worse, despite Boris's early training in aggressive behavior. I was both the smallest and was usually the last to be chosen for any team. In the spring of forty-four things improved a bit when, to everyone's surprise, including my own, I won a seriously competitive race on the school's 'field day'. This period also coincided with my first unrequited crush on a lovely classmate, Nancy Green. Greenwich Country Day was unquestionably an excellent school, but for whatever reasons, I never really thought that I 'fitted-in'.

Mother left Silver Hill for a good part of the summer of 1943. Aunt Eugenia arranged for the three of us Mother, Marty and myself to live in an empty faculty house at Rosemary Hall. It was just behind the classroom where Boris and I attended kindergarten. There were only a few people around so we had the run of the school's expansive grounds and facilities.[51] This was perhaps boring for Marty but exciting for me. Rosemary's medieval style, romantic stone buildings, with their slate roofs, battlements, and courtyards, built at the turn of the century appealed to my ten-year old imagination. One, Rosemary's little chapel, St. Bedes, was already familiar as it was the site of several family weddings and Christmas plays. It was, I was told at the time, brought from Normandy, stone by stone, though that 'fact' turned out to be serious disinformation. The Chapel was, nevertheless, charming and seemed almost a cathedral to young eyes. Marty and I occasionally played at tennis, we took sailing lessons at Indian Harbour and pottery and sculpture classes from Karl Illava at Edgewood School, near Rosemary. Further education also included Marty's sketchy introduction to what was then referred to as 'the facts of life': it was an illusory summer.

The following year 1944, Mother again came away from Silver Hill. This time she decided to rent a house near Little Compton, Rhode Island, the summer home of her long time, best friend and Rosemary classmate, June Platt and her husband Joe. June had been the cooking editor of House & Garden, an author of a number of cookbooks[52] and a designer for Tiffany Christmas cards and wallpaper. June was a lovely, kind, friendly and clever person. Joe was a bit formidable. He was an artist, an industrial designer (a peer of Raymond Lowey), but was probably best known as the set designer for "Gone With the Wind". The Platts had an absolutely splendid remodelled Cape Cod cottage overlooking grassy meadows rolling down to the Sakonnet River, where it meets Rhode Island Sound. They had added (or remodelled) two detached outbuildings, a studio for their various art projects and a large two-car garage that included an apartment for their two grown sons, John and Peter. The three buildings and an old stone foundation together created a pleasing outdoor space, sheltered from the wind, a 'sun-catcher' filled with standing and climbing roses. The site, the house and gardens could have fallen from the pages of House and Garden: it probably had.

Our summer rental was quite a different matter. Mother had rented, sight unseen, in Tiverton, some few miles north of the Platts, a house which had been constructed, allegedly, from Civil War wooden portable hospital units. This might have been true, or they could have perhaps been World War One units. The simply-constructed, unfinished, identical units had been rather haphazardly arranged. The collection, for that is what it was, created a rather leaky, fragile and spooky house but good as a summer rental. The house was partly covered with a spirited, free-for-all trumpet vine. Because of the vine the interiors were rather dim, even at high noon on a sunny day. The house was situated on the edge of a large potato field that rolled down to the Sakonnet River. You could quite easily make out the opposite bank and buildings on the Newport peninsular. In addition to the house, there were several barns and a windmill that powered the water pump for the property. I frequently climbed the windmill from which you could see for miles in every direction.

I spent most of my time, more or less, equally between the Beach Club at Sakonnet Point, swimming and jumping off its rocks, working part time at a neighbour's, weeding her garden or picking gooseberries, visiting antique shops with mother, and learning how to make angel food and sponge cakes and meringues. Marty's activities were essentially organized between the beach club and the Platts, particularly John Platt, their eldest son. He was in the navy but stationed not far away. John was quite striking in his sailor's uniform and Marty, a well-developed fifteen, took a shine to him. The appreciation was sort of reciprocal. I think this quasi relationship caused a bit of a 'hoorah' between mother and the Platts but I wasn't included in any discussions. The issue, if there was one, didn't stop us visiting or dining with the Platts. Apart from running Marty and me around, "antiquing" mother actually did some painting. A little gouache painting of a squirrel in amongst tall grasses, derived from Durer drawings still exists from this summer idyll.[53] What other time Mother had was spent visiting with the Platts reading or doing cross-word puzzles.

An evening with the Platts, in late July, turned out to be noteworthy. June had prepared one of her always-elegant meals. I do not remember the courses leading up to dessert but the dessert was a rich hazelnut torte: it was delicious. The night that followed wasn't. I had a painful stomach ache followed by my revisiting the torte. In the morning, I was still in pain and still sick. Mother decided that I had better see a doctor. As there were none in Tiverton we drove, in Mother's funny little prewar four-door Fiat 508, the ten miles to the Fall River Hospital. The doctor's diagnosis was rapid and definitive: I needed an appendectomy, "now". I was prepared for surgery and with a few whiffs of ether I was out and relieved of my appendix.

When we returned to Greenwich in late August mother had a conversation with Aunt Eugenia the result of which was a decision to send me to boarding school: but to which school and what school would take me, anyway?

In 1939 I had accompanied father to his thirtieth reunion at Princeton. At one point during the reunion, Father had me in tow while he chatted with his classmates in the bar of the Nassau Tavern. He introduced me to one of them, Sinclair Heyniger. Sinclair, looking down at me, told father that his brother, 'Lam' Heyniger, also a Princeton graduate had recently bought a school in the Berkshires: perhaps father should consider sending me there. The school was the Darrow School in New Lebanon, New York. It was designed, said Sinclair, to take students who, intellectually, could have matriculated at larger schools, such as Deerfield, Hotchkiss or Hill (father's alma mater) but who were otherwise not mature enough to succeed at these large schools. Both mother and Aunt Eugenia recalled father relating this event to them and they thought Sinclair's description was apt for me. In late August of 1944 mother made her decision and wrote to the headmaster, C. Lambert Heyniger, to ask him if he would take me. She made the point (for what it was worth) that my cousin Carl Knapp had gone to Darrow for a year before signing up for the Air Force.[54]

Darrow's application system was simple: the letter was it. Boarding schools were hardly full in the fall of forty-four. With my familial Princeton pedigree, Mr. Heyniger, who was an avid Princetonian, could hardly turn me down, I was accepted to Darrow.

The day before leaving Deer Park Aunt Eugenia, looking somewhat ill at ease, came into my room. She said she wanted to talk to me about "relationships between men and women". Mother, who, I suspect, did not want to deal with the matter, probably pushed Aunt Eugenia into the conversation (though it may just have been Aunt Eugenia, in loco parentis) I explained that Marty had already been there, at least with a broad brush though she missed a lot of detail. In any event on hearing this Aunt Eugenia did not press the matter: I think we were both relieved.

Time had been called on Deer Park and also, I would learn, soon enough, on my "childhood".

Photo of Aunt Eugenia c. 1942 when she
was headmistress of Rosemary Hall

Sketch of the Tiverton House
Marty, me and an imaginary horse in
foreground
By John Platt

Map of Greenwich
1 - Porchuck Road
2 - Grandfather's House
3 - Deer Park
4 - Indian Harbour Yacht Club
5 - Aunt Phoebe's
6 - Greenwich Country Day School
7 - Bush Holley House

PART 2

Education

1944 to 1960

5

DARROW

New Lebanon, New York
1944 – 1950

'Tis the gift to be simple, 'tis the gift to be free
'Tis the gift to come down where we ought to be,
Shaker song by Joseph Brackett unofficially adopted by Darrow

On a September morning in the fall of 1944, a week after the liberation of Paris, I found myself, in a busy Grand Central Station dressed in a blue blazer, grey flannels, white shirt and tie. A small trunk's worth of Darrow-specified clothes[55] was my only luggage. Cousin Henry, ever dutiful, was putting me on the New York, New Haven and Hartford's morning train to Pittsfield, Massachusetts, en route to Darrow. Near Danbury, Connecticut, the electric engine puling the train was changed to a steam locomotive. Thereafter the six-car train hissed, creaked and chugged, on a single-track line, originally laid in 1846, along the west bank of the Housatonic River. I do not recall if there were other students on the train - for me, this was, an interesting, even exciting trip, but a solitary one. A master, I forget who, met me at the Pittsfield station some four hours later. We collected my little trunk and drove the nine miles west to the school, located half way down Mount Lebanon, just across the New York state line.

Darrow's headmaster, Mr. Heyniger, all six foot seven of him, met us. He was standing on the dirt road that passed through the centre of the school. His presence was not a special event for me, he seemed to be always present when 'his' boys, particularly the new ones, were coming or going. Heyniger had a bone-crushing handshake but he was friendly and certainly courteous. I sensed, even then, his proprietorship of the school. It was clearly <u>his</u> school[56]. Intuitively, I knew that he was "the boss", which, I soon learned, was what everyone called him – but not to his face.

Darrow occupies the principal site of the Shaker movement in America[57]. The site was purchased from the Shakers in 1932 for a boy's school then called 'The Lebanon School', for boys. The site, on a ledge of Mount Lebanon is striking. In anyone's guidebook it would be classified as 'a place of outstanding natural beauty'. The school is actually in New Lebanon, a rural hamlet in the, still, all but forgotten northeast corner of New York's Columbia County. In 1944, Darrow owned some twenty-one buildings; dwelling houses, administrative buildings, meeting houses and barns that only fourteen years earlier had belonged to the Mount Lebanon Shaker Community.[58] The school used ten of these buildings in the so-called Church and Centre Families. The other buildings were unused and some were relatively derelict. Two Shaker sisters still lived in the adjacent North Family and there was yet another group of Shaker buildings to the south of the School, not unsurprisingly, designated as the South Family.

Mr. Heyniger assigned me to Ministry House where, previously, senior Shaker Elders lived. Now it was the dormitory for a handful of the youngest boys and was presided over by 'Doc' Velte the very English, English teacher and soccer (football) coach. Despite being a son of the Raj, Velte had a Princeton connection and because of this was somehow able to make his way from India to New Lebanon at the beginning of the war. His daughter Marguerite would turn out to be a sole classmate in my first year in this otherwise all-boys school. Darrow is a four-year school, 9th to 12th grades. I should have been in the seventh grade, but in 1944, no one was counting and I was, for some unknown reason, enrolled in an eighth grade that didn't really exist. At eleven years of age, ninety-seven pounds, four foot eleven inches tall and not physically mature, I was easily the runt of the Darrow litter.

Most of my classes were two person (Marguerite and me) tutorials except where that didn't work because of faculty availability or rather 'un-availability'. As there were only nine faculty members the available subjects were 'basic': math, history, English, science (very basic), Latin, French, religion and music. The largest classes might have only eight, or so, students. Music and religion, though less intense, meeting only once each week, provided as much of a lasting influence on me, as any other class, especially the music. Except for Grandfather's music box in the attic, music was not a big item in the Baker family. Six years of music classes at Darrow gave me a foundation in classical music that has endured providing me with great pleasure.

As for the 'main' subjects I managed to stumble through them, reasonably well, except for Latin. By some arcane calculation in my first year I managed, to achieve only a 14 (out of 100) in that subject. The note on the report explained that I had spent most of the year looking out the window. I pleaded guilty and started first year Latin again in my second year. Later, as I became more motivated, Latin would turn out to be one of my best subjects. Mr. Dakin, the Latin teacher in my senior year, even tried to persuade me to become a classics major in university: too far.

In the forties the Darrow faculty were mature and experienced teachers. Charles Broadhead, a tough but fair man with strong Christian beliefs and a Princetonian, taught history and was assistant headmaster. He had an unusual background that included sailing around the 'Horn' (in 1929) with Irving Johnson on the square-rigger, 'Peking'. He was a member of the Moral Re-armament movement of 1938 though he didn't push that on the students. Mr. Broadhead was one of my several housemasters during my six years at Darrow and he also led the outdoor activities (of which I would, in time, become a leader) such as, planting trees, clearing woods, hiking and stocking Tanner's pond with trout. Mathematics was taught by Mr. Pflaum, single, and the youngest of the faculty. He was not serving in the armed forces due to his poor eyesight. I excelled in his math classes throughout my six years. The Grigauts, French émigrés who, we presumed, had escaped from France just before it fell, taught French. Athletics was under the firm but fair control of Harry Mankhen, aka 'coach' and another Princetonian. (He was known as 'Coach' because of his former connection as coach of the Princeton 150 pound Football team.) Altogether, by anyone's standards, it was a small but remarkable faculty. It made Darrow an academically strong school capable of providing an education qualifying its graduates for colleges of student's choice including Ivy League colleges, particularly, and it probably went without saying, Princeton. Darrow, however, was not a traditional 'prep' school. Students not inclined to go to college, or not academically qualified, could, in fact, get an excellent education suitable for any future. These students, only a handful, were unusually skilled in practical matters such as farming and mechanics. They were respected for their contributions to the school's community and not demeaned for any lack of academic enthusiasm or achievement.

Sports (American football, soccer, basketball, wrestling, baseball and tennis) took place each afternoon on four days of the week plus Saturday games with competing schools. Participation in sports was mandatory (though there were some exceptions). Given my size I was assigned to the soccer squad - I would have been lost in the American football gear. Although I threw myself into the game I was not very effective. At afternoon practice in my second week at Darrow I ran into a large senior, Pierre Dupont, or he ran into me. I came out second best and fell down into a heap, hurting, but carried on in the game. After dinner that evening it was clear that something was very wrong with my shoulder and the local doctor, Cristicello (spelling may be incorrect) was called. He was a kind, elderly gentleman in a black suit, resembling an undertaker who had just walked off the set of a 'Western'. Although long past retirement he had returned to his practice because of the war. I was taken into the infirmary where, doctor Cristicello, in company with the school nurse, examined my shoulder. He determined that it was dislocated and broken in two places. He manipulated the bones back in place; very painful! He then wrapped me up with a lot of adhesive tape. Fall sports were also wrapped up for me and I was relegated to helping 'manage' the soccer team, not much of a job. Actually the team was surprisingly good as we had several South Americans who could dribble their way through a rain forest, let alone most any team we played.

The broken shoulder was not the only medical problem during that first fall at Darrow. In addition, I managed to contract a chest and sinus infection and ended up in the Pittsfield Hospital for a stay of two weeks. In present times one would probably be prescribed antibiotics and 'get on with it': but antibiotics were not readily available then. It was the combination of these medical events that permitted Mr. Heyniger to be persuaded by mother to let me take a long Christmas vacation in Florida.

The students, about forty, were pleasant and friendly. The oldest were just under draft age. Even so, there was a considerable age and maturity difference between myself and other students. Consequently, I made few friends in my first year. There was very little hazing in the school; it was not that kind of place. In addition, because of my size, or lack of it, I seemed to be inferentially 'protected' from what little bullying or hazing existed. This was not to say that I was not the target of some mild exhibitions of male adolescent sexuality.

Social contact with the opposite sex could be described as seldom and little. Once or twice in the fall or spring terms we would have 'tea dances' with neighbouring girl's schools such as Foxhollow, in Lenox, Miss Hall's, Emma Willard or St Agnes, in or near Albany. These events, formal, polite and rather short in duration, were heavily chaperoned by faculty. Over six years I recall only three 'flirtations'. One, in my first year with Ann Tilney a lovely English girl (allegedly a god-child of the king) waiting out the war at Foxhollow, a second in my senior year with Jacques Milner at St. Agnes school in Albany and the third with Helen Schoonmaker. Helen attended Shipley in Bryn Mawr and her family lived in Kingston New York. I do not recall how our paths crossed but Helen was the only one with whom I corresponded and met, occasionally, over a number of years. The relationship was a bit one sided: I pursued but Helen demurred. Other than these three graces I have no recollection of any other friends of the opposite sex during the six years of Darrow.

In 1945, after the war ended, some five (or so) veterans returned from the services to complete their studies that had been interrupted by the war. These 'students' were obviously now mature men who had been in service and, in some cases, action. While they were seniors or even post-graduate students, their arrival gave an unusually mature character to the student body. Darrow, and probably other schools of the period, were 'serious' places - adolescent frivolity was less tolerated, if at all. The typical student offences for which you could be punished included smoking, very serious (although exceptions were made for the veterans), missing classes, being late to anything, and general, unspecified, 'bad' behavior. Punishments were given in hours of manual work. For example if a class was missed you were penalized three hours, which meant you had to clean pig sties, or perform other, sometimes, menial tasks for that many hours This could leave one with very little 'free time'. It was a fair system and effective. For the most part I avoided these penalties.

By my third year the veterans had left, I was older, the school had doubled in size and some good friends were made. I become part of the school and Darrow became my 'home'.

A key program of the school was 'Hands to Work'. Mr. Heyniger had devised the program from the school's Shaker motto, "Hands to Work and Hearts to God". 'Hands to Work' occurred every Wednesday afternoon during which time the entire school worked at some physical task for the benefit of the school. We were assigned jobs ranging from such tasks as killing chickens, at the school's mini-farm, planting seedlings for future timber cultivation, moving timber piles from previously disassembled buildings (a sort of Sisyphus task) or just cleaning and performing maintenance. In the spring some students collected sap to make maple syrup. On the whole jobs requiring skilled labor were avoided – most of us were not skilled. The assignments were rotated each week limiting a potential boredom factor. The program was aimed at teaching us the benefit, and honor, of hard physical work: it worked. The school also allowed some students to work on 'Hands to Work' type projects in lieu of the otherwise mandatory sports. These projects were focused mostly around taking care of the school's aging trucks, tractors and 'historic' fire engine, collectively a great occupation for those with mechanical gifts. For the most part the students looked forward to this mid-week break from studies and sports. The program also gave the younger students an opportunity to meet and work with older students and vice versa. It was a memorable component of Darrow and continues, in a perhaps, somewhat more modest form (my opinion) today.

The school, though adopting a Shaker motto, did not, really, adopt the Shaker religious motto[59] of 'Hearts to God'. At Darrow 'Hearts to God' took on a more 'waspy' connotation. The school catalogue stated that Darrow was non-denominational: and it was. However, with its consecrated Episcopal chapel, the use of the Episcopal hymnbook and Book of Common Prayer, combined with a 'dog-collared' Episcopal priest on the faculty, this 'non-denominational' statement could have been easily challenged. We attended a chapel service every day except Saturday. On Sunday there were two, an eleven o'clock service and a vesper service. In addition, Mother had specified that I should attend Catholic Mass. On Sunday mornings I was therefore driven (in the car sense) to the rather plain, rural, Catholic Church in the 'valley', our colloquial name for New Lebanon, to attend their early Mass, which, at that time, was conducted in Latin. With my limited command of the language it went without saying, despite my earlier Catholic childhood 'catechism', that I was unable to follow the services' arcane procedures. I rose when I should have knelt, knelt when I should have risen and sat on a hard wood pew in between, daydreaming, waiting for the service to end. In another hour I would participate, quite happily, in Darrow's Sunday Chapel service. I continued with what could only be considered this religious duplication (or perhaps duplicity) for a few years. Finally there came a time, when without Mother's approval or even knowledge, I managed to put a stop to going to Mass by becoming baptized and confirmed, as a member of the Episcopal communion. Reverend Smith, the Darrow Chaplain, conducted the ceremonies in the Darrow 'Chapel' and managed the prerequisites leading to confirmation. The Bishop of Albany also participated in the rite. When mother did find out about my 'conversion', maybe two years later, she was not pleased. The event became a prickly subject for the rest of her life.[60] By contrast to the Catholic Mass, I enjoyed the Darrow Services. The Chapel, a converted Shaker tannery was on the edge of a nearly circular pond, aptly named Tannery Pond: it is a picturesque setting. The Chapel interior was finished in soft, lightly stained, pine except for its dark oak beams framing its open barn structure. A plain two-foot high wooden cross was placed in the middle of a large Shaker oat storage bin that served as the altar. Behind the altar hung a large orange dorsal. To the left (facing the altar) was the American flag and on the right the flag of the Episcopal Church. Classically, the altar was placed on a raised platform in the rear of the chancel, that itself was raised two steps from the nave. Two matching wooden lecterns stood at the leading edge of the chancel. These were sized, as were other elements of the building, to suit Mr. Heyniger. Except for the tallest among us, we students could barely see over (or be seen behind) them when we participated in the services, as we all had to. As for the pews, the hard wooden seats, designed by Mr. Heyniger and built by Ed Shilling the school carpenter were so deep (and quite body-polished) that we had to brace ourselves during the services in order not to slide into a heap on the floor.

Mr. Van Vorst, the resolute, stern, choirmaster and music teacher known by the boys, simply and rather respectfully, as 'VV', played the Chapel's electric Hammond organ. I loved the hymns, learned many of them by heart and still remember the words if not the tunes (I doubt if anyone would recognize what I was singing anyway). The vesper service with the oft-repeated vesper hymn 'Now the day is over...' and the setting sun beaming through the low western windows was particularly moving. This simple wooden chapel is one of those places whose character will always be religious, with or without a capital R, or its proper name. The 'Chapel' would be, much later, the site of the blessing of my marriage to Rosemary and, as well, for the commemoration of her death.

The fall term always ended with a Christmas service in the chapel. The space was filled with freshly cut pine trees and boughs, lit only by candlelight. It was surely not very safe but it was very beautiful. The highlight of the service, for me, was Mr. Heyniger's rendition of 'O Holy Night'. If not a headmaster, Heyniger could easily have joined the Metropolitan Opera: his voice was spine tingling. Singing was important at the school and despite my monotone, I enjoyed all of it, including the weekly sing-a-long in the Wickersham common room. I doubt if the likes of The Erie Canal, Grandfather's Clock, and Abu Ben Adam, which we all learned by heart are even known or sung today (perhaps for good reasons).

Thanksgiving was celebrated at the school: it was not then (until the late 40s) a school holiday when the students went home. The school's dining room, in the North end of lower ground floor of Wickersham was appropriately decorated for the occasion[61]. The first home break from classes came, as noted, after the Christmas chapel service. My Christmas holidays of '44 and '45 and '46 were spent in Florida where mother had rented a little cottage on Siesta Key, a few miles further south from the Gulf View Inn. Prior to leaving for these holidays I would make a visit to the two remaining Shaker Sisters in the North Family[62] to purchase a Christmas present for Mother. There were not a lot of options but a sewing box or oval carrier seemed to be well received. The Sisters were very hospitable and pleased, I think, to have a student visitor, and customer[62].

The most memorable part of these Florida trips was, probably, the 1500 mile, twenty-four-hour train ride. I travelled by train from Pittsfield, or sometimes Albany, to New York City where, at least in 1944 and 1945, a friend of the Platts ensured that I got on the Seaboard Air Line's Silver Meteor at Pennsylvania Station. At the time Pennsylvania Station was still the great McKim Mead and White Structure of 1910. I would also look across 8th Avenue to the central Post Office building of 1913, also by McKim, with its iconic inscription[63] above the colonnade. I was told that father had laid this out when he first worked for the firm: my gaze, probably, did reflect some modest familial pride.

Once on the train I was on my own. I could go to the observation car, (there often was one) eat in the dining car on its crisp white table linen, read or wander through the train. As much of the trip was at night I would do my best to get a lower berth to have a window through which to see the night scenery of dimly lit stations, military supply trains laden with tanks, trucks and guns and sometimes moonlit fields all partially obscured by the billowing, rolling smoke from the train's locomotive. It was exciting: mesmerizing.

Spring holidays were usually spent with school friends, Tim Cutler, Dick Barzin, Alan Mayers, Peter Hanke or with Boris when his Deerfield holidays coincided with Darrow's. Summers were spent, for the most part, with mother and Marty. The 1945 summer was spent in Waldoboro, Maine, near the neighbouring town of Friendship, perhaps because it was where the Whipples of the Gulf View Inn ran a summer inn or perhaps in honor of father's admiration of the iconic Friendship Sloop. He had talked of them when in a 'boat' mood. I learned to wait table for tips, (twenty-five cents was a big tip), learned that Maine water was unbelievably cold, learned how to pick blueberries from bushes and garnets from granite rocks. I sailed and rowed again. In 1946 summer was another part of Maine, Newcastle and Damariscotta. That summer we learned how to bet on Maine's peripatetic harness races. (clue: bet on horses with 'Hanover' in their pedigree) We visited every antique store in the area. I started my antique gun collection with the purchase for $7 of a Committee of Safety Musket from a store somewhere in the depths of Maine. 1947 and 1948 were spent in Old Lyme, Connecticut, first at the Old Lyme Inn and then in a cottage belonging to the late Walter Barnum[64], a distinguished yachtsman who, I believe, was a sometime sailing colleague of father. In Old Lyme, apart from some sailing, swimming and tennis, I learned the fundamentals of golf, got my driving license, and hung out with David Wycoff whose family had become friendly with mother in Florida. David's stepfather, Whitney Carpenter, was a tall, elegant and distinguished and somewhat mysterious figure fresh from the OSS of World War II. The Carpenter's large colonial house was fun to visit. It was full of silver-framed pictures of Arabs in full regalia, pictures of Mr. Carpenter doing a look-alike of T.E. Lawrence, cases with silver and gem encrusted Arab daggers and 'militaria'. Whitney was kind to me. In addition to being genuinely friendly and conversational he would periodically give me something from his collection of memorabilia. First it was a 7.65mm Luger, then a razor-sharp spear, replete with monkey hair, from the Shilluk tribe (famous, in part, for standing on one leg balancing with the aforementioned spear), and finally a dagger from Morocco. The later, he told me, was stuck into his arm while on a mission: maybe. He did sometimes tell me stories that included a wink or two.

I didn't see much of Marty during the summer. Her interests no longer overlapped with mine: at all. In old Lyme it would be fair to say that her main interest was John Barnum, Walter Barnum's son.

Each year at Darrow my marks improved and I was also able to become more of an integrated part of the school, even, in a small way, a student leader. I participated in everything, theatre, soccer, wrestling (team captain), and tennis, the outdoor club (president), the art club, mailman, as a house president and more.

The summer of 1949 was different. Marty had graduated from Rosemary in 1946 and, following Aunt Eugenia, had gone on to Bryn Mawr. In 1948, after mother purchased her apartment in 62nd street she and mother left for Paris, by ship (appropriately the 'Ile de France') so that Marty could take her junior year abroad at the Sorbonne. Mother stayed abroad during the year but returned early in 1949. In the spring mother thought that a 'Grand Tour' of Europe, or at least France, with Marty and me would be a great idea. Mr. Heyniger was at the time trying to get me to participate in the Experiment in International Living. Mother was having none of that: not surprisingly, she prevailed. In June Mother and I were on the inaugural Pan Am Stratocruiser flight to London. I am not sure how we managed to be on this flight, whether it was by accident or design (Mother had been, I believe, a friend of Juan Trippe.) I do not know. In London mother purchased a rather handsome maroon Sunbeam Talbot Ten drop-head coupe, a decision solely based on the car's looks. The car was notoriously underpowered but it was certainly good looking: it definitely suited mother.

By the time we got to London Marty had also acquired her much-loved Welsh Corgi, Taffy. We crammed the four of ourselves into the car and after a tour of London and Kent we made our way to Dover and from there, by ferry, to Calais. In Paris we stayed at the Hotel France and Choiseul on the Rue Saint Honore just behind the Place Vendome. We did a pretty thorough job of Paris sight-seeing, though the emphasis was more on getting to know the city rather than ticking off the sights. Mother's French was impeccable as it was, for practical purposes, her first language. Monsieur Grigaut's Darrow French, as interpreted by me and corrected by mother, was not so bad either; there was no language barrier.

After Paris we drove off to 'do' the Loire and its Chateaux. I cannot remember how many Chateaux we saw, it would be easier, perhaps, to count the ones we didn't see and the same could be said for the area's principal cathedrals and churches. Afterwards we 'did' Burgundy's towns and cities and a number of its Vineyards. Of the latter I particularly enjoyed visiting Pomeroy & Greno where the managing director took a shine to Mother. As a result, we were regally and liquidly, (not me though), entertained for several days.

A typical day would see us out of our hotel by mid-morning, mother driving. We would visit a chateau or two, then Mother and Marty would pour over the Michelin guide and discuss the options for lunch. Lunch, itself, was an extended event in a proper French tradition. Since I did not drink, wine did not suit my teenage palate, mother and Marty made up for it. The result was that I drove after lunch and, mostly, could choose the afternoon's chateaux, waking mother and Marty on arrival. Nights were spent at carefully chosen, 'reasonable', and sometimes bordering on 'historic,' but not too 'fancy' hotels. In the evening at dinner we would discuss French history pertinent to the day's activities, argue about the next day's plans, or, perhaps, if Marty and Mother felt like it, discuss why I was not a Catholic.

Taffy was always with us and enjoyed a pampered life of travel while eating in some of the best restaurants in France. Taffy's only problem was that he disliked anyone wearing a hat. Gendarmes, custom men and other officials were kept at bay by his aggressive, loudly expressed attitude. Marty thought this was very funny but mother and I were less sure. At the end of the summer after having seen France from Normandy to the Cote d'Azur I left to return to the States via Pan Am. Mother stayed on and ensconced herself in the France et Choiseul for the winter. Marty and Taffy went back to the Sorbonne.

My senior year at Darrow was uneventful. With mother abroad I spent Christmas with Henry and his bride, Willy (Wilhelmina) Van Neyenhoff in their newly built small house in Greenwich, off North Street. Willy, as her name might imply, was from Holland and had been a member of the Dutch underground. In the US, however, she was a model for Vogue. Willy was spectacularly beautiful. Willy was, I was told, the first model to pose almost topless for the cover of Vogue. Mother and Marty tried to keep me from seeing the pertinent issue but their efforts were in vain.

My marks in the final year were good. I vied, unsuccessfully, (no surprise there) with my classmate Bill Hudnut to be top of the class. Though I didn't win this academic competition, I was, with pretty good SATs, accepted to Princeton, my first and only choice of college. That was 'Plan A' - I had no 'Plan B'. As mother was still abroad, Henry and Willy came to see me graduate and receive the 'Merit Prize' at graduation, an edition of 'Birds of America'[65]. The citation read in part;

> *"This prize is given in recognition of your long and honorable time at*
> *Darrow... We are proud that you will be representing us at Princeton."*

Darrow was indeed a good choice for secondary school. Though I didn't know it at the time, it was a school with which I would maintain a long and active association.

Lambert Heyniger, "The Boss" conducting a sing-along (Charles Broadhead sitting in corner)

Ministry House - my first dormitory

The Shaker Dairy Barn - a site of fun and games - later remodelled by Mr. Heyniger as a gymnasium

Winning the annual cross-country race; fall1949 Bill Hudnut with the clipboard

The mailman: Daily Mail Call

Hands to Work - 1940s version 'Health & Safety' was a minor concern

The tennis team 1949 (first row left)
Exhibiting the high fashion and modern racquets of the time

Pan American 'Stratocruiser' in which mother and I flew to Europe in 1949

Mother at the wheel of her Sunbeam Talbot in Maine

I am in back seat - Marty took picture

Getting ready to row in Waldoboro Maine, 1945

6

PRINCETON

Princeton, New Jersey
1950 – 1954

"Dei Sub Numine Viget"
Princeton Motto

Following Darrow's graduation, Mother again vetoed Mr. Heyniger's valedictory recommendation that I spend the summer with the Experiment in International Living. As a result, in late May, I headed to London to meet mother for our second 'Grand Tour'. This time I travelled from New York via the 1930's Cunard liner the Georgic that had been adapted, post war, for one-class student travel. The trip was uneventful even with the full complement of cheerful and friendly student passengers. In six days or so the Georgic was turning round a big black buoy into the Mersey to disembark us in Liverpool. We transferred to London by boat train.

Mother, as planned, met me in London. This year the tour's focus would be Italy and we were in London to purchase an appropriate replacement for mother's Sunbeam that she had shipped to the States and later sold.

After much discussion, and sometimes argument, we settled (to my satisfaction) on a black 1½ Litre Riley sedan replete with wood trim and lovely-smelling red leather upholstery. It was purchased from the Riley showroom on Pall Mall, opposite the Palace of St James and around the corner from the Stafford, mother's latest hotel of choice. The Riley costing a steep (at the time) £800[66] was

83

not to be Mother's, or Marty's, favourite car. Mother subsequently 'gave' (relinquished might be a better word) the Riley to me to take back to the States on my return in September. Marty, it should be noted, was less than enthusiastic about this arrangement. She did get her own car sometime later and seemed mollified when that happened. I thought the Riley was great, if, as it turned out, a little demanding. I would enjoy the Riley for another four years.

Mother and I stayed in London for a few days and did some sightseeing while we concluded the purchase details for the Riley, rather more complicated than a car purchase today. We then drove to Dover stopping at Knole and one or two other country houses before taking the ferry to Calais. From there we drove straight to Paris where we caught up with Marty and Taffy. From Paris we headed east to Reims, Nancy and Strasbourg then turned right to go down to Zurich. In Zurich Mother, through some now forgotten connection, met up with its chief of police who, like the Managing Director of Pomeroy, decided to entertain Mother and, consequently, Marty and me. We stayed for several, not very exciting days, in a nice hotel with a room full of orange gladioli, the Chief's preferred choice of flowers.

The next serious stop before we headed for Italy was Salzburg. As I was the only Mozart fan of the three of us (omitting Taffy) this was a definite concession to me. We stayed first in Salzburg itself, at the marvelous Hotel Goldener Hirsch. I enjoyed their thick eiderdown duvets and luxurious cooking, especially the fluffy, sweet, 'surprise soufflés'. After a few days we moved to the recently reopened Schloss Fuschl on the Fuschlsee a few miles east of Salzburg. The hotel consisted of an imposing old stumpy tower and a comfortable annex. My single room was in the tower while Mother and Marty shared a room in the annex. This was a 'blessing' as the Schloss Fuschl was the site one of the longest and most memorable of mother's, (supported by Marty) 'why are you not a Catholic' harangues. Even this, however, did not take the edge off the Mozart concerts and romantic atmosphere of Salzburg and its surrounds.

We stayed at Schloss Fuschl for about a week then turned back west, via Innsbruck, to reach the Brenner Pass to Italy. On the way we tried a rather dramatic but abortive attempt to drive up the Grossglockner, Austria's highest mountain. Without going into the details, about three-quarters of the way up Mother had a change of heart and decided to quit the climb. Turning the car around on a road of hairpin turns was no mean feat and in the process mother somehow got the Riley stuck into the side of the mountain just below a hairpin turn. The Riley's tailpipe became impacted with Grossglockner earth that successfully stalled the engine. We held up traffic for almost an hour while I dug the tailpipe out and cleared it with the Riley's tire iron[67].

The Italian tour included the main northern and Tuscan (more or less) cities, Venice, Verona, Vicenza, Ravenna, Milan, Turin, Perugia, Florence, Orvieto, Asissi and Perugia, the two latter being the homes of Mother's favourite Saints, Francis and Anthony. Anthony was important to Mother due to his alleged 'ability' to find lost articles particularly, as noted, Mother's glasses. After visiting these principal cities we headed further south and did a pretty thorough job of Rome, visiting the site near the Spanish Steps where grandmother Baker kept a grand apartment in the years after Grandfather Baker's death in 1922 and the outbreak of WWII.

Our most southerly stop was Paestum the site of three Greek temples. On the way we took in Naples, Amalfi, and Pompeii. In Pompeii we hired a guide who insisted on taking us to and explaining, in detail, any 'rude' fresco or bas-relief he could find. Mother was not amused but Marty and I were. We capped this part of the trip by an idyllic long-weekend on Capri.

Looking back it is hard to believe we saw as much of Italy as we did: very 'American' I suppose. By the end of August we were heading back to Paris to drop off Marty, Mother and Taffy. I had a few days in there during which mother determined that before entering Princeton I should know the pleasures of wine. After visiting a number of good restaurants over a long weekend, she was successful. I had come to enjoy wine and knew its multiple pleasures and side effects.

From Paris I motored on to London and Liverpool to return to New York on the Georgic. The Riley accompanied me, stowed in its hold.

Princeton's fall term commenced shortly after my return. I arrived there with a car full of personal stuff and a small truck's worth of furniture, mostly from father's studio at Porchuck Road: the furniture had been in Drinkwater's storage[68]. I hardly knew what to expect upon my arrival. My only knowledge of the university had been Father's reunion in 1939 and family lore. As for classmates I knew, of course, my three Darrow classmates: Bill, Harry Hicks[69], Alan and Darrow's 1949 Contingent, Pete Conrad, Tim Cutler and Herb Hudnut. Other than these six I knew no one else in a class of seven hundred and something. Coming from such a small school as Darrow I found Princeton a bit overwhelming. By prior plan I was supposed to room with Boris who had been also accepted. Boris, however, had been taken seriously ill[70] and did not matriculate that fall. As a result I ended up in a single room in a tower of Foulke Hall: architecturally attractive but a bit lonely. Boris did come to Princeton the following year but we didn't see much of each other, the classes did not mix that much. In any event Boris dropped out in his sophomore year to pursue a career in racing. I saw very little of him during his career in racing.

The Korean War had begun that June and the potential for conscription was on our student minds. The first order of business for most of our freshman class was to sort out our position with the draft. At seventeen I did not yet have to register but, nevertheless, along with most of the class I signed up for the ROTC. I applied first for the Navy, failed there, too immature probably, but happily, with Uncle Alden in mind, I ended up in Princeton's historic Artillery unit.[71]

Over the summer mother and I had conversed at length as to what career track I might pursue at Princeton. Mother was very strong, an understatement, for anything to do with medicine or the diplomatic corps, or in fact anything other than architecture or art. She understood, as I did not, that the economics of art and architecture might not be promising. Not having any really serious predisposition to architecture (at the time) and, probably to keep the peace, I agreed that I would pursue a pre-med career. The program though not enthralling progressed well enough - until the spring term when we got to dissect frogs and other critters in biology. For me, that was the terminal point of the pre-med career track – I determined that I wasn't really into a pre-med frog program.

My marks were average. It wasn't Darrow's fault. Bill Hudnut, for example was to become our class valedictorian; it was my own lack of motivation and interest in the courses I was taking. I managed to do well in three courses: the mandatory modern language course, French, which, thanks to the Grigauts and the summer trips was relatively easy and English in which I discovered some ability in the written word and the ROTC courses, though the latter were not significant to my overall academic standing. The result, with a nod to my interest in things mechanical, i.e. cars, I switched to mechanical engineering and hoped to improve my motivation and consequently grades.

For sports, a university requirement, I tried out for the Freshman 150 pound (lightweight) crew. We ran, a lot, and rowed on Lake Carnegie in the hefty, so-called 'barge'. I made the cut and was selected for the team. Crew was essentially a year-round sport and one that I enjoyed until the fall of my junior year when I became too heavy for the 150s and too short and light for the heavies.

There was little excitement or pleasure for me in the all male University social life that first year. In age, as well as overall maturity, I was close to, if not the youngest of the Class of '54. Meals were taken in the 'commons', a good idea and a great mixing bowl in principle but in reality the 'jock's ate together, the groupies from major prep and high schools ate together and the rest us sort of mixed in between as best we could. We attended the, almost mandatory, Saturday football game. Though not a football fan Princeton had a great, unbeaten team, and probably because of that, the games were enjoyed. As an additional 'sport' I practiced climbing on Princeton's gothic roofs and towers (not that good an idea), and, though not a sport, I joined the Nassau Sovereign, a student magazine, as a writer, (a better idea).

Mother returned to 45 east 62nd street later in the fall. I would visit over the Christmas break, or when there was a debutante ball or when Aunt Christine invited me to attend a concert in Carnegie Hall. Cristina or Georgia Rockefeller (or their families) invited me, as an escort, to many of the formal 'debutante' affairs. The balls took pace mostly at the Plaza or Waldorf Astoria hotels and were fun, in a formal, let's dress up in white tie and tails, sort of way. I wasn't much good at dancing, despite lessons (Arthur Murray) - even to the staid tunes provided by Lester Lanin. The chaperoned events were not intended to be particularly romantic and they weren't.

In the summer of my freshman year I resided with mother at 62nd Street while working for the Hanover Bank in Wall Street as a potential future trainee. I do not know what possessed me to do this, I think it had something to do with the Princeton 'work-experience' program. It was a pretty dull 'experience' but it did serve to convince me, if I needed convincing, that banking would not be a future career choice.

For my sophomore year I quit the single room in Foulke and joined Bill Hudnut in a rather rundown but spacious room in Witherspoon. Although more motivated, perhaps because of Bill, the outlook, scholastically, was still pretty bleak. Bill was academically very strong, as noted, he would become the class valedictorian. We were not much of a match in the academic department. Nevertheless, we enjoyed each other's company and rooming with Bill was a much better option than being a singleton. For non-academic amusement Bill and I occasionally took the train up to New York and visited some of the Jazz clubs in the '50s', between Fifth and Sixth Avenues. Once, we even went so far as to visit a seedy Times Square dance club. We imagined that we might pick up girls but neither of us had the requisite skills, or more likely, in reality, the desire. Our ability to attract 'dates' for fall weekend football games, a big deal for many undergraduates, was slim. Although hyped up these weekends were, in my

Princeton's graduate school. I deferred entrance, however, until I had finished my ROTC commitment for active duty. In June, I stood with my friends and other classmates outside Nassau Hall to receive my bachelor's degree and, later in the day, the gold bars of a second lieutenant.

The Georgic in her New York berth

The Riley 'cooling down' - at lunch on the way up the Grossglockner

A PT23a, similar to Charlie Atherton's in which we flew to Bryn Mawr and other places

Freshman 150s Crew (Number 6) - 1951

Witherspoon Hall - In sophomore year Bill Hudnut and I had the room with the bay window (on the right side of photo) on the fourth floor - 1951 - 1952

A typical lunch somewhere in France - 1950

Patton Hall - The three windows on the ground floor just to the left of the middle entry were in our living room. Two double bedrooms were at the back.

The terrace at 62nd Street - c. 1952

Boris in his XK 120 - 1951? - Bridgehampton Races
I was Boris's 'Pit Crew'

7

ARMY

Ft Sill (Ok), Ft Campbell (Ky), and Will Kaserne (Munich)
1954 – 1957

"...the source of the bulk of our new citizen officers (will be) ... the
ROTC."

General George Marshall

U pon graduation most of us prepared to enter the services according to our various commitments derived from the ROTC. As the Army didn't need all of us at once, the commencement dates for active service were quite flexible. I elected a slot in early November. This gave me time to spend a few months in Europe after completion of my commitment to the Princeton Players summer program. The theater program, run by our cheery classmate 'Chiz' Schultz[78] was intense: almost '24/7'. The graduation celebrations were barely ended before Hugh and I were in the basement of the Theatre Intime (site of the summer theatre) preparing the sets for the first production. It was a busy two months with, I recall, three productions, *A Midsummer Night's Dream*, *The Drunkard*, and a Pirandello (*Right You Are*?). Each production required new sets to be designed, constructed and painted. We in the stage crew of four would also take on bit parts to fill out the lean cast. We roomed and ate in one of the eating clubs. We all enjoyed the experience, in an 'I am glad it's over' sort of way, despite working seven days a week, often 14 hours at a time, for very modest remuneration.

The Europe trip began in August and would complete in November. In the first part I was to join Paul (Hagan) and Phil (Cotton), another architecture classmate, in Munich where Phil was picking up a Mercedes 180. However, just before I was to leave Phil sent a telegram saying there was, "… a bicycle in the back seat". His intention was to enable me to recognize his car. However, I took his message to mean, subtly, that there was no room for me. Changing plans, I would fly to Milan, catch up with Marty and pick up the Morris Minor 'Traveller'. I would drive to Rome to meet Jim Wintersteen, (yet another architecture classmate). Jim was going to Rome to study music (in addition to being a talented designer Jim was an accomplished pianist).

By the end of July I was ready to go and left on an Alitalia flight to Milan. I caught up with Marty, Taffy and met Marty's boyfriend, Caesare, a sport journalist. Marty lived in a little flat near the centre of Milan and was still working for the American architectural firm, Pedersen & Tilney. After a few days I left for Rome met up with Jim and settled into his flat, just off the Corso d'Italia, near the Porta Pinciana.

Jim and I visited as many architectural monuments in and around Rome as we could manage, particularly if they were of the Baroque period. We talked of Borromini, Piranesi and Bernini. We visited with the sculptor Dimitri Hadzi[79] and other artists in residence at the American Academy. We entertained ourselves with eating, attending concerts but mostly, just being there. We also hoped and talked of meeting some of the attractive women we saw throughout Rome. I can't speak for Jim, who stayed on in Rome for the winter but, for me, this aspect of the visit was an unrealized and frustrating Roman fantasy.

I had time to visit with 'Aunts' Henrietta (Princess) Barberini and Marian (Princess) Chigi. Both were close friends of 'aunt' Mim[80], Jackie's wife. Although I called them all 'aunt' they were not blood-related. Both families were descended from 17th century Popes; Alexander VII (Chigi) and Urban VIII (Barberini).

Prince Enrico Barberini's large villa was located on a hill (but not one of the seven), overlooking the city. My visit included a formal lunch served at a very large, round, marble table. The Prince, a heavy-set imposing person, presided over about ten guests, chosen for their intellect and ability to converse. Prince Barberini would oversee the lunch as one might conduct a seminar. He would ask first one person what he or she thought about a current topic and then call on someone else to comment on what the first person said – no one could escape the interrogation. Italian, German, French and English were all spoken and there was always someone (fortunately for me) to translate when required. The wine flowed as freely as did the conversation – it was a task to stay both sober and alert during the two hours that the lunch lasted. Following lunch and after a short rest the Prince had his chauffer drive us into Rome for a walk about and a little 'shopping'. On this particular day we went into Gucci's, near the Spanish steps, as the Prince wanted a new wallet. As he did not carry money, when he decided to buy something, apparently it was a rare event, his chauffer would quietly appear from the shadows and 'settle' the account. It was all very interesting but not exactly relaxing.

The Chigis seemed less formal, even though the Prince held the important role of Custodian of the Conclave and Marshal of the Holy Roman Church. It was his responsibility to watch over the College of Cardinals during the election of a new Pope. The Chigis lived in a large apartment more or less in the middle of Rome. 'Aunt' Marian seemed an unlikely partner for the Prince as she came from, I believe, Macon, Georgia. I am not sure how they met or the exact connection with Aunt Mim. Marian visited mother at 45 East 62nd several times. In addition to the Rome apartment the Chigis also still owned a magnificent palace at Ariccia, south of Rome. I visited there once during the Roman sojourn. In 1954 there were still squatters (left over from the war) in one of the wings. However, the palace was so large, the squatters might as well have been in a different town. The Chigis owned the palazzo until 1988 when it was given to the Italian State.

I stayed in Rome as long as possible leaving just enough time to drive straight through to Paris, sleeping in the back of the Traveller on the way. In Paris, I was on familiar ground staying at the L'Hotel France et Choiseul near the Place Vendome where mother did her banking at Morgan & Cie. Even four years after mother had left the hotel I was still known by the manager and staff as "Madame Baker's son". The hotel in 1954 was a classic Paris hotel with creaking, polished parquet floors, lacy curtains and a courtyard where on good days you could have breakfast, a coffee or just sit and read: it was not the slick Americanized version of later years. It was musty, rough on the edges, but totally charming. The staff matched the architecture. If a hotel could feel like a home the France et Choiseul would come close.

On my drive back to Paris from Rome I wrestled with the looming reality that I would soon be entering the Army as a twenty-one-year-old second lieutenant supposed to be 'a man', whatever that meant, but certainly less than an adolescent in regard to relationships with the opposite sex. I was determined, at least intellectually, that I would resolve this personal 'problem' in Paris: it seemed an appropriate enough location.

It was for this reason that I found myself, in early November on the eve of my return to the States, tentatively and a little apprehensively, wandering the dimly lit and enticing, streets of Montmartre. I passed by one nightclub after another, lured by seductive photographs of smiling, erotically dressed women but at the same time, I was put off by the brassy, seamy, doormen-bouncers. Couldn't I just walk into one of these 'boites' without being assessed by the doormen? The answer was no. I thought I must be seen as a mark, to be taken for a ride, at best.

Torn between opposing options, the one of being a virgin lieutenant and the other of being mugged in a tacky nightclub, I opted, perhaps surprisingly, for the latter. To this end, I selected, more or less at random, one of the many nightclubs on offer. I entered feeling thoroughly conspicuous even in the dimly lit red-plush interior. Had I just made a huge mistake? Maybe, but I was too embarrassed to leave.

I watched a very average floor show, bought obligatory overpriced champagne plied by hostesses of uncertain age and looks, struggled in conversation with them and generally felt ill at ease. Nothing (whatever that meant) was happening. It was just past midnight I would be returning to New York that afternoon. I called for 'l'addition' and got up. As I did I saw a lovely looking hostess, whom I had not seen until that moment, looking at me. I returned her gaze. She came over and introduced herself saying quite simply, "I am Janine" and sat down. We fell into a simple conversation about Paris and what I had been doing: nothing much. In due course I pulled myself together, well sort of, and in my best, though hesitant, French, I asked Janine to leave with me but having no idea, whatsoever, what that might mean. Janine said, "no, I cannot". I didn't know whether to be pleased or disappointed. Janine, went on to say she was required to stay in the nightclub until it closed, and, in any event, she was not permitted to leave with a customer. I decided that, of the two options, I was disappointed: it apparently showed. There was a pause then she whispered that maybe we could make another arrangement. She suggested that we meet later, at a local hotel, after the club shut. I agreed and Janine gave me the details. There ensued an awkward discussion of some sort of, shall we say, a frank exchange and I left, as quietly as possible. I went to the hotel, paid a surly night porter for a room that turned out to be perfectly neat and tidy and even, perhaps, genteelly attractive. I lay on the bed and waited, and waited. It seemed a very long wait, though perhaps not by the clock. I began to think that I had, 'been had'. As I got ready to leave there was a light knock, Janine arrived. It was just after three am. She was startled to see that I was still dressed. She 'sussed' me out at once; "This is your first time, isn't it?" I didn't even have to answer, she knew. Janine was every schoolboy's dream; kind, lovely and exciting.

We left, some hours later, had coffee and croissants at a café and took a taxi together. I dropped Janine off at a Metro stop. On the way she told me that her family name was _____, that she was a distant cousin of the composer – I have no idea whether that was true or not. When we stopped at her metro station she kissed me. Getting out she wished me a good flight and said, in parting, "you will remember me because of my name". She was right about that, but not just because of the name.

A pleased but emotionally confused passenger got out of the taxi at the France et Choiseul. I wondered if I looked 'different' and if could the staff at the hotel 'tell'. I suspected that with their Parisian sophistication they could.

Later that day, looked after by several comely stewardesses, I was on my return flight to New York in an elegant Air France constellation. The flight was not full and I was given two bulkhead seats on which to curl up. I slept most of the way, all seventeen hours of it. I stayed in New York just long enough to pick up my smart, made-to-order, uniform that I had ordered from Brooks Brothers, get past mother's inquisitions without revealing much, at least in my opinion, and get the Riley out of its storage at Fitzsimmons garage in Greenwich.

The 1500 mile, three day, drive to Fort Sill was uneventful. Several classmates were already at Fort Sill. Among them were Paul and Phil. Paul and his wife, Bonnie, were comfortably set up a house on the edge of the military reservation. In our free time, such as it was, we saw quite a lot of each other mostly driving around visiting local sites of modest interest: not many.

The Officers Basic Course (OBC), in which we were enrolled lasted several months and was comprehensive. Its object being to teach us everything we didn't learn in the ROTC courses (a lot) and particularly to train us in the then basic weapon of the field artillery, the 105mm howitzer. The instructors were good and tough. All of them were veterans of either WWII or Korea, in many cases both. Captain Livermore, a Korea veteran, taught the best and worse courses. Best because he really knew his material and could make his subjects come alive whether they were gunnery, map reading or tactics. The worst part of his courses was the fact that they were mostly conducted in Snow Hall, after midday dinner. The auditorium was dark and poorly ventilated: staying awake was a challenge. His solution was to hit any nodding lieutenant with chalkboard erasers. He was a good shot and I caught one or two in my time. By 1954 The Korean War had ended, well stalled. Stalin had died, and Eisenhower was President. We were in a peacetime army; it was unlikely that we would be shot at. However, the Cold War was maturing and we took our military obligation and the OBC seriously.

In the Twachtman family tradition (or at least Uncle Alden's) I took easily to the artillery and was pretty good with the 105 howitzer but less skillful with rifles and handguns. My Princeton classmates and I got through OBC successfully and we even enjoyed ourselves in the process. We often took 160 mile round trips to Oklahoma City for entertainment. In retrospect I do not understand why. There was almost as little there, in 1954, as there was in Fort Sill or Lawton, Fort Sill's neighbouring town. Dallas, 168 miles away was also a weekend objective and it was more interesting. Otherwise we sort of hung out at Paul and Bonnie's house and polished the 'Desert Fox': a large, pre-war Mercedes touring car that Paul, Phil and I bought together from an officer who had brought it back from Germany. It was claimed that the car had belonged to Rommel: it may or may not have.

Towards the end of the OBC we had to 'request' our next assignment. The 'request' part didn't mean much. The options were essentially three: Korea, Germany or a stateside division. I was enthusiastic about being in the Army and was, probably, a little 'gung ho'. I mused with the idea of getting a regular commission and staying in the Army, at least for a while. To this end I requested Airborne School, as that would ultimately be a prerequisite if I were to explore the regular Army option. I also was persuaded that the airborne divisions were the 'elite' of the Army, probably, and therefore why not be with the best. My classmates thought I was loopy.

In any event I got my request and upon graduation was posted to the 11th Airborne Division at Fort Campbell, Kentucky. I stuffed my 'kit' into the Riley and set out to drive the nearly 750 miles[81] straight through without stop: a mistake. After an all-night drive, I stopped for breakfast somewhere near the Arkansas Tennessee border. Filled with coffee and feeling fine I headed off on the last leg of the journey, on route 79, that would take me to Fort Campbell. The windows were open, the rumble of the Riley's, then straight-pipe exhaust, was I thought, keeping me awake as we (the Riley and I) sped along the top of a levee. The next thing I knew, a telephone pole was passing by the wrong window and the Riley and I were prematurely airborne. The weight of the luggage in the back of the car kept us in level flight. In a few seconds we landed in a just-ploughed muddy field with nothing more than a loud 'thunk'. Belongings flew out the windows. I was shaken and stirred but unhurt and, now, certainly awake. The doors wouldn't open: the mud was too high. I squeezed out through the window and surveyed the damage. Apart from having to pick up errant belongings there seemed to be no damage at all. There was just a little problem: it was about seven in the morning, there was no one around and no way I could move the car. I was at some eight feet below the road with a steep, inaccessible embankment between me and any hope of road rescue. The only good news was that I could see a building, perhaps a mile away but at the same level as the muddy field in which I was standing. I started walking. I hadn't gone far, however, before I heard and then saw a large tractor making its way towards me. A dour, grey-haired driver looked down on me and asked the obvious in a nice southern drawl; "need any 'elp?" "Yes, please", said I.

We managed to get a chain around the Riley's rear axle and pulled, or rather dragged, the Riley out of the field and to the building I had seen. The building was, in fact, a classic country general store. Its sign announced it was in Fruitvale, Tennessee, a hamlet at best. The store was replete with a pot-bellied stove and a handful of locals who eyed me as suspiciously as, probably, I was eyeing them. I felt rather exposed and not a little apprehensive, in my now thoroughly muddied uniform, and my very strange, to them, car with its Connecticut Yankee plates.

I made a further examination of the car and apart from one slightly bent front wheel and four non-functioning brakes now packed with mud, I could find no damage. I spent the morning, changing the wheel and carefully, cleaning the mud out from everywhere, (the store let me use their hose) taking the brakes apart and washing them in gasoline purchased from the store. By noon I was able to get on the road again. During the whole time no one came to talk to me or help in any way, it was rather surreal.

There was only another three hours to drive but I was now in something of a state recovering from shock and with adrenalin wearing off. My reporting deadline of five pm was still looking possible so I stopped along the way, (I think it was in Paris, yes, Tennessee), at a barbershop to get a shave and a haircut and to change my muddy uniform. It was a 'hairy' drive but I made it and even looked presentable when I arrived at Fort Campbell. I was assigned to a BOQ that would be my home for the next six or so months. I unloaded and went to bed.

Orientation took a few days. In the process I was assigned to C Battery of the 457th Airborne Field Artillery Battalion under the command of a rather genial Lt. Col. Locksley, a West Pointer. However, before I could take up my duties I needed to complete 'jump school'. I had been forewarned to be in good shape before undertaking jump school and I was. Even so, the three-week school was a tough combination of intense physical exercise and mock jumps from platforms to practice the five-point parachute landing fall, aka the 'plf'. I found the practice jumps from the thirty-two-foot tower the hardest part of the training. Standing in the mock aircraft doorway and looking down at the ground nearly forty feet below was unsettling: the tower was my 'bete noire'. You had to jump straight out from its platform while tethered to a cable, an early form of bungee jumping. You fell until your harness caught you with a jerk just a few feet off the ground. You then slid along a cable-mounted pulley until you were dumped in a heap on a mound, thirty or forty feet away. If the instructor in charge didn't think your form was perfect, or if you shut your eyes, or you just looked 'funny' you were required to run up the tower and jump again. I was quite experienced in running up the tower before I got the 'hang' of it.

Officers of all ranks and enlisted men were treated quite equally (second lieutenants perhaps less so) in jump school. By the middle of the third week, those who had qualified got to perform their five practice jumps: we were ready for them, in fact for anything except having to run up the dreaded tower again. We jumped, mainly, from Fairchild C119s, the twin boomed, so-called 'flying boxcars'. I'm not sure whether the moniker was from its shape (probably) or, in my opinion, its take off run. When fully loaded, in the hot thin air of summer, we always seemed to be at the end of the long Fort Campbell airfield runway, before we were off the ground. The difference between being airborne and still on the runway seemed to be only a matter of the pilot retracting the landing gear and hoping for the best. The first jump was the best; up to that point you didn't know, what a plunking hard crash the landing could be: unlike sports parachuting today. Airborne school with its excellent instructors was both an educational experience and physical fitness test. I cannot say it was 'enjoyable' but I was glad to have volunteered and proud when I received my jump wings.

Following jump school I threw myself into the job requirements of being the lowest ranking second lieutenant in the battery. Mess officer, motor pool officer and general 'dogs body' officer all fell to my lot. It was all a new experience and experience is what you got: quickly.

Captain Nash, a veteran of WWII, (he had jumped with the 101st on D Day) and of the Korean War was the battery commander. He was firm and fair. A month after my posting we got news that the Division would be sent to southern Germany that fall as part of the 'Gyroscope'[82] plan. In anticipation we got down to intense training including full tactical training jumps, day and night, with our then 75mm howitzers (later we got 105s) and their prime movers. Our troops were mostly pretty tough young men. There were even some 'hard cases' drawn from the northern cities, attracted to the Airborne by the 'jump pay'. The extra pay for an enlisted man was $55 a month while an officer received $100, a lot of money in 1955. We looked forward to being sent overseas though the officers wondered how the 11th Airborne troops, drawn mostly from southern states would acclimatize to Germany and its winter weather.

Social life at Fort Campbell was almost non-existent. We were training most of the time, including weekends. In addition, almost all of the battalion's officers were married. This was a consequence of the 11th being a 'regular' division with very few reservists. My normal off-duty friend was a BOQ-mate, Lt. Dick Grube, a pilot assigned to the divisional air support group. Dick and I enjoyed eating at local restaurants, and generally 'bumming' about, though there wasn't a lot going on it that part of Kentucky. A side benefit of the friendship was Dick taking me on his 'training' flights, while he introduced me to flying. Sometimes we would 'need' to fly cross-country to places like Lexington or Fort Knox: good fun. Social contact with the opposite sex was non-existent. Dick, two other lieutenants and I did take one long-weekend away from Fort Campbell and drove to Kansas City. I opted to stay with Uncle Jackie and Mim in Independence. My pals dropped me off and carried on to do whatever was their 'thing' in Kansas City.

Jackie and Mim owned an early 20th century, white clapboard house at 620 North Delaware Avenue. I hadn't put it together before then but President Truman lived almost opposite at 610. On Saturday afternoon Jackie suggested we take a walk around Independence. To my surprise we just walked across the street where Jackie had arranged to have a coffee with the President and Mrs. Truman. We were there for almost an hour. The Trumans were cordial and warm; they could have been anybody's neighbour. They did their best to make a young, bright-eyed and rather nervous lieutenant feel 'at home'. We talked about my Army experiences and he and Jackie talked local gossip.

In the evening we went to a party given by Blevins Davis, the impresario and producer of the then long-running production of Porgy and Bess. The Trumans were there and were again cordial, greeting me as if they had known me for far longer than the hour of reality. This, undoubtedly, had more to do with Jackie and Mim than me. It would have been very hard for anyone not to like Jackie and Mim's openness, gentle humor and general enthusiasm.

A month or so before we were to depart for Germany I was called up to Division Artillery Headquarters and told to report to the Commanding General's office. There was little explanation. It turned out that I had been selected to be Commanding General's (Harrison) Aide de Camp (protem) for the next few months, at least until the Division was settled in Germany. Brigadier General Harrison, the commanding general, was a West Pointer, intelligent, and in my unqualified opinion, a good commanding general. He was not young but kept up with those much younger. I heard no complaints about him from other officers. There wasn't a lot to being his Aide, just being there would probably be a good job description.

The General was scheduled to spend two weeks in New York before embarking. I headed to New York in the Riley in time to be there before the General and his family arrived. Nearing Uniontown where, by arrangement I was to stop to see Paul, who was there on leave, the Riley's engine started to malfunction. I made a quick decision to leave it with Paul. That was the last I saw of the Riley. A year or so later Paul sold it, for $500, fair enough. Paul told me that as the new owner was driving away the right front wheel fell off, perhaps in protest.

The Aide de Camp role did get me out of a lot of the last minute hassles that were the lot of the battery officers in getting ready for the movement. It also got me a good berth on the USNS General Patch, on which the division artillery was transported. When we ran into a hurricane in the North Sea and hove-to off the port of Bremerhaven I was able to remain 'sea worthy' while most of the 11th's compliment were seasick. On arrival, the 7th Army provided a special three-car train for the use of the General, his family and Headquarters' staff. We had a nice, fast, about seven hours, ride to Augsburg, the site of the 11th's headquarters.

After a few days in Augsburg, I was relieved by the General's principal Aide and headed to Munich and C Battery of the 457th, now ensconced in Will Kaserne on Munich's northern border.

Only eleven years previously Will Kaserne, under a different name, had been the site of a Panzer unit. By comparison to Fort Campbell the facilities were pretty solid: permanent, masonry buildings, including onsite BOQs. We only spent about a third of our time in garrison the other two thirds being in the field training at places like Grafenwoehr, occasionally at Hohenfels or just on manoeuvres tearing up the German countryside. In garrison we conducted classes, tried to keep the equipment in good condition and occasionally conducted training jumps either in the Munich area, just north of the Kaserne or sometimes in Bad Tolz, on the edge of the Bavarian Alps. We had to respond to 'Alerts' set by 7th Army that tested our ability to get out of the Kaserne and become operational in the field. These 'Alerts' were challenges as our motor transportation could be rather dodgy, particularly in winter. It was probably a good thing that the 'cold war' was not hot.

Garrison time was pretty good socially. I made friends with two leftover, 'straight-leg', (the name for anyone who was not a paratrooper) lieutenants who had not completed their tours, Stanley Taben from Cornell and Charlie Watson, a

1954 graduate of Yale. Entertainment consisted of eating out, going to beer halls, visiting local historic sites on weekends and taking in the occasional concert.

The two latter activities I enjoyed mostly solo, as these were not Stanley or Charlie's thing, besides, they both had 'steady' girlfriends.

During 1955 and 1956 mother decided to spend more time travelling, seeing her friends and visiting with Marty. She also included a long visit to Munich to see me and, as it turned out, co-incidentally Marty. Marty was now staying with a titled German, a prince of some sort named Max (Maximillian) who lived in Schwabing, not far from Will Kaserne. Mother, as previously noted was an enthusiastic Francophile. Despite the Twachtmans' Hanover origins Mother was not keen on Germany but in order to see Marty and me she put up with Germany, at least Munich. Perhaps her feelings were ameliorated by the small but posh suite she had at the Hotel Vier Jahreszeiten on Maximilianstrasse. At the time the Vier Jahreszeiten was probably the best hotel in Munich and then even modestly priced. Mother brought along the Morris Minor Traveller of 1954 so that I now had my own transportation. Mother frequently invited me to have dinner with her at the Vier Jahreszeiten's elegant Restaurant Walterspeil. It was still presided over by its founder, Alfred Walterspiel the renowned chef. The clientele including mother, were quite 'dressy'. Mother never had a lot of clothes but those she had were from the best Paris designers. I usually came in uniform; sometimes even dress uniform: wearing your uniform was pretty much the accepted custom in 1956. The restaurant served, undoubtedly, the best food in Munich. For the most part I actually enjoyed the evening dinners with mother. I think she liked the fact that I was in 'service' – and – in uniform.

In mid-winter, sometime after mother had left Munich to explore warmer climes, particularly Sicily's Taormina, Charlie suggested that I join him and his girlfriend, Jennifer Rice, a Smith student on her junior year abroad, for dinner. Jennifer had a classmate, Molly Griswold, whom Charlie and Jennifer thought I might like to meet. Like Jennifer, Molly was studying German at the Goethe-

Institute in Munich. We had diner and we 'hit it off', and as one says, "…the rest is history".

When I wasn't 'in the field' Molly and I saw each other frequently. We enjoyed travelling about Munich, eating out and occasionally skiing with Jennifer and Charlie in Garmish. Molly left to return to Smith late in the summer (1956) but not before she had accepted my marriage proposal – unofficially, of course. Molly wanted to tell her parents in person. She was afraid, and probably justified, to believe, that if she wrote to them to announce that she had decided to marry a paratrooper she met in Germany that they would be on the next plane to Munich. Molly's father, Whitney Griswold, President of Yale was, not surprisingly, rather protective and Molly's mother, Mary Brooks Griswold, even more so.

Molly and I had not gone into many details about marriage; such as what are we going to do with our lives, where are we going to live and anything that was practical or pertinent: perhaps one didn't discuss these things in 1956, marriage was an end in itself. Molly had not yet met mother, though at some point she did meet Marty in Munich: they did not 'hit it off'. Marty was probably reverting to, 'I have to protect my brother', though from what she couldn't say. Mother, of course, got her Molly information from Marty. I think their combined and agreed opinion was that I was too young. While mother never argued against the marriage neither was she enthusiastic. Despite this she gave me her diamond and pearl engagement ring (originally, I was told, a gift from Elsie Rockefeller) to present to Molly. With Molly's enthusiastic agreement I had it modified to replace its two pearls with sapphires. This gift was generous and perhaps belied mother's, probably justified, reservations about the marriage - it wasn't Molly so much, it was, I believe, more her opinion of my and Molly's, general inexperience and naivety.

I was still intending, for the most part, to make the Army a career but whether this was an acceptable option to Molly I cannot recall. In any event while the Battalion Commander, Lt. Col. Kinzer, was preparing papers for my augmentation into the 'regular' army, external circumstances would intervene to determine my future in the military.

The first of these circumstances was innocent enough; an enquiry as to whether I would like to interview for Aide de Camp to the 11th's assistant division commander, Brigadier General Joseph Stillwell, son of "Vinegar Joe Stillwell". Colonel Kinzer 'declined' to let me be interviewed. He claimed he needed me for the upcoming 7th Army live fire exercises; I was, fair to say, a good fire-direction officer but not that good.

The next circumstance was General Harrison's appointment as military attaché to Greece. He asked, again through Kinzer, as protocol demanded, if I would be available to be his Aide (it was a yes from me). This request was also refused: same reasons. It appeared that my future military career might well be dependent upon the Kinzers of the army or perhaps that of his executive officer, a major who was quoted as saying; "don't confuse me with the facts, my mind's made up". I was now not sanguine about my future in the Army and I began to question my application for a regular commission and army career. Kinzer's position may have been understandable but curtailing career opportunities for a young officer was not necessarily in the army's best interests. I mulled over my options and concluded, for better or worse to finish my tour and not apply for augmentation in to the regular army.

Just before we were to go on the firing exercises for which Kinzer required my participation I came down with a mild case of flu – or so the doctors thought. To keep me 'healthy' for the exercises, I was given a 'prophylactic' shot of penicillin: bad idea. Rather than cure me the shot caused an anaphylactic reaction. Instead of being a key fire-direction officer I became a patient in the 98th General Hospital in Munich: unable to walk, with breathing difficulties and covered in hives. I would be there for six weeks. I had little to do while waiting for nature to take its course and by default became a cyclamen specialist, drawing the plants that were the favourite gift of occasional visitors.

On release I still wasn't much good for normal activities. I could not get into normal jump boots and was prohibited by doctor's orders to go on manoeuvres or even daylong field training exercises. As a result, among other administrative duties, I was given Courts Martial work for the Battalion. I spent the next six weeks, prosecuting or defending the battalion malefactors for the 'normal' offences of AWOL, misappropriation of government property, insubordination and other misdemeanours. I was pretty good at this work: perhaps too good. I successfully defended, on appeal, a trooper who was charged with 'borrowing' a jeep. This resulted in my losing 'credibility' with the trooper's commanding officer - and - Kinzer. I had 'blotted my book'. In their view the trooper was 'guilty' and I was a jerk: at best.

It was now December and I was due for a planned leave to New Haven to meet the Griswolds and get engaged, officially - or not. A MATS[83] flight took me from Frankfurt to New York where, some sixteen hours later I connected to a short flight to New Haven. A taxi took me to 43 Hillhouse Avenue, the President's House where Molly and her father met me at the door. It was immediately clear that the Griswold's were going to make a big effort for me. Molly's father had placed a full-sized stuffed tiger (borrowed from FAO Schwartz) in the front hall, a gesture to my Princeton pedigree. We were all nervous: Molly because she didn't know whether I would get on with her family or whether her parents would 'approve' of me. Likewise I was nervous because I didn't know they would approve. The Griswolds were nervous because, even while they wanted to support Molly, they were apprehensive about letting a 'stranger', let alone a paratrooper, into the family.

Molly's father, 'Whit', as he was called familiarly, was very cordial. He did his best to make me feel 'at home'. Mary, Molly's mother, was courteous but considerably more formal, if not reticent. Early on, Molly's father asked me about being president of the Princeton Sports Car Club and asked about my Princeton rowing experiences. As Molly hadn't heard this little bit of personal history I wondered how her father knew. I learned, later, that when Molly announced to her parents that she wanted to marry a paratrooper (and Princetonian) from the 11th Airborne Division there was genuine panic. As a result Molly's father called his friend Harold Dodds, Princeton's President, and had access to my records and more - so much for privacy.

The leave went well, by its end, the Griswold's agreed that Molly and I could get married. They would announce the engagement officially: we would get married in June. They hoped that they could meet mother in due course and I agreed to arrange that, somehow.

Whit also discussed my future. I told him I was giving up the idea of an army career and would apply for early release from the Army, an option that was available if one was entering a degree course; he was happy to hear that. I told him that I would take up my deferred offer of a place in Princeton's graduate school. While pleased at this he suggested that I might also like to also apply to Yale. Whit had just signed up, though not then for public knowledge, Paul Rudolph to be Yale's new chairman. Rudolph was not necessarily, as some saw him, the 'enfant terrible' of the architectural world, but I knew enough about him, to consider this option. The Griswolds also suggested that when I was out of the Army I could stay with them in New Haven. I think this was probably a combination of pure hospitality and an opportunity to get to know their future son-in-law.

It sounded like a good plan and I readily accepted. Molly returned to Smith and I returned to Munich promising Whit that I would apply to the Yale architectural school.

On my return I explained my decision to Kinzer and made my application for early release. My relationship with Colonel Kinzer seriously 'headed south'.

Within a few days I was selected, at Kinzer's request, to be the artillery range officer for Hohenfels, the primary live-firing range in Southern Germany. Hohenfels was scatalogically referred to as the aperture of Bavaria. The assignment was a nightmare waiting to happen, an invitation to disaster. Sooner or later, as everyone knew, someone would be injured on the range and only one guess is allowed as to who would be blamed no matter what the circumstances.

Only a few days passed before I was reporting to the full colonel commanding Hohenfels. In the process of the interview the colonel learned that I had applied for early release. He was, to say the very least, put out: the position was a yearlong assignment (if one survived that long). I was politely dismissed while he called

Kinzer. He had, I believe, a few choice words for lieutenant colonel Kinzer. I was back in Will Kaserne the next day, keeping my head down.

I took some accumulated leave and travelled with mother and Marty in northern Italy visiting primarily Vicenza (Palladio), Mantua and ending in St. Paul de Vence at the Colombe d'Or. Along the way I sketched, knowing that I would need at least something of a portfolio in order to apply to Yale. There was discussion of the forthcoming marriage but it was minimal, I think that while neither Marty nor Mother approved of the impending marriage they ' kept their counsel'.

I returned to Munich to find that my application for early release had been accepted. I would be out of the army in a few weeks. I sold my 'Traveller' and bought a shiny black Mercedes 219 from the Mercedes showroom in Munich and drove it to Bremmerhaven to be shipped back to the US. I collected my sketches from the trip, including the cyclamen drawings from the hospital stint and sent them off with my application to Yale. Though I had not decided on Yale, should I be accepted, I figured there was nothing to lose – which it turned out was a good assumption.

In late February I was on another MATS flight to New York and then to Fort Hamilton in Brooklyn to be processed out of active service. I still had a reserve commitment and would stay in the active reserve for another eight years.

Despite the 'shortcomings' I experienced at the end of my active duty, I enjoyed the Army experience. I should note that I never had a quarrel at the battery level. Captain Barron, my last battery CO was always supportive as were my officer colleagues. I sometimes wondered what my life would have been if circumstances had been different in the fall of 1956.

Exiting the '32' Tower

Official picture on graduation from Jump School
- 1955

Entertainment' at Ft Campbell - Dick Grube in middle
Dinner out near Clarksville, Tennessee

With Lt Linger in the C Battery HQ - Will
Kaserne, Munich
Linger was seriously injured in a jump shortly
after this was taken (I was in hospital and was
not on that jump)

"Stand in the Door" - Ready to go in a C119 - Munich

In mufti, outside the BOQ, at Will Kaserne, with my 'Traveller'

Preparing to 'move out' on manoeuvres in Germany
C Battery, 457th Airborne FA's 105mm 'Firing Battery'

My' C Battery fire direction centre and its sergeant (Clancy) and prime mover: a bit elemental but effective

8

YALE

Architectural School, New Haven, Connecticut
1957 – 1960

*"It is the unique task and responsibility of a great university such as Yale
to study that which is known but far more important to pierce the
unknown. My passion is to participate in the unending search."*
Robert Stern, Dean of Yale Architecture School (2017)

It took about a week to complete the discharge processing at Ft Hamilton. I collected the Mercedes from the Army Terminal in Brooklyn and drove to New Haven to be cheerfully greeted by Molly and her parents at 43 Hillhouse Avenue. As mother was still abroad and 62nd street rented out, 43 Hillhouse was to be 'home' until the wedding.

With all the 'hoorah' during my short Christmas leave I had hardly 'taken-in' 43 Hillhouse nor had I the opportunity to understand how the Griswold family operated on an ordinary, day-to-day, basis.

The 'house' was a large, a four-story Mansard-roofed, Victorian mansion that had undergone a Georgian makeover some few years earlier. The principal, high-ceilinged, floor was some five feet above street level and consisted of two front reception rooms, a large living room, a dining room, with a large screened-in porch, kitchen, pantry and an office for Mary Brainard, the Griswolds' private secretary. It was, as befitted its official purpose, formal. The basement or ground floor consisted of utility rooms, a two-car garage, porte-cochere and space for Peter Dino the chauffeur, butler and 'handy man'.

117

The second floor, in the American system of counting, was given over to the principal family and guest bedrooms and also a library wing, over the porte-cochere, that served as Whit's private study. The third floor had more guest bedrooms and quarters for two live-in household staff. I was allotted one of the two large front bedrooms on this floor. A formal 'grand staircase' connected the four floors as did the back stairs and an elevator.

The Yale art gallery provided suitable, and significant, artwork on the walls of the main floor. Furnishings were 'classic' American or English pieces. The house, while big, was not otherwise architecturally significant. In spite of being a formal 'President's House', I found the house warm, even welcoming. Whit, however, recalled to me that Frank Lloyd Wright, on visiting the house before receiving an honorary degree, had seemed aloof, frosty and disdainful of his surroundings. Whit said to Wright, "Well maestro, shall we jack up the refrigerator and put a new house around it?" Wright apparently found this amusing and was thereafter 'at ease'.

The domestic organization of 43 Hillhouse was under the detailed control of Mary Griswold. Mary's controlling hand matched the surroundings. The house was immaculately maintained. Meals were, 'on-time'. If you were late you could expect Mary's frosty reception at the dinner table. This included Whit who regularly whinged at the rigid time keeping. The dress code was formal, coats and ties, as befitted the times. Sports clothes were only worn of necessity to and from an appropriate event. After my Army experience none of the ritual bothered me. I easily accepted the routines and unwritten 'rules' of 43 Hillhouse.

Once I settled-in Whit took charge of my life for the next few months. He first arranged for my interview with the largest of the local architectural firms and soon I was gainfully employed as a draftsman at Douglas Orr's office, just across Whitney Avenue from the back drive to 43 Hillhouse. Orr's architectural work was competent but not inspiring. It was principally commercial although they had done work for Yale, mostly working in support of more 'prestigious' architects. In any event the office staff was cheerful and professional. It was a good place to learn basics: I did and didn't complain.

Secondly, Whit set up the prerequisite interview with the Yale architectural admission's director. A week or so later, perhaps to no one's surprise, I received notification of my acceptance to the school. The admission director did say he liked my Munich and European sketches though he would have liked to see an architectural drawing or two in lieu of flowers and landscapes. The Yale acceptance coincided with my receiving a curt note from Professor Comstock of Princeton's Architectural School saying that I was no longer acceptable to Princeton having had the temerity to also apply to Yale. I am not making this up! The decision on which school to attend had been made for me.

Thirdly, Whit looked after my continuing, non-architectural, education. From his library he selected three biographies, believing, in principle, that it was better to read about the real thing rather than fiction – the history professor talking. The three subjects were; Cromwell, Jefferson and, perhaps oddly, William Tecumseh Sherman. As I read I was expected, and did, discuss the books with Whit over dinner or at some other free moment. Books were an integral part of the household and at least once a month Whit would receive a neat, brown-paper-wrapped, musty smelling, package from Blackwell's in London containing his latest library choices. There was no television and I do not even remember hearing a radio, though I am sure there was one, somewhere.

Despite the upcoming wedding, Molly and I did not see much of each other that spring. I think the Griswolds thought that finishing Smith, properly, was more important. We talked on the phone but Molly came home only on the odd weekend to see if I was still there and to be updated on Mary's wedding plans. Once or twice I drove up to Smith in lieu of a New Haven visit.

During my Christmas visit I met the three other Griswold children; Molly's elder sister Sally (Sarah) married to Dick Leahy an oceanographer at Woods Hole, Molly's younger sister, Suzie, a student at Pine Manor and her brother Whitney, the youngest, who attended school in New Haven. I got to know Whitney better than the others as he was living at home. The Leahys came to New Haven only occasionally but I got to know them later when on visits to Martha's Vineyard: the same went for Susie. The four children were all quite different in their outlook and character. Molly was more of an athletic all-American 'tomboy', with great enthusiasm for everything she did; Sally, quite beautiful, was 'grown up' and the most sophisticated. Susie struggled to find out where she belonged in relation to her two sisters and was quite insecure; Whitney, by comparison was relaxed, sometimes to a fault, and seemed primarily focused on enjoying himself. On the whole the four children got on together in spite of various levels of normal sibling rivalry. From my point of view I liked each of them individually and related with them as a group – they made me feel included in the family.

The circumstance of the Griswold's' children being away most of the time meant that I became a third 'adult' in the household and came to know Mary and Whit, especially Whit, better than most prospective sons-in-law would know their in-laws. In fact, in time I became very close to Whit, or 'D" as his children sometimes referred to him, and came to regard him as a surrogate father. I found Mary formal, fair and courteous but not, exactly, 'approachable'. The household was clearly a 'command' and she the commanding officer.

If there wasn't anything going on at Yale that required the Griswolds' dinner presence, we ate at Hillhouse: we never went to restaurants. Dinner was always served, formally, in the dining room, at a long Sheraton table, except for Sunday nights when Augusta the cook and Mary the maid were off and we messed about in the kitchen.

As well as dinner all other meals were taken in the dining room. At dinner, Whit sat at one end Mary at the other and I in the middle. Guests were a rare event. We ate under the watchful, and commanding eye of the Duke of Wellington[84]. (I do not know why Wellington was an appropriate choice for the dining room.) Dinners were preceded by a fifteen to thirty minute drinks 'hour' at which the days' highlights or family matters were discussed. Drinks were not fancy, no Pimm's or martinis, normally just sherry or whiskey. At five minutes to seven Mary would remind us that dinner was at seven, which meant that if you wanted another drink you had better get it. Wine was not served so we brought in whatever was left of our pre-dinner drinks. At precisely seven we sat down and with her foot stretched to the point of nearly falling off her chair, Mary pushed the floor buzzer for dinner to be brought in by either Mary or Augusta. Dinner menus followed a set pattern by which you could tell the day of the week. Monday might be ham, Tuesday, lamb, Wednesday, beef, and so on. Desserts followed a similar pattern. The dessert following the beef meal was always trifle, perhaps Whit's least favourite dish. Trifle always rankled Whit and each time it was served he would make some negative remark. Mary would offer a strong retort about how difficult it was to run the household, what procedures were best for Agusta and Mary. Whit would ask, logically, why trifle had to be part of the procedure. The conversation would sputter along with verbal thrusts and parries or cease altogether until one of us broke the ice, and it was ice, with a new topic. When it came to the trifle wars Whit would try to draw me onto his side by telling Mary that even I didn't like trifle (which was more or less true) – I did my best to develop a diplomatic strategy between the two camps. I doubt that I pleased either side. Notwithstanding the menu selection, the food was very well prepared, wholesome and tasty.

Conversation normally ran to Yale subjects, personalities of any kind or what each of us did that day. Sex, religion and politics were avoided, either by accident or design: I do not know which. Most of the time conversations were just tense but sometimes they were fraught with Mary and Whit taking opposing positions. I often felt like a spectator at a tennis match. An example was a conversation on travel: On one occasion, I remember, Mary had gone to New York, for the day, by train. She remarked that she enjoyed the train trip in the parlor car as she was not bothered by anyone. She could read and be alone in her own world - fair enough. Whit retorted that he never went first class because he enjoyed meeting people and talking with them. In the process he effectively accused Mary of snobbery. Thus ensued a feisty verbal exchange of views. I found these 'fights', and they were fights, uncomfortable. On reflection, though, the fights didn't seem to affect the protagonists as much, perhaps, as they did me.

After dinner, normally lasting about an hour, we retired to the living room for coffee. Whit almost always played his flute and Mary often accompanied him on the piano. The music was mostly classic selections though Cole Porter, Rogers and Hart and Gershwin were often featured. Whit was an enthusiastic flautist. However, he may not have made the first cut if he had tried out for the New Haven Symphony. By nine we were off to bed, perchance to read.

Breakfast was served at a smaller table at the room's north end. Whit often used the breakfast hour for a one-on-one meeting with a guest, who may have (or mostly did not) spend the night. It was an opportunity to have an informal discussion on fundraising, a new building, or new policy. I sat in on some of these tete-a-tetes when invited. Over time I remember meeting Dean Acheson, the former Secretary of State, Justice Potter Stuart, Whit's classmate Paul Mellon, Irwin Miller, Chairman of Cummins Engines, Congressman and later Mayor of New York, John Lindsay, Bishop Paul Moore and the architects Philip Johnson, Gordon Bunschaft, Eero Saarinen and Ed Barnes. Though I was rarely drawn into the conversations I was an attentive listener.

As the forgoing list suggests, Whit went out of his way to introduce me to the architects he would employ for Yale's building program that in 1957, was in high gear. Whit was interested in my point of view even though I was by no means any kind of expert, to put it mildly. I did enjoy being asked and enjoyed meeting the architects, probably the avuncular, pipe smoking, Eero Saarinen most.

Whit had a group of close friends on the Yale faculty and a number of them often 'dropped-in' to 43 Hillhouse. Top of this list was 'Uncle' Tom Mendenhall, Master of Yale's Berkeley College and later President of Smith. The Kublers, Dunhams, Coopers, and Hennings were also in this group[85]. These stalwarts of the Yale faculty and New Haven social set also made up the core of the parties that the Griswolds sometimes attended or were given by them. A highlight of any of these was a 'sing-a-long' where Whit and selected others would perform classic Cole

Porter, Rogers and Hart, or Gershwin songs[86] with 'clever' new words, (more often than not written by Whit) about a current Yale subject such as fund raising. The performers enjoyed themselves as much as their audience, probably more.

As June and marriage neared, the Griswolds encouraged a visit from Mother. Although still abroad, Mother agreed that this was an appropriate necessity and she returned to New York. After some negotiations she arranged to have lunch with the Griswolds in New Haven. The meeting was polite, uneventful and unenthusiastic. Mother announced that she and Marty, as well, would be unable to attend the wedding. I do not recall the excuse but she hoped that she would be well represented by other members of the family: she didn't think anyone would miss her anyway. Mother returned to New York, the same afternoon, as soon as she thought it was politically polite: it wasn't a long stay by anyone's clock. Some years later mother let on that she liked Whit but found Mary hard going, I suspect the feeling was mutual.

Molly graduated from Smith in June and Mary and I went up for the event. Whit was too involved in Yale's own graduation activities to attend. Plans for the wedding had been in full operation for some time, organized capably by the Marys, (Griswold and Brainard) without much (read any) input from me, or, if I recall, Molly. Under the circumstances it was to be a fairly large affair and the requirements for Molly and myself were, mostly, to be there and look happy.

The wedding took place in the afternoon of the 16th of June in the packed Chapel of the Divinity School. Hugh Hardy was my best man and my Princeton classmates Paul Hagan, Charlie Atherton and Phil Cotton, were ushers as were Dick Leahy and Whitney. Syd Lovett, Yale's Chaplain officiated. The reception was at Hillhouse Avenue.

Mother was correct; she was well represented by her family and truthfully, she was not missed, except by her own family. If anyone else thought her absence peculiar they didn't let on. Among the Twachtman members were Uncle Alden, Jackie, Mim, Aunt Marjorie, Emery, Peggy, Elizabeth, and Bitsy. The Bakers were also well represented by Aunt Eugenia and cousins, Henry Jessup, John Jessup and

John Baker. On the Griswold side it seemed that most of the senior Yale faculty came as well as most of Molly's mother's family, the Brooks. There were few, if any, Griswolds at the wedding. As a matter of fact I (think) only recall meeting Whit's brother once (not at the wedding), and Jock Whitney, a cousin, but no other Griswolds.

I recall few details of the wedding day; as the author Carlos Zafon says, "weddings always stay more clearly in the memory of others". I recall no hiccups and, (I was told), it was a 'memorable affair'. After the reception, or perhaps while it was still going on, Molly and I left for our short honeymoon in Norfolk, Connecticut happily driving away in the 219.

I am not sure why we picked Norfolk, perhaps we didn't, more likely the Griswolds did. In any event Norfolk was hot and humid. The historic Inn in which we stayed was pleasant but unromantic – even boring. We visited some Griswold friends or perhaps they were distant relatives and bought a Hitchcock chair. I think we enjoyed ourselves, though I am not sure – perhaps, like weddings, one is also not supposed to remember the honeymoon? We came back, as planned, after a few days, so that I could continue earning at the Orr office to help pay for Architecture School. Apart from a small Baker legacy, Mother had paid my way through Princeton but on this venture I was on my own – Mother was still negative about architecture and was unenthusiastic about contributing to what she thought was my career delinquency. I believe she wished that I had remained in the army. In any event, in addition to my own savings I received significant help from the US Government. I was technically a Korean War Veteran and qualified for the benefits of the GI Bill. I earned additional funds as well through my participation in a local unit of the army reserve.

Molly and I initially lived at Hillhouse until we could move, later that summer, into married graduate student's housing in the Quonset huts out by the Yale Bowl. These 'huts', were constructed for married students after the war ended. They were quite fun to live in and justified the old phrase, "…there is nothing so permanent as temporary housing." Each unit, half the length of the hut, consisted of two little bedrooms, a tiny toilet/shower and a kitchen-dining-sitting etc. room. A pot-bellied, coal stove was the heating source. They were hot in the summer and breezy in the winter but the rent was cheap and everyone got get along well. We even made a few good friends. It is perfectly possible, though not obviously so, that this experience with the Quonset Huts would subliminally add to my life-long interest in prefabricated housing.

The highlight of the summer of 1957 was my initial introduction to Martha's Vineyard. From the first day that we met in Munich, Molly spoke about the Vineyard. As a consequence the Vineyard had taken on an almost magical aura in my mind. I looked forward to the visit. In late June we drove up from New Haven and took the ferry, the 'Islander', from Woods Hole to Vineyard Haven. The trip, of about an hour's duration, was pleasant, invigorating and in the first instance, expectant. The Vineyard in 1957 lived up to Molly's description – the island <u>was</u> magical. It was low-keyed, family oriented and very New England. On the island, one could be excused for becoming suspended in time and place.

The Griswolds' home was a renovated and enlarged shingle-style cottage in Lambert's Cove, on the North shore to the West of Vineyard Haven – the Griswolds had owned it since the late twenties. It wasn't a large or prepossessing house but it was homely and a great vacation getaway. In addition to the main house there was a guesthouse that served as Whit and Mary's apartment, a shack later to be turned into a little house for Whitney, a garage and a four by four shed which served Whit as a study. He sequestered himself in this box every morning to write his articles or books on his Smith-Carona and just think, without being disturbed by phones or visitors and remote from the hubbub of the main house. A clay tennis court completed the property's facilities. The house overlooked Lambert's Cove, Vineyard Sound, the Elizabeth Islands and in the far distance, Buzzards Bay. The views were spectacular. 'Lambert's Cove', as the property was colloquially called, was anyone's ideal summer home. Molly and I occupied a room on the second floor, under the eaves.

Lambert's Cove was also the site of my first architectural commission (if one forgets the design of my mobile fire-direction centre for Charlie Battery of the 457th Airborne Field Artillery Battalion in Munich). Whit, and to a lesser extent Mary, wanted to get a better view of the cove from the guesthouse living room and asked me to have a go at it. We agreed to knock out a corner of the house and replace it with a multi-paned window generally matching other details in the house. Roger Engley, the Griswolds periodically used local builder, made the alteration. It wasn't a big deal but the Griswolds liked it, particularly Whit, and the result was deemed a success.

Mornings at Lambert's Cove were for tennis, possibly swimming at the cove itself, (an easy ten-minute walk through two scruffy fields), shopping, perhaps nine holes of golf at Mink Meadows (Mary's favourite), or a visit to another part of the Island. We would all gather back at Lambert's Cove for a one o'clock (prompt!) lunch. Whit would join in the afternoon activities. These would sometime involve an outing in Whit's twenty-three foot 'bass boat'[84]. These outings, more often than not were for fishing, for flounder or bass, but sometimes to go to the Elizabeth Islands or Woods Hole or just for 'messing about'. Whit's boat, I cannot remember its name, was a classic New England working boat with clean lines, clinker-built by the skilled local craftsman and small boat builder, Eurford Burt. Whit would say that Eurford Burt was the only person he knew whose name, "… sounded like a fart in a bathtub". Whit did have a slightly scatological turn when he wanted. He and Molly used to fall about with self-inflicted laughter making up words derived from the German 'fahren'. Mary did not approve of this - which made it all the funnier.

Mary's family, the Brooks, were also ensconced on the Vineyard some miles to the east at Oak Bluffs at what was called 'Cousins' Corner'. There were lots of Griswold/Brooks get-togethers during the summer.

For a special treat the Griswolds went to what was called "the shack" on South Beach. "Let's go to the Shack" would be the rallying cry some mornings. It only really worked when the weather was perfect and everyone was bored with alternatives. 'The shack' was literally a one-room rickety shingle sided frame building on the littoral dune defining South beach. It served as a unisex dressing room and storage for beach gear. It was reached by rowing across a salt pond in a dilapidated dingy. Nature periodically rearranged the shack's location during the winter storms but never, in my time, destroyed it. South Beach is one of the great beaches, probably of the world, and although I am not a beach fancier, too much sand, even I liked "the shack".

We stayed on the Vineyard for only a week or two that first summer, but it seemed longer. The rest of the summer was spent in New Haven, on my part working for Douglas Orr and for Molly's part getting ready to move and then moving into our Quonset hut.

Architectural school started in September with Paul Rudolph chairman, as Whit had promised. Our class consisted of about thirty students, all, but one, male. Architecture, among other professions was, in 1957, male dominated. My classmates got on well together and a few of them, Alex Grinnell, Warren Cox and Ivan Poutiatine would become good and long-standing friends. Most of our class would last the three years of the program.

The architectural school occupied the top floor of Louis Kahn's Art Gallery, one of Whit's first, and most courageous architectural appointments after becoming President in 1953. The open plan, trapezoidal concrete ceiling, concrete block walls, steel and glass fenestration, the triangular stair in a concrete drum of Kahn's Art Gallery all made up a studio space that could arguably be one of the great architectural teaching spaces of any age. The Art Gallery was by later standards not Kahn's most finished work but it was a building of great humanity, and one was always happy to be there, it was an afternoon out with your favourite aunt or uncle. The late Peter Millard of the full time faculty and perhaps our class's favourite design studio 'critic', would use Khan's building as a teaching tool as a violinist would use the bow.

At Princeton, as noted, I had found some academic studies somewhat of a struggle; at Yale I relished all of them. It was probably as Whit would often explain a question of 'motivation'. The school attracted both good students and outstanding visiting critics to lead design studios, lecture and teach. Whether it was an architectural history course by Scully or Kubler, Engineering by Henry Pfisterer or Herb Siegel, Tunnard's city planning courses, or studios by Rudolph, Barnes, Johnson, or Johanson the courses were always engrossing: we looked forward to attending. There was even opportunity to devise one's own courses, in art, forestry or city planning which some of us did. As a class and even as a school I think we all felt privileged to be there.

It was a dynamic period in modern architecture, and we felt, and still believe today, that Yale was (and still is) a leading educational player in the world of architecture. Griswold regarded architecture, as he did other disciplines, as part of a liberal education, not a trade. The school clearly reflected his belief and the work of the Yale graduates from this Rudolph period would in time demonstrate the soundness of the belief. An analysis of the work of the architects graduating during the Rudolph years is impressive.

Visiting critics included Louis Kahn, Mies, (arranged by Phyllis Lambert) [85], Jim Stirling from London and Kenzo Tange from Japan and Philip Johnson. Johnson, not surprisingly, was a frequent visitor. Also, among these leading practitioners of the time was Peter Blake, then editor of Architectural Forum and previously curator of Architecture at MOMA. Peter came as a housing critic in the second year: his visit would turn out to be serendipitous.

The typical day at Architectural School was, not surprisingly, busy. Mornings were taken up by classes and lectures: primarily the mandatory engineering, and architectural history courses, as well as one's selected optional courses. The afternoons were given over to the design studio where we worked individually on assigned design exercises or 'problems'. For example we might be asked to design, a school, a housing project, individual house or whatever an appointed design critic selected. As we progressed through the three years the 'problems' become more complex and would require several weeks to complete. The design studios would be monitored by a full time faculty member, for our class, most often Peter Millard, and be supplemented by a visiting critic. Millard's teaching aim, as well as those of the better visiting critics was to draw out the talent from each individual student, much as a psychiatrist gets a patient to talk, rather than 'teach' the student how to design. This required a good deal of patience on the part of Millard and others. There was little chance that our design work could be completed in afternoon studios alone. Evenings and weekends would find most of the students in the studio struggling with rapidographs, glue and cardboard, to finish their drawings and models. Design discipline, as ever, was in short supply so towards the end of each assignment the studios were often occupied all night as we each struggled to finish our designs by their deadline – it was the 'charette' of the old Beaux Art, nothing had changed. In the spring term of the third and final year we were required to prepare a project of our own choice. Mine was a laboratory for the Woods Hole Institute, the program being provided by brother-in-law, Dick Leahy. Among the reviewing critics were Philip Johnson, Paul Rudolph, and Vince Scully. Their combined comments, I recall, were not rapturous and could be summed up by competence, not brilliance – fair enough.

The fact that I was the President's son-in-law was, for the most part, ignored by both students and faculty. There was no secret about the relationship, and certainly no special favours. I never felt the connection affected anything I did or didn't do. In addition to the architectural studies, occupying the role of a newlywed, new father and an active role in the local reserve artillery unit I worked on *Perspecta,* the seminal Yale Architectural Journal. At the end of our second year I was elected to be its editor and took on the task to publish *Perspecta 6.*

Perspecta did, and still does, hold a unique position in architectural journalism. As the architectural historian, Henry Russell Hitchcock said in his introduction to *Perspecta 6.* "*Perspecta* has never offered the last word on any subject, but quite often it has uttered what (in the context at least) was the first word. This is a service which the professional journals burdened with other intellectual responsibilities, have in our country been reluctant to perform, and one which the scholarly journals, by their very nature, are vowed not to attempt." While *Perspecta* has faculty advisors it is very much run by the students. They agree on the 'context' of the issue, select and arrange for the contributors in support of that 'context', design the artwork, find the funding, publish, distribute and sell the publication. For part of the time, the work, for practical purposes, is full time.

In the spring of the first year Morgan was born. I cannot say that this was our precise or even strategic family plan, but Molly and I and the Griswolds were delighted. Morgan's name (actually Mary Morgan) was selected from amongst a number of Welsh names deriving from the Brooks family. We elected to call her Morgan much to mother's dismay – she thought the name dreadful and that it would lead to peculiar nicknames. I liked the name and still do – I think we all somehow adapt to our names and Morgan did. It would be hard to imagine Morgan with any other name. Now that we were three the Quonset hut got a little crowded and the Griswolds pushed for us to live somewhere that perhaps, in their belief, was more 'appropriate'. As a consequence, in 1959 we moved into a garden apartment off Prospect Street not far from the Divinity School - or for that matter, Hillhouse Avenue.

Graduate studies were not brilliant for home life but the school wasn't programmed for that. Molly looked after Morgan, visited with the family and generally waited for something to happen. There were discussions about volunteer work but mostly she endured a lot of frustration and boredom.

I worked for Orr in the summer of 1958 while Molly and Morgan spent most of their time on the Vineyard. I drove up most weekends. Also in the summer the Leahy's took a long shot risk and hired me to design a house for them at 'Seven Gates' an up-market 'development' on the Vineyard. The basic plans were produced over the summer and later developed around my academic responsibilities. The house was an amalgamation of the Leahy's strong design requirements and my rudimentary understanding of the 'Shingle Style' with a little bit of Wright thrown in. The house was constructed by Roger Engley during the winter of 1958-9. In any event, the Leahys liked the house and, so far, it has served their family for three generations.

The second summer, (1959) was spent in New York. Following the completion of Peter Blake's design studio, a housing project in New Haven, Peter offered me a summer job working for his firm Blake & Neski. It was not an offer a student architect could refuse. A classmate helped us find a small apartment on Lexington and 91st over a liquor store. We went to sleep while its large multi-coloured flashing neon light blinked 'liquor' long into the night. The apartment belonged to an action-painter who was spending the summer in the Hamptons. We set up our temporary home and from there I commuted by subway to Blake and Neski on southeast corner of 50th street and Third Avenue. Their office was on the third, top, floor of this small, walk up, brick building. A hamburger joint conveniently occupied the ground floor. It was all pretty modest. Peter's partner Julian Neski, familiarly known as Joe, ran the office as Peter, holding the full-time job of editor of Architectural Forum (then owned by Time Life), was rarely there. The only other employees were a part-time secretary and Vernon Gibberd an intelligent, pleasant, and talented, import from the UK. He worked with Joe and I worked with Peter. Joe was a fine architect and a superb draftsman with a refined sense of detail. He also had a marvellous sardonic sense of humour. We worked hard and enjoyed ourselves in the process.

Peter and Joe's work consisted primarily of beach houses in the Hamptons, though they also had a commission for a Lutheran Church in Hollis Queens and a Synagogue in Livingston, New Jersey. The houses were simple, very carefully planned and detailed and modestly priced: they were definitely modern with a Bauhaus pedigree. The job was a perfect, practical opportunity for a fledgling architect. My work, that summer, was to prepare the working drawings for Peter's new house at Sagaponick. Peter would show up, periodically, to give me, or if I was not there, leave, cryptic notes and drawings on graph paper indicating what he would like me to do. After a while I learned to interpret them and we got on well.

During the summer I contracted mononucleosis and was holed up in the apartment for several weeks. We learned, as I leaned against a freshly painted wall how this painter worked. He had covered the remains of his not yet dried paint splatters with a thin coat of white paint which when leaned against produced T-shirts of striking multi-coloured patterns. I'm not sure how much Molly and Morgan enjoyed the summer but they, at least, got to spend some extended time on the Vineyard. In September Peter invited me to return, after graduation, to Blake and Neski, on a 'permanent' basis. He also offered, an option: that I join him as a writer at Architectural Forum. The highlight of the summer was Molly's announcement that she was pregnant.

Jamie was born on March 25th, some two months premature. His life, as it is said, 'hung in the balance' for some weeks but we had the full attention of the Yale-New Haven medical faculty. After almost two months we were able to bring a small but healthy Jamie home. It was an emotional time.

When it came to graduation there were two prizes awarded, one was for excellence in academics, the other for excellence in academics, service to the school and leadership. I received the latter. Yale was a great experience and would provide a solid foundation for my architectural career.

Molly on Martha's Vineyard - 1956

43 Hillhouse Avenue, New Haven
Formerly the President's House

Whitney Griswold in his study c. 1957
- a much used photo

Our thesis jury: Philip Johnson, Paul Rudolph,
Vincent Scully

Molly leaning on the 219 in Norfolk on our honeymoon

A typical Quonset Hut at Yale -
(a neighbour's)

Cousins 'Bitsy' Fraser and her mother Elizabeth (Pell)
Fraser and Uncle Alden - Outside Hillhouse Avenue, after
the wedding

Announcement from the New York Times

The Leahy House, Martha's Vineyard - 1958 - almost complete
(still in the family in 2019)

PART 3

WORK

1960 TO 2005

9

APPRENTICESHIP

New York
1960 - 1964

"I am glad God ... gave Death a
Job taking care of all who are tired of living."
Carl Sandburg[87]

In order to obtain an architectural license in New York, or any other state for that matter, one first had to spend three years working under the immediate supervision of a licensed architect – in other words you had to be an apprentice in the medieval sense. Peter had offered me two opportunities, one working for Blake and Neski, a normal apprentice route, the other as a writer for *Architectural Forum*, Time Life's architectural publication. The latter job was very well paid, the former less so. Whit and I debated the options but came to the conclusion that it was better to be an author than a critic. I therefore chose to return to Blake & Neski with the intent to complete, at least, the statutory apprenticeship.

After a short look around the east side, Molly and I found an affordable apartment on the top floor of six-story building at 17 East 95th street, between Fifth and Madison. Although rather run down, the two-bedroom flat had large south facing windows and some character. We learned quickly that we were not alone in the apartment but shared it with an army of cockroaches. Nevertheless, we settled in. By the end of June Molly, Morgan and Jamie went off to the Vineyard for the summer.

It was about this time that Whit was diagnosed with colon cancer. An operation was required. While it was declared successful, Whit ended up with a

A Pewter Spoon

colostomy. I think he considered this the worst aspect of the cancer. He recovered, initially, in New Haven but as soon as possible Whit was taken to the Vineyard. As Whit was the focus of the family his illness put a serious strain on everyone, especially Mary. I do not know what went on in private, away from the children, but Whit appeared, to me, to be quite uncomplaining about his illness and its longer-term implications. He was back to work as soon as possible. I do not recall that Molly and I talked much about his cancer: we maintained a collective protection of denial.

On almost all weekends, I joined Molly, the children and the Griswolds flying up to the Vineyard from LaGuardia on Fridays or sometimes Thursday evenings in the DC3s of Northeast Airlines. During the four day weeks I made up, and then some, the missed hours of a Friday by working into the evenings. Joe and Peter were quite relaxed about this as long as I got my work 'done'. I would normally work from eight am until about seven pm then go for an omelette or salad at the Brasserie in the basement of the Seagram's Building. The Brasserie, designed by Philip Johnson, had booths and an up-market diner-like counter where one could get efficiently fast service from comely women dressed in physically complementary Alsatian[88] costumes. It was an uplifting place to eat.

After dinner I would return the four blocks to the office and work a few hours more. On occasion I would pull an all-nighter in order to feel extra-justified in taking a late Thursday night or early Friday flight. On one such instance, on a hot summer Wednesday, I went home to change and came back to have a late dinner in the Brasserie. As I was sipping a glass of wine, awaiting my dinner, a platoon of the ancient 95th street army chose that moment to march out of the left sleeve of my jacket onto the counter. There was a bit of a 'klefullfel' with my waitress. It was some time before I felt 'comfortable' returning for dinner.

Work was very similar to that of the previous summer. The office still consisted of Joe and Vernon and occasionally, a part-time secretary. Peter came in when he wanted. There were new house commissions to draw up and visits to Long Island to attend to construction matters. Apart from Architectural Forum Peter was often asked to write for other publications. Sometimes, when he didn't have the time (or inclination) to prepare an article he would ask me to write the odd piece for the likes of Funk and Wagnalls, and even once the Manchester Guardian. I enjoyed the writing but invariably got caught up in competing deadlines between architectural and editorial work. Taken all together one couldn't have asked for a better job for a new architectural graduate - but it was not to last.

About a year after I joined Blake and Neski, Joe and Peter had a falling out. I do not know the details but suspect it was over the fact that Peter was rarely around or it could have been because he was, on occasion, around – I simply do not know. In any event within the year Blake and Neski was over. This presented an economic and job problem. However, almost at the same time as the firm was breaking up I received a call from Darby Perry, Darrow's then chairperson: a call that would determine not only my immediate opportunities, it would have, in a then unforeseeable way, a significant impact on my future.

Darby, a Darrow alumnus and Princeton graduate, introduced himself and then said, "… I understand you are an architect". "Close enough", I responded. He told me (what I already knew) that from 1938 up to his death, Heyniger had sketched, on the back of an envelope, so-to-speak, almost all the school's planning and renovations.[89] He was, in practice, the school's architect. Since Heyniger's death the previous year Darrow was without this facility and now needed to find a Darrow-friendly architect. Darby thought I was the only Darrow graduate who was an architect. "…It would be nice if the school's future architect was a Darrow graduate" he mused. "What a good idea!", I thought.

He asked if I could meet with him and Nick Philip, another trustee, engineer, and a graduate of Darrow and Princeton, at the Princeton Club: "… as soon as possible?" "Yes", I responded, with enthusiasm.

We met the following day. Darby, at the time, was the publisher of *American Heritage* and an avid amateur military historian. Nick was a part-time apple farmer, scion of an historic Dutch family with an estate just south of the town of Hudson. 'Thin as a rail', usually nattily dressed in a slightly worn off-white suit with tired but polished shoes Nick could have walked out of a Graham Greene novel. Apart from apples, he was a civil engineer with Tibbets-Abbot-McCarthy-Stratton and worked on international projects of grand scale, projects that most often had an agricultural component; in fact agriculture was Nick's real specialty. Darby and Nick were both WWII veterans and some ten years older than I. We were all, however, Darrow and Princeton graduates; we got on immediately. I explained to Darby and Nick that although I wasn't a licensed architect, I could work with Peter. That would take care of any appropriate legality, if, in fact, there were any. Nick and Darby may have interviewed others for the job, I don't know, but in a day or so I was informed that I would be the school's architect. That did not imply a long-term post it was in reality only the school's architect for Darrow's immediate requirements. My first assignment would be the renovation of the Second Meeting House into a library, a memorial to C. Lambert Heyniger. A second would be the renovation, into a dorm of what the school called the 'Medicine Shop' (I think the Shakers may have called it the 'Drug' Building).

This was my 'first', serious, non-family, commission and it would provide the modest income permitting me to work, essentially on my own, but with Peter as my licensed 'mentor'. Peter would look over my shoulder and give me 'crits'; he was, in fact, very good as a critic. The modest fee income from the library, plus that from the simultaneous Darrow commission for the conversion of 'Medicine Shop' combined with some on-going projects from Peter, would provide almost enough income to support the family for about a year.

In developing the requirements for the Library and Medicine I worked closely with Darrow's new Headmaster John Joline, another Princeton graduate and contemporary of Nick and Darby. John was a scholarly, serious, fair-minded person: a good client too. He was detail minded and demanding but he also gave me design latitude. John was strong-willed and Darrow's Board normally agreed with him. When you got to know John, you would learn that he had a quiet, somewhat sardonic sense of humour. I liked him. He carried on Heyniger's customs and traditions despite the rapidly changing style and ethos of the student body. He and his family, his wife Jean, daughter Bitsy and son John Jr. became good friends. John and I would come to work together on Darrow matters and projects throughout his tenure. He even asked me to remodel his house in Duxbury, which I did with pleasure. I always was given a room in his 'official' residence, Whittaker House, when staying overnight at the school and this turned out to be often.

The Library construction was completed for the opening of school in 1962.[90] Ed Schilling, Darrow's long time, aging, in-house, carpenter-artisan, executed the renovation work. Ed had worked with Heyniger, renovating buildings, building furniture, whatever. It was Ed who had built, to Heyniger's specification, the 'too-big for my bottom' benches in the Chapel. Ed was a skilled craftsman, a taciturn but gracious 'New Englander', even if he actually lived in New York State. He had been friendly to me when, as a student, I visited him in his workshop in the basement of Wickersham. In another life he could have been mistaken for one of the Shaker brethren. The Library was Ed's swan song and he retired shortly after the renovation was completed. While Ed was building the library, Mike Dimana, Ed's understudy, took on the remodelling of the 'Medicine' building into a dormitory. Mike would turn out to be a valuable asset to the school and was employed by Darrow until he retired some twenty years later. He complained a lot but 'got the job done'. I supervised the library and Medicine House construction on a weekly basis, beginning what would be, over many years, probably more than 1500 round trips from New York to New Lebanon, taken on the Taconic Parkway or old route 22, the two principal options.

After the Library was completed and in use, Peter thought it worthy of publication[91], notwithstanding what might be considered a little 'conflict of interest'. The library was published in *Architectural Forum* and based on this project alone, I was included, a few years later, in "40 Under 40",[92] the Architectural League of New York's exhibition featuring "Young Talent in Architecture". More than a third of the architects selected for the exhibition were Yale graduates, perhaps not surprising as the principal selectors were Robert Stern, (who some years later became Yale's Dean of the Architectural School) and Philip

Johnson. In any event the exhibition was a fortuitous moment in a nascent architectural career.

While this work was going on Peter and I had to figure out how to meet the office overhead that he had inherited after his split with Joe. Apart from the income generated from the Darrow projects, Peter attracted two acquaintances, George Lewis and Harry Buttrick who agreed to share the 50th street space thus minimizing the overhead burden. We created a loose association between ourselves calling it, 'The Office of George Lewis'. George, a Harvard graduate, was older and had been a practicing architect since before the war. Harry was also a Harvard graduate of my vintage. Apart from Darrow one of our first joint projects was the renovation of a brownstone, in the 90s between Park and Lexington. The client was Robert Bicks an ex assistant attorney general in the Eisenhower Administration. At about the same time, Peter introduced me to Bob Motherwell and Helen Frankenthaler. That started what was to be more than a decade of work on their houses and studios, particularly their town house on east 94th street. I enjoyed this relationship and it continued even after Bob and Helen split up. Bob, a very positive person, was generally laid back and philosophic when things went wrong and enthusiastic when things went right. More than once he said to me, "Jim, it's what you don't do that will haunt you, not what you do." Up to a point, I still agree with him. One of Bob's special requirements was his 'Motherwell-blue' ceiling colour: getting his blue just right could drive painters to distraction. Helen was, perhaps even more demanding. If anything was not to her liking, and that could be a lot, I would hear from her - day or night, early or late. On the other hand she could be most generous (Bob gave me three inscribed lithographs and Helen on lithograph and a painting) – it was perhaps a love-hate relationship. All in all "The Office of George Lewis" was a happy place: we enjoyed each other's company. I would continue to be close to George until his death.

In November 1962, just months after the opening of the Heyniger Library, Darrow's dining hall, (the Heyniger-converted Church Family Wash House) burned down. Though the fire was of suspicious origin no cause could be ascertained and no definitive conclusion made as to the origin of the fire. I met with John to decide what could be done, architecturally.

We agreed that the Shaker 'Dairy Barn', that Heyniger had converted to the school's gymnasium should be used, at least temporarily, for the dining hall until alternatives could be sorted out. Mike DiMana went to work and in a few weeks there was a kitchen and the basketball court was a dining room. The students were bussed to the local public high school for basketball. We started thinking about building either a gymnasium or a dining hall. We hadn't been long into that process before the question became redundant.

Just after Christmas vacation, in January 1963, the converted Shaker Dairy Barn burned to the ground in a spectacular night-time conflagration. On this occasion the police lost no time in declaring that the fire was arson and they set about to find the culprits. Since barn burning was sometimes considered a rural recreation for miscreants this was not an easy task. The most likely culprits were the local 'barnburners' or students but the police had little evidence to point in either direction. When they learned that I was hired to design a replacement building, and consequently a 'beneficiary' of the fire, they were interested enough to interview me! Fortunately this bizarre idea didn't gain credence and in spite of forensic efforts and interviews the police did not find the culprits.

Darrow was in crisis. It had neither dining-hall nor gymnasium. The students had now to be bussed for meals as well as to the gymnasium. Fortunately, Berkshire Farms, a high profile, joint private and publicly funded, then a sort of reformatory (today it provides "services for youth") provided this neighbourly culinary help. Berkshire Farms was located only a few miles away down route 22. New Lebanon's high school continued to share their gym. All this was a strain, but it worked.

The Darrow Board, led by Darby Perry, had only two choices: shut down or go on. By February the Board had agreed that the school would go on. It would replace the lost facilities. We collectively decided that we would build a new multiple purpose building containing both dining facilities and gymnasium. It would be constructed on the on the site of the Shaker Dairy Barn. The decisions were really 'no-brainers'. In the meantime a better solution than bussing the students to Berkshire Farms three times a day had to be found.

New York's Senator Keating intervened: I do not remember who contacted him. In any event Senator Keating managed to divert a prefabricated structure destined for an army base in Alaska to be used, by Darrow as a dining hall until a new building could be constructed. The large flat-packed building arrived within a few weeks. I worked with Mike Dimana for a number of days, surveying the site and sorting out the basic layout so that Mike could assemble it. The building, later to be called the 'green shack' because of its colour, was located just west of where the Dairy Barn had stood. Though it was agreed that 'The Green Shack' was a 'temporary' loan, as it turned out, the army decided they didn't need it. After its use as a dining hall it performed multiple uses for almost forty years. It was demolished in 2001: yet another example in the history of 'temporary' buildings.

The design concept for what was, within the year, to be called, not surprisingly, 'The Dairy Barn', was sketched on a place mat while I was having lunch in a restaurant just a few doors down from Henry Pfisterer's office on Whitney Avenue in New Haven. I was there as we had hired, Henry Pfisterer, my erstwhile favourite engineering professor, to be the 'Dairy Barn's' structural engineer.

The Dairy Barn's site had a significant slope and in sketching the concept I found there was room to place a little 300-seat theatre, under its dining hall. Joline liked the idea. The concept sketch was upgraded for appropriate presentation and accepted by Darrow's board.

By working late into many nights the construction drawings for the building were sufficiently completed so that the building could be priced and construction begun when the frost was out of the ground. George and Harry occasionally helped but it was sometimes easier to just draw by myself rather than explain and debate. I hired my Princeton classmate, Hugh Hardy, to work on the building's theatre. Hugh after a stint as a set designer with Jo Melziner had now opened his architectural practice specializing in theatre work. Apart from professional contact

Hugh and I saw each other frequently as we were near neighbours. Hugh, Titziana, his wife, Molly and I frequently had dinner together. If it was at Hugh's we would be entertained by his brisk, show-time piano: his repertoire of Cole Porter, Rogers and Hart, Hammerstein and more was legendary.

Construction on the 43,000 square foot 'Dairy Barn' began in April. Remarkably, the Dairy Barn was operational by mid fall. This was most probably due to a good relationship between the key parties: architect, school and contractor, the Macomber Company from Boston. It was constructed for less than $12 per square foot, even then, an extremely modest cost[93]. The school paid for it from the insurance proceeds on the lost buildings supplemented by gifts from alumni and friends known as, "Operation Phoenix" and some borrowing. The 'Dairy Barn', is now past its 50th birthday having probably served more than 2,500 Darrow students in this period. It is now in the process of being upgraded and will probably serve Darrow for many years to come. Curiously, in a book on barns published in the seventies the Dairy Barn was included as a "renovated Shaker Building": I am not sure what that says about the design. I have taken it as a compliment.

While all this was going on Molly and I decided to move from 95th street with its omnipresent blattodea family, the erratic elevator and the ever-present smell of the old, badly maintained, oil-fired boiler: we had had enough. Molly had recently received a family legacy and in consultation with the Griswolds and financial advisers it was concluded that it would be a good investment for Molly to use some funds for a down payment on a house. We found a modest, four-story, sixteen-foot wide brownstone at 178 East 93rd street, between Lexington and Third avenues. It was in need of renovation, which suited us. We, bought it for around $100,000. Molly made the down payment and we took out a mortgage for the renovations and the balance of the purchase price. The renovations were thorough but practical and modest in detail. The top floor was given over to a one-bedroom apartment, for rent. The third floor was independent and could either be rented out or used by us for an office and space for an au pair. These two floors were served by the building's main staircase. The first two floors were made into a duplex for ourselves. On the first floor Morgan and Jamie each had equally sized, small bedrooms, overlooking the garden. Molly and I had a reasonable-sized bedroom in the front, facing the street and the four of us shared a small interior bathroom. We opened up the ground floor to the garden, with a south facing glass-wall and French doors. A new galley kitchen was installed facing the street. A small interior stair connected our two floors. There was also a, pretty grim, but useful cellar. It was a tremendous improvement on 95th street and quite comfortable.[94]

Harry Buttrick suggested Louis Danzico, a local, (local in that he had a workshop at 90th street near First Avenue), cabinet-maker cum builder for our contractor. Like many craftsmen turned builder. Louis and his workmen were skilful and produced commendable final results. Getting there, however, was not "twice the fun" as an old ad states. Ask Louis to meet you at eight or nine, or any time you may have agreed to, and you could give pretty good odds he wouldn't be there. His billing and project administration was often wishful thinking but, in the end, he was essentially honest, cheerful, accommodating and most importantly, the quality of his work was excellent. We used Louis for a number of years on renovation projects until he died or drove us loopy: I am not sure which came first.

Having their own rooms and a place to play outside was a big improvement for Morgan and Jamie. In due course, we employed an 'au pair' for the children, Cartiona Shafer, a cheerful and enthusiastic student at Chapin. I think Catriona was the daughter of friend, of a friend of Molly's.

By 1963 Morgan was ready for school and Jamie was not far behind. We were fully engaged in the middle class debate of which school was best and how to get the children accepted. If you wanted a good education the public school system was not really an option: certainly in our part of town. In other parts of the city the system could be, in fact, pretty good. It was the usual post-code lottery; even then it was difficult to get into good schools. In due course we opted to apply to the Madison Avenue Presbyterian pre-school and kindergarten and were accepted. This meant we also felt 'obliged' to attend their Sunday services. Fortunately, David Reed, the presiding minister was an articulate sermonizer and although I did not consider myself a Presbyterian I ignored any hypocrisy. The Griswolds came from a New England, protestant background so what bothered me a little didn't bother Molly at all. The fundamental educational grounding of the Madison Avenue Presbyterian Church School meant that by the time Morgan was ready for 'real' school she was accepted to Nightingale Bamford. Later Jamie would be accepted to Collegiate. Morgan, perhaps, had a slightly more difficult time getting into a good school as she suffered from dyslexia. When Morgan was just learning to talk we observed, not immediately it is fair to say, that even simple words like 'saw' were interchanged with 'was'. Understanding Morgan at times was frustrating to us, but certainly more frustrating to Morgan. We sought advice from Whit but his advice in this area of learning was not one of his strengths. At the time it was thought that Morgan's 'speech impediment', (the word dyslexia was not in familiar usage at the time) might be psychological. Whit had little time for psychology or psychiatry and really didn't want to discuss it. His view was either just to get on with it or to make an assumption that the problem would go away. Molly and I concurred that we had to get to the heart of the problem. By her tenacity Molly found an organization in New York that was pioneering in what was then an undefined field. The organization, (I do not think it exists any more), can be credited with minimizing the effect of Morgan's speech problem.

In between renovating 93rd Street and working on Darrow projects, I continued participating in the active reserve. On coming to New York I was transferred from my 76th Division unit in New Haven to the 77th Infantry Division Artillery Headquarters on west 42nd street. Its commander, Brigadier General Varian, was a courteous and amiable lawyer by profession and a veteran of WWII. On reporting, General Varian first thought about having me as his aide but then decided, perhaps as I was now a captain, to appoint me as the Division Artillery Headquarters Commandant. Thus I took on what was, in effect almost a half-time job. Headquarters Battery had almost two hundred enlisted men and some fifteen officers, though only four would be reporting to me. The rest were senior staff officers reporting to General Varian. We met once a week, one weekend a month and for two or three weeks in the summer, at Camp Drum in upper New York State, near the Saint Lawrence River. As a commanding officer there was a lot of additional work in between meetings. It was a challenge, but one, though time consuming, I found rewarding: the remuneration provided was helpful too. One longer-term benefit was meeting my executive officer, Howard Schneider a graduate of Cornell and lawyer. Howard would become a close friend and represent me in a number of personal and business matters over the coming years. One of the highlights of my stint as 'Commandant' was leading Headquarters Battery down Fifth Avenue on Armed Forces Day.

Molly and I saw mother infrequently. It was pretty clear that neither she nor Molly were that fond of each other: an understatement. Mother was also not what one would call a 'typical grandmother'. I am sure she was very fond of the children and liked to see them at 62nd street. I cannot remember, however, that she 'babysat': even once. Her visits to 93rd street might not, by my recollection, even justify the s on visit. She did like to buy clothes for Morgan and Jamie and she painted a picture of a squirrel, in the style of Durer, for Morgan and a picture of Noah's Ark for Jamie, but that was pretty much the extent of her involvement.

Despite her feelings Mother did try, quite often, to entice us to 62nd street for dinner and a game of bridge with her old beau from the twenties (pre father), David Forgan. David was an old roué but I rather liked him. He had moved back to New York from Chicago. I am not sure how he and mother met up again but that is unimportant. David, who was not very well, gave mother a purpose: to look after him. In addition to mother, bridge, was not Molly's idea of fun. The few evenings we did go to 62nd street resulted in three handed bridge, and arguments thereafter with me, from both Molly and mother as to each other's behaviour, it was a lose, lose situation. To this day I am not sure what the problem was between them. Possibly on Molly's part a prejudgment based on Mary's view, possibly on mother's part a prejudgment on what she thought was best for me. In any case the situation was not helpful to anyone's relationship and was a source of continuing angst.

In the winter of 1963 Whit's cancer returned. In between our normal activities Molly and I and the children visited New Haven as much as possible. In the process we got to know Yale's new Provost, Kingman Brewster, who had been hired as a strong back up to Whit after his first bout with cancer. Kingman and his wife Marie Louise had moved into the Provost's House, next door to 43 Hillhouse. Whit was now at home and Kingman was a frequent visitor. Whit was clearly the final stage of his illness. In April we were called up to New Haven, Whit was worse, in fact he was dying. All the family came round and we did our best to be supportive of one another. On the morning of April 19th Molly and I were asked to go up to his room to see him. Whit was lying comfortably enough in bed but by this time he was gaunt, if not skeletal. We were only there for what seemed a few moments before he drew his last breath. A moment only matched by what I had experienced when my father died - I felt I had lost my own father, again.

It was a sad but busy time most of the details of which have, not unsurprisingly, faded from memory. Whit's funeral was held in Yale's Battel chapel with Syd Lovett and William Sloane Coffin conducting the elaborate and moving[95] service. A magisterial Dean Acheson led the long, academic, sombre and elegant funeral procession from the Chapel through Yale's 'Old Campus'. Whit was buried in the nearby Grove street cemetery. Without knowing it at the time, Whit's funeral was the beginning of the end of a short but significant 'chapter' of my life.

In June I was 'head-hunted' by the architectural firm of Kahn and Jacobs. Kahn and Jacobs was a large firm with an over thirty-year record of doing large-scale projects, of competence but not, by many standards, elegance, mostly their work was in New York City. Ely Jacques Kahn, a small elegant, slightly Poirot-like, (David Suchet version) was a Beaux Arts trained architect and had, essentially, retired. Bob was a larger than life, a brash, 'I can get it for you wholesale' type, but, nevertheless, very professional, architect. The Kahn and Jacobs staff was skilled in their basic trade of office buildings and apartment houses, even if the designs were not award winners. Bob was determined to bring together new talent in order to change the firm's image. I was one of two or three designers to be selected to lead a new design team.

George Lewis, Peter and I had a number of long, 'heart to heart' conversations whether or not to take up the offer. In the end we concluded that I should: at worst, "it would be good experience." George would now handle, the day-to-day work on the 'Dairy Barn' construction but I 'stayed in touch' throughout the construction period. By the time I moved to Kahn & Jacobs in late July the 'Dairy Barn' drawings were all but complete and the construction well under way.

Working at Kahn & Jacobs wasn't as much fun as working at 50th street but there was a compensation: good pay. The staff, particularly those in the design department, were welcoming but it ended there. I only made one good friend at Kahn & Jacobs, Henry Halevi, a competent designer and all-round nice person with a good sense of humour and carefree attitude.

My initial assignment was to manage the African Pavilion for the upcoming World's fair in 1964. This was an odd assignment as the 'pavilion', actually a series of round tented huts had been already sketched out by a set designer. My job was to turn his sketches into something that could be constructed. The contractor was Crow Construction and the project manager was, by coincidence, my cousin Carl Knapp. He and his compatriot at Crow, David Wudunn would factor in and out of my New York architectural career for many years. Twin brothers and entrepreneurs Roy and Ray Graham, were the clients. The Grahams were impossible to tell apart, even at fifty, they had, remarkably, gained weight and lost hair in the same places. This led to some confusion as to who said what to whom and when: confusion, which I think they rather enjoyed. If you really wanted to tell them apart you had to surreptitiously check out their hands, Ray had lost part of his left hand little finger in an oil-rig accident. The Grahams were ex oil wildcatters who had turned their oil entrepreneurial talent to entertainment and hospitality. I would in due course become their architect on a future project.

In early summer, 1963, after the requisite three-year apprenticeship I took the New York State architectural exam. The exam is a three-day event. Two days are given over to testing one's knowledge of architectural history, structural engineering, mechanical engineering, building detailing and professional ethics, law and management. The third day is a twelve-hour 'design problem'. An applicant had to pass each section in order to pass overall. Fortunately, if you failed any section, you could just take that section over again in six months time. However, if you didn't pass all the sections within something like two years one had to sit the exam from the beginning. I passed everything but the design section. This was regarded, curiously, as an indication of a 'good' designer. The problem was, it was said, that a 'good' designer spent too much time getting an acceptable concept and then did not have time to develop the concept in sufficient detail to be acceptable. We all, anyway, those who had failed, moaned and groaned about the 'unfairness' of the 'incompetent' examiners but succeeded only in winding ourselves up. In any event, the following spring, I took the going advice, did a miserable design, worked it out, and passed the exam. Being a licensed architect didn't immediately change anything: there was no extra pay.

I was working on the African Pavilion in the Kahn and Jacobs design room on the early afternoon of November 22nd 1963. (It is quite extraordinary how one remembers a major event years later.) The office was collectively stunned to silence, we all listened, with incredulity to radios or phoned our family or friends. The office was shut within the hour and we drifted home in a nearly silent city. It was not until after Kennedy's funeral that the office returned to normal.

At nearly the same time mother's friend David Forgan died. Mother dealt with this as she did so many other things, she said nothing and went about her business, such as it was. It was obvious, however, from the few visits we had thereafter that she was depressed. Her depression was compounded by a fall outside 62nd street that left mother with a damaged knee. While surgery was not recommended, or, perhaps, not elected, she was left with a substantial limp and required the support of a cane. The winter, unsurprisingly, started early, cold and wet. It was too much for mother. With little consultation with me and none, to my knowledge, with Marty who was still in Milan, she determined to sell 45 East 62nd street and move, at least for the winter, to Barbados. Mother apparently had some acquaintances there and at least, 'Sandy Lane', where she was headed, was reputed to be 'comfortable'. Most importantly, for that moment, it was also warm. It all happened rather quickly. The apartment was sold for a mere $66,000 (I hate to think what it would sell for today) to a member of the wealthy Phipps family.

In the spring of 1964 the New York World's Fair opened. It was pretty tawdry by comparison to my childhood recollections of the fair of 1939. Only a few buildings were of any architectural merit, and only one, Johnson's New York pavilion would remain as some sort of icon. The African Pavilion was jolly but unremarkable. In the last days before it opened I managed to fall, or more accurately, flip off one of its smaller pavilions breaking my left wrist in several places. Despite the cast I was able to continue drawing and worked on my next Kahn and Jacobs assignment, a science building for the New York State University at Geneseo.

In June Molly and the children went up to the Vineyard as usual. This was the summer following Whit's death. The atmosphere around Lambert's cove was quite different without him. There was no one to balance Mary's new singular family dominance. Whit had not only been the centre point of the family but also he brought the 'aura' and 'excitement' of Yale into the family. What had been a busy, sometimes almost frantic, in-the-limelight, family was now, by comparison, one that was turning in on itself, looking to find a new focus. Molly and I began thinking that it would be a good idea to move out of Lambert's Cove and get a place of our own. With Whit around this may have been a fleeting thought, without Whit, it was a constant thought.

In July I received a letter from mother telling me that she had tired of Barbados. It was now very hot and humid, the winter people had left and mother was finding life dull. She thought that a nice little villa on a northern Italian lake would suit her better, perhaps "Locarno, the Swiss end…", she proffered. She would be near Marty, away from what had become, to her, a dreary, depressing New York and return to her European roots. The idea had spirit and romance. I wrote that I thought it a good idea. I probably also thought that getting along with mother was easier at a distance and Italy, with Marty nearby, was better than Barbados.

So it happened that on the afternoon of Wednesday, July 22nd 1964 I met mother at Kennedy Airport[96], when she disembarked from a Pan Am flight from Barbados. Although still suffering from the knee affliction, and in need of a wheelchair for any distance, Mother seemed quite buoyant, even excited about the Italian (or Swiss) prospect. She had written to Marty and, according to mother, that end of things seemed to be in order. Marty would meet her on arrival and they would go looking for a place for mother to make a new home. I took mother to the closest airport hotel where she could spend the night. We had dinner and arranged that I would return in the morning to take mother to Pan Am for her flight to Milan. We sent Marty a follow up telegram confirming her arrival time on Friday the 24th. On Thursday, as planned, I was back at the airport having breakfast with mother and chatting about the past, present and future until it was time for her flight. I put her on the flight, actually taking her to the plane in a wheelchair and saw her off. Later that day I flew up to the Vineyard to join Molly and the children.

It was a normal, busy summer weekend: swimming with the children, tennis, beginning to look for a house and discussions with Mary and Augusta about a proposal for the remodelling of the kitchen at Lambert's Cove. Just before dinner, on Saturday, the phone rang. The Children were in the front room playing, Mary was at her desk, Molly and I were having a drink. Mary answered the phone, it was Marty, Mary handed me the phone.

> Me, "Hello"
> Marty, "Are you sitting down"
> "Yes"
> "Mother is dead"
> "What … ?"
> "She's killed herself in the hotel (Principe et Savoia); there's all hell to pay!"
> (That was one of Marty's phrases when she didn't quite have a handle on what was happening) – how soon can you get here?"

"I don't know, I don't even have a valid passport."

"Well, send me a telegram when you know – get here as soon as you can – bye".

Marty, like myself, didn't waste words. Stunned, was the only apt word to describe my reaction.

Mary went into action: she was very good in a crisis. One of her friends, a classmate from Smith, was head of the passport agency. Mary got hold of her immediately. By midday Sunday morning it was arranged that I would get a passport waiver and take an Alitalia flight to Milan in the evening. The consulate in Milan would arrange for a new passport once I was there.

On Monday morning after a sleepless but comfortable (Alitalia upgraded me to First Class) flight, I was ushered through immigration and customs at Malpensa as a VIP. A taxi was arranged and in an hour or so I was at Marty's. She was then living with her long-term beau, Caesare Carrasatti, in a small apartment in downtown Milan not far from the Duomo. Marty showed me the day's main Newspaper, the Corriere della Sera. On the front page in the bottom middle, under the banner "Rich American Widow found dead in the Principe et Savoia", there followed a picture (Mother's grim passport photo), and an article describing her 'probable' suicide under 'suspicious' circumstances in one of Milan's finest hotels. According to the article she had taken an overdose of sleeping pills and had left a note. The police were investigating. It was understood that Signora Baker had family in Milan and the police were contacting them. Considering there wasn't much to go on the writer had embellished enough to make it a rather fulsome, intriguing, if not factual, article. It was almost August and there was not much else to write about.

The article, however, was the extent of our knowledge. Marty, apparently, had not received mother's telegram as she had left early Thursday for the weekend. As mother had Marty's address in her belongings, the police had been able, with the help of Marty's concierge, to locate Marty in the country. The police had summoned Marty to meet with Milan's District Attorney. The meeting was arranged for Tuesday morning so that I could be there.

As Marty's flat was too small for me to stay there, Marty had arranged for me to stay in her friend Renata de Millevillles's flat a little further out from the Milan's centre. Renata was an aristocratic but impoverished friend from Marty's days in Munich and I had met her there. I had the run of Renata's charming flat as she was staying with a friend elsewhere. It was a helpful housing solution.

The meeting with the District Attorney was testy. Although I could understand a little Italian, actually that's very little, I couldn't speak it and Marty had to translate everything. That turned what might have been a generous hour's meeting into a three-hour saga. The District Attorney, possibly because he didn't have anything else to do, was making as big a deal out of the matter as possible. There was no doubt that he thought it possible that both Marty and I were somehow involved in mother's death (which in a sense was true) and that her death might not be suicide (which wasn't true). According to the paper mother, after all, was a "rich widow".

Mother's note, not to put too fine a point on it, could be characterized as " to whom it may concern." The gist of which was, sadly, "… I do not want to become a burden to my children." The note also included the instructions for her funeral. She wanted a Catholic Mass, to be cremated and to have her ashes spread on an Italian lake. Apart from the fact that suicide was illegal, masses couldn't be said for those who took their own life, cremation was not permitted for a catholic, and, in Italy at that time, ashes were not permitted to be cast about, it was all just fine! The District Attorney informed us that he was holding mother's body until he was satisfied that there was no "foul play". He informed us that we needed a lawyer, as, under the circumstances, the paperwork would be, even for Italy, quite difficult. It was all not very promising. Perhaps the American Consul could help? In any event I had to get a passport. Marty went to find a lawyer I went off to make an appointment with the American Consul.

I met with the rather officious consul the following day. Having received instructions from the State Department he had someone deal with a new passport: so that was fine. As to mother, that was another matter. He couldn't interfere with the Milan police. However, assuming that there were no "problems" and we could get possession of the body, he suggested, "smuggling" Mother to Switzerland where matters of this sort were "less rigorous": some help.

While I was meeting with the Consul, Marty found a lawyer thorough one of her friends. We met with him the following day. His office was astonishing. It was quite large but nevertheless you could hardly see his desk. Every square foot of floor space was taken up with stack on stack of legal papers, all atilt at different angles and just waiting, it seemed, to fall into a general heap. They were all bound with coloured ribbons and seemed, to that extent, rather festive. For a fee of a 'wadge' of lira notes he agreed to take on the task of getting mother's body released and taking care of the Italian bureaucracy. I couldn't converse with him, but since Marty didn't complain, a rare occurrence, I think his fee must have been fair.

By Thursday mother's body had not been released and we were no closer to resolving that which, certainly in theory, could not be resolved, the funeral arrangements. We were in Marty's flat discussing what we could or should do when there was a knock on the door. On opening, a short figure of a rather comfortably robust man, wearing sandals and the robes of a Franciscan friar was revealed. He was Brother Franco. He had heard, (it was never made clear how), that we had a 'problem': he was there offering to help in any way he could.

He would turn out to be, without being facetious, a 'godsend'. First, he arranged a meeting with Milan's Cardinal. It took about five minutes with the pompous, scarlet clad, Cardinal for us, Marty, Brother Franco and myself, to get a pre-emptive and abrupt "no" to a mass, forget the rest, entirely.

Next, Brother Franco and the lawyer went to the District Attorney. Their intervention was more successful, or perhaps the DA had tired of the matter and had moved on to something more interesting. In any event, as long as a family member would identify the body it could be turned over to the civil mortuary and a funeral could be planned. I did the identification of mother's now, decaying, naked body. Brother Franco, robes and sandals, drove me around Milan in his 500cc

Fiat Topolino with élan and abandon. He was a fearless driver, which is more than could have been said of his passenger. Clearly, God was on his side.

After nearly two weeks of Italian bureaucracy Brother Franco conducted, as mother had requested, a mass for her soul. It took place in a little church the name and location of which has since passed from memory. It was a short but moving event attended by Marty, Renata, Caesare, myself and a few members of the public, who just happened to be there and appeared interested. Brother Franco clearly believed in God not the Cardinal, though he did have a few choice words for the latter.

Brother Franco also made the arrangements to have Mother cremated in Milan's Cemeterio Monumentale. Mother's body had by now been placed in a simple pine coffin, but it had not been embalmed and in the heat of early August it was rank. At the entrance to the cemetery the coffin was placed on a small two wheeled, 19th century cart, pulled by a casually uniformed attendant wearing a tired visor cap. From the entrance we proceeded, at a slow walk, down the cemetery's main earthen road to the crematorium, located at the furthest possible point, perhaps a half-mile, away from the entrance. Brother Franco led the sad procession, the cart came next and Marty, Renata and myself followed behind. We passed by 19th century marble monuments to the left and right; weeping angels, marble tears, sad marble dogs, weeping marble women and men, weeping willows, anything that could weep did – in stony silence – except, every revolution of the cart's wheels produced an unearthly squeak. After about ten minutes Marty and I exchanged sympathetic glances and we both started to giggle, it had been and was still all too much. A few passing visitors looked at us, askance. I actually think Mother would have giggled too; maybe she did.

We got a grip on ourselves by the time we reached the crematorium. We were halted there by a uniformed official, raising his arm like a traffic cop. We had, it turned out, a penultimate task to perform, a task for which we were unprepared. It seemed that a family member had to identify the body before it was sent into the furnace. Marty and I looked at each other – which of us would do it – I started to make a move but in my hesitation Brother Franco walked forward and told the official that he had known mother for some years; he would do it. You could see that the crematorium official didn't believe him but who was he to question the word of a Franciscan Friar?

Standing outside the crematorium, we waited for a half hour or more, while its chimney spewed mother's remains into Milan's troposphere. The ultimate task, which was required of us, was to identify the remains, following cremation. This task fell to me. The remains, on a still smoking steel tray were more substantial than one would have expected. One understood why the Italians didn't want them 'scattered'. The uniformed attendant swept up mother's remains placing them in a metal box to be put into a niche in the crematorium wall, where, I presume, it still is[97]. When the 'event' was finished we made our way to one of Marty's usual restaurants and raised a glass, (or two), to mother and to each other.

We gave brother Franco a contribution for his order and thanked him profusely. He said simply that he was doing the job God gave him to do. He disappeared as he arrived; one moment he was there, the next he wasn't. Mother would have approved of him, he was, after all, a Franciscan, mother's favourite order.

I kept in touch with Molly during the two weeks leading up to the Mass and cremation. At some point we decided that a 'break' was appropriate after the trauma of Mother's death. Mary agreed to take care of the children and Molly joined me in Milan. At more or less the same time Peter Blake had heard about Mother's death and had somehow managed to reach me by phone in Milan. It happened he was staying in his holiday flat in La Spezia. He suggested that we join him there for a few days. Molly and I agreed and we headed south to La Spezia.

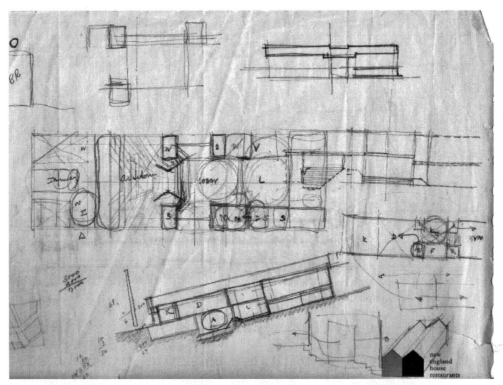

Sketches for proposed 'multi-purpose building (later called the 'Dairy Barn') made at the New England House, New Haven - January 1963

The 'Dairy Barn' as completed - photo 1967?

Motherwell/Frankenthaler House, East 94th Street

Heyniger Library - 1962

178 East 93rd Street - 1964 - (demolished in 200?)
Mitchells are last door to the right
(Next door neighbours to right unknown - typical New
York)

Greeted at Martha's Vineyard Airport - 1962
In the 1960s Northeast Airlines had a direct
flight to Martha's Vineyard from the Marine
Terminal at LaGuardia

In discussion with the excellent First Sergeant Reyes - Camp
(now Fort) Drum - 1964

10
BAKER & BLAKE - 1

New York
Part 1 - 1964 - 1968

"... no one is ever told what might have been."
Simon Barnes[98]

La Spezia, located on the Mediterranean coast, two hundred and fifty kilometers south west of Milan, was what one imagines an Italian seaside holiday destination to be. It was throbbing with people of all ages, crowded with cars, full of restaurants and stalls selling garish souvenirs and plastic beach paraphernalia. We actually were heading for Portovenere an historic seaside village, just west of La Spezia where Peter had his flat consisting of a few small irregular rooms in an ancient stone tower. The flat was charming and eccentric but just big enough for Peter and his winsome, willowy wife, Petty. So Peter arranged for us to stay in a small hotel nearby for a few days, sleeping, eating, drinking, sunning, and swimming, probably in that order. On our second day while we lounged on a local beach Peter suggested that we rent inflatable rafts or li-los. While Molly and Petty chatted, Peter and I paddled away on our li-los. It turned out that these inflatable rafts were only a plot, designed to get me alone. While we were bobbing gently in the relaxed Mediterranean swell, out of earshot, he revealed his plot.

He wanted to form an architectural partnership with me as his partner. It was an offer, that in an Italian manner, I couldn't refuse and I didn't. We did not discuss details. We agreed, however, that it was to be an equal partnership: Peter's suggestion. Peter also proposed that it be called, alphabetically, Baker and Blake. The name would help to imply 'equality', despite the obvious differences in age, experience and status between Peter and myself. When the proposal was revealed to Molly, she was supportive (at least I think so) but I do not recall that we discussed the matter at any great length. We held a celebratory dinner that night with Peter, Petty and some of Peter's friends. We departed the following day with Peter and I agreeing to meet to sort out details in New York, later in the summer. I was, to say the least, excited.

Molly and I drove back to Milan to see Marty and to receive her unsolicited apocalyptic warning that since I was mother's executor she and I would end up in a fight and probably never speak to each other again! She suggested that Uncle Alden and Mother fell out over the settlement of grandmother's estate[99] but I have no evidence that her statement was factual: we had seen a lot of Uncle Alden following grandmother's death and I do not recall any animosity, but who knows now? It wasn't exactly a friendly farewell, but maybe it was just Marty getting in a pre-emptive strike. As it turned out there were no 'problems' but then, perhaps, was I too 'fair'? Marty also said that she would be leaving Milan for Rome, something that she had talked about and which the last few weeks in Milan had helped to confirm.

After our goodbyes to Marty and Milan we headed north to the Brenner Pass and Austria. Molly and I had agreed, in Portovenere, to treat ourselves to a nostalgic visit to Munich. Once in German speaking countries I looked forward to being relieved from my duties as a laughable Italian linguist. I was to be disappointed. Molly, only seven years previously a fluent German speaker, 'locked up' leaving me to struggle with my inadequate 'US Army' German. Though it was better than my Italian I think she thought my linguistic efforts were funny: they probably were. As it turned out our nostalgic visit would last only few days. We both found Munich changed. It wasn't what we had known, or remembered and we were happy to depart for New York. We caught up with the children on the Vineyard and went about getting back to 'normal'.

Peter and I met in September. We decided not to rush matters and take our time finding an appropriate office. Its location would be very important for Peter.

For convenience, it had to be either near his editorial office at the Time Life Building or his apartment on 55th street between Fifth and Sixth Avenue. Also, since neither of us had a lot of spare cash beyond the $10,000 ($75,000. today!) we had each agreed to put in, we decided to wait until we had some work in hand. We agreed, too, that Peter would not give up his job as editor of Architectural Forum and I would assume the responsibility of managing the partnership. This suited me and it made economic sense. We would, at least, at the outset, need to support only one partner's salary. I continued to work at Kahn and Jacobs while we looked for an office and an appropriate project or two to prime the practice. My 77th Infantry Division friend, Howard Schneider drafted a short 'partnership agreement' to be signed when the time was right, which it turned out, was soon.

Peter, in his search for an office, discovered that Carnegie Hall had one or two studios for rent. These studios were located in the interstitial space between the two-story trusses spanning the hall. The studios were constructed to provide space for acceptable artists; musicians, painters, dancers and photographers. In 1964 architects were also included as 'acceptable'. The studios were brilliant: many were sky-lit and many had two story high west-facing windows. We settled on 810 Carnegie Hall. We could see the Hudson from its west-facing windows: well, in truth, we could see New Jersey and therefore we knew <u>where</u> the river was, close enough. The vacant lots then used for parking and which permitted the view are now filled-in with large, vacuous buildings obscuring any view, at all and, in any event, the studios are now, apparently, only history.[95]

It was time to tell Bob Jacobs my plans. He was understanding and supportive. I was not cut out for the more corporate architectural world represented by the Kahn and Jacobs type of office and Bob agreed. We parted company amicably.

Access to the Carnegie Hall's studio floor was by the Hall's original, water-powered, piston-driven elevators. They hissed their way up and hissed their way down. The elevators were manually operated by aging, uniformed, cheerful staff. Some of the elevator men, nearly as old as the elevators themselves, had been there for their working life. On the ground floor, at the 56th street entrance, the one we used, was the Carnegie Tavern. This was a genuine German-American relic of the turn of the century and was mostly used by local artists of all disciplines. Grey-haired, white-apron wearing, German-speaking, waiters served you, with a Germanic flourish worthy of Munich's Hofbrauhaus. Schnitzel a la Holstein for $3.00 ($23.00 today) was my favourite of the many ethnic German dishes. We ate there in its dark smoky interior when entertaining a client, a potential client or whenever we could find any modest justification. Occasionally we splashed out at the Russian Tea Room, just a door or two down from Carnegie Hall on 57th street. Mostly though, lunch would be sandwiches from the Carnegie Deli, eaten at our desks.

In 1964, as we were setting up the office, Peter's book, *God's Own Junkyard*, was published. It was a small, heavily illustrated, volume decrying the rubbishing of America's countryside and its main-street. The book was (and still is) a hit with many civic-minded citizens and organizations. It led to Peter being invited to give lectures to sympathetic civic groups. For the most part these groups were local to New York. An exception, however, was a civic group led by Lester, ('Bud'), Glen in Manistee, Michigan. Bud was the owner of Glen of Michigan, a successful national manufacturer of women's sports-wear and jeans. Bud was in his 50s. A smallish, wiry man, with close-cropped grey hair, he was seriously energetic, humorous, in a sardonic way and a pre-Nike, 'just-do-it' pusher. He wanted to get the best from anyone working for him and this definitely included the architects he hired. He drove a huge, classic, Cadillac convertible, which choice perhaps said something about Bud's persona. Bud had just remarried. His new wife, Ruth Milliken, was part owner of the eponymous Michigan department store chain and sister of Bill Milliken, Yale '44, a contemporary of both John Lindsay and David Mitchell. Bill was Lieutenant Governor of Michigan.

Bud invited Peter to lecture Manistee's 'great and good' with the idea that Peter would stimulate the town's 'movers' to improve its image. The lecture was a success and shortly after, Bud hired Baker & Blake to prepare a study for the improvement of downtown Manistee. Bud also asked if we would be interested in doing something with his 'fifties' modernist house, overlooking the eastern shore of lake Michigan. He had constructed a 'classic' one-storey house, in a style not too dissimilar from the Blake and Neski houses of Long Island: flat roofed, open-plan, large windows and sliding glass doors. His house was pretty much a bachelor's pad. However, with Ruth now on the scene he needed to add an appropriate bedroom wing for himself and Ruth. The house renovation became my responsibility while Peter took on the urban planning project: he found it more challenging.

As well as good clients, the Glens soon became good friends. I would, in time, design two more houses for them[100] after Bud sold his business and the Glens moved from Manistee to Birchrunville, Pennsylvania. Ruth's brother, William, became governor of Michigan[101] and Bud and Ruth, as a gift to 'Bill', hired me to redesign the governor's offices in the Lansing Statehouse. Some years later Peter Glen, Bud's son[102] who lived in Sniffen Court in Manhattan, also became a friend and client. Bud would never allow anyone other than myself to visit or even talk to them about their projects. When I once suggested that one of our architect employees, Baldur Peter, was better qualified than I to visit a site for a specific task he replied, "I want to dance with the leading lady not with the chorus line." He was a keen observer and listener. He once remarked on a visit to our office, "Jim, it's too neat, you need more work." If I had a best client award to present to one of my many good clients during almost fifty years of practice Bud would be on the 'short list'.

Almost at the same time, as we acquired these first two Glen projects the Leahys bought a house in Chestnut Hill for which we were hired to do renovations. Peter's friend Craig Ellwood, a cheerful, not to say bon vivant, friendly and amusing, gifted California 'architect'[103] asked us to be his East Coast partner and he would be our West Coast partner, should we need one: more of an architectural exercise in ego than practicality. Craig was a specialist in light-weight steel structures in the Miesian tradition. He had lots of contacts and we would, in due course, work together on a number of projects including the New York headquarters for the Xerox Corporation. These projects, as well as on-going work at Darrow, more than justified Baker & Blake's launch.

Peter and I signed our agreement, gave a small party in the office and opened 810's doors for business. Even with our substantial investment and early clients we were seriously under capitalized and without even more commissions our 'shelf-life' might be short. However, the economy was good, we had excellent, if untried, credentials, we exuded confidence and more projects came across the transom. Our first technical employee, a talented draftsman (and later architect), was David Wong, fresh from Hong Kong. David, the name given to him by Catholic missionaries when he escaped from Mainland China[104], became a close friend and valued member of Baker & Blake. David would later change his not politically correct 'David' to PC, for Pak Cheung. We also hired a secretary, Anne Ryan, an intelligent, cheerful, even bubbly (but perhaps a little 'scatty'), professionally trained ballerina from Boston. It was a funny mix but we all got on and dug in to make Baker & Blake work; and it did.

I joined the American Institute of Architects and soon became involved in the activities of the New York Chapter. It was during my summer with Blake and Neski that I was first introduced to the Chapter. At that time, I recall, the Chapter rented a dimly lit room on a cross-town street, just south of Grand Central, between Park and Lexington Avenues. It seemed to be a place where architects could socialize with each other and have a drink: quite informal. Only a few years later, when I joined, the Chapter had become, by comparison, quite business-like and professional. Its offices were now on 40th street, opposite Bryant Park (co-incidentally where father had his New York office) and it had a full-time director, my friend from 50th street days, George Lewis. I was soon on the Chapter's board and then elected to be the Chapter's treasurer, (to this day I am not sure why) a position I retained for four years. Being 'treasurer' was an unlikely position for me but the job wasn't all that 'clever'. With a little luck the finances of the Chapter improved significantly. George, who was to be the Chapter's executive director for more than twenty years, maintained that I was the best Chapter treasurer, ever: who knows?

Peter who liked to teach in addition to his other work was on the adjunct faculty at Cooper Union and Pratt. As he was often too busy to take a class he would ask me to sub for him. I found this substitute teaching enjoyable. When I heard that City College had initiated an Architecture program and was seeking adjunct staff to fill out their faculty requirements I applied. They accepted me as a lecturer and design studio mentor. Thus began what would turn out to be a twenty-five year, rewarding, teaching experience: rewarding in the friendships made, student and faculty alike, and, also, in the additional, and steady, income teaching provided.

Overnight I had become, over-committed; something had to give. The army reserve was enjoyable, though often a hard slog, and it was now getting repetitious. More importantly, its requirements interfered with both the architectural practice and City College. My reserve obligation was more than fulfilled. With some regret, I resigned, put my uniforms away and turned Headquarters battery over to my capable friend and colleague, Howard Schneider.

* * * * *

In 1964 Darrow was still an all-boys school, with an enrolment nearing 190 students. The rather bullish question then was, 'could the school expand'- even further? Apart from the educational and marketing issues of enrolment the board wanted to know how and where the physical plant needed to change as a response to any increased enrolment. The school still only occupied the Church and Centre families but had its 'eye' on acquiring the North Family property from Hugh Sphon, a vice president of General Electric in Pittsfield. The North Family could certainly be part of the 'where'.

Spohn had bought the North Family at auction[105], for about $40,000, in the early nineteen sixties, 'promising', in return for the school not bidding against him, that he promised to give the ten remaining North Family buildings and some related land to the School while keeping the Great Stone Barn, his real interest, for himself. He wasn't hurried in making good his promise but John Joline and others kept at him until there came a time, around 1966[106] when he did donate the buildings and their associated land to the school, perhaps garnering a nice tax deduction in the process.

The planning process started in 1964 and required me to again make numerous visits to the School and to Darrow Board meetings for discussions. The Board met in John Joline's office, formerly Mr. Heyniger's, in the northeast corner of the first floor of Wickerhsham. The room had not changed much since Heyniger's death in 1960. Heyniger's roll-top desk was still there, against the north wall, as was a large Shaker table that served as the headmaster's working desk. Two large lamps made from Shaker jugs provided primary illumination. The Headmaster's chair was an old, leather padded, swivel chair possessing an alarming habit of taking a sudden backward tilt if you moved about too much. Against the desk, forming a T, was a quite massive, contemporary conference table. Its unfortunate design did not permit the Windsor or even the ladder-back chairs scattered about the room to be pulled underneath. It was a guarantee that if you were sitting at the table you would either end up with bruised knees, pinched fingers or both. Those, in the know, elected not to sit at the table. A Shaker bench and a large Shaker hymnal cupboard completed the furniture collection. Benjamin Young's tall clock, a truly impressive Shaker cupboard with doors and drawers, and an alphabet board from the Shaker's schoolhouse were in the secretarial anteroom to the headmaster's office[107]. It was an eclectic space, an interesting balance between a museum and a homely, functioning office. I liked it. The office is now split into the admissions office suite and the Shaker artifacts are long gone and all but forgotten.

In addition to Darby, the Board's chairman, and Nick, there were usually about eight other trustees at the meetings. Among these were, Dave Thompson, later to succeed Darby as chairman, John Sprague, President of Sprague Electric, a delightful articulate artist, Austin Purves, a friend of Heyniger's, Austin Haight, a lawyer and local naturalist. I do not recall the others nor do I recall Frank Boyden, headmaster of Deerfield and a long standing trustee at any meeting that I attended in the 1960s. The board was quite 'old school', tweedy, conservative and with a definite Princeton tilt[108]. At one meeting, following a presentation, Nick and/or Darby said that it seemed silly for me to be attending all these meetings as the school's architect, shouldn't I be a trustee? There was a short discussion about either creating a new category of alumni trustee or filling out that category, I do not remember which. In any event, there were no great formalities, I was made a trustee on the spot: I would be an active trustee for more than forty years and now am a trustee emeritus.

* * * * *

Over the next two years numerous commissions were obtained from varied sources. David Mitchell, our neighbour on 93rd Street became managing director of S.G. Warburg. He hired us, to do his first, and as he expanded, his second and third offices. David was a tall, mostly bald, Yale graduate and navy veteran. True to his Scottish background, he could be quite dour. I don't know how many times over forty years he told me that the economy was going to 'tank', and sometimes it did. But despite his pessimistic streak I always found David to be thoughtful and kind. He was enthusiastic about (in his opinion) my architectural 'talents' and could have passed as a promoter of our practice. David is also definitely on the short list for 'best client'. In addition to our architectural relationship, David would, until his death in 2010, provide very considerate, and considerable, personal and business counsel. Although a banker by profession, I regarded him as an entrepreneur as well as friend. David was always suggesting that I, or someone else should get together with some other person he knew and see 'what happened'. His New Year's Day parties at 174 East 93rd were legend. He invited most everyone he knew, friends and relatives as well as a good selection of New York's shakers and movers, to the eight-hour, wall-to-wall gathering in his house. His guests would come any time after two pm and stay until eight, or later. He would push through the crowded rooms making sure that guests would meet at least one or two other persons who might have mutual interests. One of his recommendations would, in fact, come to materially alter my professional career. I always looked forward to meeting with David, no matter what the occasion. David's wife Frannie was a bit more restrained in her enthusiasm but she was also very kind and generous. They had four daughters, one of them Caroline, was Jamie's age and she, Jamie and Morgan sometimes played together. David and his extended family provided a pretty good illustration of a Scottish clan.

In addition to the Glen, Darrow and Mitchell work, I was hired[109] to lecture on architecture by The New York State College of Ceramics at Alfred, in the town of the same name in the Southern Tier of New York State. Alfred is a private college to which for administrative purposes the state funded College of Ceramics is attached. Although I did lecture and conduct a seminar, the position was a 'cover' to help Professor Theodore, 'Ted', Randall, prepare a formal program and political case for a new ceramic arts building. I think the original contact may have been made to Peter at the Architectural Forum. The college's existing facilities were distinctly underwhelming for an arts program. In due course the program, a sketch design and model were submitted to the New York State University and its Construction Fund (SUCF). Two years later, in 1968, $6,000,000 (about $35,000,000 today) was approved for a new 135,000 square foot building. Perhaps not surprisingly, Baker & Blake were appointed as the architect.

The College of Ceramics 'teaching' assignment required me to travel to Alfred at least twice a month. The most uncomplicated, and certainly the cheapest, way of getting there was to take the Erie Lackawanna night train from Hoboken, New Jersey to Hornell, New York. This was quite marvellously archaic and reminiscent of my childhood trips to Florida. One first had to take a ferry from Manhattan across to Hoboken, the site of the Erie Lackawanna Terminal. There you boarded 'The Owl' the overnight sleeper to Chicago. Sometime after midnight 'The Owl' left Hoboken and wound its way, very slowly, along the Southern Tier of New York. The train arrived the next morning in Hornell, the nearest station to Alfred, at about

10 o'clock. Ted would meet me there and drive the eleven miles to Alfred. I would stay with Ted for two or three days while I worked on the proposed facilities program, prepared the prototype design and provided a lecture or two on architecture.

Peter and I both contributed to procuring our architectural commissions, individually and collectively though Peter initially had the edge, a question of equals but one was 'more so'. One of my contributions came through Irwin Miller, Whit's friend and Yale Corporation member. Miller, Chairman of the Cummins Engine Company, and one of America's greatest architectural patrons, saw that we got work from Cummins Engine Company. He wrote to me once telling me how to succeed in Architecture, saying, in summary: "stay on budget, stay on time, maintain interest in all the little details and bring something to the table that the client couldn't imagine was possible". It is good advice and I have always tried to follow it. I have often included the dictum in the many student lectures I have given over the years. One of Peter's friends was George Dudley a well-known architect and influential player in New York State. It was through his influence we obtained several additional projects from New York State agencies, including the Binghamton Rehabilitation Centre a project for New York State's Department of Health and Mental Hygiene.

With threes large projects we needed more staff and, consequently, a larger office. We moved down the hall to Studio 828: much bigger. It even had a mezzanine. At the same time Anne Ryan left, to return to Boston and other pursuits. Anne was replaced by another Anne: Westbrook. Anne II turned out to be terrific. She was hard-working, enthusiastic, competent and pragmatic, she essentially took over most of the administrative and financial responsibilities for two years until, for personal reasons, she moved to London where she worked with Vernon Gibberd of Blake and Neski and later, for many years for Frances Lincoln, the publisher. She married John Fraser, a Cambridge graduate and a gifted architect. Anne and John would remain a good friends, I often stayed with them on my later trips to London. Sadly Anne died of cancer in 2008.

As Darrow's Master Plan was being developed it became clear to the Board that Darrow's underwhelming science facilities needed improvement. Science and space exploration were on educator's minds, science was the highest priority. 'Improvement' was an understatement. The then existing facilities in the basement of Wickersham were not much different from what they were when I entered in 1944. Spurred on by Darrow's trustee, John Sprague, the Board agreed to build a proper science facility. Baker & Blake was appointed to provide the design. Jay Walter, our newly hired designer, would work with me on its design.

Jay was a California architect turned jazz drummer or, perhaps, the reverse. Needing work to supplement his music income he, literally, wandered into our studio one day looking for part time work. We 'hit it off' as they say and he was hired 'on the spot'. Very quickly part time became full-time. It turned out that Jay and I would work together, on and off, for our professional lives. He became a good friend of the family and would even keep and play his drums in my home (his apartment was too small and his neighbours, apparently, unappreciative). He was also a competent pianist, a Bach enthusiast. He, too, sadly died of cancer, in 2008. Despite changes in how physics, chemistry, biology and math are taught, the Science Building, now updated and fifty years old, continues to adequately serve its function.

* * * * *

It was during the summer of 1966, while I was visiting the school to discuss the Science Building that the mystery surrounding the Darrow fires of 1962 and 1963 was solved. John, Jean and I were having dinner one evening in the dining room of Whittaker House. We were about half way through when the phone rang. John left the table to take the call in the library. Jean and I, being nosy, stopped talking and listened but could only make out bits of John's end of the conversation that, as I recall, was rather terse. John could be a little abrupt. The conversation went something like this;

John, "What?", pause
"Who?", pause
"Where?", pause
"Stay there, I'll call the police!".

When he came back into the dining room John looked as if he had seen a ghost. He sat down and in a rather deliberate, quiet manner said, "I know who set the fires," and no more. He got up again to call the police. It turned out that a Darrow graduate sitting at a bar, somewhere in Florida, overheard another drinker boasting about how he and two friends had nearly put a school out of business by setting fire to two buildings. The graduate made four from two and two and called John. The following morning the New York State Police hit on the overheard drinker and with the information gained then arrested the other two. All three confessed. As the arsonists were minors at the time of the crime, the whole matter was kept secret. Even as a board member I did not learn who the perpetrators were, nor who had called: I did not try to find out.

* * * * *

My work commitments were not lending themselves to a reasonable home life. I was deemed a 'workaholic', by Molly, and others. At the time, I defended myself but, in retrospect, I was probably guilty as charged. I left for work early, worked late and often taught evening classes. In addition many of our projects were "out of town" requiring time-consuming drives or 'overnights'. I had the AIA obligations and to cap it, often spent time in the office on weekends to catch up. I did not see Molly much and the children less. I saw Morgan and Jamie in the morning, before school, and would try to get home to see them at dinner; but this didn't always happen. Assuming I was home, I saw and played with the children but mostly on weekends. This work commitment was not unusual for young architects in a similar position but that is not an excuse and I do not give myself high marks as a father during this period. I was often short and frequently became unnecessarily angry, often with the children. My reactions to Morgan or Jamie's minor childhood infractions tended to be over-the-top. Morgan and Jamie were, in fact, well behaved, charming and fun to be with. When I got angry with the children I was mostly getting angry about something else though I didn't realize it at the time. I was proud of the children and loved them: unquestionably.

Molly seemed frustrated during this period. She did not have a job but wanted one. She appeared to be uninterested in my work, vicariously or otherwise, not that she had to be interested. I do not recall Molly ever visiting our offices. Given the time I spent in the office I believe Molly came to resent my work and other commitments. It also would be fair to admit that I was unable to relate to or share Molly's frustrations. We probably, naively, didn't realize the strains that my work on the one hand and Molly's boredom on the other hand, was creating. Curiously, Whit, before his death, with prescience, more than once, warned about the potential deterioration of relationships between couples when one was involved in an active professional life and the other was left at home. Whether it was fair or not he cited Mamie and Dwight Eisenhower as a dramatic example of this 'problem'. Rather than look to find personal time together or seek resolutions to our growing 'problems' Molly and I buried ourselves in activities; we found that easier. In New York we became involved in the NAACP and fringe political activities involving John Lindsay who had become Mayor in 1966. On the Vineyard we moved out of Lambert's Cove, buying and renovating a delightful little Cape Cod cottage at Indian Hill. I constructed a small but geometrically complex barn, mostly by myself, as well as renovating the property's little pond, earning Mary's sobriquet, "capability Baker". Molly and I, mostly Molly to be fair, were activity organizers. Tennis tournaments, sailfish racing, days at Lambert's Cove beach or the 'shack' were orchestrated with Molly's energetic enthusiasm. We mostly followed her lead. A major event one summer was 'The Bird Drop Ball' a dance we (and in this case it was a definite 'we') organized in the old steamship dock in Oak Bluffs. We probably had nearly two hundred guests of all ages and all enjoyed a costumed boozy evening of dancing and home-produced entertainment.

In 1966 Molly and I agreed to increase the size of our family and soon our third child was 'on the way'. Around the same time, for some reason, Jamie became fascinated in pigs – perhaps it started with a large stuffed pig I bought for him. Anyway, we 'borrowed' a piglet from a local farmer and looked after it for the summer. (The piglet went back to the farmer at the end of the summer.) We learned that little pigs are very strong, very noisy and that their antics can be amusing. Jamie called the piglet Charlotte. Charlotte was to become the inspiration for 'Toinki the Super Pig' a small book I wrote as a Christmas gift for Jamie in 1967.

Because of our almost hyperactive life, Molly and I rarely shared intimacies, of any kind. We often had life-style disagreements as well as more abstract arguments. Once I even walked out of a restaurant during an argument over the Vietnam War. Though, perhaps improbable, Molly was pro war and I antiwar, at least at that moment. Some of our arguments were action-packed and at least once I ended up in hospital having sliced my foot kicking the glass out of a garden door. I suspect, in a way, we were both walking in our parent's footsteps: if something bothers you, don't talk about it. We may have given the impression of a happy family but we were not. Counselling might have helped but Griswolds didn't do counselling and the Brooks didn't do divorce, either. This, 'it's not <u>my</u> problem' attitude would eventually change but only when it was too late.

Molly and the children still spent most of the summer school holidays on the Vineyard. I still joined them on Thursday nights and stayed, mostly, until Monday mornings. Thursday the 27th of July 1967 was just a normal Thursday and I arrived as usual. Molly was now in her eighth month of pregnancy, due in the third week of August. Our plan was to return to New York within the week in order that Molly could be delivered at Columbia Presbyterian. We had already selected names for the forthcoming child. In the event of a girl, she would be named Catriona, a name we first came across because of Catriona Shafer the children's 1963 au pair. We liked the name and its Scottish and literary connections. I cannot remember what a boy's name would have been. In any event we didn't make it to New York. Catriona arrived safely at the Martha's Vineyard Hospital, after a rather rapid drive from Indian Hill, on Saturday the 29th of July. Not surprisingly we remained on the Vineyard during August.

Despite the excitement and distraction of Catriona's arrival matters between and Molly and myself continued to deteriorate We were at loggerheads on a daily basis. Postnatal depression may have been a contributory factor but in 1967 this was not well understood and the subject never came up. At some point, back in New York, doctor Dalton, who had been our family doctor for some years, and Aunt Christine's before that, was consulted. He suggested that I meet with a colleague of his, Doctor Wilkie, a psychiatrist. I took his advice.

Wilkie was a classic Freudian psychiatrist. He was, in appearance, non-descript, of medium height, balding and wore rimless glasses. He spoke quietly (and infrequently) causing me to ask, "what", frequently (and I wasn't hard-of-hearing). In the several years (off and on) I saw him he never raised his voice, even for inflection. Hollywood would have probably cast him as an accountant, not a psychiatrist. His office in a little back room on the second floor of an anonymous brick apartment building on the northeast corner of Park Avenue and 72nd street was modest in the extreme. In a way it matched Wilkie's appearance. There was no receptionist, nor any semblance of formality. One waited in the hall outside his office and entered when he opened his door, he would stand back a little, nod very slightly, and say, "Mr. Baker" almost as a question. He allowed ten minutes between appointments in order to avoid patients meeting each other and to make end-of-session notes: he kept his client's woes in copious notebooks. (One wonders what happened to them after his death in 2007.) The ten minutes of separation didn't always work and sometimes his patients passed. In this event you might nod, just slightly, perhaps in imitation of Wilkie, but say nothing, at all. "Well, how was it?" was not an option. In the many times I went to his office I never saw anyone I knew or in fact anyone twice, it was a little weird. In the office there were two seating options, a chair opposite Wilkie's or a classic psychiatrist's couch on which you would lie with your head facing away from his. The couch, though it included a small backrest, was flat and uncomfortable and not conducive to sleep, unless you were exhausted, I did succumb once or twice. Wilkie was a smoker. He lit up when he felt like it and though he kept the one double hung window open, top and bottom, even in winter, his office always smelled of cigarette smoke. Besides the window itself, a standing lamp provided the only other illumination. On the walls there were a few unmemorable prints, all in all, there wasn't much to focus on – except, of course, one's thoughts.

You talked whenever you wanted, or, sometimes not at all. Dreams were ok if you were in a pinch as to what to say. Wilkie was totally non-committal; good or bad were not in his consulting vocabulary. Nevertheless, over time one knew that he was honest, ethical and on the side of his clients. He could even be subtly amusing at times, if he thought it appropriate. Through gentle comments he could steer you in what would likely be the 'right' directions. The realization of any decision would always be your realization, your decision not his. I couldn't list Wilkie as a friend, he was always too professional and he never talked about himself. I knew more about him from his obituary[110] than I did from several years of close contact. Did Wilkie have an influence on my life - in all sorts of ways and was seeing him educational? There is only one simple and unqualified answer: yes.

Initially, I sat in the chair opposite Wilkie, telling him how I saw my 'marriage problems'. After only a short while he suggested, that it would be best for the marriage if Molly would also "see someone" and that even joint meetings might be appropriate. I discussed this with Molly, but Molly, following her father's opinion of psychiatry, had no enthusiasm for this proposal. Molly thought any 'problem' was my 'problem' and that I should get on with it. I did.

Molly and I continued to have arguments, sometimes stopping just short of violence. Though Wilkie was, a noted, quite neutral, there came a time, when after reciting a previous night's events, the one where I ended up in hospital having kicked out the glass door, Wilkie stated, categorically, (one of the very few times he actually made a suggestion) and without qualification that I should leave 93rd street, "<u>now</u>", before something really regrettable occurred. I did, spending the next week in a hotel near Carnegie Hall. The situation was pretty grim: seriously depressing. I do not know what Morgan and Jamie were told nor can I imagine what they thought about the situation – it couldn't have been good. What had gone wrong? Perhaps we got married too young, were too emotionally immature or some related combination, (thoughts of mother): it was a different age a different time. Wilkie provided two observations. One was, "if you keep rubbing yourself with sandpaper you will eventually bleed, if you keep it up you will bleed more, until, in fact, you bleed to death." The second was even simpler (and less sinister), "if you don't dredge a canal it silts up and eventually the water doesn't flow at all". The 'canal' that was our marriage had 'silted up'.

Alex Grinnell[111], my Yale Architectural School classmate, friend and associate of Baker & Blake and his then wife, Kate, invited me to stay with them in their spare bedroom. I took advantage of this kind offer and spent some time with them. In due course I found a charming, and slightly Bohemian one room flat over the Blue Angel nightclub on 9th street, between Fifth and Sixth. Molly, for her part, moved out of 93rd Street and its memories. She determined that a clean break, with distance, would be appropriate and she, with the three Children left for London in the fall (1967) for the winter. They settled in a flat in Queen's Gate Terrace and Morgan and Jamie were enrolled in the American School. Trina was of course too little for that. Basil Henning, a retired Yale master and friend of Whit's was in London writing a history of Parliament. He and his wife would provide a base line for Molly. A formal separation agreement was drawn up and signed. The agreement, perhaps, wasn't quite the end of the marriage but it was certainly the beginning of the end.

I immersed myself in Baker & Blake. We were now not only busy we were, perhaps, frantic. We had the commission for Alfred, one for the Rehabilitation Centre in Binghamton and two housing projects for the New York State Urban Development Corporation. There were, as well, as a number of smaller jobs. Baker

& Blake now consisted of eighteen professionals, two in administration plus Peter and me.

The first step in the design process for the College of Ceramics was to research existing buildings of a similar nature. As there were not many such prototypes in the US, I persuaded the State (State University Construction Fund: SUCF) to fund a tour of appropriate European facilities. Not surprisingly one of these facilities was the Royal College of Art in London. Other facilities were in Copenhagen, Stockholm and Helsinki. Peter endorsed the idea of the trip and asked me to interview Alvar Aalto in Helsinki and to visit the USSR to see what there was, if anything, of publishable merit. This was all quite satisfactory and I accepted Peter's suggestion. Appropriate arrangements were put in place and I left New York in early March, 1968.

I stayed in London for a week, seeing Molly and the Children as well as visiting the Royal College of Art. Copenhagen and Stockholm were visited and after I flew to Helsinki. I stayed there for about a week visiting Arabia, Marimekko and other design studios in company with a kind friend of Peter's. I visited Aalto twice, both times in his studio. He enjoyed a drink or two during lunch and my appointments were all scheduled after lunch. I found Aalto quite avuncular and friendly, rather mystical in his description of his work, and quite free with his conversation. I said little but he talked a lot, which was appropriate. I visited many of his buildings, as well as those of his contemporaries such as Timo Penttila. I liked and was inspired by Aalto's work even before I went to Helsinki. I liked his work even more after experiencing it. Peter's colleague took me to dinner in the country with some of her friends and we attended a concert at Helsinki's City Theatre. The visit was thoroughly entertaining and educational.

After Helsinki, I flew Finnair to Leningrad arriving on a cold and snowy March morning. An Intourist agent met me and delivered me to the Astoria Hotel. The hotel put me in the mind-frame of Tolstoy and Dostoyevsky. If I shut my eyes, even now, I can see red draperies, red plush upholstery, red carpets, crystal glass, and taste vodka and caviar. It may have been an austere time in 1968 Leningrad but it wasn't in the Astoria.

The following morning, in the guise of an architectural journalist I had a pleasant, formal meeting at The House of Architects, a stylish, late 19th century town house: trust architects to find an elegant situation! I was there as an Architectural Forum writer to 'interview' some eight Russian architects. The eight architects an interpreter and I sat around a large, green beige covered round table. I think we discussed the state of architecture in Leningrad. As vodka and cognac were freely flowing at eleven o'clock in the morning I am not so sure about the discussion. In any event several architects later took me to visit some large but grim housing projects. I also visited the Hermitage on two successive days, saw the cruiser Aurora and went to a terrific one-ring circus. I walked for miles around the city dutifully followed by an Intourist 'guide'. I left after four or five days flying to Moscow on Aeroflot. I was ill with a sinus infection at the time and the unpressurized plane was amazingly uncomfortable, excruciating if I remember correctly. I vowed not to fly Aeroflot again.

Moscow was bitterly cold and I stayed in the Hotel Metropol, near Red Square. I visited with a cabal of architects at the Moscow House of Architects, only the address was different from that the House of Architects in Leningrad. Larger, ungainly, and leaky housing projects were visited as was what Peter referred to as the "cold cuts"[112], otherwise known as Lenin's tomb. There a guard, hotly, (it was the only 'hot' thing I experienced in Moscow) chastised me for keeping my freezing hands in my pockets. I spent time meandering through Gum where I bought some toys and an iconic fur hat, visited churches and walked around the Kremlin. I had more 'fun' in Leningrad. I found Moscow a bit inhospitable. After a few days I was happy to be leaving.

Intourist had booked me on Aeroflot, via Berlin to Paris where I would connect to a New York flight. However, with respect to my vow, I managed to cancel Aeroflot and arranged to take the overnight sleeper to Berlin where I would get a flight (not Aeroflot) to Paris. Somewhere along the way my Intourist 'guide' who had shadowed me for most of my visit to Moscow got 'lost'. By the time I boarded the train at Moscow's Belorussky station it appeared, that I was on my own.

The trip, taking more than twenty-four hours, was brilliant. I played chess with the car's porter, conversing, (more or less), in French. The porter was quite the better chess player but he seemed to enjoy beating me so we played, a lot. In between I watched, lulled by the sounds of the steam engine and the clickity-clack of the track, almost mesmerized, as the flat snowy countryside slid past the window during the day and the moonlit night. I drank endless cups of teas prepared in the sleeper's steaming samovar. At Brest-Litovsk I watched the while the train was lifted to remove the train's Russian trucks and have smaller ones installed for the standard European gauge. Some three hours later I was walking around the Warsaw station and environs during the train's long stop there. We finally arrived in a cold and dark East Berlin, the final stop, around eight in the evening. There, Kalashnikov-armed, uniformed and plain-clothed policemen and officials boarded the train to check our papers before allowing us to disembark.

There was a little 'problem'. Intourist, apparently, had really 'lost' me. I wasn't supposed to be there. The Berlin end of the Soviet system was not expecting a 35 year old American male, travelling alone, in Berlin. My documents (and theirs) said I should have arrived in Berlin by plane the day before. No one on the German side spoke English very well, and as a result our mutual efforts to communicate were dodgy. My German was not up to explaining why I didn't like flying Aeroflot.

My luggage, passport, wallet and contents of my pockets were examined and then taken away. I was placed under guard. A young, but stern-faced, uniformed policeman, stood over me while several plain-clothed policemen muttered to each other in the corridor outside the compartment. I was a little unnerved, no one had any idea where I was. Should matters go badly I had no clue as to whom to call or what to do. I did the only thing left, sit, wait and pretend to be calm.

After about an hour a clutch of officials returned with my belongings. One of the plain-clothes officials, rather triumphantly, held my wallet in his hand and slowly pulled from it a pack of my recently engraved, and elegant, if I may so, calling cards indicating that I was an architectural correspondent, a good cover. Between each card was a thin sheet of tissue paper. On the paper was a faint, ghosting of the card's printed face which, when you looked at it from the wrong side it appeared to be some sort of code as the ghosting was backwards and hard to read. I struggled at some length to explain this curiosity and ultimately was successful, or, alternatively, perhaps the East Germans got bored. After some further interrogation they gave up the questioning, put me in a taxi and told the driver to take me to West Berlin. I found my way to the Hilton where, fortunately, there was a room. The next morning I would fly to Paris connecting with a flight to New York.

After only a few hours sleep I was up, arranging with the hotel's concierge to take me back to East Berlin, Schonefeld, where the flight originated. It was not easy to arrange this but finally a driver was found and I was in the back seat of a black Mercedes 180 taxi heading back east through some check-points and tank-traps to Schonefeld. When we got to the airport it was a bit eerie, there was hardly anyone around. The taxi driver agreed to wait while I sought out someone who could tell me what was happening. It transpired that the airport was closed, because of expected "unrest", though "unrest" was not explained. In any event, there were no flights; back to the Hilton: they still had my room.

The day turned out to be quite exciting. "Unrest" turned out to be a euphemism for demonstrations. I saw it as an opportunity to get some pictures and went out to look at the "unrest" with that intention. Inevitably I became caught up in a fleeing crowd chased by policemen on horseback and a mobile water cannon. Not what I had planned though I did get some good pictures. In the afternoon I engaged in a more peaceful pursuit and visited the new lion cubs in Berlin's zoo.

Later, back in New York I wrote up a report on ceramic teaching facilities for the State and provided Peter with an outline of the Russian and Helsinki visits. Peter and I agreed there wasn't much, architecturally, about which to write, but the trip, for certain, was memorable.

185

In the spring of 1968 we had projects in western New York, Maine, Martha's Vineyard and points in between. Visiting them took hours. In a moment (looking back) of not very clear thinking I came up with the idea of learning to fly in order to 'simplify' transportation. Peter sort of gave his approval to the idea. This was enough encouragement to enrol in the flight school at Teterboro Airport, just north of the Newark Airport. My flight instructor was a professional clarinettist who split his professional time between filling in with the Metropolitan Opera orchestra and jazz evenings at Village venues. His pastime was flying which he did whenever he could. As an instructor he could fly and get paid, a satisfying solution. He did, however, claim to be selective in who he agreed to teach, he did not have a death wish.

My lessons were scheduled for one day a week and were always the first one of the day. I was at Teterboro by six am and in the air in one of the school's Piper Cherokees by six thirty. By eight-thirty I was back in Carnegie Hall. After about ten hours of instruction I was permitted to solo. The event was memorable as the Cherokee's radio failed, requiring me to make emergency wing signals to obtain permission to land. It worked out: I didn't panic or crash. In due course I passed the required written test and was granted a license to fly under visual flight rules. On longer trips my instructor flew with me in a more substantial, and faster, twin engine Piper Aztec. I flew a reasonable number of hours over the next two years, flying when it made sense economically and, maybe, sometimes when it didn't.

When Molly and the children returned from London she determined to move to Boston to be near the Leahys in Chestnut Hill and perhaps more importantly to get out of New York. New York was never Molly's town. The move commenced what would turn out to be years of difficulty in seeing the children and of making alimony and support payments with accusations and counter accusations on both sides – but all that was to come.

There was some talk of reconciliation but it didn't go far. I did not consider myself happy but at least I felt free of 'sandpaper' and more relaxed. I concentrated on work.

The Darrow Science Building - 1967

Making a presentation to the Darrow Board for the
Science Building - In the Headmaster's office - 1966

Late work at 810 Carnegie Hall - 1964

11

BAKER & BLAKE - 2

New York 1968 - 1974

"...this is not the end. It is not even the beginning of the end."
Winston Churchill

In setting up the partnership, Peter and I had agreed to allocate each project to one or the other according to its source and/or our available time. While Peter and I shared similar principles of modern design[113] I was, after all, his 'mentee', our 'design management' styles differed. Peter's approach was top down, mine bottom up. Peter's top-down approach required Peter to come up with a design concept for the project in question. He would illustrate the concept by neatly drawing, in single line, (usually with a ballpoint pen held, in an odd way between his, index and middle finger so that the barrel appeared between the knuckle of these two fingers) a plan at a small (very small) scale, on graph paper. Peter made few, if any, elevations or sections. He would present this little drawing, to me or later to his chosen designer. He was enthusiastic in this task. His tongue darted in and out of his mouth, viper-like, sometimes seriously distracting the listener as he presented his verbal rationale for the design. Peter then asked the respective recipient to "work it (the concept) out" as he left to return to his Architectural Forum offices.

In a few days Peter would reappear to see how his 'concept' had, in reality, 'worked out'. Though Peter's ideas were often very sound, almost inevitably Peter would find that the development of his concept wasn't exactly what he had expected. Either the surrogate designer had inputted his or her own ideas; the concept wouldn't fit the program, (Peter didn't necessarily let the client's program

188

get in his way) or, as often happened, Peter had mutated his own concept. Peter's method, 'sort of', worked when I was his surrogate, especially on simple Long Island beach houses. For the most part I understood Peter's 'design intent' implied in the little sketches. On more complex projects Peter's top-down approach didn't work as well, (if at all), especially when one of our designers (though some of them were <u>very</u> good) did not understand Peter. There was a lot of room for misunderstandings. These 'misunderstandings' inevitably led to bad 'feelings', all around. Peter would be 'put out' and his designated 'designer' discouraged (if not angry). I was left to sort it out - a diplomatic, time-consuming, and costly, exercise.

My bottom-up approach was more, one might say, democratic, though that is, perhaps, a curious word to use with 'design'. My intent was to hire the best, most sympathetically inclined (of course, to our view of design), designers[114] we could find and work with them. The hope was that the best design would emerge from this process. On Alfred, for example, I worked with Jay, we mostly saw eye-to-eye and, except for having to sometimes corral him on cost issues, we got along fine. This method didn't suit Peter's more autocratic nature, and to be fair, it sometimes didn't work that well – democracy being difficult even (or perhaps especially) in design.

In order to try to patch up the cracks that 'design' caused in the partnership Peter and I came to a reasonable compromise: Peter agreed to spend more time in the office and work more closely with the senior employees, especially the designated project managers who were responsible to either Peter or myself for the day-to-day development of the design as well as the preparation of construction documents and administration of the construction. For a while this worked quite well. Alex Grinnell worked on Binghamton with Peter and, initially, this was quite satisfactory.

In due course, however, Peter fell back into the habit of spending too little time in the studio. He wasn't terribly enthusiastic about Alex and looked to me as his personal 'project manager'. At that point Peter's process didn't work: there was insufficient time to cover Peter's responsibilities and run my own jobs as well as the office. There were difficulties and I often found myself an unnecessary mediator between Alex, other staff and Peter.

Peter's response to these management problems, was to write acerbic memos to my attention, usually all marked and underscored "<u>urgent</u>" – as a matter of fact, now that I think of it, I cannot remember one that was not "<u>urgent</u>". Peter's pen spoke for him, he was not as good at verbal discussion or debate.

Anne Westbrook set up a file marked "Shitty letters from Peter" as a repository for these missals. Some were, intentionally or not, quite funny. Peter was after all a good writer and his negative references to one or more individuals as being "cement heads" or other epithets, while generally inaccurate, could be amusing. Later, his accusation that I was related to Alex (I am not) and that we were 'plotting' against him was farcical. Anne's file became quite heavy and, ultimately, ignored. I still have most of it.

Despite these internal partnership distractions Baker and Blake continued to attract projects, though not as large as Binghamton or Alfred. Fred Hussey, scion of a New England whaling family and aviation aficionado hired us to design a heliport for 42nd street, a private airfield in New Jersey and a museum to display his extensive collection of WWI aircraft. Fred's projects were what some architects think are the best, they were never built. No leaking roofs, no cost overruns, and no delays only wonderful optimism for what might be. The Museum project was fun. The project discussions took place at his home in western New Jersey. To get there Hussey would have his little Bell helicopter pick me up at his 42nd street office and return me here after the meeting. I had great opportunities to look over and touch his WW1 aircraft collection. Hussey asked us to hire an expert aviator advisor for the technical bits of exhibition. Not knowing historic aviation experts I discussed the problem with Don Gold a literary agent with the William Morris agency. Don, whom I met through contacts of Anne Westbrook had interest in getting '*Toinki the Superpig*' published but he also seemed to know lots of people across many fields and had an interest in aviation. He called one morning asking me to send him a check for $100 to cover the costs of his proposed advisor to fly in from Ames, Iowa.

Don, being somewhat secretive, wouldn't tell me his name. In due course the 'advisor' arrived at Carnegie Hall. He was dressed in leather flying gear including a flowing a white silk scarf (I am not making this up). He turned out to be a brilliant, seat of the pants, biplane pilot, who regaled us with stories and technical information. Richard Bach was, as Don promised, an appropriate advisor. Don was in the process of getting Richard's book, *Jonathan Livingstone Seagull*, published.[115]

There were several private house projects, including one for the President of Alfred[116], but, like Hussey's projects, not all were built. They did, however, contribute to an interesting and eclectic practice and helped the cash flow. Our interior work, various apartment renovations, offices for The National Football League, City Investing, the Xerox Corporation and others were profitable and quite free from partnership debate as Peter had little interest in them. Work on Alfred Ceramics and the project at Binghamton absorbed a lot of the office time and in due course, unfortunately, became loss leaders. I continued to be responsible for Alfred and Peter did stay on top of Binghamton. We were busy, still reasonably profitable, and optimistic for the future. As for the future David Mitchell was giving us some gloomy forecasts while he was also optimistically hiring us to do another office for him.

On returning from London, Molly and the children did move to Cambridge. Given the proximity to her sister Sally and the Vineyard, Cambridge was a good choice. As predicted, it did mean that my communication with the children was going be difficult and it was. We proceeded with the divorce process. Howard Schneider represented me and Sam Hoar, a lawyer from Boston, represented Molly. The discussions over terms were emotional and acrimonious. The final divorce agreement satisfied neither of us - perhaps an inevitable outcome. In Molly's opinion, although she got the houses and most of the chattel goods, she did not get the fiscal support she wanted. From my point of view the alimony and support payments seemed to be based on someone else's hypothetical income, not mine. As it turned out I could not keep up with the agreed payments. As a partner in an architectural practice I did not have a fixed salary but only took periodic draws mutually approved by Peter and based on our actual profitability at any given month - to say the least this varied, greatly. There were late payments (or no payments) all leading to consequential problems. The visitation provisions were, in my opinion, onerous and complex. In sum, the agreement was, too little for Molly and too much from me, in other words, fairly typical. Nevertheless, it was signed: perhaps we both just gave up? In the summer, Molly and the children 'moved' to Idaho in order to obtain the divorce. Idaho had relatively simple divorce laws by comparison to Massachusetts or New York but there was one drawback, you had had to 'live' there. However, the residency requirements were quite short and by late summer the divorce was final. For Molly the acrimony arising from the divorce never abated, even after four decades.

Sometime during the late spring (1968) I attended a small, late afternoon concert at the Vanderbilt Mansion at Hyde Park. I cannot remember why I was there, perhaps it was because it was Mozart or perhaps it was just a stop off on a return trip from Darrow? During the orchestra's rendition of Eine Kliene Nachtmusik my eyes wandered from the performers to the audience. Catriona, the children's ex 'au pair', and her mother, Margaret, whom I had previous met on a couple of occasions were sitting only few rows away, a complete surprise. During the intermission we met and caught up. I had not seen either of them for, probably, four years.

After graduating from Chapin, Catriona had gone on to Vassar where she was now finishing her senior year. Catriona would be working in New York over the summer and we agreed that we might 'give each other a call'. We met several times during the summer and I visited with her parents at Bard College, in Annandale-on-Hudson. Fritz was Bard's Episcopal chaplain as well as a professor of philosophy. During the visit Margret made an unusual proposition: would I design a house for them? Margaret had only three requirements for a house: it had to have an octagonal living room, (a Hudson River oddity[117]), it had to be <u>very</u> economical and it was to be constructed on Bard property[118] along the Sawkill River. Margret had picked the site. Otherwise I could design anything I wanted, at a price – the price was that there would be no charge for the design. Cheeky, but that was Margret. I accepted the challenge. Fritz made little comment and had little input (if any), in the ensuing discussion – the current popular word, "whatever", comes to mind.

Margaret turned out to be an enthusiastic client; indeed she seemed enthusiastic about everything she touched. She was a concert level pianist and taught the instrument, privately. Her interests were catholic but tended to be mostly related to art and literature. Margaret was the author of several books, the main character of one, Saintly, appeared to be a thinly disguised version of Fritz. By comparison to Margaret, Fritz was taciturn (but then most people were compared to Margaret). I came to respect and like them both. I never had any deep, or long conversations with Fritz whereas I did with Margaret. Fritz was highly respected by both his students and the Bard faculty. In addition to being Bard's chaplain, Fritz was rector of the local Episcopal Church, St John's. He was, I thought, an intelligent, thoughtful sermonizer. On Sundays after church he could be found sitting in his car somewhere along a road, not too far from Annandale, reading the Sunday paper, Fritz also liked his privacy.

The concept for the Shafer house emerged during a design-intense Sunday afternoon in my 9th street apartment: the house would be a carved out cube floating above ground on the edge of the river just where it became a boisterous waterfall. The house would be constructed only of elements that could be found 'on-the-shelf' in the local lumberyard[119] and it would be self-built.

Margaret liked the concept and I proceeded to develop it, in my 'spare time', over the winter. The house (aptly named "Stream House" by Margaret), was constructed the following year with the help of Paul Shafer, one of Catriona's two younger brothers and a number of volunteers from Baker & Blake. All in all I think it took about six months to build, working mostly on weekends. The construction cost was seriously economic. The finishes were sparse and while the construction quality could be faulted it was a good result. The living room, wasn't a classic octagon as specified, but it did have eight sides. The house was selected as a 'Record House' in 1972, received several other awards and was published in a number of magazines in the US and abroad. I received requests to provide designs for the house from as far away as India.

The work in the office was steady. The two large projects, Alfred and Binghamton were in construction and for both projects their construction turned out to be difficult. Elia Construction from Buffalo was the lowest bidder on Alfred. Their reputation preceded them to the extent that the Construction Fund tried, briefly and unsuccessfully, to disqualify their bid. Before the first shovel of dirt was turned we were up to our necks in meetings with Elia's and the Construction Fund's[120] lawyers going over the two hundred or so drawings and a thousand pages of specifications while Elia's lawyers looked for reasons to increase their bid. After much wrangling a political solution was agreed behind closed doors (we were excluded) and construction got under way. It was to be a very difficult two years. The details no longer bear recitation or elaboration. Suffice it to say that the project started with lawyers and ended with lawyers – many, years later (seventeen, I believe). I do not even know the exact legal outcome but I do not recall that Baker & Blake or its insurers paid anything to anybody save for legal fees – it was a grim, and stupid, business. As noted earlier, a good project requires a good architect, good client and good contractor. Alter any one of those and you are in for trouble: we were in for trouble from the outset and even the cleverest of lawyers do not build buildings. Notwithstanding the legal difficulties Alfred was finished more or less as it had been designed. The good news is that, over the ensuing years, I have met students and graduates of the college who found the building exciting and a good environment for education. The construction story also provided me with anecdotes for many years of lectures in my management course at City College.

The construction of Binghamton was less confrontational but even that ended with lawyers due to an excessively deflected concrete slab over the building's auditorium. This problem was either a technical fault in the engineering design or failure of the contractor to place reinforcement correctly or to provide the correct concrete mix. As any of these possibilities had nothing to do with the architectural design, we watched from the side-lines – even now, as in Alfred's case, I do not know the outcome. The matter became even more complicated by the death of the principal and highly reputable, structural engineer, Aaron Garfinkle. In the end it was lawyers for the engineer's estate that had to defend the matter. Also, as with Alfred I have never heard of any complaints relating to the architectural design of the building. Despite the difficulties and arguments between Peter and myself over design I believe both projects were a credit to the office.[121]

In the fall Catriona left for a job in Barcelona. We corresponded frequently and agreed to meet in Barcelona for the Christmas holidays. We did, and after Barcelona we visited Marty in Rome. Marty liked Catriona so that was good. Somewhere in a snowy Italy, it may have been Orvieto, or Ostia, I proposed to Catriona and the proposal was accepted. Catriona and I were married in a (small) civil ceremony, at the Shafer's home, just about the same time Neil Armstrong stepped onto the moon. Actually the local justice of the peace, a mason, joined us in "holy masonry", he seemed unable able to say 'matrimony'. In view of my divorce and keeping with Fritz's rules (or perhaps more the Episcopal Church) we were not married in Bard's Chapel tough Fritz did conduct a service of Blessing following the "masonry" service.

The pre-wedding celebrations of the night before were elegantly hosted by Chauncey Stillman in the gardens of his rather magnificent estate, 'Wethersfield' in Amenia, New York, not that far from Annandale. 'Wethersfield' was designed in the style of a large Georgian vicarage with extensive formal gardens. Consisting of some 1200 acres of farmland it had some sixty miles of coaching roads, driving being one of Chauncey's pastimes. Chauncey's daughter Elizabeth was married to Catriona's elder brother Stephen. As a result, Margaret had become a close friend of Chauncey[122]. Though I didn't know it at the time, Chauncey was related to Elsie Stillman Rockefeller[123], mother's Greenwich neighbour and long-time friend.

Sometime during the spring, before the wedding, I moved from 9th street after finding a charming (though somewhat impractical) little duplex apartment, the bottom half of one of the little 19 century Queen Anne style houses, in Henderson Place. Henderson Place is a tiny mews at the eastern end of 86 street, where it meets Carl Schurtz Park. The apartment was a little odd, the kitchen and bedroom were in the basement (or ground floor), a few feet below street level. The first floor consisted of two rooms, allegedly a dining and living room but which we used as a spare bedroom for the children's visits and as a study. We lived mostly in the kitchen and bedroom. There was a tiny garden in the rear of the property that overlooked a similar house twenty feet away owned by the Nixon's daughter Trica and her husband.

Another neighbour was Arne Naess, nephew of the owner of one of Norway's shipping fleets. Arne at the time was married to a svelte, and friendly Swede, Filippa, and lived in the ground floor flat of the modern high-rise apartment opposite our house. We got to know him quite well, so well in fact that he commissioned us to do an office for him. All went well with the project until Arne's African Grey parrot got out of its cage (that I had designed) the night before he moved in and attempted to wreck the office – actually, he made a pretty good job of it. Though Arne was not amused we stayed friendly. As I had to admit to at least some failure in Parrot-cage design, the repairs were costly to us. I went off African Grays.[124]

There are people that do not read newspapers but I am not one of them. I almost always bought the New York Times and read, or at least looked at it from cover to cover. Thus, one day shortly after Catriona and I were married, I chanced on a familiar face in the business section: Boris. In retrospect perhaps I should have passed up the paper that day but I didn't. Also possibly I should not have found his number and not called him but I did. By such happenings are our lives changed.

Boris, after leaving Princeton had become a professional racing driver. He won a F1 race, placed in some and crashed in others. At his peak, he indicated that he was a member of the Formula 1 Ferrari team. When age (or one too many crashes) stopped his career he was left with some 'silver' and a fluency in the Italian language, women and manners of Italy. Boris had then turned to property development. He used an inheritance (I never knew how much) from his mother Sonia to buy a large plot of land in Northern Westchester and had successfully, (and profitably), turned a rough and tumble site into what today would be called luxury housing. It was this success that earned him a place in the financial section of the New York Times. Boris also had interests in or had worked in Jamaica though I do not remember why or what: perhaps, I never knew.

We met and after 'catching up', Boris suggested a number of "opportunities" in which Baker & Blake could make money by working with him. One of his schemes focused on building low-income housing in Jamaica and the second was a "mystical", (his word) project in Italy.

The Jamaican project seemed quite straightforward; Jamaica was sponsoring an international exhibition of low-cost housing. Boris, for some reasons that I cannot recall, knew Manley, the then Prime Minister. Boris figured, correctly, that he could get Manley to invite Boris and his architect friend, (me) to submit a proposal. What Boris failed to tell me was that the 'proposal' meant a full sized house to be constructed near the National Stadium in Kingston. The most successful solutions would be given contracts from the government. Boris was buoyant about 'winning' given the involvement of "such a talented firm as Baker & Blake", or words to that effect, and we believed. Boris also once told me not to believe a developer's hype.

The "mystical" project was just that: Boris described how, while "under the influence of some mind altering material", he was boating (or floating) in the waters of the Liparian Islands[125]. There he "had a vision" of the beautiful, abandoned island, Filicudi, as a Shangri-La of tourism. He proposed that we "take a look, it really would not cost much and, of course, I could visit Marty". Boris was at his persuasive best and that was pretty good if you forgot the nagging feeling that you might be being 'conned'. Nevertheless, I agreed to discuss both "opportunities" with Peter.

Peter, understandably, was sceptical. However, Boris's Italian proposal had the advantage that it was in Italy. Jamaica was a competition and Peter was always up for a competition. We had entered in the course of the partnership several: unsuccessfully (I might add). Peter agreed that we might take, "just a little look". I did not realize it at the time but the "little look" would lead to another road taken in my architectural career.

In Jamaica, it was our understanding that to be successful we had to come up with a building method other than the standard cement block or concrete systems that dominated the market at the time. I believe it was the architect Steven Winter, who had worked for us for a time, who suggested a system that had been developed in Texas a few years previously, based around the use of paper honeycomb. After some digging we tracked down Leonard Cowan, a Californian, then working as a house builder in Las Vegas. Leonard it appeared had rights to the system's patents as a result of a Byzantine lawsuit or two. We reached Leonard on the phone to discuss our interest in the system. Even with Boris's sales pitch Leonard refused to come to New York. So, as the saying goes, Boris and I went to the mountain, aka Las Vegas. Between one thing and another, I do not recall that we slept at all during the three-day visit, we came away convinced that Leonard's system was brilliant and was just what we needed. The system was light-weight, used only plywood or gypsum board on either side of a paper honeycomb core. Two story houses could be constructed, only one trained technician was required for the construction process, and mechanical integration was simple. It had been tested and met current ASTM[126] standards, and it was very inexpensive. We estimated that we could build finished houses in Jamaica for less than $7 a square foot. Even then this was very economic. There was only one problem – the system required the construction of an on-site 'factory' to laminate the materials together: and, of course, there was no such 'factory'. Leonard had estimates in hand of up to $250,000 for the factory's design and construction. While we knew (or thought) that the system was what we needed, we were not even close to having access to that kind of money. Leonard's optimistic, (he almost always was optimistic even in the face of overwhelming evidence to the contrary) parting shot to us as we left to return to New York was, "… of course I could build it myself for much less!".

That was Leonard. We discovered, over time, when working with Leonard, that just when you thought everything was going 'pear-shaped' he would find a solution. Leonard was a prototypical American who might have fallen out of a Norman Rockwell painting. He was the understated hero who could be portrayed fighting off German fighters with one hand while with the other holding a plane together with bailing wire, saying, "just doing my job". He was a veteran of the Korean War, flying on B29s as a non-commissioned technician. He had been shot down (at least once, some said it was twice) behind North Korean lines and, evading capture, had made his way back to fly again. He never really talked about the war or his Air Force career, or, as a matter of fact about anything personal. He was in pain for the latter part of his working life as a result of stopping a heavy building panel, caught in a gust of wind, from falling on an employee saving his employee's life. The accident had separated all the ligaments attaching his right arm to his shoulder. The damage couldn't be repaired but Leonard just adjusted how he did things and got on with his life. You would not have known he had a problem. Leonard and his wife Rhoda were an inseparable pair, he would never travel anywhere without her. Rhoda's prize possession, other than Leonard, was the immaculately restored pink Ford Mustang Leonard had given her, on their wedding day. Leonard was deadly honest, opinionated, stubborn and highly moral. Leonard would not put up with anyone, for very long, who did not meet his standards. I worked with Leonard, on and off, but mostly on, for nearly thirty-five years. His stubborn streak finally killed him as he refused to stop smoking even after his lung cancer was diagnosed. He was working (mostly with me) up until a few days before he died in 2001.

With regard to the factory, we took Leonard at his word. I do not recall where the money came from or how much it turned out to be. I think we all chipped in something, some more than others, but in any event before long, Leonard had moved East to Connecticut. We rented a small industrial unit near Stamford and Leonard was soon constructing what my City College colleague, Allan Talbot[127] dubbed, "the great house-building machine."

Fired up with dreams of future profits (and perhaps, a little glory) Boris, Peter and I agreed to set up a share-holding company that would more fairly reflect the varying interests of the individuals that had succumbed to this emerging, intriguing, entrepreneurial plot. The company would be called, (with appropriate immodesty), IDC, the International Development Consortium[128]. In addition to Boris, Peter and myself, the initial shareholders included Nick Philip, my fellow Darrow Trustee, representing the environmental and agricultural disciplines and Arthur Houlihan, a well-known Westchester real estate broker. Leonard had an appropriate 'special employee' status. IDC Industries, a subset of IDC owned the 'Great House Building Machine', reflecting differing ownership interests of the machine, itself. It was agreed, probably by default, that I would be the President of the various IDC companies. Without knowing it, though still practicing architecture traditionally, I had become an accidental entrepreneur.

About this time, while in the throes of all this heady activity I awoke one morning with a rather red, itchy and painful right eye. In a few days it was worse and I called on my friend the ophthalmologist, Fran L'Esperance of 77th Infantry Division days. Fran, whose specialty was pioneering work in laser eye treatments, decided the problem was not in his purview and passed me on to Dr. Arthur DeVoe, head of ophthalmology at Columbia Presbyterian. His diagnosis was herpetic keratitis. So began a year of treatment including three lengthy hospitalizations. The associated pain was often quite remarkable. There were times when the prescribed analgesic drugs left me 'floating' in space. In between hospitalizations I did as much work as possible but 1970 was part-time year for me. At the end of treatment, some two years later, most of the vision of the right eye had been lost. In the long run, however, the body adjusts and the sight loss became less distracting. I did have to give up flying, probably no great loss.

Despite the medical problems work preceded on the Jamaica project and by some miracle we raised enough money, again, to build a model house. We shipped panels rather than the machine, doubting that we would get the machine back once it was in Jamaica. The panels were made partly from bagasse board a local Jamaican product made from sugar cane residue. Leonard built the house in three days using local, unskilled, labour enticed off the street by our offer of unlimited 'red stripe' and a few day's pay. All in all, I believe it was a good, early example of environmentally friendly, sustainable, low cost housing. More than 100,000 Jamaicans visited the house over the three-day exhibit and ours was clearly the most popular of the dozen or so examples.

Did we get a contract? No. But the housing minister said "no" very slowly keeping us looking and working in Jamaica in hope and expectation, not reality. We also interviewed and proposed projects in Venezuela and Honduras where we had, now forgotten, contacts. The Jamaican government, as well as those of Venezuela and Honduras, after stringing us along for a time, decided that they wanted houses built of concrete, after all. Lessons learned (and relearned); government-housing officials are traditionalists and don't want to take chances.

Leonard was a little put out after the year's effort in the Caribbean. We lent him the machine and he went off to Texas for a couple of years to construct, privately, several hundred houses with the "great house building machine", it did work. Alex, a believer in Leonard and the system stayed in touch with Leonard for some ten years and I would stay in touch with Alex.

We visited the Kingston exhibition site some fifteen years later. Our house was the only one still standing, looking pretty much as it did fifteen years earlier. An old man and his goat occupied the house; both seemed happy. We understood that the other houses had been demolished following damage from hurricanes.

Meanwhile Boris's "mystical" project, now simply called Filicudi, was maturing. We recruited support from Michele Michahelles[129] an Italian Architect who had recently married Rosalind Aldrich, Catriona's closest friend and Alden's Godmother. Michele, a talented architect and multi-linguist was very helpful in the planning and architectural work, dealing with Italian officialdom and with his contacts. We modified the IDC system to suit the Italian conditions and design criteria. Alex Grinnell got Kate's father, Brantz Mayor then a vice-president of Boeing enthused. Brantz was Boeing's marketing director and was for one reason or another in charge of Boeing's joint venture with the Sicilian builder of Aliscafi. Brantz also introduced us to Dr. Tony Benis, a retired director of the Banco Commerciale d'Italia and he, in turn, became a Filicudi enthusiast. Nick Philip took on the ecological and environmental aspects of the project. Margaret Shafer introduced us to Hart Perry the financial director and senior vice president of ITT then the owner of Sheraton Hotels. Catriona's brother and sister-in-law, Stephen and Elizabeth Shafer became investors in the project. My job was to try to pull these diverse personalities and interests together into a coherent whole. It was a jigsaw, for sure, but you could see a picture emerging.

Our first Italian visit started in Rome and included most of the IDC gang. Meetings were held with the Casa per il Mezzogiorno, (the development bank supporting projects in southern Italy), generally referred to only as the 'Casa', "Italia Nostra", the Club of Rome, the Belle Arte for environmental and cultural support and the Banca Commerciale. Even if these groups thought we were a little loopy they didn't let on and we received cautious enthusiasm from all of them for the idea of turning Filicudi into an ecological tourist destination. In our favor was the fact that having once had a population of 4000, Filicudi now officially, 'supported' only 185 persons. In fact, at the time we came to Rome, the island actually had a population of only nineteen, consisting of four natives and fifteen, exiled, Mafioso. The 181 other Flicudians had left in protest but not before they had, according to the national press, "rioted". One can only imagine that a "riot" on Filicudi, was something of an oxymoron. Apparently the Filicudians destroyed anything useful on the island: cigarettes, wine and food. The government sent in eight truckloads of troops to put down the 'uprising', but since there was no landing beach or roads, this action was of limited use. The fifteen Mafioso were ultimately removed and the island was returned to its somnolent routine of fishing, eating, pastoral pastimes and waiting for something to happen, or not.

Each of the groups with whom we met advised us on what we had to do to obtain approval – actually the phrase used was more interesting; we had to get a "nulla osta" from them. In practice, this meant we had to do whatever they wanted so that in the end they had a 'no objection' to our proposals: they saw no point in sticking their necks out to tell us what to do.

To obtain these "nullas" from the officials in Rome we had to map the island, prepare complete development plans, demonstrate the project's marketability, have an approved hotel operator in place, plan the infrastructure, obtain government grants, get an appropriate agreement for land expropriation,[130] and provide evidence of external capital financing; in other words 'no problems'. We also had to demonstrate that a transportation system could be established: enter Brantz Mayor and his local friend Rodriquez head of the Aliscafi company. Also fundamental to Rome's approval was the understanding that we had the support of the province of Messina, the commune of Lipari and any other "interested" parties in Sicily: again, no problem!

While meetings with all these parties, at least the Roman ones, were taking place, Catriona and I stayed with Marty in her little house and garden in Prima Porta, on the outskirts of Rome. Marty was still living, more or less, with Caesare, and their son David, or 'Davidino', depending upon his behaviour. There were also about fourteen Welsh Corgis wandering around. Marty both showed and sold the latter and, remarkably, Marty was able to make a modest living from this activity. The house was full of dusty silver cups and ribbons demonstrating both the number of shows attended and the quality of her Corgis. David was four at the time, already handsome and charming, fortunately rather Twachtman-like (as opposed to Caesare-like). David did behave a little peculiarly, in that he would often choose not to talk to me but to bark: slightly disturbing. Marty just ignored it, probably the correct approach. He did eventually become verbally articulate, at least in Italian. I guess if your playmates are dogs you need to communicate with them. Marty's house was attractively furnished, in a Twachtman manner, that is to say, arty, but a little run down. Most of the furniture was from mother's New York apartment. I recall when 'antiquing' (our made up verb) with mother, when she would spy something she liked, the fact that the object of desire had a crack or a chip or had been reconstructed didn't make any difference. If the object pleased mother, that was it, the resale value was not a consideration. Keeping with this tradition Marty had mixed collections of slightly chipped china, tables propped up where a leg was missing and lampshades turned so that you would miss the tear, burn or hole. Cleaning was notional. Marty's dogs, fortunately mostly friendly, had the run of the place. It was hard to move around the small house without tripping over one or another of them. Actually the place was more of a kennel with humans than the other way round. Getting sleep was a challenge; inevitably one dog would wake, bark, then the others would follow. Marty would throw open her shutters and shout, "shut-up". This would get the neighbours, canine and humanoid, going and they joined in the cacophony. After thirty minutes or so of this, peace would break out - until the next row in an hour or so. Eventually, some years later, Marty moved out to a more bucolic setting in the north in a little hamlet, near Agazzano, south of Piacenza. Prima Porta was quieter. I think Marty's neighbours may well have 'urged' her to move.

Marty sometimes cooked, she was a good cook, but for convenience and to reduce domestic pressure, we often ate out. It was quite cheap at the friendly local trattoria and there was less competition with the dogs, easier by far. After animated discussions with the owner-chef we ordered whatever food was recommended on that day. The food was well prepared and the wine flowed freely. We all enjoyed these leisurely though noisy dinners.

Notwithstanding that it was good to see Marty, staying with her was something of an experience of mixed blessings. A short stay was pleasant enough, a longer one a bit of a trial. As the applicable saying goes first prize was one night, second was two nights. I generally found a reason after a day or so to stay in Rome at a comfortable hotel: early morning meetings were a good excuse. Marty was probably just as happy not to have us though she protested. On occasion she came to our meetings to translate. A second factor in not staying with Marty was Marty's carry-on, usually fuelled with or by the local wine, in matters religious, old personal matters, Molly etc. Marty was still not fond of Molly (even though we were divorced) and still thought I should be a Catholic. Marty and I thus continued our love-hate relationship of childhood: in this my patience was limited.

Marty, unfortunately, had her own marital (and/or non-marital problems). When Caesare and Marty got together, in Milan, Caesare was married, although he was not living with his estranged wife. The laws of Italy did not, at that time, permit a divorce. However, sometime during the period while we were coming and going for the Filicudi project the laws changed. One day Caesare came home and announced, "Marta, I have good news, we can get married!" Marty replied, "I have bad news, I don't want to". Caesare, apparently, was a little put out. Shortly after this event, one Sunday afternoon, he absconded with David. Marty was not to see David again for nearly ten years despite her efforts through legal and diplomatic channels. Marty left David's room as it was on the day he disappeared: it was a little eerie, Dickensian and dusty.

A typical visit to Rome for meetings with banks, the Casa etc. would take up a week or ten days. While we all enjoyed Rome, we always looked forward, more, to visiting Filicudi. On the first trip, Boris couldn't wait to show us the Island, 'his' island. The 'us', as I recall, in addition to Catriona and myself, Boris and his girlfriend Jinkie ('partner' wasn't in play then), included Alex Grinnell, Rosalind and Michele, Tony Benis, and Nick Philip. Getting to Filicudi was a bit of a slog. First we had to fly from Rome to Reggio Calabria, there hire a car and take the ferry to Messina, where we would spend the night. Messina was also the base for our Sicilian professionals, the civil engineer Nello Ferlazzo and his architectural counterpart, Roberto Romano[131]. These gentlemen were, effectively, i.e. "we recommend these individuals to you", appointed by the Casa to look after the Casa's interests as well as playing an important role in the design and logistics of the project. Both were very supportive and helpful. Roberto could be a bit reticent and pessimistic but Nello was always enthusiastic and optimistic about the project and also seemed quite connected in maters Sicilian.

It was only a forty-minute drive from Messina to Milazzo, from where the Aliscafi left for the hour-long trip to Lipari. The drive could be exciting. There were two options: one over a 'mountain' pass and one around the coast, for various reasons they were evenly matched, if not in distance, in time. As we needed two cars (because of the number in our party), Boris would challenge me to see who could get from Messina to Milazzo first. We would flip for the routes, the rest is fairly obvious, Boris would win unless he got stuck behind a lorry. I don't think we would get away with that craziness today and I am not sure why we did then.

We stayed on Lipari for a day or so to deal with the mayor's office and to hire a fisherman and his boat for the almost two hour trip to Filicudi. The fisherman would stay with us all day and ferry us back in the evening, at the time there was nowhere to stay on the island. The boat was a rather robust open fishing boat and we hoped for good weather; we usually got it.

Filicudi was all Boris said it would be. Strikingly beautiful in all aspects, Filicudi appeared, on approach, as a large green whale sunning itself on the water. The eastern end was a high promontory the site of a protected pre-historic settlement. From this the land dropped down to a saddle, a fertile area for agriculture, the ground then rose to the west, it was here in the lower to middling heights that most of the abandoned houses were located. Further to the west the land rose to a high inaccessible mountain before it sharply dropped back into the sea. The main, active settlement, was on the south side. Apart from a few houses there was a pier and a very modest trattoria. It was here that we landed, ate lunch, and arranged for local guides and 'transportation'. The latter consisted of a handful of docile donkeys. The donkeys provided a pretty uncomfortable ride so for the most part, we climbed and walked and walked. Over our two-year's of periodic visits we got to know every nook and cranny of the island.

The trips to Filicudi and environs were enjoyable if not always fun. We worked hard but Catriona and I also took side trips to mainland Sicily visiting Palermo and the Greek temples at Segesta. We visited Naples where Michele had friends, supporters of the Filicudi project, who lived in Emma Hamilton's impressive house, Villa Emma, on the coast, and Torre Nova, Michele's father's 15th century house, on the Tuscan coast.

In 1971 Catriona was happily pregnant and on the 13th of June, 1972 in Columbia Presbyterian Hospital Catriona gave birth to Frederick Alden: Frederick for Fritz and Alden for Uncle Alden. The trips from then on became just Boris or possibly Nick Philip and myself and, apart from visiting Marty, there was no sightseeing. It was all business.

The work on the Filicudi project went on another year absorbing nearly half my working hours. We met with the great and good of Italy and, as well, the not so great and not so good. The work was sometimes ecstatic, sometimes depressing, largely depending upon the reaction of the various bodies having a say on our proposals. By 1973 the "nullas" were positive, that is to say, in order. We were invited to Rome to sign agreements that would put the Filicudi project in play. To that end Boris and I left New York for Rome via London on Monday the 15th of October. The plan was to lay over in London and proceed to Rome during the week and take it from there. We were appropriately excited.

London was as far as we got. On Saturday, the sixth, Egypt attacked Israel and on the 16th-17th OPEC established an oil embargo. Nello called and told us to hold up until he could find out what was happening in Rome. On Thursday the 18th he called to tell us that the Government was putting everything on hold. In very short course oil prices went up as much as 70%, Italy stopped moving and went dark. Not surprisingly in quite short order the Italian government aborted any energy consuming projects, Filicudi among them.

There were significant unrecoverable losses all around. We tried to revive the project during the next year or so, but momentum (and funding) was moribund. Filicudi, for us, was finished and Boris, Michele, Nello and others faded, albeit slowly, into an Aeolian sunset.

The worldwide energy crisis also contributed to a worldwide recession. Architectural projects went 'on hold' or were abandoned. Apart from anything else, and there were a lot of 'anythings', the recession was the coup de grace for Baker & Blake. Our major domestic projects, Alfred and Binghampton, were complete or nearing completion and there was precious little in the pipeline. There were few good reasons to continue a partnership where partners had differing objectives and in which the partnership had had become acrimonious. Perhaps, too, it was time for the mentee to break loose from the mentor. For me, a split from Peter would be a relief from the almost daily frustrations of his angry "urgent" memos and letters. Howard Schneider was called on to manage another 'divorce', like the previous one it was difficult. The terms of the dissolution gave me most of the on going Baker & Blake projects, such as they were. Alex and I set up a successor office, Baker-Grinnell to handle the work. Alex and I divided the project responsibilities. Boris disappeared: I am not sure what happened to him. We earned some income but it was not sufficient to recover the losses incurred from Filicudi. We were in an end game. I needed substantive work to (let's say), survive.

Philip Johnson had heard about my situation and contacted me. He was looking to find a partner level practice manager. He interviewed me over a long and pleasant lunch at the Four Seasons restaurant, with the view that I might be it. While it was an exciting prospect it didn't feel right. Despite the failure of Filicudi and the Jamaican ventures the projects had exposed me to what was a broader, more exciting arena for an architectural career. With some misgivings I suggested to Philip that I was not the right person.

It was David Mitchell who came to the rescue. At some point, it may have been at David's 1972 or 1973 New Year's Day party, David had introduced me to Marietta Tree, Llewellyn Davies's partner in New York. Llewellyn Davies, known colloquially as 'Prof' was the principal partner of his London based planning and architectural firm with its New York office; Llewellyn Davies Associates (LDA)[132]. There were other offices too: Sidney, Bahrain, Beirut, Tehran and Toronto[133]. The firm could arguably have been considered the world's leading town-planning firm. We had a number of meetings leading up to a final one in September 1973. Llewellyn Davies, Marietta Tree and I met at their offices at 410 East 62nd Street. It was a good meeting and in due course I would be invited to London to meet others in the firm. Alex concurred that our nascent partnership was not a 'goer'. He agreed to finish up our odds and ends in the event I was to join LDA.

One of the last jobs Baker-Grinnell acquired as the recession was taking hold was a planning exercise for New York's Alleghany County. This was courtesy of Ted Randall and was a 'fall out' from the Alfred project. The Alleghany project wasn't really my thing but it was a reasonable carrot to offer LDA. We agreed to joint venture the project with LDA. It was on this basis and perhaps the fact that LDA thought I might be useful, that LDA[134] brought me on board, pro tempore, as an independent consulting architect. There would be further discussions, probably in London, to iron out all the details. In the meantime LDA would provide a relatively steady, (with reason, I was only paid for the actual time I spent on LDA work) paid employment but also it would allow me to continue to work on Darrow, the Lassell house in Greenwich, a job with Jim Polshek and to wind up other unfinished business. My architectural career was about to take another 'new' road.

A Pewter Spoon

Prime Minister Manley addressing visitors outside the IDC House in Kingston, Jamaica - 1970?

North shore of Filicudi - 1971 - (Photo taken during our survey of the Island)

Filicudi Discussions: with Boris and Rosiland Micahelles a lighter moment at Rokeby (?) Michele took the picture - 1970?

With Catriona at the Lassell House Greenwich - 1973

Glen House, Birchrunville, Pa. - 1971

Shafer House - Annandale-on-Hudson - 1970
A Record House of the Year 1972

Bard's Student 'Dorms' - 1972
Recipient of a HUD (US Housing and Urban
Development) award for Innovation in Housing

College of Ceramics (middle building) - Alfred
University
(Contemporary photo)

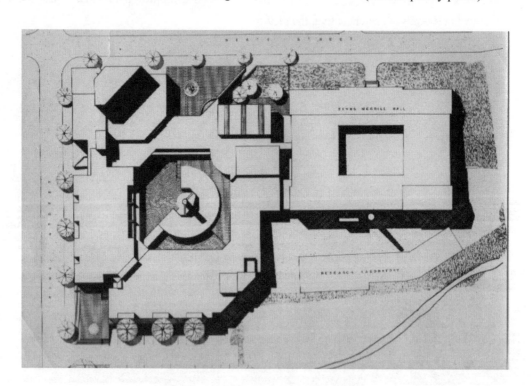

Site Plan - College of Ceramics - 1970
(Existing Binns-Merrill Hall on right)
Construction cost would be about $35,000,000 in 2018

12

LLEWELLYN DAVIES (LDA)

New York – London – Kingston - Havana – Beirut - Tehran – Manama

1973 - 1978

"Forward, forward let us range, ... forever down the ringing groves of
change."
Alfred, Lord Tennyson

"It is a truism that no row is ever about what it is about."
Simon Barnes

Llewellyn Davies Associates, (LDA) was not the only change. Alden was almost two, at least he was getting there. Henderson Place, though charming, was now somehow becoming smaller, not really, but not suitable for the three of us. Catriona and I agreed to move if we could find larger, affordable, accommodation. A solution was soon at hand.

Sometime during the Filicudi saga I was introduced (I cannot remember who did this) to one Otto Teitler, a small, intense man with a recent MBA from Harvard. He had an alleged Israeli military background (maybe), a short man's ego and a persuasive, and sometimes wheedling, tongue. His business career, post Harvard, seemed to have revolved around the Central African Republic, according to a medal and certificates he showed me. Somehow, Otto had heard of the Filicudi project and was, I presume, impressed (this was before the project 'tanked'). It must have been this, otherwise why would he have asked me to look at a tract of land he controlled on Sal, one of Portugal's (at the time) Cape Verde Islands? We agreed to a modest fee plus expenses to cover a preliminary evaluation. It turned out to be a pleasant, but bizarre, holiday for Catriona and myself. Alden went to stay with Margaret and we flew to Lisbon the only source of flights to Sal. We puttered around Lisbon for several days while we waited for the once a week midnight TAP 727 flight, via Bissau, to Sal. We arrived in Espargos, the capital city of Sal, in the darkness of early morning where we rented the only car available, an old, open-sided, 'deux-chevaux'. We drove for about a hour over an unpaved road through, what could only be called a desert, to Santa Maria the most southerly point on the island where we had arranged to stay in its small Pousada.

We arrived as a beautiful dawn was breaking, there is almost always a beautiful dawn since it is virtually always sunny on Sal. The little, six room Pousada had 100% occupancy, actually 120%, as it was the overnight, layover accommodation for South African Airways crews on their flights from Johannesburg to London and vice versa. This meant that some occupants, I am not sure how they were chosen, were rousted out so that the early morning newcomers, like us, could have a room. The sheets were changed but the beds were warm.

The Pousada was quite basic. Some of the rooms were no bigger than a closet, at one point we had one that I believe <u>was</u> a linen closet. There wasn't much to do. As Coleridge wrote, "The fair breeze blew, the white foam flew, …" that was it. We were lulled all day and night by the clack-clacking of wooden windmills pumping sparkling clear sea water into salt flats where salt crystals would form on strings. The air was so clear that you could walk for hours towards the single lighthouse on the horizon, but never reach it. Eating was the principal and only offered entertainment. On the first night we were told to expect a specialty, turtle's feet. We were duly appalled when we were served up this 'delicacy'. Great laughter ensued as the guests watched us trying not to retch. The joke was that the 'delicacy' was actually a mussel-like crustacean, the form of which mimicked what we thought was turtle's feet. It was the only joke on offer.

We took the 'deux-chevaux' to explore the designated site, visit various other salt flats, (they are all about the same) and a small mountain near Pedra Lume on the east coast. Though the weather was literally perfect, all of the time, we concluded that Sal was definitely a pre-tourist destination. We were at least a generation too early. We stayed the 'required' week waiting for the once a week 727. We were definitely ready to return, we had 'done' Sal.

We got to the airport about one thirty am, in plenty of time for the four am flight, turned in the car and went to check in. To our amazement the departure lounge was chaotic. A disorderly throng of pushing, shoving and shouting would-be passengers struggled to get to the single counter. We never made it: not even close. The Lisbon plane arrived and left, without us. We re-rented the 'deux-chevaux', returned to the Pousada, and were lucky to get the, still warm, beds of a linen closet. At breakfast the Pousada's inmates, after looking at our long faces, said that if we were very lucky we might be able to get passage on the supply steamer later that month: "ha ha", this was their second joke!

As it turned out, three days later we were able to get on an extra flight to Lisbon and to New York from there. I thought of Uncle Jackie and Mim and what their Lisbon experiences may have been in 1940.

I told Otto that he should wait a few years, maybe forty, before pursuing any tourist investment on Sal. Otto thanked me and said, no worries as he had another idea: he was full of ideas. He had bought an old-law tenement at 538 East 89th street, sort of a door up from Gracie Mansion. The building was in total need of refurbishment. This was his 'idea': if I would do the planning and architectural work and agree to manage the building I could renovate, at my own expanse, a duplex apartment in the back of the building. It sounded vaguely reasonable and after some discussion with a doubting Catriona I accepted Otto's proposal. Catriona was less enthusiastic, correctly suspecting that Teitler was a little tricky. We had a little 'to do' about it. In fact, Catriona and I were having a number of disagreements and 'to-dos' on a number of now forgotten subjects. One took place in a First Avenue restaurant, in the fifties that catered to a particular New York social sector. After a fairly raucous exchange between Catriona and me, one of a pair at the next table remarked, "see, I told you, mixed marriages don't work!"

To do the construction at 89th street, Otto hired a builder, Frank Osso whose only real claim to anything was that he was indeed a west-side builder. He had completed a number of beguilingly cheap (but otherwise appalling) renovations. The part that appealed to Teitler was 'cheap'. Osso was from Calabria and was a fair representative of Calabria's reputation for hard-headedness. (His name was probably a clue that I missed along the way). I drew up detailed plans and specifications for the building. Otto and the building department respectively approved them and construction began. It was a 'disaster' from the start. Frank paid no attention to my drawings and specifications nor did he follow any of my quite straight-forward instructions. Frank didn't even keep my carefully drawn plans on the job. One day, not long into the job Osso summed up the situation: "Professoooorree, you makka all da plans you want, I'm a'gonna build it my way!" I did, he did and Otto didn't care.

The construction of my duplex in the rear of the building was done in part by me, part by two City College students (mostly Joe DiMonda), and in part by contractors I knew and trusted, anyone but Osso. The result was an unusual two-bedroom flat with a dug out 'garden', actually a steeply terraced garden, something one might have found on Filicudi. The work was never really completed nor the flat furnished. Otto decided one day that the deal should be, since the flat was so nice, that I pay some rent in addition to my 'sweat' equity. Though I cannot remember the amount he wanted to charge it seemed to me a lot and was not the 'deal' we made.

At the same time that trouble with Otto was brewing Catriona and I were having more 'hoorahs'. To varying degrees these were fuelled by my travelling absences generated by the new work at LDA, the Teitler problem, the financial shortfall from the failed Filicudi project and the recession. It was a very emotional and unhappy time for both of us. Alcohol consumption, either a contributor or evidence of our problems, didn't help. In retrospect, while I can 'reasonably' explain why Molly and I split up, I cannot 'reasonably' explain what actually caused Catriona and my relationship to deteriorate. Perhaps it was more me, my ego and my drive to 'succeed'. I think we kept Alden out of most of it, but I'm not so sure.

There were two outcomes: one: Catriona and I separated with Catriona moving to a flat, just around the corner at 87th and York (this allowed me to see Alden easily, if not frequently). Two: Otto and I agreed to let the New York courts sort out our differences; we could not do it ourselves.

The dispute with Otto took almost two years to resolve, (the New York Civil Courts can move very slowly when you are not in a hurry (Otto wasn't) and even if you are! However, there was really no resolution. The judge essentially took Mercutio's position, "A plague on both your houses." If either of us claimed a pyrrhic victory it would be an exaggeration of the result. I got my expenses, had a row with my lawyer (I didn't think he represented me very well) got seriously angry and Otto got the flat back: eventually. Some years later Otto was walking down 63rd street while I was walking up the street, we were on a collision course. When Otto saw me he scooted across the street. I think he thought I might attack him, in fact I was considering it. Otto was not a 'nice guy' but on my part I allowed myself to be conned, not for the first or last time.[135]

The only good news at the time was that the work with Llewellyn Davies was beginning well. I met with Llewellyn-Davies again in London and, at Marietta's insistence, had a further 'interview' (I am not sure that that is quite the right word) with her and her husband Ronald Tree[136]. The interview was at the Ritz, in a cheerful and luxuriously furnished suite overlooking Green Park. The lunch was elegant, long and alcoholic. If it was a test to see if I could hold my liquor I passed, but not out, though it was a close call. If the meeting had been a test of anything else I also passed. The arrangements with Llewellyn Davies were very good financially and I had the effective rank of a director but without the duties and responsibilities going with the position (perhaps they didn't want me at their table?). I would have primary responsibility for designated international projects. This meant that though I would be considered a New York employee I would, most likely be called on to work away from New York. This was fine by me and it turned out to be the case, soon enough. It was agreed, or confirmed, that I could finish any non LDA work commitments in hand and continue to perform work for a few selected clients; for example, Darrow. This assumed that any other work would not interfere with Llewellyn-Davies' work.

My continued interest in AIA matters resulted in my being selected as a National Director of the American Institute of Architects.[137] This would turn out to be a time-consuming task[138]. To make time commitments even more difficult I succeeded to the Chair of Darrow's Board when Bill Hudnut, my roommate from Princeton, decided to step down when he was elected to Congress[139]. Fortunately, Llewellyn Davies was supportive of both these extracurricular activities or at least they made out as if they were.

The remuneration at LDA, based on time spent on their jobs, was good, better than what I had been able to earn through Baker & Blake. My immediate 'bosses', but in most ways equals, were Brad Perkins, the managing partner of the New York office and Paul Buckhurst, the head of planning; both became good friends. Brad also became my teaching partner (along with his friend Fritz Reikoph) at City College and took my lectures and seminars whenever I was away. Bernie Spring, formerly Chairman of the Princeton Architectural School, was now the dean at City. He was very supportive of the management course I had developed and as long as it was well covered (it was) he didn't complain about my periodic absences on overseas work. Bernie even created a special title, 'Visiting Professor of Architecture' and he was also instrumental in supporting the recommendation made by others that I be elected to the College of Fellows of the American Institute of Architects.[140] I duly received this honor at the 1976 Convention in Philadelphia. The citation read, in part, that I had "materially contributed to making the City College School of Architecture a centre of educational excellence".

The first real project offered to me by LDA was a planning project in Jamaica. It came through the London office. Given my Jamaican experience this seemed appropriate. Peter Kerr-Jarrett, the owner of Barnett Estates, an historic and major landowner in Montego Bay, needed help in reorganizing his land holdings. The assignment was to provide a land use plan for some 6000 acres of sugarcane, hamlets and housing. In short course I opened a Llewellyn Davies office in Kingston. Roy Case[141] an architect friend from IDC days agreed to look after the office on a day-to-day basis. The work carried on, at a Jamaican pace, for almost three years. The Kerr-Jarretts became good friends and I often stayed at one of their several guesthouses. Jamaican politics, growing bananas, sugar cane and sorghum became very familiar subjects.

On my visits to Jamaica, Carol Tinsley, aka 'Fuzzy', sometimes accompanied me. 'Fuzzy's' nickname derived from her henna-dyed, curly hair. 'Fuzzy' was a friend of Boris's, I had met her sometime during the Jamaican IDC venture. After separating from Catriona, I looked her up. We were mutually attracted. 'Fuzzy' was catholic in her physical preferences and lived her own life, we never moved in together. Notwithstanding a somewhat distant, sometimes awkward relationship, when 'Fuzzy' thought that I had 'looked' at another woman, say in a supermarket, she would go into a 'fit' and storm off – sometimes for days at a time. Although 'Fuzzy' was not 'beautiful', in a classic sense, she possessed striking looks, was very bright, and dressed and walked in a way that attracted men's attention - from at least a 100 meters. She achieved particular attention when she wore one of her diaphanous blouses. On more than one occasion I found myself having to stand up to some man's unwanted attentions. She was a passionate, eccentric woman and it was, perhaps consequently, a tumultuous, roller-coaster relationship. The ride lasted for about a year.

While Jamaica was underway Llewellyn-Davies acquired, through American Express Middle East the assignment to analyze the campus of the American University of Beirut (AUB), perhaps Beirut's largest landowner, with a view to releasing land for development. AUB's land was on well landscaped, steeply rising ground, facing north and so overlooking the Mediterranean Sea. It was a stunning environment in which to place a carefully planned development.

Llewellyn Davies, at the time, had an office in Beirut, in the up-market Hamra district, to support, planning and architectural work for the principal Beirut hospital[142]. Paul Steele, an affable and amusing, hospital architect, and a Londoner ran the office. Paul lived to the east of Beirut, in a pleasant house with a grand balcony overlooking the city. At the time of this assignment, Beirut was a chic (in a romantic mid-east way), thriving, cosmopolitan city.

My job was to prepare the physical plan for the university, program its needs and identify sites that could be sold off, suggesting both appropriate uses for them as well as architectural massing. Brad and American Express worked the numbers. There were numerous meetings with AUB's president, Samuel Kirkwood, the administrative staff and faculty, marketing people, bankers, city planners, utility providers, and potential users of the site - in fact, with anyone who had an interest in the site, then or in the future: there were many interested participants.

It was a stimulating assignment and required me to visit Beirut a number of times. We (i.e. on occasion including 'Fuzzy') stayed at the Mayflower Hotel as it was more central, less expensive and more interesting (the Mayflower was the hangout for most foreign newsmen) than the grander St George down in the harbour. We, got to know the city and its environs quite well and found time, on weekends to visit Tyre, Petra in the Bekaa Valley and Damascus. The food and wine were good; it was a fine time all round – while it lasted.

By early 1975 Lebanon, however, was heading for civil war. At night, from Paul Steele's balcony you could hear gunfire and watch tracers arc over the Beirut sky. By morning the city was relatively calm and the inhabitants went about their daily business. Meetings often took place in bullet-marked, sandbagged buildings with Kalashnikov-armed militia on guard. On one occasion we had to clear a meeting room of spent shell casings and broken window glass but this didn't seem to affect anyone's input - planning work went on as if nothing was happening. Our work only stopped when BA refused to fly into Beirut and when the head of the Engineering department, one of our client's chief representatives, was murdered.[143]

While the AUB project was underway I was asked to go to Tehran to discuss a housing project in Ahwaz for the NIOC[144]. After a briefing we flew down to Ahwaz, in Iran's Southwest. The town, now a major city, was then a bustling, growing, 'frontier' town built around the oil industry. At night the main entertainment for both the locals and visitors was to go to the oil fields and dance in a wide circle illuminated only by the light of the burning gases of the oil wells. The shadows cast and the noise from the flames gave a remarkably eerie quality to the event. On the work side I gathered information and set about designing a prefabricated building system for the NIOC workers' housing. Other members of LDA did the town planning. It was a brief but interesting project but, given the political events that followed, I am, again, not sure whether any of our work was ever implemented.

After Ahwaz I was offered a project with the Llewellyn Davies office in Manama, the capital of Bahrain. (By this time Fuzzy and I had gone our separate ways – I think we both knew from the beginning it wasn't going to be a long-term relationship; too stressful.) The Bahrain office consisted of about ten architects preparing housing policy studies and performing various other planning and architectural tasks for the Sheikdom. A subset of this work was to be my special project, the development of a system for self-build houses. After, IDC and Ahwaz this project was right 'down my street'.

His Highness the Sheik, (we actually called him his 'shortness' because of his stature, or lack of it), wished to provide housing for 'deserving' (i.e. selected by him) Bahrainis and had sought Llewellyn-Davies's technical help. The idea was to provide these 'deserving' individuals with a small plot of land and a 'building kit' with which they could build their own house.

This was a different kind of assignment. The AUB and Ahwaz projects involved lots of people. My work on them was part managerial, part political and part 'hands-on' design. The Bahrain work was one-off and all 'hands on'. Except for help in preparing presentation documents it was a singular operation. The better part of six months in 1975 and the first half of 1976 was spent in Bahrain preparing the specialized report, (actually a book), entitled, somewhat facetiously, "1001 Designs". I got to know Bahrain well, studying, in detail, their housing stock from 'barristis'[145] to their ugly new palaces. In the end the Sheikdom was provided with a design kit of six basic house types, each of which had its unique variations and all of which used common, easily accessible components. The result provided, through permutations and combinations quite close to the 1001 options advertised in the title.

The project was well received by Dr. Kanoo the Bahrain project director and Sheik Kahlid, the ruler's brother and housing minister. Implementation was not part of the assignment and I left Bahrain after a formal presentation. I was told, sometime later, by an independent source that the housing ministry used the work, at least to some extent. The project was selected by the USIS[146] as an example of work by US architects working 'overseas' and was exhibited for several years at venues in the US and abroad.

Outside of work, there was precious little to do in Bahrain. Camel races on Fridays, visits to the souk and the occasional visit to the 'Sheik's Beach'. The latter was only available to his immediate family, friends and designated foreigners, which we were. The office staff all extolled the virtues of this beach and arranged for my visit at the earliest opportunity. Oddly, when we arrived, my companions, Kelvin Jones and Chris Colbourne demurred from going in the water. I, however, jumped off the end of the pier into about 12 inches of luke-warm Gulf water. I proceeded to wade out to deeper water – after about 300 meters the depth increased only to about 30 inches, I could see Chris and Kelvin on the dock laughing heartily. At this point something went whizzing by me, then another and another, I was in a school of flying fish! To avoid the razor sharp wings I had to crawl back to shore. General boredom can create curious jokes. Kelvin and Chris, however, become good friends and we passed our time, apart from working twelve or more hours, seven days a week, inventing practical jokes to bait the rather pedantic, martinet of an office manager. In the end we decided we felt sorry for him and declared a truce.

Further LDA work, lasting more than a year, included a prototype blood fractionation facility for the American Red Cross. This was a very complex project. I travelled, with Dr. Harlan Anderson of the Red Cross, to fractionation plants in Scotland, Sweden, Holland, Germany and France in order to understand the process. (We were banned from visiting similar plants in the US out of commercial spite. I was told that Harlan's name and picture hung in the security offices of the US plants, as did mine.) It was educational, technically, and as an additional fillip, we were well entertained. LDA put together a multifaceted report of which my prototype designs were a substantial part. Dr. Anderson, a financial representative, John Smith, from Booz Allen and myself made a presentation of our report to the full board of the Red Cross in Washington. In the end, a few years later, the Red Cross decided not to go into competition with existing commercial ventures. Lengthy, expensive thoughtful, but unimplemented reports were as often as not the end product of LDA work.

One of the more complex and high profile projects awarded LDA around this time was the preparation of the plans for Shahestan Pahlavi, a major new town (city) on the edge of Tehran. This was the Shah's pet project. It was a huge project requiring a major staff input. While I was available and could have been involved, I was given, instead, the job of managing LDA's input into a major hotel in Isfahan for Pan American's Intercontinental hotel chain. The hotel's design was a joint venture between, Kamran Diba, the Shah's architect brother in law, LDA and Davis Brody[147], the excellent New York architectural firm that had become partners with LDA in New York.

I knew Lew Davis, Sam Brody and their partner Alan Schwartzman from Baker & Blake days. Sam and Lew started their partnership in the 1950s and rose to architectural fame through ground-breaking housing projects in New York City. Lew was quite acerbic, Sam laid back, and Alan totally professional and detail-minded, he looked after the business side of the practice. Davis Brody was one of a handful of really good New York architectural firms of their time. It is still going strong today as Davis Brody Bond. Sam, Lew and Alan were always friendly and I enjoyed their company though I never knew what they really thought of my unconventional architectural career. But as far as managing the Isfahan job they were quite happy to leave me to it. Soon after LDA and Davis Brody joined together we moved from LDA's 62nd street office to a joint office at 130 east 59th street, an even more convenient location for me.

The Isfahan job lasted through most of 1978, until the instability and ultimate fall of the Shah's reign called a halt to its construction. While it was active the project required numerous visits to Tehran and Isfahan for presentations to the local owners, discussions with Kamran Diba, Tishman the construction manager and other specialist contractors. In Tehran I would stay at the Intercontinental Hotel for a few days meeting with Kamran Diba, or mostly Costas Kondylis from his office then take the one-hour flight, usually on a Monday, to Isfahan and return to Tehran on Friday. Isfahan is an interesting city with impressive mosques and other intriguing architecture. It was, and I guess still is a place to visit. I would stay at the luxurious Shah Abbas Hotel, a former caravansary. Apart from the meetings I would take time to take in the sights in and around the city and environs: there were many. The return flight on Friday could be dodgy. Iran Air often oversold our preferred late afternoon flights. On one occasion a visiting colleague, Bud Frankel, from Tishman and I were 'bumped'. We couldn't get any hotel rooms (Isfahan was a popular tourist destination) so that we could stay over to Saturday. We were left with only one option; to hire a taxi and drive the four hundred and fifty kilometres to Tehran. We got one of our Farsi-speaking colleagues to negotiate what was, we thought, an exorbitant price and we got underway, around four. The driver spoke no English and we no Farsi.

The road between Isfahan and Tehran was mostly under construction. Today the trip would probably take four or so hours, in 1977/8 it was more like six hours. For a time we bumped along in the driver's black, clapped-out Mercedes 180D on the unimproved side of the four-lane highway-to-be. After a while, however, the driver tired of this and decided to use the paved side occupied by oncoming traffic. We remonstrated with him as best we could, but he ignored us. We hunkered down and braced ourselves awaiting an inevitable crash. On making it to the first rest and refuelling stop at Kashan we found someone to translate our objections to our driver's homicidal style. The driver listened to the interpreter; there was a thoughtful pause before the driver replied with a shrug and a brief statement. "What did he say?", we asked. The translator replied, laughing, "We all have to go sometime!"

On the way we witnessed the awful aftermath of three recent head-on collisions, but it wasn't our time and we made it to cosmopolitan Tehran by ten, still in time for a well-earned, we thought, dinner of caviar, steak and vodka: lots of it.

With all this overseas work my miles piled up mostly with BA and Pan Am but also, in no particular order, Eastern, TWA, Air West, Air Jamaica, Iran Air, Air Canada, Delta, Frontier, Nordair, Canadian Pacific, Piedmont, BEA, SAS, Alitalia, National, Northwest, Alleghany, Cubana, Gulf Air, American, United, Aero Mexico, Mexicana, Iberia, TAP, and Ward Air; those are only the ones I can remember, there were probably more.

Flying in the late seventies was quite comfortable and occasionally elegant. Though I was most always booked in tourist or Y class, given that I was a 'frequent flyer' (to say the least) I was often upgraded and could use the first class lounges at most airports. A typical month in 1975 included a flight from New York to Jamaica, then to London, on to Beirut, Tehran, perhaps Ahwaz, Isfahan or Shiraz, later to Bahrain then back to New York via London. In between, when in New York, there flights to Washington for the AIA or to other US cities where the AIA Board would meet. During my time on the Board the latter included Philadelphia, Portland, Memphis, Denver, San Diego, San Antonio, Kansas City and Mexico City. I was away so much that for a period, after giving up 89th street I was without a home base and stayed in hotels, clubs, with friends or, on occasion, even sleeping on the comfortable sofa in LDA's conference room. I rarely saw the children.

I returned to New York in the fall of 1975, specifically to see Morgan, Jamie and Catriona and participate in Darrow and AIA Board meetings. Fortunately, these meetings were often back-to-back and never coincided. I also found the time to find a rent-stabilized, two-bedroom, apartment on the top floor of 105 East 63rd street, a block from mother's apartment. Mr. Lebwhol, an elegant old-world gentleman, owned the apartment building. He always dressed formerly, in a sort of mid European thirties style, usually in a light grey suit, highly polished black shoes with a long grey overcoat hung loosely over his shoulders, all of which was topped with a homburg. He was well spoken, polite and helpful and did his best to be a good landlord. When he died a few years later his widow Jennie took over. She was everything that her husband wasn't and the landlord-tenant relationship was, thereafter, tough going. In any event, the apartment would be my New York home for the next twenty-five years. It wasn't a well-finished apartment, the roof leaked, windows collapsed, cockroaches abounded and the several successive supers never spoke English, but the apartment was quite large, had great light, views, for its location, and, the location was terrific.

Retuning to New York from the AIA Board Meeting in Washington on the Eastern shuttle I 'managed' to sit next to a strikingly good-looking, dark haired young woman wearing (among other clothing) a South American native cloak and oversized dark glasses, the fashion signature of the time. By the time we reached New York Noni (Fiona Nichols) from Solihull (a Birmingham suburb) and I were friends. Noni, a budding professional photographer, artist and writer, was on her way back home from a long visit to parts of South and Central America where she had been studying and photographing indigenous Indian tribes. When, in January 1976, when I returned to Bahrain, Noni accompanied me. We were not to stay an 'item' long, in part for geographic reasons, but we had an interesting time for about a year. By September Noni was in her London flat and I my apartment at 63rd street. We still exchange Christmas cards.[148]

Early in 1976 my father's first wife, Marion Lindley died. I didn't know her and I am not sure how I found out she had died. However, in the complicated Dickensian legal arrangement of the twenties, she had become the 'measuring life' of a small trust left by my father for Marty and me.[149]

Having grown up sailing at Indian Harbour, having the model of father's next boat on which I had worked as a child on a shelf for thirty-four years and having an odd hankering for a possible long-distance sail, perhaps the Caribbean, or an

Atlantic crossing, I had often thought about owning a boat. My share of the remainder of the trust was just enough to accomplish this.

The boat I selected was a Westsail 28, a descendent of a Colin Archer design[150], cutter rigged, double-ended with a long deep keel, capable of being safely sailed single handed, even by a relative amateur. Though the Westsail 28 design was smaller it was, on principal, near to the hull model on my shelf. I would christen her 'Seven Bells', my recollection of the name father had chosen for his next boat. The hull was made in Long Beach, California. I visited the plant there twice, while also visiting Alden who was now living with his mother in Sierra Madre, on the outskirts of Los Angeles. When finished Seven Bells was then shipped by rail, to Wrightsville Beach, North Carolina where the final fit out and rigging was completed, and this is where she was launched and where she was moored for the next three years.

Seven Bells was a mixed experience. There was great enjoyment for a lot of the time. She served as a weekend and holiday retreat but there were also great frustrations. Enjoyment came in a number of ways. The obvious one was being heeled over in a good breeze on a hot (or even cold) day with spray flying, or alternatively, coasting quietly, at sunset, into a solitary sheltered bay off the Intercostal Waterway, dropping the anchor, and relaxing with a drink and fixing dinner as the sunset faded into night. Although I could, and did, sail her single-handed I enjoyed much more sharing the experience with one or another, child and/or partner. Enjoyment for me was also polishing, cleaning, painting and making Seven Bells look 'smart': it did. Frustration came from Seagull engines that didn't start and shipyards that did not keep appointments or meet schedules. Frustration came too from not being able to use the boat as much as I would have liked. Frustration notwithstanding, I had 'Seven Bells' for seven years, quite symmetrical.

LDA's 62nd street offices were fairly basic. The building was designed for light manufacturing and there were few traditional offices. Work-space divisions were, for the most part, created by 'Homosote' backed, grey steel book shelving. My office space was next to those of Brad and Paul. The shelving height was such that if you were sitting down, your office life was quite private. However, if you stood up you could see into your neighbours' office and it was all quite public. The system was workable and certainly, it permitted good and frequent communication.

One morning while I was deeply involved in the preparation of the Red Cross project, Brad's head appeared over our dividing partition. "Want a trip to Cuba?" he queried. Thus started a project that would become, in due course, another milestone and another road taken.

US businesses were not permitted to work in Cuba but Llewellyn-Davies was a multi-national organization and had Canadian branch office in Toronto. It was this branch that had been hired by the Canadian arm of Tower International a firm owned by Cyrus Eaton Jr., or 'Cy', as he was called familiarly. Cy was a son of the late industrialist of the same name, (ex 'Jr.'). Among other major investments Eaton senior had been the primary owner of the Chesapeake and Ohio Railroad. He was Canadian by birth and a serious believer in international trade; with every country. He traded with the Soviet Union and other Soviet Bloc countries at height of the cold war. He considered this the best way to keep the peace or, at least, to avoid all-out war. For this he was reviled by the 'right' in the US, particularly during the hysteria of the McCarthy era. Khrushchev said Eaton was his "favourite capitalist". He awarded him the Lenin Prize. Even before Eaton senior's death Cy was, himself, trading with the Eastern bloc countries; he had taken on his father's mantle and perhaps more. One of Eaton's specialties was the ability to finance the construction of hotels – a 'hard currency' earner for Soviet Bloc countries. By 1976 the political environment had softened enough so that Cuba, certainly a Caribbean version of the Soviet Bloc, could be considered a possible future market for 'western' tourism. Because of Eaton's experience and soviet connections, Castro had invited Eaton to Havana for discussions on improving Cuba's tourism facilities. The outcome of these discussions led to an invitation for Eaton to partner with the Cuban tourism section, Intur, in order to develop a singular resort that would cater to American and European tourists.

Because of the prohibition on US firms working in Cuba Eaton needed an architectural or engineering firm from outside the US. Canada was the logical choice, both because Canada had good relations with Cuba and because Eaton (through his father's interests) still had, a foothold there.

The resulting selection, by Eaton, of the Canadian branch of Llewellyn-Davies was a logical choice. In addition to the obvious fact of being a Canadian company it encompassed a European and US component. Notwithstanding the trading prohibitions, as there were no tourism or hotel specialists in the Canadian office, because of my Filicudi and Jamaican experience I became the logical (possibly only) candidate for the work. Technically and legally, I was a consultant and advisor to a Canadian firm and was not therefore working directly for Cuba: a subtle distinction.

To reinforce the Canadian face to the project it was agreed that I would travel to Cuba, on at least the first trip, with John Carson, the taciturn manager of the Toronto office and a Canadian and trained city planner. Our visas were obtained through Cuba's interest section in Washington. I found out later, through my Yale architectural colleague and friend, Warren Cox, that certain US "officials" had contacted him (and others), in order to find out why I wanted to go to Cuba. I think (but do not know) that the State Department's 'official' position was that while they would not 'approve' my travel to Cuba they would take no action if I did. It was sort of a US version of the Italian 'nulla osta'.

There were no commercial flights from the US to Cuba so one had to go via either Canada or Mexico, unless of course one wanted to go by Spain. The plan was to meet up with John in Toronto and take the once-a-week, three hour and a half, Air Canada, flight to Havana. We would meet up with Eaton there.

In the meantime I had to tidy up other projects I was working on and make arrangements for my City College classes to be handled while I was away. My management and design classes at City College, continued. Brad (and others) covered for me when I was absent, at least most of the time. Teaching, for the most part, was a pleasure and I was considered a good teacher by both students and faculty. The students, in their annual faculty evaluations, gave me high marks. Norval White, a full-time faculty member and a Princeton architectural graduate a few years before me, was responsible for preparing the School's catalogue. In this he referred to me as City College's "distinguished professor of management". I liked the sobriquet and tried to live up to it.

One of the side benefits of teaching while running a professional practice was the opportunity of hiring good students, a sort of first crack at the employment market. In heady days of full employment, when it was hard to get good staff, this could be a real advantage. As manager of Baker & Blake I hired a number of my students as did other faculty members, theirs. It was not unusual to meet ex-students on the streets of Manhattan and sometimes employment opportunities arose from these chance meetings.

It was not that surprising, therefore, that one afternoon in the fall of 1976, as I was returning from a meeting near Lincoln Centre, and before the Cuba trip, I 'bumped' into Valery Goldberg, an ex-student of my management class and a graduate of the City College School of Architecture. Valery was a friend of Joe DiMonda.[151] She and Joe had usually sat together in the back of my management class. They were, occasionally, a bit inattentive now and then sharing something between them that, to them, was amusing. This minor distraction had not bothered me, both were good students and both were very employable. We chatted for a few minutes. Valery, told me she was working for Bernie Rothzeid, another City College professor. She told me that she was starting to look for another opportunity as her work with Bernie was nearing completion. LDA at the time was looking for additional help in their graphics department to support 'my' Red Cross project and another of 'my' projects, Timber Ridge, a housing development, in Orange County. I offered to check with Brad or Paul if a position was open. I would let Valery know, one way or the other. I did as I said. Valery was interviewed by Paul and was soon working for LDA. Although Paul was Valery's 'boss', for practical purposes, she was assigned to my projects and we got to know each other a little better. One evening we were working late and when we finished, I suggested a drink. It was a pleasant early fall evening and we decided on the bar of the Tavern on the Green. It turned into a quite romantic evening. We became an 'item' not long after; we had 'fallen in love.' By mid 1977 Valery had moved into 63rd street and in February 1979 we were married. It was a small, but I think elegant, civil ceremony held in the apartment.

Valery's father, Aaron, a large, reserved man with rather fixed views, was a senior analytic chemist working for a medical department within the New York City Department of Health. Her mother, Catherine, was French, quite petite and some years younger than Aaron. She was from a professional family in Verdun. They had met there, while Aaron, a lieutenant in the U.S. Army, was stationed nearby. They were married not long after the end of World War II. Catherine was, perhaps, more open-minded than Aaron though she did keep a 'little black book' of slights and oversights, apparently, I have been told, a characteristic of many middle class Frenchwomen. Valery, born in 1954, was their only child. French was the language of the Goldberg household and Valery was fluent in the language. The Goldbergs lived on the corner of 93rd street and Lexington Avenue, about 100 meters from 178 East 93rd, we must surely have passed each other on the street years before. Despite some obvious concerns of the Goldbergs, Valery <u>was</u> twenty-one years younger than I, they accepted, if not approved, of our relationship. Religion was not a problem. While Aaron was Jewish he did not attend Synagogue. Catherine was Catholic but did not attend church. If the Goldbergs had any concerns over age or religion I was not aware of them.

* * * * *

The children were growing up. Morgan was accepted at Vassar, Jamie was in his last years at Brown and Nichols in Cambridge and Trina was nearing graduation from Buckingham. Alden visited during school holidays. In warm weather these holidays were mostly spent aboard Seven Bells, first in North Carolina and later in Connecticut. Catriona was very supportive and encouraged Alden's visits. There was none of the visiting problems that continued to haunt the on-going, ragged relationship with Molly. Alden and Valery got along very well: so did Morgan, Jamie and Trina.

While my new employment arrangements were economically beneficial funding child support and tuition fees was still difficult. 'Misunderstandings' with Molly, usually over money or visits meant that thousands of dollars were spent on lawyers. This didn't improve either emotional or financial matters. Apart from periodic late payments the relationship with Catriona was significantly less problematic. Despite improved remuneration, fiscal requirements constantly exceeded availability. I was usually playing 'catch up'.

* * * * *

In mid-October John and I were on the Toronto to Havana flight. We were greeted at the Havana airport by Gines Castroman, (no relation to Fidel) Intur's pleasant, not to say cheerful, polite, head of protocol. We were whisked through the formalities and driven to the famous (or infamous) Riviera Hotel, a time-warp relic of the murky high life of the Batista days of the fifties. We met up with Cy and Clara Reece his chief negotiator in its Lapidus-like lobby[152]. We spent the afternoon chatting in Cy's suite and 'prepared', as best we could, for our first meeting with the Cubans on Monday.

Cy was in his mid 50s, quite tall, around six feet plus, with greying hair. He appeared, characteristically, thoughtful, polite and, at first, quite formal. Later I would learn to appreciate his rather slightly cynical sense of humour. (Cy had been a B25 pilot in WWII. On his unit's first bombing mission over Holland his plane was attacked by German fighters, hit by flak and shot down. He was badly wounded but nevertheless was able to bail out near the Dutch coast. He, the only survivor, was picked up by Dutch fisherman and turned over to the Germans. The only comment he made about this part of his life was, "I spent the war a guest of the German Government."

Cy dressed fairly neatly, in dark Brooks Brothers suits in a sort of off-hand way, there was nothing 'showy' about him. He could have lost a few pounds and as a result his pants hooked up above his waist always looked like they belonged to a shorter man, not terribly becoming. Having said he was polite Cy could, on occasion, be quite short if he thought someone was being stupid or officious. This characteristic was not one of his strong points and often embarrassed his colleagues, including me.

Clara, of uncertain age, but, let us say, probably in her late 40s, was a short, robust figured, redheaded woman of mixed Romanian and Hungarian heritage. She was reserved, (but 'suspicious' might be a better word), at least at a first meeting. She could be quite sarcastic, about anyone, and rarely combined her sarcasm with any redeeming humor. Clara was a master of at least seven languages, Slavic, obviously, but also English, German, French and a little Spanish. This was one of her several strengths as a negotiator. Another was the ability to intimidate (or at the least make them mad) "the other side", as she referred to anyone who was not on Eaton's "team" (and even some who were). She was loyal (to a fault) to Eaton and regarded anyone who she thought might not be as, "an enemy". Her attitude of course did not mean she, herself, wouldn't argue with Cy.

In time I was to get to know Cy and Clara very well. Initially, however, they were Mrs. Reece and Mr. Eaton and our relationship was precise and professional.

We were to learn, rather quickly, that any schedule prepared for us by Intur was only an intention. Meeting times and venues changed frequently. We were often summoned to a meeting on a moment's notice. But on Monday there were no changes and we met with our Cuban counterparts to be briefed on the 'project' that was to be known simply as 'Cayo Sabinal'.

The four of us, 'Cy', Clara, John and I were outnumbered, more than four to one. There were architects, planners, engineers of every sort, marketing people, economists, environmentalists, hotel people of various disciplines, translators and others of unknown professional (or not) background. The project concept was to take the Cuban island, Sabinal, on the north coast, off Camaguey Provence and turn it into a 'destination resort', the hot-topic, tourism concept of the seventies. We learned, in English and Spanish about flora and fauna, geodetic characteristics, weather trends, employment resources, construction resources, transportation, professional resources and anything else anyone from the Cuban side could imagine we should know about. The meeting actually lasted the better part of two and a half days and included late night dinners and entertainment. John and I filled up notebooks of facts and figures.

Cayo Sabinal was Filicudi under a different name; 'been there, done that' or as Yogi Berra[153] would have said, "it's déjà vu all over again!" Although the project was large and complex, I was more than 'up for the challenge'. We did not stay long on that first trip and returned at the end of the week to Toronto and I from Toronto to New York.

The next Cuba meeting was in November. It was arranged so that we could explore the site and begin to determine building and infrastructure locations. Intur arranged for a flyover and a 'reconnaissance' of the island from the sea as well as several days of on-site investigations.

Our group was made up of the key Cuban professionals from the first meeting led by Roberto the principal architect, our translator Juan, and what seemed to be a few of the ill-defined 'hanger-ons'. Cy and Clara did not participate in the visit to Sabinal. They stayed in Havana and were involved in meetings regarding finance. We flew from Havana to Camaguey in a big, single engine Russian biplane, a WWII, Antonov AN2. The plane was quite 'boxy' a sort of flying lorry, a brute of a plane. There were not enough bucket seats for all of us, so some of the group stood on take-off and landing: it was pretty casual.

Before landing at Camaguey's grass-strip airport we made several long and low passes over Sabinal to get an initial look at the large, approximately twenty-five miles long by five miles wide, undeveloped island. The only structures were a fishing shack, a large lighthouse at the southerly end and a dusty road connecting the lighthouse and fishing shack to a causeway and small wooden bridge to the mainland. Another road, actually more of a track, led to the north end of the island where there were some small boats moored alongside wooden docks. There were large bays opening into the sea, inland lakes and varied vegetation. Sabinal appeared to provide a good working palette for a destination resort.

After landing back at Camaguey we had a Cuban, i.e. quite extensive picnic lunch in a hangar. After lunch our group was taken to the little docks we had seen at the north end of the island. We arrived not much before three. The weather, which had been partly cloudy all day, now looked like rain, but the temperature was warm for November and we were comfortable.

The plan was that we would go out through the north pass to view the twenty or so miles of beaches from the sea and re-enter the bay by the east pass overlooked by the large lighthouse we had seen from the air: maybe a two hour outing, at the most At the local fishing port, Nuevitas, we would be picked by the minibus, taken back to the airport and flown in the AN2 back to Havana, all in time for an eight or nine o'clock dinner; a good plan.

A Russian, twenty foot, (more or less), open aluminium hydrofoil launch was moored at the rustic landing. A young Cuban, the boat's pilot, was standing by. The boat was designed for about 8 people, our group numbered twelve. With a lot of enthusiastic discussion and gesticulation we managed to squeeze the twelve into the launch, (sort of six pounds of potatoes in a four-pound bag) and headed out through the pass. John and I were seated, quite comfortably in the stern with our translator, Juan, just in front of us.

Once clear of the shallow pass, the pilot opened the throttle to bring the boat up on its foils and attain its cruising speed of, we had been told, perhaps twenty knots. The engine responded with an enthusiastic roar, but there was no lift, the bow only dug into the water, we were overloaded. A slightly melodramatic discussion ensued. Juan translated it, in a shortened version he told us, "no problem it will just take a little longer, plenty of time to make dinner in Havana". As we motored into the Old Bahama Channel, the sea became a little rough. The pilot turned to starboard (southeast) and we moved along at a reasonable speed, just off the reef line, perhaps a quarter mile off shore. We scanned the shoreline, bracing ourselves against the corkscrew roll of the boat caused by a following sea.

Soon the sky became quite dark and we were hit by a squall, obscuring our vision and getting us pretty wet. The sea got up a bit during the squall so we slowed and the pilot turned into the wind and sea to keep the boat more stable. It got much darker. Some of the Cubans bailed as the waves occasionally broke over us. When the squall passed we could no longer see the shore and the dark clouds overhead dimmed what was left of the afternoon light. The pilot turned the boat back to what he believed was the correct bearing.

Our Cuban colleagues remained in high spirits and jabbered on. John and I, however, exchanged looks of some disquietude; we were losing faith in the competence of our young pilot. There was now periodic light rain, wind and somewhat rougher water. I enquired of Juan, (quite discreetly I thought), "does anyone know where we are?" Juan had a muffled conversation with Roberto. The answer was, "well, sort of", not very reassuring. We now learned that since this was to have been just a shoreline trip our boat, inexplicably, had no compass[154]. It became quite clear that the pilot, apparently, had become disoriented during the squall and only 'thought' he knew where we were or where we were heading. In good weather we could probably see a mile or so from our little boat. In our present conditions it was probably less, even if you were standing up. The pilot was depending, for direction, on the light from the setting sun, unfortunately, that was now only a memory; night was approaching fast descending us into a general blackout. There was no moon and with the heavy clouds not even a significant nautical twilight. We had only a flashlight for illumination but there was nothing to illuminate. Time passed it was now after seven, we should have been in Nuevitas. There was now growing concern for our fuel supply. Our normally ebullient Cubans were quiet. We slowed down even more to conserve fuel and maintained just enough headway to keep us steady in the not so smooth sea. Juan and Roberto allowed that they were a little concerned on another matter; we were in an area used by anti-Castro raiders from Florida to land in Cuba.

Another hour passed; conversation was now quite hushed. In addition we were getting hungry. Dinner in Havana seemed a long, long way off. "A light!" someone shouted, "it must be the lighthouse!"; much jabbering. The boat was turned towards the light with a little more headway. The light grew stronger but it didn't seem like a lighthouse to me, or John. In fact, in another thirty minutes we all saw that the light was the stern light of a Cuban fishing boat working, they told us, a few miles off the coast.

That was the bad news, but not all of it: the fishermen were understandably suspicious of us. We did look a motley bunch, wet, dressed in shore clothes, and in a small, open, not very seaworthy boat. The fishermen wouldn't let us on board just in case we were, not who we said we were. We could be escapees or decoys for raiders. The good news was that the fishermen let us tie on to their quite substantial boat. In addition they gave us some good, strong Cuban coffee, a few biscuits and radioed the Cuban coast guard. Most of us were relieved, in one or another way.

Sometime later we heard the throb of powerful engines. The dark grey and black hull of a Cuban coast guard patrol boat loomed out of the darkness, with its heavy calibre, deck-mounted, manned machine gun trained on us. The boat, a substantial wooden cabin cruiser, converted to patrol boat use, made two passes around us before its two-man crew moored alongside the fishing boat and boarded. Roberto and the pilot also went aboard. We could easily hear the big palaver that ensued including frequent gesticulations towards John and me. In due course Juan informed us that the coast guard had agreed to tow us (as we were now low on fuel as well as navigationally blind) into their station at Nuevitas or at least to the fishing shack on Sabinal. A win-win solution for them; they would have saved us or they would have captured us, either way they couldn't lose.

A towrope was made fast and we were towed, slowly, into the black night. An hour or so passed, the waves were getting a little shorter and sharper, and we slowed even more. Juan said we must be nearing the reef off Sabinal's coast and we had to be careful lest we damage the boat's foils. Apparently we had a choice, stay just outside the reef and let the reef serve as a guide to the southern pass (the lighthouse, we had been informed by the coastguard, was unlit due to the perceived seaward risk) or alternatively to find a spot to get inside the reef in order to reach the fisherman's station. There was a lot of looking in the water with the, now useful, flashlight. We soon saw the coral reef beneath us and we could just make out the foam from the breaking waves on the beach.

John and I had our heads over the side when all of a sudden there was a bang, a jolt and the sound of an engine racing. Our boat heaved over and we banged into the patrol boat. We sorted ourselves out and looked see the scene illuminated by the flashlight. The patrol boat's stern was tilted up, out of the water, with the boat's propeller still turning. The bow of our boat was jammed under its stern. There was consternation, shouting and flapping about. As our boat was pushed and pulled free, the stern of the patrol boat settled back in the water. It was plain to see that the patrol boat was filling with water. A projection in the reef had torn out the patrol boat's bow and she was sinking, fast. The boat's crew scrambled over its stern and swam to us and we pulled the coast guard crew on board. There was blood everywhere; the crew had been badly cut on the reef. The rescued were now the rescuers. Untied from the patrol boat we drifted towards shore the foils just clearing the reef. The 'win-win' solution was turning to 'lose-lose'.

We grounded about five meters off the beach and disembarked into the water. By luck, or it may have been the navigation skill of the patrol boat skipper, we had arrived close to the fisherman's station. It was now after midnight, the sky was clearing and a faint light revealed the superstructure and deck gun of the patrol boat, awash on the reef.

The shack, that night, housed two fishermen. One went off in an old pickup with the injured crew to get them to a hospital and get assistance for us. There was no radio or phone at the shack. We waited and waited. A faint pre-dawn light was appearing when a minibus arrived. We were driven to the airfield and flown back to Havana in the AN2 that was still waiting for us. Gines met us at Havana and seemed very pleased to see us in one piece. We split up, the Cuban group went their way and we back to the Riviera. We cleaned up and met Cy and Clara for breakfast.

We were told, later, that the injured coastguards were recovering but we were never told what happened to them or to the hapless young pilot of our boat.

That was all we were to see of Sabinal on that trip. In the balance of the time remaining in Havana we attended more meetings, mostly about marketing, visited more of the historic quarter of Havana, several schools and other points of interest. I returned via Mexico City and then to an AIA Board Meeting in San Antonio.

The Cubans we met impressed me; they were all courteous, friendly and often quite humorous. We were well entertained. Mojitos flowed freely and all descriptions of fulsome Cuban meals were consumed. While the Cubans we met professed pride in their country they didn't flog it. I heard few complaints about the US; but there was clearly a distinction between Americans and American political policy. The countryside was remarkably beautiful, colourful, still the Cuba of Winslow Homer's watercolours. The historic Spanish colonial architecture was faded and often run down but colourful and sometimes quite powerful. New Soviet style architecture, mostly housing, was grim and inappropriate; it could have been in Moscow. The occasional new buildings designed by Cuban architects, however, could be quite appropriate and in context. The 1950 American car fleet was ubiquitous and would be for some time to come. The fifties cars, the faded hotels and the older colonial architecture helped to create a feeling of being suspended in time.

The Cayo Sabinal project report eventually ran to some 300 pages of technical data, marketing plans and financial projections all supported by numerous architectural and engineering drawings. It would take nearly two years to complete and cost, in today's money, more than a $1,000,000. By the third trip to Cuba the Canadian component of the work was quietly dropped and I ran the project from LDA's offices in New York, there were no problems.

We made multiple trips to Cuba during the next two years. None were quite as dramatic as the second, except perhaps the one when the Cubans arranged to borrow ponies from the Camaguey 'caballeros' so we could more easily get around the island. Good idea but the spirited ponies didn't like the work, or us, and decided to go home with their riders, including most of our engineering staff. Sam Brody and I avoided the rush as our ponies were still tethered when the stampede for home started. There were several hospitalizations as a result of unhorsing, our engineers as well as the Cuban technicians, but no one was seriously hurt.

'Cy' was very pleased with my work. Over the two years we developed a very good working relationship. Towards the mid-point of the project 'Cy' asked me to visit him in Cleveland for the weekend. He picked me up at the airport and drove me to his very comfortable, large 'farm' just outside Cleveland. It wasn't actually a 'farm', it just looked like one, but without any animals, except the odd dog or two. With its white fences and New England detailing it was more of a Hollywood movie set of a 'farm' staring Jimmy Stewart. Cy's amiable, bright wife Mary came from the same Hollywood script.

Much of the visit was given over to quiet persuasion, (Cy could be quite relentlessly persuasive) as to why I should join him. I would be President of a subsidiary company, Park Tower and would have the primary responsibility of developing hotels for his group. Park Tower, at the time was a company registered in Bermuda with only one part-time employee, Michael Kiesser, the former Manager of the Southampton Princess. Eaton made the point, however, that I could develop the company into whatever I (and of course subject to Eaton's approval) wanted it to be. We agreed that I would not move to Cleveland and that, in the immediate future, I would continue to work from LDA's offices, an agreement Cy would make with Richard and Marietta. When the time was right we would open an office in New York. 'Cy' was often in New York on business and had wanted to have a New York office for some time. This was all fine by me. The remuneration would be better than LDA and, as further incentive, I would earn 10% of the profits accruing to Eaton on any projects that I managed: potentially, this could be a large sum.

It was an appealing challenge. I told Cy I was very interested but that I wouldn't change without the express approval of Llewellyn-Davies. I was, so to speak, their man in Isfahan as well as Havana. 'Cy' agreed. A few weeks later 'Cy' came to New York and met with Richard and Marietta. At the end of their private meeting, I was invited to join them. Richard, and Marietta gave me their professional 'blessing' saying that they thought it was a good opportunity; they thanked me for my work and wished me well. In a volte-face I became their client, or at least, their client's representative. As they say on British Rail, "all change".

On a visit to Marty - 1977ish
L-R: Marty Valery, David

Making an informal presentation in Bahrain - 1976

Ground transportation on Cayo Sabinal
Sam Brody (back to camera) and Roberto the
Cuban project architect (The frisky ponies were on
loan from local Cuban cattle ranchers)

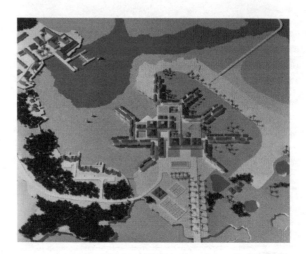

A portion of the presentation model for Cayo Sabinal
Design in collaboration with Davis Brody/LDA

The AN2 type of aircraft we used for aerial survey of Cayo Sabinal

Seven Bells - near Wrightsville Beach, North Carolina

City College - Design Studio - c 1977

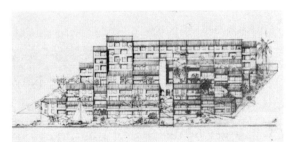

Proposal for tourist development in the Dominican Republic - 1977. One of a number of proposals made in that country - nothing came of them

13

EATON & PARK TOWER

New York, Cleveland, Havana, Eastern Europe, Manila and Shanghai[155]
1977 – 1983

*"It was an expensive and high-risk line of business, he had a taste for that
– always trying to hit a home run instead of a single. He got himself
overextended."*
John Eaton[156]

The metamorphosis from the consultant side of projects to the client's was gradual; it was indeed "all change", but slowly. I didn't move my office, I still ran the Isfahan Intercontinental Hotel project, and needed to tidy up loose ends several other LDA projects. Cayo Sabinal, however, took up most of my professional time. I was, for all practical purposes an independent consultant to both LDA and Eaton. This satisfied all four parties, LDA, Davis Brody, Eaton and me. The only change on the Cayo Sabinal project was that Eaton paid me for my work on that project. I continued to receive remuneration from LDA on their projects: it was financially quite satisfactory.

Maurice de Rohan,[157] the recently appointed Managing Director of LDA, (Brad had moved on to run the New York office of his father's firm, Perkins and Will) agreed the various details with me. Cy was quite laid back and concurred with whatever Maurice and I agreed to, he wasn't bothered. There were probably some conflicts of interest but these were beneficially ignored.

During the discussions with Cy I had expressed concern that part of his job description for me presumed an understanding of project financing: sources of funding, balance sheets, financial projections and business plans. The preparation of relatively sophisticated financial documentation was not within the more mundane financial experience of a small(ish) architectural practice [158] Eaton assured me, however, that the financial projections required were not complicated and, in any event, he would show me what I had to do. His commitment in this respect was one of the aspects of the proposal that gave me enough comfort to accept his job offer. I didn't want to move from a 'comfort zone' to a 'failure zone'.

The first 'financial training' meeting took place, in Cy's office in Cleveland soon after the completion our employment arrangements[159]. Cy and I sat down in his conference room. He had some papers with him but as he did not refer to them I presumed they were just props or something else. For my part I had a notebook and pencil at the ready.

He explained the essence of his business. Over more than two decades Cy had developed an intimate understanding of the socialist (communist) way of doing business. He claimed (and he was probably correct) that he was only one of a few people in the US that knew how to conduct profitable trading with the soviets or soviet bloc countries. His main competition, if he had any, was Armand Hammer who was doing the same thing, more or less, and, I understood had been a partner in some of Cy's father's ventures. Due to his father's success, Cy had a lot of clout with the Soviets and Soviet bloc countries. Part of this 'clout' depended, to a great extent, on the soviet's belief that Eaton was wealthy, very wealthy. Everyone knew Eaton senior was a billionaire, or at least a multimillionaire. It was common knowledge that Eaton, senior, had made and lost fortunes. Was Eaton Jr. wealthy, really wealthy? I never knew. Cy never threw money around and I never heard Cy say he would finance a project. He always told his potential project partners that he would or could 'arrange' the project financing. 'Arrange' was a useful word, it covered a range of possibilities and I suspect many might-be partners thought he was just being modest. He looked and acted as if he had money. I never heard Cy explain to a partner at home or abroad, what, exactly, Cy meant by 'arranging the financing". Cy did, however, provide the most difficult part of project financing, the significant up-front costs of getting projects 'together'.

The fundamental starting point for an Eaton project was the reality that the soviets and soviet bloc countries needed 'hard' currency, dollars mainly, but pounds, marks or francs were also acceptable. They could earn 'hard' currency by manufacturing goods and selling them to the west or earn dollars through tourism, hence the appeal of quality hotel construction. An obstacle, probably the main one, for the soviets and soviet bloc countries to earn 'hard currencies' was the reality that these countries made few products of acceptable quality nor did they have, Western standard hotels. (Anyone having travelled in Eastern Europe in the sixties and seventies could attest to that.) Eaton offered the soviets opportunities to joint venture the development of both factories and hotels.

For example, Eaton built a modern tire factory in Eastern Europe for Dunlop. Eaton 'arranged'[160] the financing for the hard currency component and provided the technical 'know-how', always a critical piece of the project puzzle. The soviets provided the land for the factory, the necessary infrastructure, labour and local materials to construct and operate the plant. In the end, Dunlop had a source of cheaper, but now quality tires. The country therefore gained a profitable market advantage. Eaton received his compensation from Dunlop in accordance with the terms of a negotiated agreement between them. Such an agreement could last, perhaps, ten or more years. This description is a bit simplistic but nevertheless is broadly correct. There were all sorts of complications to any project; just for example; who owned the land, or the physical plant, what were the political consequences, did a project fit the country's economic plan, would the financing guarantees be acceptable to lenders, how would the local labour be priced, would Dunlop agree to provide sufficient product uptake, etc.?

Hotel projects were developed in a similar way. Eaton would 'arrange' external hard currency financing, (mostly through export credits), sufficient to purchase the foreign construction components, (typically about 50% of the construction cost of a hotel), arrange for a hotel operator, (for example, Intercontinental, his Bucharest hotel of the early seventies or Hilton his Prague hotel of the same period) to run the hotel. Eaton would have the architectural plans prepared, and oversee the hotel's construction. For these 'services' Eaton could receive fees form the operator, product suppliers but, <u>primarily</u>, would receive an income stream from the 'hard currency' earnings of the hotel over an agreed period of time. The actual ownership of the hotel would be a tourism-based 'soviet style quango' of the host country. Along the way, the owner would provide the required land, infrastructure, labour and financing of local costs.

Eaton's business plan was based on a high risk and high reward strategy. There was always the high cost incurred in putting a 'deal' together (sometimes as in Cuba it was <u>very</u> high) and there were more opportunities for failure than success. But when a project worked it could be, financially, <u>very</u> rewarding, or as was often said in socialist countries, 'interesting'. (The soviet bloc and China hated to talk 'profit', much too capitalistic).

Cy explained that his business plan for Park Tower assumed, first, that we would continue work on Cayo Sabinal. A second element of the plan would be to 'package' new hotel projects in Eastern Europe that might be identified by Tower International. A third element would be to assist Cy in any other non-hotel projects, when and if appropriate. Up to now I had not been involved on the financial side of Cayo Sabinal, now I would be. Cy, during our meeting, made the financing seem quite simple, in practice it would turn out to be simply complex, maybe that's what he meant. As Aleksander Orlov would say, "simples".[161]

After an hour or so of discussions when Cy and I were getting down to the 'nitty gritty' of project financing, Paula, Cy's helpful and bright secretary, came into the conference room. She told Cy that a problem of some magnitude (unspecified to me) had arisen and that it needed his immediate attention. Cy left, I waited. In due course Cy came back and said he needed terminate our meeting (at least for the time being) in order to take care of Paula's 'problem.' I asked him, "When would we meet again? He answered that we probably wouldn't. He was sure I could figure out what I needed to know out as "we went along". He didn't expect that I would have any problems. He also mentioned, almost in passing, that

I would be accompanying Clara, in the next two weeks, to Eastern Europe: Prague, Zagreb, Dubrovnik and probably other places.

That was it, it would be, as they say in the Army, on-the-job training, the best kind of training there is. I returned to New York, went back to work on Isfahan, the Red Cross and Cayo Sabinal. I arranged for the necessary visas and tickets and prepared for the coming trip.

The first stop would be Prague. The plan was for me to fly to Vienna, pick up a rental car and drive to Prague to meet up with Clara at the Hotel Jalta. I made a reservation with Hertz for a modest car for pick up at Vienna's airport. However, on arriving from New York, early one morning, there was no 'modest' car. Hertz, instead, gave me (at the same price) the biggest, latest and blackest Mercedes they had. This would turn out be both good and bad news.

The drive to Prague was pretty easy except for the Czechoslovakian border. The border was reminiscent of East Germany. Lots of grim-faced, heavily armed guards, little communication and long waits while officials just stared, silently and inexpressively, at me or other travellers. I had very little sleep on the plane and the delay and consequent stress at the border had its effect. Clearing the border took more than an hour. As I pressed on to Prague I struggled to stay awake. Finally, on reaching Prague, my body gave in (or up) and as I slowed for a red light I fell asleep at the wheel only to wake up a split second later as I bumped (albeit very gently) into the car in front of me. Its driver and his companion jumped out, their contorted faces promising battle. Definitely awake now, I too got out. I was travelling in a dark suit, nicely polished black shoes, and, as it was quite cold, wore a heavy, black, great coat, all topped by a wide brimmed black fedora. I stood, as if a zombie, by the door of the great big, black, shiny Mercedes, (its Austrian license plate obscured because of the little 'bump'). The two grim Czechs approached but stopped short just before reaching me. They stared at me, and at the car, then gave each other ill-defined but knowing slightly fearful looks, turned and jumped back into their own car speeding off through the still red light. Thank you Mr. Hertz. I found the Hotel easily (it was on Wenceslas Square), met Clara and got some needed sleep.

Apart from seeing Prague and being well entertained, as usual, the trip was inauspicious. We were asked to make a proposal for a hotel and trade centre (in due course I did) but nothing came of it. I found our potential Czechoslovakian partners rather dull and hard going. We stayed for four or five days.

On the way back to Vienna I was pushing the 'Merc' pretty hard as we were running late for our flight to Zagreb. At one point we came over the top of a hill on the road to Vienna, at something around a hundred miles an hour to see an Austrian police roadblock, dead ahead. Two policemen were standing in the road waving little wands with red discs. The police dove for cover as I hit the brakes and came to a screeching, smoking, halt. The police recovered and ran to our car, shouting, angrily. I rolled down the window and turned to Clara, "say something to them", I pleaded. Clara slid down in her seat, becoming as invisible as possible. "I don't speak German!" she said, lying. I was stuck struggling with my Germano-English. In the end I coughed up a few hundred Austrian schillings. Clara stayed 'shtum'. She never said anything about the incident, at least not to me. We made our flight to Zagreb.

In Zagreb we met up with Nuno Boric, Eaton's man in Yugoslavia. Nuno, a rather solid, stolid Serb operated from the small Tower International office in the renovated Intercontinental Hotel, a successful Eaton project of some years before. (What he did from day to day when we were not there was a mystery to me.) Nuno gave us the update on the politics and possible hotel opportunities in Yugoslavia. He also gave me a pretty good tour of Zagreb. The best opportunity he told us seemed to be in Dubrovnik, others were in Bled, Bohinj, Belgrade and Sarajevo. We arranged to meet all the appropriate local hotel operators. Our first stop was Dubrovnik.

It was another one-hour flight to this very attractive medieval town on the Dalmatian coast. We were there to discuss the development of a large, 350ish room, new hotel and casino south of the town. (An odd coincidence to my visit to Dubrovnik was that only a few years later, cousin David Twachtman painted, and sent me, a little watercolour with an image of Father's boat, the 'Dog Star', sailing off Dubrovnik. On the reverse he wrote that Father told him that he had wanted to sail the Dalmatian coast. He also reminisced that father had paid for his (David's) sailing lessons at the Indian Harbour Yacht Club.)

The Dubrovnik project appeared to be a good opportunity and I duly prepared preliminary plans and spent time with Cy developing the financial projections. As Cy had claimed they were not all that difficult. We got the proposed hotel 'packaged' but were thwarted in the end; in part by archaeologists (the proposed site was an ancient monument), in part by an earthquake that materially altered a key part of the site, but mostly we were frustrated, in my opinion, by the Yugoslavians, their federal government as well as their quasi-governmental hotel organizations. Even then, (it is now part of Croatia) the Yugoslavians didn't get on amongst themselves. They were difficult, unrealistic and generally hard headed. It didn't help that most of those we met were without any appreciable sense of humor.

We looked at other potential projects in Yugoslavia and visited the recommended opportunities in Bled, Bohinj, Belgrade and Sarajevo. Though the visits were culturally, and historically interesting they did not produce any tangible results, just a lot of talk. We visited Yugoslavia a number of times over several years, mostly in pursuit of Dubrovnik: without success.

On subsequent trips, in addition to Yugoslavia, we visited Bucharest (for a possible new hotel), Sofia, and several sites in the south of Bulgaria, Moscow and Leningrad (St. Petersburg). Except for Leningrad, where Eaton made headway financing a hotel constructed by a Finnish contractor (I was only peripherally involved in that one) nothing came of our efforts. If I had thought the Yugoslavians difficult the Bulgarians were worse. Our meetings always consisted of at least a dozen or more Bulgarian architects, engineers, accountants, managers and party officials. They often ended up in shouting matches. Clara was more than adequate in holding up our side and, I think, rather enjoyed the battle, I didn't. I did, however, enjoy the Bulgarian landscape, especially the rugged south but not the then not so Grand Hotel in Sophia in which we stayed during our 'negotiations'.

The failure of Eaton to produce beneficial projects in Eastern Europe, despite his and Clara's efforts was in part the inability of Eastern bloc countries and their government sponsored tourism agencies, to 'get their act together'. One group would hold the land, another the money, a third the construction permits. Whatever decision might be tentatively made at a meeting would have to be ratified by some anonymous political committee with whom we had no contact. There sometimes appeared to be more disagreement within the host country agencies than between the Eaton side and the principal local partner. But another part of the failure, I believe, was due to Eaton's growing frustration and decreasing enthusiasm (even anger) with his 'might be' socialist partners and also, in part, a lack of Western enthusiasm for Eastern European financial risk.

This broad lack of enthusiasm resulted in Eaton's taking a laid back approach to projects in the Eastern Bloc countries. In some instances I thought he was sometimes sending us on a merry chase just to keep Clara happy; she of Eastern European background could be pretty insistent. Clara had a nice flat in Belgravia and working in Eastern Europe, in some ways, was justification for that. By comparison, Cy's attitude to Cayo Sabinal remained aggressive and he continually worked hard to achieve a positive conclusion.

* * * * *

The change of employment from LDA to Eaton coincided with changes to my 'extracurricular', non-work-related occupations. My term as an AIA director would be completed in 1979. Apart from attending on-going Board and committee meetings and the annual Convention, two, time-consuming, tasks remained. The first was to sponsor and lobby for the award of the 1976 AIA Gold Medal to Philip Johnson. There were some difficulties with this due to Philip's alleged (or real?) past affinity for Germany in the run up to World War II. In my opinion, though the objections were understandable, they were not relevant to Philip's contribution to architecture. The majority of the board agreed, (eventually), and Philip received the award in 1978. The second task was to complete the work as chair of the committee on the reorganization of the AIA. I did. The report was approved. Like some (or a lot) of the LDA and Eaton work I am not sure whether any of the recommendations were implemented. After completing my term as an AIA main board director, I continued as a trustee of the AIA Foundation, taking an interest in the AIA archives. However, this was 'small beer' by comparison to being on the main Board.

* * * * *

Given my on- going overseas travel, doing an appropriate job as the Darrow chair, was impossible and I soon relinquished this responsibility. Hans Solmssen, another Darrow graduate, five years my junior, succeeded me. Despite the handover of the chairmanship, I was still continued to be very much involved with Darrow and continued as chair of the buildings and grounds committee, a serious time commitment. The new (in 1975) headmaster David Miller and I struggled to keep the schools facilities in one piece. It wasn't easy and not always successful. There was never enough money for the required work so the Board practiced what was called at the time 'deferred maintenance'. It sounded like we were doing something, though we were not. It was only a recognition that maintenance work was required and would be completed when it was affordable. The result was obvious, the buildings and grounds were minimally maintained and consequently degraded. I worked closely (and frequently) with David to do what we could and got to know him and his wife Bonnie very well. They became good friends and the Millers, Valery and I would spend a fair amount of time together, both in and outside of school business (Valery pitched in and helped me prepare documents for bathroom renovations and the like).

Dave was physically large and somewhat overweight. He was an intelligent, cheerful, affable, enthusiastic, thoughtful headmaster. He also had a good sense of humour (I think any head needs one). He had the unenviable task of presiding over a now co-educational school in the nineteen seventies. Drugs, sex, smoking and alcohol were on the daily menu. It was a fragile time for Darrow (as well as other schools). Dave did what he could in this era of cultural change and rebellion. Getting enough, let alone good, students was difficult. Fund raising for scholarships and operations was a struggle; it was a trying time. There is no doubt that the academic quality of the students diminished as did discipline and good behaviour. In later years Dave was criticized (in hindsight) by some trustees and alumni for letting the school's standards 'slip'. There is no question that they did: he was 'in charge', his watch. However, I do not concur with the many who made David a singular 'scapegoat'. I think the devaluation of standards was inevitable, perhaps more of 'a sign of the times' rather than any individual failure. In any event, Darrow continued to survive, barely, but it did.

* * * * *

The design of Cayo Sabinal moved ahead and the time came to hire additional professional help, both architects and engineers. The architect assignment was a no-brainer, LDA with Davis Brody. Engineering was a bit more complicated but we hired Amman and Whitney who were already working on Isfahan. I met up with cousin Carl. Carl's employment career, following Crow Construction and the African Pavilion found him, in 1976, working for Amman and Whitney, the major New York engineering firm famed for, among other projects, the design of the George Washington Bridge. Carl introduced me to them with his thought in mind that I could get them hired for Isfahan. In due course I had introduced them to Wally Rutes, the tough, irascible, manager of Intercontinental construction projects and Don Colombo Wally's calm (by comparison) Isfahan project manager and to Lew, Sam and Maurice de Rohan. Amman and Whitney were more than technically qualified; moreover, they had existing offices in Iran. They were hired and to keep matters simple, since we were now familiar with their staff, it was logical to hire them for the engineering work on Cayo Sabinal. This was the beginning of a ten-year working relationship with Carl as well as Amman and Whitney. David

WuDunn, one of only two outstanding estimators (of the many) that I have known was still in the picture with Carl. David consulted to Amman and Whitney as well as to other leading New York construction entities. David's estimates were, in my opinion, accurate and informative. I was happy to be working with him again.

During the Eaton years there were perhaps fifteen trips to Cuba. Some were technical and design meetings but as many were business or marketing based. On the marketing side we hired Bob Warner or more precisely, his firm. Bob, a 1960's Darrow graduate owned a high-end hotel marketing company. His work and our relationship were quite reasonable until one of his deputies, Walter Johnson, technically qualified but a bit of a pompous show off, decided to take a risky high dive from a Cuban fishing boat that was being used for our entertainment by the head of Intur, Gongora. The dive was risky. Gongora, one of the few 'tough Cuban cookies' we met during the Cuban exercise thought Johnson might have killed or maimed himself leaving Gongora and Intur in deep sand or something akin. Johnson didn't know, as he leapt from the mast, that his swan dive was really a swan song. Gongora suggested, firmly, that it might be better if Johnson were to 'disappear' from the project. The event rather soured our relationship with Warner's firm. Further involvement was limited and Cy, under the circumstances, was reluctant to compensate Warner. There was a bit of a hoorah. I do not remember the outcome, though I believe it wasn't good. Cy, to my relief, kept me out of the loop.

During the process of working on Cayo Sabinal I got to know Cuba's geography pretty well. In addition to knowing the nooks and crannies of Sabinal, and of course Havana, we were taken on tours of Cienfuego, Trinidad, Camaguey, Santa Maria, Guama and the Isle of Pines and we visited places of interest (or not), schools, medical facilities, villages, and some alligators in between. The Cubans also saw that we were well entertained. On one night when Cy and Clara had dinner with Fidel, the Cubans brought out Fidel's older brother, Ramon, to host our 'technical' staff at the Tropicana. I sat next to Ramon. He was bearded and dressed in fatigues and looked like one might expect Castro's older brother to look; as a matter of fact he could have been mistaken for Fidel.[162] He was mainly interested in farming and for most of the evening that was the subject, in between the lively Tropicana revues. We did not talk politics. He came across as intelligent, informed, courteous and cheerful, unlike the youngest of the Castro brothers.

Later in 1979, when the technical side of the Sabinal project was completed, Gongora asked us if we would be interested in redeveloping the Hotel Nacional in Havana, Barlovento, once a marina resort west of Havana, and a hotel at Varadero: Cy was. We prepared three more proposals. The proposals were mostly prepared by me, say 75%, and the balance was prepared either by Paul Buckhurst or an engineering consultant. The added cost was minimal but the potential quite significant. Cy, understandably, saw this as a 'no-brainer'. These smaller proposals were not as sophisticated as the proposal for Cayo Sabinal but they were acceptable to Gongora. I personally visited almost every room and space in the Nacional over a period of several weeks, a somewhat boring task. In addition, with some minor exceptions, I prepared 'concept designs' for the proposals; that was more fun. Perhaps I was a bit 'Toad like' but I enjoyed the work and, as one says, 'it kept me out of trouble'. Despite a certain enthusiasm on everyone's part nothing came of the new proposals, just more exercise books to put on 'a shelf of uncompleted projects'.

In pursuit of the financing of Cayo Sabinal, Cy and I made frequent trips to Canada seeking ways to 'arrange' the financing. In 1979 Canada was the logical (and nearest) choice for financing. Canada had good relations with Cuba, a lot of Canadians used Cuba as a destination resort ('cheap and cheerful') and there were Canadian funds (mostly belonging to insurance companies) frozen in Cuba. We made presentations to banks, mostly the Royal Bank, appropriate insurance companies, AIG, Sun Life, and Confederation Life. As well, we made presentations to a plethora of wealthy individuals and businesses that might (or as it turned out didn't) have an interest in Cuba such as the charter airlines, Wardair and Nordair. We also worked extensively on the export financing part of the project with Ian

Macdonald of Canada's department of Industry, Trade and Commerce. We became quite familiar with Canadian financial infrastructure.

I was sent, also, on two, one man, trips to Spain to meet with Juan Entrecanales (a contact of Brad Perkins) and head of one of Spain's largest construction companies, a possible contractor for the Sabinal project. Juan was an elegant, smart, charismatic character. He put me up at the Ritz and would lend me his car and driver when he thought it would be useful. While his interest in Cayo Sabinal didn't materialize I learned quite a lot about construction in Spain and Madrid. Cy was right, I did learn how to make proper financial projections and present them. I actually enjoyed this work, even before the advent of Mac computers. The Cuban adventure(s) continued into 1983. Travel became easier. The State Department cleared us for private charter flights so we flew from Miami, generally in various types of twin-engine Pipers with which I was familiar from my flying days. While administratively complex, due to restricted flight times and paths, it was much easier to reach to Havana from Miami. I enjoyed the flights and often had the co-pilot seat. Clara hated little planes, big ones too. The only plane Clara like was the Concorde, probably because the flight time was shorter and it was luxurious. As I often travelled with Clara that meant I too had the pleasure and excitement of travelling on Concorde. Prior to any flight, even Concorde, Clara fortified herself with little vodka shots that she kept in her handy handbag. Cy, when he was with us on a Cuban trip would sit in the rear (despite his experience as a pilot) and, if he felt like it, would wind up Clara on the risks of flying. I suspect there may have been some undefined quid pro quo for these charter flights; perhaps some general information on Cuba passed along to an appropriate agency, quietly, after trips – but I could be wrong. Valery came along on at least two Cuban visits and this added to the enjoyment. The Cubans liked Valery and she and Cy got along well. I am not so sure about Clara, at least there were no squabbles.

One of the wealthy individuals that Cy met in Canada was Karsten von Wersebe. Karsten had recently immigrated to Canada and had founded a real-estate development business, aptly called York Hanover (York the early name for Toronto and Hanover, capital of lower Saxony, Karsten's birthplace). In addition to office buildings and shopping centres the company owned and operated several hotels in Canada. In Karsten Cy had found an ambitious individual, a developer with apparently deep pockets[163] open to the challenges Cy offered him. (In retrospect Cy's challenges reminded me of the old joke, "first prize is one night in Philadelphia, second prize is two nights".) Cy needed additional funds for the professional work on Cayo Sabinal. The project was large enough to whet any entrepreneur's appetite and potentially profitable enough to absorb additional partners. Partially, because of the Canadian connection, Karsten (and/or his colleagues) was 'up for Cy's offer of a 50% share of Park Tower (Park Tower was the beneficial owner of the Cayo Sabinal development rights) for a sum in the order of $1,200,000 (about $4.5 million in 2018) plus commitments for additional capital when needed. In addition, Karsten agreed that he would (and could) provide further investment funds[164] for specific projects he liked. The Karsten 'deal' was, for Eaton, good (and timely); Clara, however, (never one not to offer her opinion), objected to Karsten. In my opinion, Clara's objections were twofold; one stemmed from a general, "I don't like Germans", arising from of WWII experiences and the other because Clara found Karsten 'suspicious', as she found anyone who might, in any way, get between her and Cy. But needs must, and one day in 1977 Cy telephoned to tell me that Karsten had agreed in principle to Cy's offer to be a 50% owner of Park Tower. The full agreement was subject to meeting me and conducting due diligence on our projects, both Cuba and Eastern Europe, but particularly Cuba. The three of us met in New York at Park Tower's recently opened small office for just me and my efficient and pleasant secretary, Terry Fimano, within Perkins and Will's[165] large offices on Second Avenue, near 42nd street. The office and its modest rent were thanks to Brad's friendship and the tacit understanding that Perkins and Will would have first shot at any architectural work Park Tower generated, at the time for example, the hotels in Cuba and Dubrovnik.

The meeting was cordial and 'successful' and Karsten agreed to become Cy's partner. That meeting, and several subsequent meetings resulted in a number of modifications to Park Tower's business plan. First, while Park Tower would work on Cy's projects (particularly Cuba) Park Tower would also look to develop domestic (this included the Caribbean) projects as these were potentially more in Karsten's personal interests – I think he saw Park Tower as a good entry into a US market; second, Park Tower would take on additional staff as required[166]; third, Park Tower would move to larger premises as soon as appropriate (Karsten didn't see my relationship with Brad in the same way as I did.); fourth, our monthly operating funds would be sourced from York Hanover and, fifth because of that, Karsten would take the hands-on partner's role in overseeing Park Tower's day to day operations and project development for anything other than the Cuban and Eastern European projects. Cy was not that enthusiastic about these changes, they obviously meant he lost a lot of control: in fact, most. He realized, however, that 'he who pays the piper calls the tune', and, by necessity, concurred in the changes.

There were a number of positive features to these arrangements. By taking on domestic projects, for which we had, potentially, more control and ability to fund, Park Tower could, at least in theory, generate income sooner and, probably, more easily. Relying on income generation from socialist country projects was a long-term strategy and Karsten sought to balance this strategy with his shorter-term strategy. I was up for this. A definite negative feature of the changes was that I was now serving two equal partners; with Cy I had an intellectual and, even, an emotional tie, (despite some periodic misgivings, I really liked Cy) but I had a fiscal fastening with Karsten. It was a business arrangement that, in time, would prove untenable.

I soon found it was not that easy to work with Karsten. It was not that he didn't treat me fairly or respect my work, he did, but it was impossible to 'read' him. He was rarely enthusiastic or, for that matter, negative about projects, the complete opposite of Cy. Cy could wax lyrical about a project, even without any apparent justification. He would be able to enthuse his partners, colleagues and employees beyond any reason. Karsten had neither praise nor criticism - about anything; he was a 'cool customer'. He was a man of little humour; perhaps none would be more accurate. In his requirement for extreme detailed project analysis he was quite Germanic (no surprise there!). I did learn from him in this respect. Perhaps, at the time, had I known more about my own ancestral Hanoverian[167] past we might have had a better relationship. As it was we both moved around each other with extreme caution. I think Karsten wanted me to like him, if for no other reason than to ingratiate himself to Eaton, with whom I, obviously, had a close relationship. For my part, like Cy, I was mindful of who was paying the piper and did whatever I thought was appropriate to satisfy, and, as well, tried to second-guess, Karsten.

Karsten was an ambitious, single minded, workaholic. He travelled all over the place pursuing deals. As a result, once we had concluded the initial, but thorough, 'get to know each other' meetings, he delegated periodic, bi-monthly (sometimes weekly) contact with me to two quite sycophantic assistants, Gisela Laubitz, a sort of accountant and Steve Rosenburg of unknown professional (or not) background. These two, while necessarily polite, were never really helpful. Their primary interest seemed to be keeping in Karsten's good graces. If this meant making trouble for me that was ok. In due course Karsten also hired a semi-retired banker, (I cannot remember what bank or what position, he could have been a teller for all I knew) George Kendall, to watch over us. George was supposed to help on the financial side of the business. In reality, he came to the office around ten, read the Wall Street Journal and New York Times, had lunch, spied on us if he could (we made that as difficult as possible) and went home when he felt like it. Apart from these individuals we were pretty much left on our own to explore development opportunities.

We were soon looking at a variety of projects. Peter Sampton, a partner in Gruzen and Partners in New York and an AIA compatriot, suggested we look at the possibility of building a hotel in Raleigh, North Carolina[168]. Cy was not particularly interested but Karsten in due course flew down to Raleigh in his Lear Jet, met the players, looked at the site and agreed to invest. I was able to 'arrange' the hotel's financing with the help a good mortgage broker, Andy Elfmont, and my friendly bankers, Mike Fitzpatrick and Doug Duval of the Bank of New York. Aetna would provide the long term financing. Radisson agreed to manage the hotel. The 365 room Radisson Plaza was constructed and served downtown Raleigh and its Convention Centre for some forty years. It is now a Sheraton hotel and has been fully renovated.

We developed a condominium, the Clarendon[169], south of Palm Beach. Roy Case (and his friend, Digby Bridges[170]), both now emigrated from Jamaica to Florida, were the initiators. Roy and Digby did most of the design under the aegis of Baker Amman and Whitney, an A&E company that we formed for the purpose.

The largest and most complicated project for Park Tower, outside of Cayo Sabinal, was our proposal for a hotel at St George in Bermuda. Michael Kiesser identified the opportunity, it was well known to anyone in Bermuda that the Government wanted to find and appoint a developer to create a new hotel on government-owned land overlooking the very pretty harbour of St George. The project was full of political intrigue as well as internal intrigue. Michael Kiesser was not without his unhelpful Germanic guile and was often marching to his own tune. Jim Woolridge, the late bubbly tourism minister was nominally in charge for the government. However, the Governor General and Bermuda's Prime Minister were available to influence the project when needed. In addition, almost everyone else had their opinions. In fact, we met, at one time or another, most everyone of any influence in Bermuda.

I enjoyed the Bermuda project, not only because it was a good project, but also because I remembered father talking about Bermuda. One of father's artefacts in my possession was a photograph album of pictures he took on his own visits to Bermuda. These included pictures of some of the 'first families' of Bermuda, most still extant and pictures of St George.

In addition to developing our own work Park Tower was hired to work on York Hanover's hotels in Niagara Falls. In our domestic sphere, in addition to Raleigh, we made proposals for hotels in New York City (Times Square), Charlottesville and Atlantic City. Cy had brief, intense but seriously misguided belief that we could enter the casino business. In the Caribbean area (not counting

Bermuda) we explored, to one degree or another, resorts in St Lucia, the Cayman Islands, the Dominican Republic (three projects), St Thomas and a casino project in Antigua. In between these domestic and Caribbean projects we continued to pursue Eaton's (or Clara's) Eastern European projects. Each of these projects required interface with governments, country, city or state, each required concept designs, preliminary financing plans, marketing studies and more. And for something entirely different we were invited to Manila (though I am not sure exactly why) to participate in planning a tourism project west of the city.

The latter project involved a large tract of land at Limbones southwest of Manila (looking north to Corregidor) for the Martels, a politically correct (in a Marcos sense of the term), wealthy, Manila family. The first trip included myself, Paul Buckhurst for planning, David Wudunn for construction costs, and Fred McKewon our Cayo Sabinal environmental engineer for the environmental impact assessment. The four of us set out together from JFK on Pan Am to San Francisco where we would change to Pan Am's flight to Manila. In view of our frequent flying, Pan Am upgraded us to first class. This was absolutely fine except that by the time we arrived in San Francisco some six hours later Fred was, as the contemporary stand-up comic Michael Macintyre might say, completely 'bungalowed' – but we didn't know it. There was not much time between planes and the four of us hurried across the airport to the appropriate gate. We were not paying much attention; just hurrying along, and we didn't notice until we got to the gate that Fred was missing. We went back over our route, we paged him, checked every toilet, every shop and persuaded Pan Am and the police to look, but it was futile, Fred had vanished. Last call for Manila came, we (Paul, David and I) made the decision to leave and left money and details in the hope that Pan Am would find Fred (or vice versa) and sort things out.

We arrived in Manila the following morning and were met on the tarmac by our host and client Jose Martel. He was very keen and excited to tell us that we had an important, and formal, government reception that evening on behalf of the project. Immigration proceedings were waived and we proceeded to get our baggage. There was a little problem; no baggage, it had gone somewhere else; it certainly was not in Manila. The only clothes we had were what we were wearing. No worries, Jose knew a tailor who could fix us up for the evening. We were rushed to the tailor, measured and assured that we would have our suits delivered to the hotel by six pm. We then proceeded to the hotel, (owned by the Martels it should be noted), and were surprised to be greeted by Fred, now perfectly sober. He had somehow managed to get to Manila before us, <u>with</u> his baggage. Paul, David and I were a little 'put out'.

The suits arrived as promised – mine looked and fit as if it had come from the wardrobe of 'The Man in the White Suit' - just before the suit disintegrated. The reception, however, was fine even though we looked like the three stooges, plus Fred, no one said anything.

We were regally, though that may not be the appropriate word, entertained on our visit. We had two government helicopters, 'Hueys', a significant boat (for entertainment, lunches, swimming etc.), and on and off road vehicles at our disposal. Lunches and dinners were elaborate. The visit lasted some two weeks. We made another, but less stressful, visit to finish our preliminary report. The Martels seemed pleased. Jose stayed in touch with me for several years and we often met when he was in New York to catch up on the project and chat. The last time I saw him he told me that the project was proceeding, though slowly. Given the changing politics of the Philippines, probably very slowly.

As Karsten had forecast we added to our staff and moved from our little Perkins and Will office to 488 Madison Avenue. The office there, overlooking the north side of St.Patrick's Cathedral, was rather grand, designed some years before by Florence Knoll. Our key staff now included the non-residents, Michael Kiesser and Frank Codella, my secretary, Terry Fimano, Bill Dowling previously the marketing director for Princess Hotels, Harry Phol his assistant, Feresteh Bekhrad[171] from Tehran, a project manager and Behrooz Nournia, an Iranian architect and friend of Feresteh who helped on presentation and design. Preliminary or concept design was done 'in house' under my aegis but anything more than that was farmed out. The former Princess financial officer, Arnold Chubb, became our chief financial officer, kept us financially straight. He and his assistant, Charles Regent (previously from LDA) helped to prepare financing plans for proposed projects. Esther Regent, also ex LDA, was our office manager.[172] Following Llewellyn Davies' death in 1981 (also, for all practical purposes the death-knell of his New York office LDA) Paul and three of his colleagues set up their own planning firm, Buckhurst, Fish, Hutton and Katz. Their first office was a sublet of from Park Tower and their presence provided an (almost) in-house planning department. Park Tower was a busy, lively and interesting office. With the exception of Bermuda and the brief essay into casino business, Cy showed minimum interest in Park Tower's 'domestic' projects but that was ok. Working with only one partner was easier than with two. Then came China.

For a several years, Cy had been expounding on the coming opportunity of working in China. He saw, correctly, that China would be a great opportunity for his particular skills, especially at the beginning of China's rapprochement with the west. In late 1979, he called me to say that a Chinese group had invited him to come to Beijing to discuss the possibility of building a major hotel. He, naturally, expected me to come to China with him and, of course, Clara, he thought the trip might take three or four weeks. Great as that sounded the timing was miserable. We were in the midst of the Raleigh financing, Bermuda was in a critical planning and political phase and the Clarendon was just under construction. I discussed the matter with Karsten. "No way!" was the least of his comments. He wanted nothing to do with China. He had not signed up for a China risk.

Karsten had growing confidence that Park Tower would satisfy his domestic development ambitions and be fiscally sound. Karsten's position was that if Park Tower got strung out with projects in China it would put him and his investments in Park Tower and its projects at risk, which was probably true. There ensued two or three weeks of testy contradictory telephone calls from Cy, Clara and Karsten. To the best of my knowledge Cy and Karsten did not, themselves, discuss Cy's China ambitions with respect to Park Tower and expected me to make my own decisions. To go or not to go, that was the question. While I was sympathetic with Cy, and wanted to go, I concluded that reason was on Karsten's side and I declined. Cy, to say the least, was unhappy. Clara, too, had a few select comments, typical Clara, she never failed to get her 'oar in'.

Cy went to China and was given the contract to build the 'Great Wall Hotel'. It was the first 'Western' joint venture hotel project in China. The architect was Welton Becket, the architect for Cy's aborted Moscow hotel of some years before[173]. Cy's focus on China completely obscured any on-going interest in Park Tower and its domestic projects. As well, his interest in Eastern Europe and Cuba, waned. Nevertheless Park Tower ploughed on with its projects and I kept Cy informed of our progress, even if he was not interested.

Not many months passed after Cy's China trip before the inevitable happened. Karsten, in buying a 50% interest in Park Tower had bought into the Cuba projects, the US opportunities and (to a lesser extent) he accepted the Eastern European market; but definitely not China. He now wanted out of the partnership, he declared that Cy had effectively breached the agreement by focusing his attention on China. The ensuing split was drawn out. It was an emotionally fraught, tedious legal process and took months. Karsten, initially, was interested in keeping me on but Cy still wanted my services, despite the Chinese imbroglio (he, more or less, forgave me my China 'indiscretion'). I was pulled first one-way, then another. In the end, despite some misgivings, Valery, for example, was not too sure what was best and we had a long debate, I stayed with Eaton. Karsten made the separation as difficult as he could.

When the legal ink was dry Park Tower (the name only) remained with Cy as well as the Eastern European projects, such as they were, (which was not much) and Cuba. Terry Fimano, my long-suffering secretary and I were again Park Tower's only staff. Karsten got every other project and might-be projects; Clarendon, Bermuda, the Raleigh Radisson and a shelf full of 'maybes'. The projects now became York-Hanover projects.

Was this always Karsten's Plan B? I don't know. In any event, Karsten put Feresteh in charge; he sublet most of the office and, in short course, made most of the remaining staff redundant. I wasn't too keen on Feresteh's move to Karsten. I felt she had been a little duplicitous during the separation negotiations, but that might be either sour grapes or unrealistic New England ethics.[174] The three projects, the Radisson, Clarendon and Bermuda (now the St. George Club) were in good shape and were completed by York Hanover. The 'maybes' were, to the best of my knowledge abandoned.

Back to square one (or even minus one); I still had a job (although now needing redefinition), I was still in New York, and I still had a secretary. But I had nothing to do and no office in which to do it. Another trip to Cleveland's Terminal Tower and a meeting with Cy followed. We needed to develop our Plan B.

Plan B: I remained as President of Park Tower in charge of myself and Terry. I would take on responsibility for developing any new hotel projects in China (the Great Wall Hotel would not be my project – good news to me, I wasn't thrilled with the idea of taking over such a large project in mid-stream) and I would continue work on Cuba and any, viable, Eastern European project. Initially I would work from home but if an office was needed due to bona fide work, that would be considered. My personal financial arrangements would be the same but any funds for pursuing projects would be severely limited. Cy was entering a phase of fiscal austerity. Plan B was a simple, workable plan, even if it was a 'come down'.

* * * * *

On the home front everything was perking along very nicely. After LDA shut, Valery took up an alternate career, cooking, she was already a good, but not professional, cook. After attending a culinary institute, she became an executive chef with two Wall street firms (not at the same time). We ate well. There was always food left over from lunches, Valery only did lunches. Apart from this Valery had a few private architectural projects. We got along well, very well. The children appeared happy with Valery, or at least they appeared to have no objections, another 'nulla osta'. Marriage was inevitable and in February 1979 as noted this took place in a small ceremony in the 63rd street apartment.

The foreign travel was a bit of a strain on us but the fact that Valery came along on the some trips, Cuba, Bermuda and Europe, provided something of a balance. In the winter we often went skiing (cross country), staying, rather regularly, with the Millers at Darrow. In the spring, summer, and fall we were on Seven Bells, which, after bringing her up through the Intercostal Waterway, was now moored at Westbrook, Connecticut.

Morgan graduated from Vassar in 1980 and Jamie from Yale in 1982. Morgan stayed in Cambridge. Jamie studied history and enlisted in the Marine reserve at Yale. Molly wasn't too keen on the marine bit and was outspoken in objecting to my "persuading Jamie to join the Marines". I didn't, it was Jamie's idea. Yale received the Commandant's trophy, in 1982, on behalf of Jamie having been the outstanding officer candidate that year. I attended his graduation ceremony at Quantico and was a proud father watching him lead his class in the formalities and receive two out of the three awards given to members of his class.

Valery, Alden, Trina and I visited Bermuda on a working holiday that started out well but had a grim ending when Trina was attacked near our project site at St George by a young prisoner on day release. Trina, as is her wont, was stoic about the event but was obviously affected. Molly was, understandably appalled. In due course Trina and Molly returned to Bermuda for the legal formalities. I was kept out of the loop as I was, rightly or wrongly, treated as responsible.

Trina, after graduating from Buckingham went on to Dana Hall, a choice made in part because she could keep a horse there. After Dana Hall came Mount Holyoke, still more horses, as well as art. Alden continued his summer visits and sometimes also holidays and I also managed, from time to time, to see him in California.

After sailing around the Eastern end of the Long Island and Connecticut waters for several years Valery and I concluded that we had 'done' Seven Bells. Too much money and hassle for too little pleasure. We had enjoyed Seven Bells but it was time to move on. Seven Bells would be sold and the funds used for a 'place in the country'; that, to us, meant Duchess or Columbia counties.

We knew both counties primarily because of Darrow and Bard. Moreover, at the time, the counties were quite affordable. Though we drove the back roads of most of both counties every weekend we could not find what we wanted, perhaps we didn't know what we wanted. But in 1981 an unusual opportunity arose at Darrow that would settle the matter and affect life for, certainly, the next twenty-five years.

One of the most derelict of the Darrow's North Family buildings was its Forge. Despite its Shaker pedigree, because of its condition, it was under condemnation threat by the town's building inspector. The school had no foreseeable use for the building, or funds to renovate it even with the sale of Seven Bells Valery and I did not have enough to complete is renovation. Notwithstanding, Valery and I saw it as an opportunity. Could we restore the building into a residence while saving it for posterity? We were enthusiastic and optimistic about the idea, even if we were a bit naive. Maybe we could talk the school into letting us try under some conditions, it was worth an ask.

There was some interest from outside the school's immediate community to buy the structure for use as a workshop but the proposal for that use came with some significant conditions. Valery and I made an alternate proposal to Dave and the board to lease the building and convert it to a residence – it would be our 'place in the country'.

Dave liked our idea the best. He considered it a win-win proposal and thought the Board should consider it, "they can always say no" was his bottom line. The proposal went to the Board at its next meeting. After a short discussion (I was not present), the board agreed to the transaction. Several of the trustees told me afterward that they thought we were crazy and took bets as to how long it would be before we gave up. In any event they posited that the school had 'nothing to lose' the worst-case scenario was that Darrow would be back where it started.

The building appeared to be a wreck, the result of nearly eighty years of mostly neglect and some misuse. The Forge hadn't been occupied or used (except by Darrow Students for various unlisted extracurricular activities) since the 'turn of the century'. There was no power, no water, no sanitation, the foundations had collapsed, the chimneys were falling apart and the south wall of the building was, essentially, missing. Moreover, there were only a few windows in place; a lot of undergrowth, a lot of dirt (almost two feet in the main room) and it was home to swarms of bees and local fauna. Otherwise the structure was in pretty good shape, seriously. The slate and metal roof was original (1840s) and didn't leak, so apart from rotting sills there was no internal rot in the frame. The frame and roof, in fact, were about all there was that was sound in the building, but that, it turned out, was enough.

When we started work we had not yet closed the sale of Seven Bells so, as usual, we were short of cash. We went down to the little Taconic Bank in the valley to see if they could help with some temporary funding in order to get the basic utilities, water, power, a waste system, completed or at least started. We saw the friendly manager, Art Huls and explained to him who we were and what we were doing. He asked, only, if we knew anybody in the area. "Dave Miller?" we offered. Art confirmed this with a telephone call and that was good enough. Art opened an account for us. I put my signature on a short loan agreement, and Art made an opening deposit, on the spot, of $10,000. That was the way the local bank supported the community in 1982.

We stayed with David and Bonnie almost every weekend while we worked to bring 'The Forge', to a 'campable' condition. It would take several months of hard work, before we could achieve even this. By 1982, 'Seven Bells' had been sold, for a good sum, providing the necessary funds for basic renovation and we were soon able to live in the Forge on weekends. It was a bit rough but Valery and I had our 'place in the country'. The doubters were confounded.

* * * * *

My teaching at City College continued, no change there. But by 1980 my commitment to AIA matters was all but finished. This might have meant more personal time but this was not to be, both because of the Forge but also because of, what might be called, an elaboration of my role as a Darrow trustee.

At every trustee's meeting almost half the time was given over to discussing fund-raising, a constant need in order to try to balance Darrow's budget. With Darrow's limited graduate constituency and in part, its location in a low-income part of Columbia Country, raising annual, let alone capital funds was difficult. In the early years Darrow had depended on the fiscal resources of its Headmaster, Heyniger. The funds required to replace the buildings lost in the fires of 1962/63, the so called 'Dairy Barn', were largely insurance payments, supplemented by the positive (and also desperate) message that if funds were not raised to replace the demolished buildings the school would close. Fund raising for the 1967 Science building was another single purpose effort primarily led by the trustee Peter Sprague.

The unique selling points for these fund-raising successes were not applicable to the year on year need to cover Darrow's operating deficit. There was generally a short fall in each year's budget, met, more often than not, by borrowing more money against the value of Darrow's plant (buildings). By the early eighties Darrow's debt was substantial and growing year on year.

From the beginning, Darrow's greatest physical and fiscal asset was its historic Shaker site and buildings. These, of course, were, at the same time, its greatest liability. The buildings and site required constant maintenance and improvement. Some buildings, especially those in the recently acquired North Family (including, of course, the Forge) were in danger of collapse or serious degradation. In any event some of us, specifically Steve Howard, a former faculty member but now Trustee and myself lobbied to find a way to capitalize on Darrow's Shaker buildings and site.

Steve and I proposed, in principle, that Darrow create a separate, not for profit, organization that would own the buildings but lease them back to the school for a notional rent. The new organization's main purpose would be historic preservation, not education. The organization would be a public benefit not-for-profit entity therefore eligible to raise funds from sources, including government preservation resources, not available to private schools, a key point.

While there were lots of 'unknowns' to the idea, the concept had potential for a win-win result. Perhaps understandably, not all the board greeted the proposal with either universal or unmitigated enthusiasm. There were two main objections; first, though the school would retain beneficial use of the buildings, it would have to sell its primary fiscal asset; the second: Darrow would be involved with the various governmental, state and federal, agencies concerned with historic preservation - a potential conflict with the academic use of buildings. The debate was long and testy but, though the vote was not unanimous, the proposal was passed.

The new organization that would be the future owner of the site was, after some lengthy discussion, called Mount Lebanon Shaker Village, aka MLSV. The initial board was composed of several key members of Darrow's board, including Hans Solmssen, Darrow's Board Chairman, Trip Samson and Debbie Solbert, local interested persons and some carefully selected Shaker specialists and historians. Among the latter were; Professor Michael Coe of Yale, Michael's alter ego Ernie Wiegand an industrial archaeologist, Charlie Flint a Shaker furniture specialist from Lenox, Don Emerich a Shaker expert and New York State historian and Mary Black, director of the American Folk Art Museum. I would be the new organization's President and Chairperson.

Thus started an organization that would be instrumental in saving the school, though we didn't know it at the time. The new organization almost immediately took up any remaining free time that I might have and then some. In 1982 David retired as headmaster and was replaced by Jerral Miles. Jerral embraced the MLSV concept and he and I began a good working relationship. Though Jerral and I (as well as most of the MLSV's trustees) saw the new organization as synergetic not everyone did. In time this would become a problem.

While all the Darrow/Forge 'business' was going on a bona fide project emerged that justified removing the Park Tower office from the apartment, much to Valery's (and my) appreciation. As a result of Cy's success in Beijing with the Great Wall Hotel Cy was invited by the Chinese investment authorities to meet with the Jing Jang hotel group, the principal hotel organization in Shanghai. There was no question that this would be 'my' project. Though there was precious little funding available a proper office was required though the likes of 488 Madison Avenue would not be an option.

AIA connections, again, helped to solve this 'problem'. It was Bob Gatje who came to my aid. Bob was a former New York City AIA Chapter president, friend and partner in MBA (Marcel Breuer Associates) the successor firm formed after the Breuer's death. Bob had been a colleague of Joe Neski's when they were both associates in Breuer's office and I had known Bob since that time. We met, had a few discussions and agreed that I would sublet, for a nominal sum, a small portion of their office, a spare conference room for me and a front desk for Terry Fimano. The deal included the quid pro quo that if we generated projects in China requiring architectural services, MBA would be appointed their architect. Cy agreed. In due course I settled into MBA's cheerful, busy, offices at 15 East 26th street, overlooking Madison Park and continued looked forward to my first trip to China.

Cy's China projects had grown in importance and scope. Hotels were only one opportunity. There were potential deals for paper mills and, most importantly, agricultural projects. Cy created a joint venture, (Farmland Eaton World Trade), with one of the largest US farm cooperatives. Bob Bergland, President Carter's former agricultural secretary was hired to run it. Cy was clearly 'on a China roll' and the future seemed bright.

My first trip to China, in April 1981, was as part of Cy's 'delegation' consisting that consisted of Cy and Clara, various Farmland personnel, Bob Bergland and myself. We flew to Tokyo where we discussed China matters with a

271

few banks and then flew on to Beijing. I got to see most of the tourist sights there, as that part of the trip did not involve hotels. However, we all ate together in the evening and I was kept abreast of the day's happenings, subject of course to being aware of probable Chinese eavesdropping. We were, essentially, a happy, enthusiastic group. I got on particularly well with the affable Bob Bergland as we shared an interest in sailing. In the back of my mind I was conjuring up a proposal to build sailboats in China. On the first trip I kept these thoughts to myself but I was nevertheless keen to get Bob's opinions. For some reason all this bothered Clara and she tried to pick a fight accusing me of toadying up to Bob – Cy told her to 'shut up', and she did, more or less. Clara did tend to pick a fight when she had nothing better to do, it was just part of her red-haired, feisty, Romanian ethnicity.

After Beijing we flew to Shanghai where we were comfortably put up in one of the several elegant VIP guesthouses that were former residences of foreign consuls or wealthy foreign families. These buildings were typically European designs of the thirties. They had been only minimally maintained; 'shabby chic' would be to describe the best of them. They appeared suspended in time, a little creepy. One, in particular, reminded me of scenes from the 1987 movie, 'Empire of the Sun'. On other trips we occupied the presidential suite of the Jing Jiang hotel itself[175]. The Chinese authorities treated us, certainly outwardly, with deference. A typical day would include, usually in the morning, a pro-forma visit to a construction site, or a possible hotel site, or some building organization. After lunch, usually on our own, there might, or might not, be a meeting with the Jing Jaing group. These meeting were usually impromptu and the subject varied from meeting to meeting. If it was technical I would most likely be on my own, if it involved financing Cy and Clara would be leading the discussions. The Chinese would inform us of a meeting only a few hours (if that) before the event. There were also frequent large 'Banquets'. The Chinese would entertain us first and then protocol would require that we, in turn, would entertain the Chinese. In the 'free' evenings, after dinner, most often late into the night, or early morning, I would type up a memorandum, proposed contract or interim protocol agreement, based on the day's discussions. These memoranda, prepared in multiple carbon copies were prepared on my handy, portable Olivetti 'Lettera 22' that accompanied me, like a modern day laptop, on all my travels. The memoranda would form the basis of the next day's (or perhaps the day after) meetings. The Shanghai visits would last anywhere from a week to two weeks. There were lots of activities but also a lot of waiting for a meeting, we were kept 'on edge', probably 'on purpose'. Our emotions varied from elation to despair, with stops in between. The waiting drove the not-too-patient Clara loopy. Cy was more phlegmatic about the waits though on occasion he did get fed up and told the Chinese what he thought! Cy could, and did, 'blow' from time to time. However, during my seven-year stint with him I was only once the recipient of these periodic 'hoorahs', that was when I didn't go to China in the first instance – but that 'blow' had been an extravaganza.

Over our several visits I saw most of Shanghai, often on my own. I was not aware of being followed but I may have been. Clara and Cy didn't participate in my perambulations either because they were not that interested or because they had other meetings to attend.

The proposed 600 room Jing Jiang Hotel would be the primary focus of my work for two years. The basic 'deal' was that we would provide the concept design in collaboration with a designated engineering firm in Shanghai, purchase and supply all the foreign components for the hotel, train the key hotel staff and provide the foreign component financing, in total about $50,000,000, then. It would be a formidable task.[176]

The US financial institutions were not yet up for Chinese project financing and the UK institutions were 'iffy'. The project looked like a non-starter until Bob Gatje put me in touch with Mario Jossa, the Italian born, American-educated, French architect who ran MBA's Paris office. Mario, a delightful, articulate and thoughtful person, let alone an excellent architect, had developed a broad network of professional friends in construction and project financing during his long career in France.

Mario made a few enquiries on our behalf and suggested several French banks that might be interested in financing a Chinese project including the Banque Worms and Paribas. I discussed this with Cy. It didn't take a lot of persuasion; I was sent off to Paris, with Cy's blessing.

The MBA office on the Boulevard du Montparnasse, near the Port-Royal Metro station was convenient and it had room for a half dozen architects. At the time, apart from Mario, there was only one other architect working there, so there was plenty of room and I had a desk in the front of the office for two years. It was a friendly place with lots of drop-in visitors of various nationalities, some of whom I got to know quite well. Although he wasn't really involved in the Shanghai venture and received no remuneration, Mario took an active interest in the project and he was free with his introductions to contractors and others who might play a role in putting the Jing Jiang project together. Designs for the proposed hotel were produced in New York by Marcello Gatica, a member of MBA's staff and myself. These in turn were taken by me to Paris to develop the hotel budgets.

On some of my Paris visit I sometimes stayed with the Solberts (Darrow and MLSV Trustees) who had a marvellous flat on the Ile Saint Louis's Quai d'Orleans or with Michele and Rosalind Michalles who were now living in Paris in a flat near the Luxembourg Gardens. It is my recollection that I introduced Michele to Mario. That was one of the better outcomes of the Paris period; they became long-term partners and friends. At other times I stayed at the Hotel Lutece or at other small hotels in the vicinity MBA's office. On the couple of occasions when Cy and Clara came to Paris I upgraded to the Plaza Athenee, only as a matter of convenience, of course. Actually, I liked the slightly shabby garret rooms or the small hotels: more romantic.

The next two years (more or less) were, in a word, exciting. Mario's French connections were indeed interested. Mario also introduced me to Francois de Nerciat, a lawyer who had good contacts with a number of bankers. Despite my worry that Francois might be a bit dodgy we became friends. I also stayed with him once or twice and we shared meals and visits to Jazz clubs, the latter mostly at his insistence.

At the Banque Worms we were introduced to Michael de Courcel. Michael came from a distinguished family and was a cousin of Jacques Chirac, soon to be mayor of Paris and later President of the Republic. We became working friends and sometimes sharing meals together. Michael even invited me to dinner in his quite sumptuous flat near the Trocadero. The Banque Worms became sufficiently interested in supporting our efforts and Michael joined us for some of our meetings in Shanghai. Unfortunately Cy and Michael didn't quite hit it off and Michael's interest, and that of the Banque Worms, cooled. DeNerciat then introduced us to Patrick Le Febvre of the Banque de Paris et des Pays-Bas and they took over the financing efforts where Worms left off.

The Jing Jaing project went well and we were able to 'package' the hotel design, financing and procurement. In between working on the hotel we even reached a preliminary agreement to manufacture 'my' sailboats.

Just as everything was going so well and optimism was high the hotel 'stalled'. We were told there was a problem with the site, the current users were refusing to relocate and the authorities (whomever they were) were averse to take action. Then we were told the Chinese Trading Company and the Bank of China that had oversight on the hotel financing said they didn't like the interest rate on the hard currency loan. There was always a palaver about interest rates. In late 1982 the Jing Jiang Group advised us there would be an "indefinite delay". It was all reminiscent of the "Dead Parrot" skit from the Pythons.

As a gesture the Chinese (broadly speaking) gave us the Hua Ting hotel to finance and Eaton apparently received a modest fee. I say "apparently" as I was not involved and do not know one way or the other.

Despite Eaton's 'deals' looking attractive to the Chinese with protocols attesting to that none were closing, for undetermined reasons. Eaton was finding it financially hard going, there was precious little income from any source. Pay-checks and reimbursements were delayed. I undertook to pay Terry for a while but ultimately had to make her redundant. My Eaton short fall exceeded $100,000 ($250,000 today). Valery and I were getting pretty nervous; so was MBA.

The Cuban projects were 'technically' still 'alive' but with no funding we couldn't continue. I understand that Cayo Sabinal is a now nature reserve; I suspect that is how it will stay. The other projects, and more, have been developed and tourism has flourished, except from the US; maybe one day.

Cy's unbridled enthusiasm got him overextended and did him in. He also had some bad luck. The phone between New York and Cleveland fell silent. I could not reach Cy; I was told he was "unavailable". It was not long, however, before I was officially notified that Cy had been declared bankrupt. It was all over. I did not hear from Cy, or even Clara again. It was only years later that I learned that Cy, in addition to bankruptcy, had also suffered a stroke. All of the Eaton projects, of course, terminated, there was no one to take them over. I became a claimant in the bankruptcy but there were no assets: I was on my own and all but insolvent myself.

I looked for gainful employment opportunities: there were some. One came from the Marriot hotel chain. They were looking for someone to lead their hotel design team. After a long day of interviews at their Washington office I had to conclude that the corporate design world was not for me and withdrew. Marriott may have concluded the same but we didn't get that far.

I met with cousin Carl over a sandwich to see if he had any ideas. Carl was now working for J. Rich Steers a heavy engineering/construction company. Carl said his boss, Dick Steers, was tiring of his role as the fourth generation of his family's company. Dick had apparently discussed with Carl the idea that building houses might be an alternative to bridges. Carl, having started out his construction career building houses thought this might be a good idea and he had an good (at least I took it as good) idea of who might be helpful.

In any event within the week, since I didn't have much else to do, I visited with Dick and Carl at Dick's office in 17 Battery Place. His large, old-fashioned office was in a corner of the building and had a stonking 180-degree view over New York's harbour. Dick was a graduate of Princeton, class of '46: that was a good start. He talked of his frustrations and weariness of heavy construction and was wondering what house building might be like as an option. "Maybe we could build some houses together, in Princeton?" was his sort of rhetorical remark towards the end of the meeting. He then suggested that I could have a desk in one of the back offices. He wasn't offering me a job just a friendly gesture towards Carl's cousin. Who knows what might happen?

It seemed like a good idea, to Valery as well. I took up Dick's offer, settled with MBA on friendly terms (under the circumstances), put my paraphernalia in a couple of boxes and moved from Madison Square to Battery Place.

The North Family Forge c. 1972 - even worse ten years later

Jing Jiang discussions - Shanghai - 1980 - to my left is the 'Boss' to my right their architect - others include the interpreter (nearest camera) and various technical specialists

Relaxing with Cy in the Presidential Suite of the Jing Jiang in Shanghai

Cy and Clara with Gongora (on right) and Marketing Director (?) - Varadero, Cuba

The proposal for the Radisson Hotel in Raleigh, NC. It was a little 'simpler' when constructed

Proposed Hotel, Frank Sound, Grand Cayman - not constructed

One of a number of proposals made for hotels in the communist bloc.

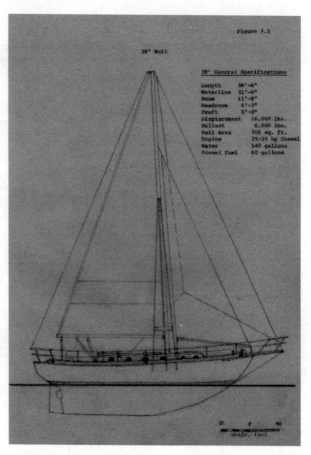

Proposal to Shanghai Investment and Trust Corps to build yachts (Any resemblance to 'Seven Bells' is 'purely coincidental'). Design by Herb David and JB.

14

SPRINGLAND

New York and New Lebanon
1983 - 1990

"It's not only up to you – you need a bit of luck as well."
Anon

*"It was the best of times it was the worst of times ... it was the spring of
hope, it was the winter of despair."*
Charles Dickens

J. Rich Steers, Inc. was a well-established, New York heavy engineering and construction firm. It could trace its lineage back to 1851 when J Rich and George Steers, Dick's great grandfather and great, great uncle, designed the yacht America. The company was responsible for many historic public projects in New York City and the Eastern Seaboard; bridges, piers, a good deal of New York's East River drive and other infrastructure. Under Dick's management it had undertaken the construction of the massive foundations of the Verrazano Narrows Bridge, several contracts for the Washington and Atlanta rapid transit systems and numerous smaller, but still large by any measure, infrastructure projects, mostly in New York.

Steers' principal work in 1983 included contracts for the Atlanta Rapid Transit System, a major pier in the East River and a sanitation facility on the North River (aka the Hudson). Heavy construction of this sort was a tough business. It required extensive capital in equipment and a sophisticated and experienced, engineering staff. It often cost Steers more than $250,000 (in 1983 dollars) to bid on a major project with only a one in three or four chance of obtaining the contract. To be a successful bidder on a large project, a heavy engineering firm, such as Steers, had

281

to come up with an innovative approach that would give them an economic edge, a unique selling point. Steers had that capability. Bidding was never only a matter of assessing the costs and adding a small profit margin. Once a low bid was achieved a contract needed to be negotiated. This meant dealing with hide-bound (and sometimes dodgy) bureaucracies, unions and in some (possibly many) instances other even less savory 'organizations'. When the New York City government tried to get to the bottom of corruption in its construction industry (as it, periodically, does), the city's lawyers called on many of its leading contractors, including Dick to testify. Dick told me that no contractors (certainly not Dick) appeared before the investigation commission. I asked Dick why he didn't testify; he responded, with the slightest of smiles, that he valued his life more. Steers' projects were so complex that almost all ended up in some form of litigation. Prominent on Dick's desk was a thick book entitled, "How to Make Construction Claims" (or something to that effect). Like Eaton's, Dick's business was high-risk.

It was small wonder that Dick, nearing his sixtieth birthday, was looking for less stressful construction opportunities: projects that could use his own engineering and entrepreneurial talents, those of some of his 20 key employees and, as well, his extensive construction equipment, or as they say in the trade, 'iron'; trucks, earth movers, a precast concrete business, tugs, cranes and barges. Was building houses a realistic option?

The first weeks of my desk tenure at 17 Battery Place were uneventful. Part of the understanding with Dick was that he didn't want to get too involved with something new in case a latent Eaton project materialized (though that possibility was in fact not possible, I could not convince Dick) I sat at my desk in the accounting section, had periodic lunches and 'what if' chats with Dick and/or Carl. Carl's role with Steers was that of business procurement and PR. Carl as we all knew had 'connections' and he could talk your socks off, a mixed blessing. I managed to earn a little on some small architectural projects, worked (pro bono) on Darrow matters and worked on the Forge. My finances were dodgy but with Valery's income we managed to keep afloat: just.

During the first months at Steers I got to know Dick's professional staff. Most regarded me with some suspicion, believing that in one way or another I might represent a threat to their job. Their suspicions were justified

During our luncheon conversations, Dick and I had determined that Princeton was the most likely location to for housing prospects and it wasn't long before Dick decided that he and I should take a trip to Princeton. Princeton, the township, was one of the most desirable places to live within commuting distance of New York and it followed that Princeton must have an active, high end, residential market. Dick was an enthusiastic, well connected, 'Princetonian'. Several of Dick's classmates were of some standing in the community: Princeton made sense.

Our first trip was organized around lunch at Princeton's Nassau Club[177] with Reeves Hicks, one of Dick's classmates. Reeves, an intelligent lawyer of local note and friendly personality knew everything you needed to know about real estate in Princeton. I got to know him quite well and liked him. Reeves gave us a generally positive outlook but noted two substantial problems. The first was finding land (affordable or not) and the second was if you did find appropriate land could you get permission to develop? Princeton had a reputation for 'nimbyism' and Princeton's planning board, reflecting this popular political position, could be relied upon to take a negative position on any proposed development. Reeves, however, knew the planning board and thought he could, nevertheless, get approval for a properly planned, 'good' project. Reeves also had a 'handle' on several available properties.

One of the properties, just off Route 206 leading out of Princeton, but still in the Township, had just come on the market. Reeves thought we should have a look. The property belonged to an historic Princeton family named Russell. Its location, just within Princeton Township, near the governor's mansion, was terrific. It was, however, pricey, around $3,000,000, not exactly, in Dick's opinion, 'affordable'.

We looked it over after lunch: a windshield survey. The property itself seemed somewhat nondescript, consisting of about sixty acres (large for Princeton) of deer-infested, mostly scruffy land but, still, it had some good trees and an interesting looking derelict mansion. Even considering some of its shortcomings we thought the site was essentially good. Dick and I tried not to be too enthusiastic. We agreed that we should, at least, explore the site's development potential. Dick was quite excited and so was I. Dick, like Cy, could get pretty enthusiastic (or not), quickly. He asked me to get on with due diligence. This was 'good news'; I had an assignment (more like a mission) and was now gainfully employed – at least for the time being.

I needed planning help - professional non-prejudiced but friendly third party oversight of the property's development potential. Paul Buckhurst and his firm, Buckhurst, Fish, Hutton and Katz, (quite a moniker) had moved from Park Tower's offices and were now, conveniently, located not far from Battery Place. I introduced Paul to Dick, a satisfactory meeting, and we agreed to hire them to give us a first look at the site's potential. I undertook to examine the housing market with the help of Princeton's estate agents. The market analysis was perhaps the easy bit. In 1983 there was a shortage in the Township (thanks, in part due to the aforesaid 'nimbys') of quality, high-end housing. Paul advised that local planning laws permitted one acre zoning 'as of right' but if we designed the development as a 'cluster', providing smaller plots for each house, while providing more contiguous open space within the development, the planning board could grant a higher (not specified) overall density. While there was no precedent for this approach, the three of us (Paul, Dick and I) thought this was a good option. We 'crunched' the numbers. The preliminary results, though probably subjective, were positive; to no one's surprise. It appeared to us that, with some luck and a rising market, a reasonable profit projection might be in the range of $3,000,000 on a project cost (then) of about $30,000.000. This clearly whetted Dick's fiscal appetite. The best results obtainable from a heavy construction project of that magnitude could not match this projection, even taking into consideration that we might be, well, optimistic.

There was of course one very large problem; there usually is at least one - the cost of the land. The lawyers for the Russell estate would not countenance our purchase 'proposal' that we would pay the asking price IF we received planning permission. Their unmovable position was; "…you want the land? "Buy it." – end of message.

It was a seller's market. At a price of $3,000,000 this presented a high risk. With planning permission for the number of houses we wanted to build, at least 60, the site was worth more. Without planning permission the value was considerably less. We worked and reworked the numbers while continuing to try to negotiate a better price and/or conditions of sale. In the end, Eaton-like, Dick took the plunge, raised the funds and bought the land. We were in the 'development business'.

We formed a new company that, at my suggestion, was called 'Springland' the name of the 18th century Baker farmstead near New Brunswick. 'Springland' sounded both gentle (for a developer) and upbeat, plus the name carried a modest historic rationale. As Dick was putting up all the money and taking the BIG risk we agreed that he have 90% of the ownership and I, 10%; fair enough. I was to be President and Dick, Chairman. We agreed my salary, substantial for an architect (even now) and more than what Eaton had paid me; when he had. Dick was unsalaried as he was still running J. Rich Steers. A car was even thrown in. I was pleased and very optimistic, as was Valery. Although patient and supportive during the Eaton saga Valery had had enough of Eaton's mostly forlorn promises and unfounded, as it had turned out, optimism.

Dick and I agreed that Springland would, at least to start, only focus on Princeton. We would use the capabilities of J. Rich Steers in construction, particularly on project infrastructure, but keep our options open on building construction. Dick saw architecture design as a question mark. He agreed that Springland should design 'some' houses but he thought, and I agreed, that sixty or more houses all designed by one architect, me, might be a bit much. We selected two friendly architects (Roe Eliseo and Jerry Ford)[178] to join us in design. With a strong recommendation from Reeves we selected Pete Callaway, the most upmarket Princeton realtor, to market the project. As for planning Dick had come to like Paul Buckhurst and was amenable to Paul's firm continuing as the project planner. We agreed with Paul that we would use the cluster zoning option as the design basis for the project.

We made our first presentation to the Planning Board about two months later. It was a disaster. I cannot remember one person testifying on our behalf. "The project's too dense", "there will be too much traffic", "I've walked my dog there all my life", "it ought to be a park", "Princeton doesn't need more housing for the rich", "what about the deer?" were only some of the negative, or plaintive, comments. We encountered the "I'm on board, pull up the gang plank" brigade. It was, often, the latest incomers to the Princeton community that made the most noise. The planning Board turned us down, unanimously. But, they did say we could make another application in response to the negative comments.

Dick was beside himself: he could make a pretty good show of being 'beside himself'. He could see his investment evaporating before his eyes; heavy construction was looking good again. "Why did I persuade him to get involved?" "Crikey", what else could I say? Fortunately for all our sanities some of the "old guard" in Princeton told us, quietly, (they had not testified for or against us) that they thought we were on the right track; "it is always like this to begin with", they said.

Back to the drawing board: revised plans, detailed traffic studies, more marketing support to establish housing need, detailed conversations on Springland's contributions to improvement of sewers, roads and recreational facilities, (we agreed on two tennis courts) and on and on. Traffic was a big problem. In the end we had to effectively split the site in two to break up the presumed traffic loads, overkill in our opinion: compromise is development's middle name.

We prepared sufficient drawings for our proposed houses to demonstrate our design intent. The architectural proposal was to provide five plans, by the three architects, with the understanding that each could be "adjusted" (within reason) by clients to suit their individual requirements. The clients would pick a site, pick a house type and make such 'adjustments' to the house type as they 'required'. It was sort of a very upscale Bahrain. It was an architecturally labour-intensive approach requiring a full set of drawings for each house, but then, we were in Princeton. By doing this we could imagine a development achieving some sort of balance between uniformity and individuality. It was an unusual approach but one, we thought, both appealing and saleable. It set us apart from other developers, giving us, at least in our opinion, a market edge, an 'unique selling point' over the typical standard plans of the competition.

Our two Princeton based, (more or less) architectural firms, my classmate Jerry and Roe Eliseo, each provided a design. I provided the three other designs; there had to be some point (fun) to being the developer! Not to put too fine a point on it, my approach was eclectic. My design recipes were in parts derivative of Porchuck Road, a few McKim Mead and White houses (perhaps Grandfather's porch?) a bit of Lutyens, with a dash of 'new'. We avoided the developer's tendency to name the designs and called each simply A, B, C, D and E. The Planning Board liked the concept.

For our second presentation we hired good graphic designers and Pete Callaway's slightly 'above it' real estate firm was on board to add a certain, local, cachet. We had the best local site engineers, the best energy consultants (my former partner Alex Grinnell now of Steven Winter Associates[179]), and the best environmental engineers. We had, in fact, sixteen, excellent, if expensive, consultants; Dick was not exactly happy with the expense but there was a lot at stake and he concurred with a 'full on' approach. We talked to community shakers and movers and slowly gained their support. The area would be developed sooner or later and perhaps we were seen as the best of a generally bad lot! We called the project, 'Russell Estates'. Though developers, including us, tend to name their projects after what is no longer there, I think that the name went down well in the community. We covered all the bases (and then some) and made a revised, 'classy' submission.

By comparison to the first, the presentation went well. There were still the usual objections that we had heard the first time but we were better prepared and had reasonable rebuttals for all of them. Traffic and sewer issues remained but we could see approval was only a matter of time and some further compromise. It was frustrating to Dick, to be sure, but he was feeling better. We worked with the Township and Borough Engineers and found acceptable solutions to their remaining objections. There were several, more amenable, hearings and we made progress. Objectors and objections fell away or were, at least, neutralized.

We started planning the next steps, the construction of a model home. Dick wasn't too big on this because of the cost but Pete Callaway convinced him that we couldn't sell anything unless we showed potential clients the quality of our product; it made sense. We agreed to build the most conservative of the five designs submitted to the Planning Board, a sort of 'Georgian' brick pastiche (my design) that we thought would provide a non-controversial start to Russell Estates.

Arthur, aka 'Artie', Spanarkel our treasurer and Dick's former senior accountant helped persuade the Nassau Savings and Loan Association to provide construction funding. Artie was Springland's 'Mr. Fixit'; he was as adept in obtaining the best price for tires as he was in creating a 'good-looking' balance sheet. He also had a finely tuned sardonic sense of humour which could come in handy. Having funding in place for such a large project was a necessary part of the overall presentation to the Planning Board. A 'smoke and mirrors' approach to development was unacceptable in Princeton, quite right too.

In late August 1984 we made the final presentation to the Planning Board and on the 10th of September received approval, with expensive but acceptable conditions. Valery marked the occasion by giving me an appropriately engraved silver letter opener from Tiffany. I still use it.

With all the Planning Board's requirements the development costs were now greater than we had initially thought. However, the increase in potential sales revenue from escalating house prices and the cluster zoning bonus, perhaps eight houses, kept the overall projected profit target in balance. We started construction.

Dick got into the first phase of construction with enthusiasm. Site infrastructure, clearing, building roads, installing sewers, drainage, gas and power distribution networks was his 'thing'. Dick provided heavy trucks, a bulldozer and a backhoe from his New Jersey yard. He liked to put his 'iron' to work and particularly enjoyed charging its cost to the project. We appointed one of Dick's site superintendents, Marty Stachowski as our field superintendent for infrastructure. Marty would also be responsible for constructing foundations for the houses. He was tough and he was good, even if he wasn't much of an administrator. He kept all his receipts, (there were hundreds each month), in a large cardboard filing box. At the end of each month Artie had to sort them out, it was sort of a giant raffle draw. Artie wasn't too pleased but that was the price to pay for Marty's otherwise exemplary performance.

When the site infrastructure work was well under way Dick, cousin Carl, Artie and I conferred on how we were going to actually build the houses. There were few good contractors around, or available, and those that were, were expensive. We decided that we could, and probably had to, do it ourselves otherwise the estimated profit would just be passed to a third party builder. We recognized, too, even if we were to do our own construction, that getting good house framers and carpenters, in the construction-active Princeton area market would be difficult. We agreed that we should look into prefabricating the house structures. We gave Carl the assignment to look into this and he came up with a good timber-frame fabricator, Snavely, a long-established lumber and timber-building fabricator from Lancaster, Pennsylvania.

When Pete Callaway heard we were going to fabricate the structures off site he threatened to quit. He claimed his clients would not buy a 'prefabricated' building even if the prefabricated components were only the shell. He, like many others, incorrectly harboured the idea that prefabrication was 'cheap', and poor quality. To the contrary, in good hands it was the best possible, quality solution in that market place. Callaway and Springland 'compromised' over the prefabrication - if you call bringing in the manufactured panels under the cover of early morning darkness a compromise.

We now needed a good project manager. I suggested an ex-student, Jim Banks, a Glasgow-educated, detailed minded (even perhaps a bit 'anal') 'Brit' who had been in my graduate management class at City College. Dick liked him and he was hired. We hired an unpretentious, even-tempered architect (a rara avis), Eric Hoskinson, to lead the architectural side of the business (under my direction, of course!). The architectural staff would in time expand to more than a dozen very capable architects and designers. Various sub-contractors and individual workmen were employed for the site infrastructure. We still needed a good carpenter crew for frame erection and finish work. Jim Banks found the right hands-on carpenter/construction manager, Bill Harley, who at the time was working for a competing developer. We 'enticed' him to join our team. He stayed with us for almost six years. By October we had a management staff of ten and a twenty-person construction team. Springland was 'in business', a design-builder as well as a developer.

Harley had the first prefabricated frame for the model house erected in less than a week. Structural frame erection in three of four days became the norm for the project. The general public seemed serenely unaware of how we were building the houses. In due course, however, Callaway and potential clients recognized the quality of off-site manufacturing. A year or so into the project, when Snavely's plant went on strike, our clients refused to accept on-site 'stick' framing and waited for the strike to be settled.

We were about halfway complete on the model house when Callaway suggested that we should actually have two 'model' houses. He thought that while the conservative one was fine, a lot of his potential clients would want something a little more exciting. He was correct. Dick agreed, but not without appropriate grumbling and moaning. We decided on the so-called 'A' model constructing it adjacent to route 207, on one of the least attractive sites. House 'A' was a lot different, a Baker design that included big spaces and an open-ended plan with many variations.

Along the way while the two houses were still under construction, Callaway asked how we were going to 'decorate' them. We had not thought much about it but pretty quickly came up with an economical proposal; I would do it, 'with a little help from my friends', including Valery. I thought that the first house, the conservative one should look as if it had been furnished with 'Aunt Emma's' hand-me-downs, that is good quality furnishings though a little worn, 'shabby chic'. This seemed, at least to me, to be the Princeton upmarket style, at least then. The 'A' house would be a bit more modern. The only realistic place to find these kinds of furnishings was, in my opinion, the UK. I suggested that Valery and I go on a buying trip to London.

Dick thought I was kidding, if not unhinged. However, when Callaway backed the idea and Dick saw that the pound to dollar ratio was quite favourable he agreed: a bit reluctantly. We settled on a budget and Valery and I were off.

It was a grand and successful trip. There existed at the time a company called 'Passport' set up just for people like us. A 'Passport' agent met us in London, took us around to antique shops in London and the Home Counties. When we agreed on a purchase. 'Passport' would pay for it, arrange the pickup, consolidate the current purchase with previous ones and arrange the transport to Princeton. The pound was worth about $1.25, the purchase prices fair and Passport fees reasonable. It was altogether a good deal. Passport may have made a little money 'on the side' but the furnishings were still good value.

One of our first stops was an antique store in Woodstock an Oxfordshire market town and site of Blenheim Palace. Valery and I were attracted to one shop by a 19th century burled walnut music room grand piano in its window. We thought it would look good in the conservative living room of the 'C' house. The owner apologized telling us that the piano, having rather worn, wooden pins, was almost impossible to tune. He rather discouraged our purchase. At a negotiated price of about £1,000 we were not concerned. Though puzzled by this purchase he cheered up and asked, "Would you like another? I've just received one that's all in pieces in the back room. I know it will go together, because we took it apart. I could let you have it for the same price, and it will save me from having to put it together!" We went into a storage room and pealed back some of the piano's wrappings. The rosewood case was handsome, from what we could see of it and we thought it would be just right for the living room in House 'A' and no one had to play it. We agreed to his offer and added it to our growing collection. Apart from these pianos we acquired dining tables, chairs, pictures, carpets, sofas and designer artifacts, nearly two containers full of 'stuff'. The buying trip ended in Paris where we obtaining some 'bargain' paintings from the attic of one of Valery's cousins who owned an art gallery. We finished the trip by visiting Venice and then Marty in her new home near Agazzano. (I think Marty's actual town, more 'hamlet', may have been Pecorara consisting of a petrol pump and small trattoria cum mini food store.)

Marty had settled in a little 'farmlet' on the edge of a rather large tomato farm, typical of the area. She was now living with a 'partner'; Ephesio. A former test driver for Fiat, Ephesio seemed a little dodgy but he was pleasant and he and Marty seemed to get along well enough. The 'farmlet' was without running water or electrics: fortunately, though, there was a well, and buckets. Hand washing was done in the house but showers had to be taken outside, behind the house, using multiple buckets, essentially a two person operation. Fortunately it was September and still quite warm. Electricity was provided, on an as needed basis, by a petrol generator: sufficient for a few low-wattage lights. Marty usually turned it on every evening at dinnertime. Candles were 'de rigueur' in the bedrooms. Despite these shortcomings the 'farmlet' was almost charming. It was certainly even 'great' as far the twenty or so dogs were concerned. They could run around and bark their heads off and no one cared, except perhaps the inhabitants of Marty's house. There were several outbuildings, rough structures, once used for storage. Marty enthused over one that she thought Valery and I should renovate as an Italian pied-a-terre. We thought, "maybe not" but we played along. In the few days we were there we kept busy helping Marty to get settled: cleaning, painting and moving furniture around. We also participated with all the neighbours in a two day, rather gruelling tomato harvest and enjoyed the festive bacchanalian harvest-dinner afterwards.

Marty liked Valery so there were no conflicts: we had a good time, probably the best visit ever. Sadly, David was still missing: he did not come up as topic of conversation.

* * * * *

The two containers of furnishings followed soon after our return to New York. We furnished the first model houses and almost immediately received positive responses, but not necessarily the ones we wanted. One response went something like this; "…we like the house, very nice, but it's a little conventional for us. But, by the way, would you sell us the furniture?" At least we knew how to decorate! Meanwhile the construction of house 'A' moved along we hoped that it would be more appealing. We furnished it with an Anglo-American touch. When the house was opened in early December we decided, after a few grumbles from Dick, that it was time to have an official opening for Russell Estates. We decided on a Christmas party to be held in the just-finished 'A' house.

Steve Howard, (the former Darrow teacher and trustee) was now head of the American Boychoir School in Princeton[180]. He agreed to provide some vocal yuletide entertainment with one proviso. His music director, James Litton might want his own piano. By now the mysterious rosewood piano, from the back room in Woodstock, had been assembled in the living room and tuned. It seemed to produce the right notes (at least to me) it was after all a Bosendorfer. In view of this I suggested to Steve that perhaps their own piano tuner (who was also the University's) might retune it and give Steve (and Litton), the nod; or not. I didn't look forward to telling Dick we might have to replace the piano for the evening if we wanted the Boychoir. The piano was duly retuned. Fortunately the University's tuner said that the piano was <u>very</u> good. He even took serial numbers off the piano and told me he would let me know what he found out about its provenance. Steve was given the nod (apparently good enough for Litton), the piano had 'passed muster'.

The night arrived; the Boychoir was appropriately arranged around the piano, the guests, lots of them, happy with a drink or two, filled the house. I made a brief welcoming speech (thanking everyone for their support during the planning process! I think it sounded sincere) and introduced the choir. Litton started to play. He stopped, looked down at the piano with a thoughtful face, then looked up and around to the now curious and silent audience - I thought, "this is it; he's going to walk out." He addressed the guests (a pretty sophisticated University-based crowd) and said, "I stopped because I want you to listen to this piano, it is one of the best sounding piano that I have played!" He played on a bit, solo, before he brought the choir back in. Whew! Dick gave me what I took to be a rare smile of modest pleasure or relief.

The party was a success, so was house 'A'. House 'A', in fact, became our biggest seller, so much so that about halfway through the project we agreed not to build anymore (despite the variations) lest Russell Estates take on too much uniformity. By the time we made that decision I think we were, already, on to house type 'H'.

Some weeks later the University's piano tuner called me. He told me that our piano was a mid-nineteenth century piano with a pedigree and was valuable. He believed it had belonged, at some point, or at least played on by Liszt (or maybe it was Schumann or Brahms, I do not remember). Dick didn't care he was just thrilled to learn it was valuable. We sold it soon after to a collector for a sum exceeding the cost of all the furnishings, transportation, duties and other expenses that Valery and I had incurred on our trip, and, we still had all the furnishings! You get lucky sometimes. Russell Estates was also off to a good start and sales were strong.

* * * * *

Weekdays were spent between our office at Battery Place and the Princeton site. Running a project of the size and complexity of Russell Estates was time consuming and would remain so until the last house was sold. Weekends however, were another matter. Valery and I would usually leave for the Forge early Friday afternoon, getting there in time to have super at the eponymous 'Lenny's', in the valley. Lenny was an escapee from Brooklyn who had given up his business there (a butcher I think, though something nags at me that he may have had a shoe business, hopefully not at the same time) and had moved to New Lebanon. He had taken over the town's late nineteenth century schoolhouse and had turned it into everyone's favourite local restaurant, good, basic food with an Italian edge. Eating there was a social as well as a modest culinary occasion. It was here the weekenders and locals met to catch-up: you could be entertained too. Later on in the evenings, after the dining crowd was thinning out, Lenny would take to his old upright piano and accompany himself in his favourite operatic arias. Nessun Dorma was his most popular; he had a very good tenor voice and I can hear him now. The Niemands, Arno and Brenda, often met us there, more by custom than plan. Arno and Brenda, who had been an editor with American Heritage, were our best local friends and we saw a lot of each other. Arno had a business in New York manufacturing cardboard mailing tubes and high quality boxes for perfume. Arno and Brenda had remodelled a late-Victorian house on West Street in New Lebanon into a very comfortable, handsome, weekend retreat. In time it became their principal home. Arno had become a trustee at Darrow during David Miller's administration, which was how we met. Arno was my favourite trustee. We sat together in meetings and often entertained each other with sotto voce wisecracks.

Both Brenda and Arno also became trustees of Mount Lebanon Shaker Village when that was founded and they were great supporters of that 'institution', in fact, during my tenure as President and Chairman of the 'Village' they were my 'mainstay'.

The 'Village', in fact, was doing quite well. We became 'legitimate', that is to say chartered by the New York State Regents and we earned charitable (tax exempt) status by becoming a 501C3 organization with help from our admirable lawyer and trustee, Peter Solbert. The board met frequently in the Forge and we attracted some interesting members. In addition to those already noted we added John Castellani, a Darrow graduate and former Executive Director of Mount Vernon and Cheryl Bell, a banking executive. We raised sufficient funds to hire part time directors. First it was John Castellani, then June Sprigg, of Hancock Shaker Village, and finally Andy Vadnais who split his time between the Village and his role as a Darrow history teacher. With the help of Joe Bruno[181] our State Senator of long standing and a parent of a Darrow graduate we raised money every year (almost) to repair North Family buildings. The great stone barn was stabilized with the assistance of a colourful local engineer (a collector of old construction equipment), Bill Craib[182]. The Wash House foundations were improved and the building was opened as a visitor's centre. The carriage shed was stabilized, Tim Rieman, the outstanding maker of Shaker furniture, improved the Granary for his shop (with our help) and the agricultural shed was renovated with funds from Joan Davidson and the Kaplan Foundation. (Joan was a good friend of Mary Black and lived near Annandale. I had met her some years before through the Shafer's.) We opened the North Family site to visitors during the summer with the help of local volunteers as guides. Our local directors, Lore Squier, Brenda and Arno pitched in too. We developed a site guide and good graphics. Charles Flint undertook to write and publish, on behalf of the Village, the seminal catalogue on the Darrow collection of Shaker furniture. The Village was an active, vibrant entity in the eighties and more was to come.

However, not everyone was happy. As the Village grew and achieved a certain 'status' with its modest accomplishments, some on the Darrow Board saw this as some sort of undefined 'threat'. Darrow was struggling with its debt, low enrolment and a slightly 'tarnished' image of a school that was seen by many as a 'used to be good' school. Neither the money the Village raised, nor the energies expended by its directors benefited Darrow, directly. Some Darrow Trustees and administration saw the Village 'success' as being on the 'back' of Darrow. "Darrow owns the buildings not the Village" (true) was a barely suppressed murmur.

Jerral Miles formerly head of the Potomac School had replaced David Miller as Headmaster in 1984. Jerral was upbeat about the Village. He saw the long-term potential benefit to Darrow, as in fact had David Miller. Jerral and I spent time thinking of ways in which the relationship between the school and the Village could be improved and become more, let's say, 'obviously' mutually beneficial.

Darrow's listing as a National Historic Site and its ownership and use of its Shaker buildings was, as was often repeated, an appealing asset for the school. However, Darrow's ownership was also a liability, there were simply too many buildings to maintain. The concept of a working relationship between the Village, a 'public' organization, that could access public funding and provide public access, and Darrow, a 'private' organization, was seen by some of Darrow's constituency as a 'problem', but by others as an 'opportunity'.

By the late 1980s Darrow's standing debt had grown to a million dollars, more or less. The money was owed to two Albany banks that had provided the school with mortgages secured by the assessed value of its buildings and land. The borrowed money had and was being used to meet annual operating shortfalls. However, the cost of servicing this debt ensured that year on year Darrow could not balance its budget and had to borrow yet more money. The Darrow board began to consider the possibility of having to close. A closure would of course, co-incidentally, in the opinion of New York Sate's department of Parks and Recreation put the entire Mount Lebanon historic site 'at risk'.

Jerral and I explored the possibility of the Shaker Museum and Library buying the North Family and merging with the Village. The museum's extensive Shaker collection consisted to a large extent of artifacts from Mount Lebanon. The trip hammer from the Forge, just as an example, was on exhibit there. All the exhibits were, however, exhibited in non-Shaker farm buildings. The concept of the museum with its extensive, unique, collection of Mount Lebanon objects moving to Mount Lebanon seemed an obvious 'fit' to all concerned.

I met with the Shaker Museum Board in Chatham and explored this possibility. Though there was definite interest, the majority of the Chatham Museum's Board were still emotionally and intellectually tied to their 'historic' and 'off the beaten track' Chatham site. The proposal was seen as premature. We looked for another option and I had the germ of one, derived from the Forge experience.

Suppose the Village owned all the buildings and provided long-term leases for those buildings that Darrow needed? I met with John Middlebrooks of the New York State Parks Department to essay the idea. The North Family would become the core of the 'public Shaker Village'. The concept was bold, if not brazen. The Village was a very young organization but it had a good board and it had demonstrated a certain ability to raise funds, open the site to the public and repair and renovate buildings[183]. The idea got John's attention. He tried it out on his superiors and came back with a preliminary, but positive response. The idea fit in with the aims of the then Environmental Quality Bond Act (EQBA) that provided federal funds for a wide range of environmental projects including historic preservation.

John, Jerral, (as well as others) and I met a number of times, often on the back deck of the Forge, to discuss and shape what would in time become a formal proposal to the State under using the provisions of the EQBA. The concept was simple, at least in principle. $2,000.000, the assessed value of the buildings and land, would be paid to Darrow for the purchase. The money would come from a $1,000,000 EQBA grant and $1,000,000 from matching funds (an EQBA requirement) raised the by the Village less, perhaps, the prepayment of the value of Darrow's long-term lease.

The transaction, if consummated, would mean that Darrow would be subject to a number of physical controls over the buildings owned by the Village but leased-back to Darrow. The Darrow Board's fear that the 'upstart' Village would in fact control the site was anathema to some Board members as well as some in the school's administration, perhaps understandably. The two million cash injection would, however, go a long way to keep Darrow operating, a matter that by 1990 was becoming moot[184].

The Darrow Board debated the proposal and, with some misgivings, such as, the very reasonable question, "can the Village raise $1,000,000", agreed to proceed.

The Village board also agreed, with its own, similar, concerns about raising the required funds. It was, however, worth a try. The responsibilities to which the Village would be committing were substantial. With the help of John Middlebrooks and the Village staff, Andy Vadnais and Rich Chafka, we finished the proposal and made the application for a grant of $1,000,000 to the State Parks Department. We would now have to wait while the proposal went through the necessary State and Federal bureaucratic processes. In the meantime we started exploring our own possibilities of raising the $1,000,000.

* * * * *

With the activities of the Village taking time, weekends at the Forge became long-weekends and then short weeks in New York. Russell Estates was now ticking over nicely without any daily involvement from me. Dick had become, for all practical purposes, the managing partner for the project, he enjoyed that. Being less involved with the daily events in Princeton, I soon became interested, though I cannot specifically remember why, perhaps because I wanted an excuse to stay upstate, in local development opportunities in the Berkshires. In 1984-1987 the Berkshire market in second homes, mostly condominiums, was, at least by Berkshire standards, buoyant.

The Springland staff, now some twenty professionals strong, was not overworked and there was sufficient management availability to take on another project. One conversation with Dick led to another and soon he and I were examining an attractive, forty some odd acre, tract of land overlooking Richmond Pond in Pittsfield. Known as the Scace farm, it was being marketed by Pierre Joseph, a local Lebanese émigré. Pierre imaginatively combined real estate opportunities with his liquor store on Route 20 just a few hundred yards west of Hancock Shaker Village. Valery and I frequented the store, in part because Pierre sold a wine that came in nice wooden boxes in which Forge workshop 'stuff' could be stored: the wine was ok too. Pierre, slight in stature, likeable, even a jolly fellow, was a bit of a 'wheeler-dealer', maybe skip the 'a bit'. While he tried to take on some local bucolic colouration, his heart, mind and manner seemed not far from the souk: my London friends would have called him, a 'wide boy'. Dick and I, nevertheless, rather liked him. Pierre did have his contacts, humour and his wine selections and prices were competitive.

With the help of Kim Burbank a Darrow trustee who had become my lawyer (and friend) we negotiated a fair price for the Scace farm; subject this time to planning approval. We hired Paul Buckhurst, again, for planning. I would do the architecture, no surprise there. Kim was well connected in Pittsfield.[185] He would guide us through the planning process.

Our initial proposal was for a development of about ninety condominiums designed in a New England (with Shaker overtones) style. If we had thought the opposition in Princeton was bad we were taken aback by the ferocity of the 'antis' in Pittsfield. Every neighbour and neighbour's neighbour was a 'nimby'. The local girl-scout troupe owned land adjoining the property on the south boundary. They led the charge against us. At the first hearing in the Pittsfield town hall we were ambushed by the whole troupe of some twenty-odd, uniformed young girl scouts arranged in order of size and age. Their negative testimony started with the youngest. The nub of their testimony and that of all the other objectors was that they all liked the farm the way it was and thought any development would be environmentally detrimental and 'damage' their campsite. If I recall correctly the only testimony on our behalf was from Pierre. He thought the proposal was "great" - I think his testimony was the final nail in the presentation coffin.

The Eagle, (the excellent Pittsfield paper), the next day carried headlines on the first page of its second section describing how the girl scouts sank Springland's proposal. Dick was not happy and wondered why I had decided to build in Pittsfield: I wondered too.

As in the first presentation in Princeton we were invited to re-present our proposal taking into consideration the objections. There was no way we could easily rebut the main objection, essentially for us to 'get lost'. We just had to quietly

300

present our best case. I proceeded to meet with the neighbours, Kim worked with the town council, I'm not sure what Pierre did but he claimed to work 'behind the scenes'. Paul Buckhurst prepared revised presentation documents with a lower project density and a wider 'no build' area on the Girl Scout's boundary. We also agreed to extend the local sewer and water lines - at our expense.

At the second presentation we were still turned down but the board was now divided and the vote split. We received support on our environmental, architectural and macro-project economics. Meanwhile an adjacent property came up for sale, part swamp and part good dry high land. I told Dick we should buy it, quick. "Why?" he asked, rather petulantly. "Because we are going to give the swamp to the girl scouts as a nature reserve and sell the high ground", I replied.

The negotiation with the girl scouts was low-keyed, delicate and successful. At the final hearing the girl scouts even testified on our behalf. We received unanimous approval for what we now called South Pond Farm: as noted before, historical names, are always good. The <u>Eagle</u> wrote a short, complimentary editorial on our behalf. It was quite a turn-around.

With Artie's continuing magic persuasive accounting skills we obtained a construction loan from the First Agricultural Bank. The introduction to the bank had been made through the late Tom Plunkett a long term Darrow trustee, local person of note and an officer of the bank.

We started construction quickly using two local firms, Petricca for infrastructure and Louis Allegrone for construction. We agreed with Pierre that he could market the property. Two of the three decisions turned out to be serious mistakes. First, Allegrone, a good, high quality contractor, wanted (or 'required') more money to build one of our units than for what we could sell it. Second, we soon found that Pierre was not up to marketing and selling what, for Pittsfield, were high-end properties. His sales objective was to negotiate a low buyers-price, thus creating a sale at any cost (to us). His clients were also, not exactly, up-market. His market strategy was Pierre wins Springland loses: not good. We dismissed both Allegrone and Pierre. Allegrone, understood and was pragmatic about the decision.

Pierre, however, was apoplectic. He sued us for breach of contract and we had to settle with him. Dick was not happy. We did stop buying wine from him: that was the only legal revenge we could think of.

Andrea Sciolla our excellent, tough, director of marketing for Princeton now relocated to Pittsfield to lead our marketing and sales program. She and I oversaw the "merchandizing" of the model unit. The furnishings consisted of some contributions from the Forge, Shaker reproduction furniture made by Tim Rieman and odd pieces, including paintings, from the Caropresso auction house in Lee. The model house was quite elegant and was featured in a national magazine.

Jim Steers (Dick's son) joined Springland, moved to Pittsfield and became South Pond's project manager. With Alex Grinnell's help I located Leonard Cowan and he also relocated to Pittsfield to join us as our builder. We hired Louise MacDonald wife of Darrow's business manager as a sales person. We had a very good South Pond Farm 'team'. Sales increased and we started to 'look' to a profit.

By 1986 Princeton was in its final stages and South Pond Farm was 'looking' successful. Kim now introduced me to Brian Fairbank. Brian was chief executive and co-owner of Jiminy Peak the ski resort in Hancock, Massachusetts, about a ten-minute drive from the Forge. Brian was just beginning a condominium development of his own. For a number of reasons, mostly location and a different client profile, Brian's proposed development was not in direct competition with South Pond Farm. Kim, who was also Jiminy's lawyer, thought we could help. It can be very 'friendly' in the Berkshires.

We met with Brian and got on well. Brian liked our designs for South Pond and liked the idea that I was (more or less) local. Dick came up to visit with Brian and they too got on well. Within a month or so we had agreed a partnership with Jiminy Peak. Springland would manage and construct the new condominium project and share in the development profits (or losses). Jiminy would market the project. The project would be called Mountainside. Subject to planning it would consist of about a hundred, single family, stand-alone, 'high end', condominiums.

At the same time we were designated by Pittsfield to be the developer of a downtown office building, the so-called "Parcel 3" project. Meanwhile there were continuing commitments to MLSV, Darrow, City College, the American Arbitration Association and Barnard School in New York where I was also a trustee. It was, perhaps obviously, a bit too much. The commitments if they were to be met, didn't leave much time for what might be a 'normal' life. Weekends were spent catching up on work, working on Mount Lebanon and Darrow and working on the Forge. Valery was now very busy, herself, gainfully employed as Deputy Commissioner of Buildings for Manhattan, quite a plumb job. Despite the pressures Valery and I enjoyed our life together. Then the elephant in the room trumpeted.

In 1986 Valery and I had been together for ten years. We got on well and enjoyed being and working together. There were few arguments: in fact I cannot remember any. But, there was an elephant in the room. It made itself known one evening when Valery told me she wanted to have a child: now. It was a non-debatable statement, not a suggestion. It should not have surprised me but nevertheless it did, at least in its timing. My panicky and negative reaction was inappropriate and unfortunate, to say the least. I do not recall exactly what I said but whatever I said was not well received. Valery and I were at an immediate impasse. The impasse was both obvious and catastrophic for our relationship. To make matters worse we were by any other measure still 'in love'. The movie "It's Complicated" comes to mind, not because its plot was similar but simply because the matter was complicated. The impasse was so bad that within a very short time Valery had moved out, (not on my account), renting a small apartment on 68th street, just off Third Avenue. Despite this we kept in close touch and after a short time met each other for dinner or an event, it was a strange time. We, easily agreed to meet with a thoughtful psychologist, Fredda Bruckner, who had been recommended to us, I believe, by Dr. Willkie. After the first meeting Fredda announced that the matter was indeed, "complicated". Fredda postulated that the 'matter' had as much to do with age, Valery was now 32 and I 53 and the changing relationship from inequality to equality, as it had to do with children. In addition to our joint, frequent and emotional visits with Fredda I also saw Dr. Willkie: again. I think his opinion was much the same as Fredda's but then I never quite knew what Willkie thought, about anything.

It was a difficult, emotional and drawn-out saga. There were times when it seemed Valery and I would get together again (I having, in due course, agreed to a child) and times when getting together seemed only a remote possibility. I am not sure what the children thought about the saga, perhaps that would classify as another elephant. They kept their own counsel. There appeared (to me anyway) to be some support for my initial 'position', I wasn't the children's best concept for a father (a fifth child, "no way!" was all but a slogan.) but also for Valery's desires. The children liked Valery and liked us together. They were upset. The 'impasse' would last nearly ten years and it would negatively affect any well-meaning, nascent relationships during that time: another story and certainly a digression.

In the meantime my work and commitments, (as noted, there were plenty), were my principal solace and distraction: that and finishing the renovation of the Forge with the help of Terry Lamphere, a local stone mason/builder and a hundred thousand dollar lmortgage from the Troy Savings Bank.

By mid 1987 Russell Estates was all but complete and it was turning out to be as profitable as predicted. We were three quarters through South Pond Farm and 'cautiously optimistic' on its financial outcome. Jiminy Peak was progressing nicely. In addition to these projects Joe Bruno, had cornered me, actually we were sitting shoulder to shoulder in the chancel of the chapel – (he was the commencement speaker) at Darrow's graduation. I was representing the trustees. He told me, sotto voce, that he owned a property near his house in Brunswick (near Albany) and wondered if we would like to look at it. Joe gave an impression 'that one hand washed the other', if he was helping us with Mount Lebanon (he was) perhaps we could help him. There was no 'quid pro quo', just a "could you…" – fair enough. I agreed with Joe that we would take a look at the property. Dick came up to meet Joe and take a look for himself. The site, of about twenty acres, near Joe's own house, was a rather barren high field with good views and a lower portion of similar size. Not bad, not great, but the price was right, nothing, until houses were sold. Dick and Joe got along. I, too, got along well with Joe in a sort of formal way: though we would never be 'drinking buddies'. Before we even knew it (so to speak) Springland was building the first phase of 'Windfield Estates'. Joe and I met from time to time to discuss our various mutual interests. On several occasions Joe tried to get us involved in other projects but we resisted the temptation. He continued to be supportive of the Village work and endorsed its various application(s) for appropriate State funding for restoration. Joe was a consummate, colourful, Republican politician of the right though he tolerated my more liberal views, I was a registered Democrat. He became majority leader of the New York Senate but ran into trouble later in his career when he was indicted for 'fraud' (not, thank you, related to Darrow, Mount Lebanon or Springland). He was, eventually, cleared of all charges. He is now retired.

Meanwhile, back in Princeton Jim Banks was getting nervous that he might be out of a job when Russell Estates finished. On the basis of our success with Russell Estates, Jim set about lobbying Dick to start two new projects in Princeton. I was not enthusiastic about this, mostly an intuitive feeling but also because the sites proposed by Jim were second rate. My arguments were compromised by the amount of work that we, (mostly me to be truthful) had developed in the Berkshire area. We even had renovated part of the Brethren's workshop just behind the Forge to use as our local Berkshire office. I lost the argument. So in mid 1987 we now had two more projects, Willow Creek and Blackwell Farm. Our work was well managed by a capable staff of now about fifty good professionals and other construction and administrative staff. From a personal viewpoint I was, yet again, overcommitted: on all fronts.

* * * * *

Monday the 19th of October 1987 was a pleasant, warm Indian summer day, the height of the leaf season in the Berkshires. I was in New York; it was one of my days to lecture at City College. As I drove up to the 138th street campus I listened to the five o'clock news. The main and almost only item was the fall of the value of the New York Stock Market. It had 'crashed', losing over 22% of its value. The event was to be called "Black Monday" and it was the beginning of the end of a buoyant US housing market: full stop. That certainly included Princeton and the Berkshires and it was consequently the beginning of the end for Springland. On that sunny October day the luck part of our work had run out.

Sales at our properties didn't stop on Tuesday but they did slow: almost immediately. It would be two years before they came, maybe not to a halt but certainly to a trickle. The sales situation was not sustainable for Springland. As sales fell off we stopped building on 'spec' and although there were still units under construction we no longer required our large staff and needed to reduce our overhead, quickly. Making some (and eventually all) fifty employees, including Dick and myself, redundant wasn't pleasant. One of the first redundancies was cousin Carl. Dick decided that Carl's services were unnecessary, a correct assumption, and he let him go[186]. Carl thought, that it was my personal decision and he chose not to speak to me again: he didn't.

* * * * *

1987 continued to be an ill-fated year. On Friday November 6th I received an unexpected telegram[187] from Caesare (I had not seen or heard from or about him for more than ten years) saying that Marty was ill and could I come to see her. (Ephesio was gone, apparently, he was in jail, I never knew the details.) The telegram had been sent to an unknown address in New Jersey but, somehow, after a delay of two or three days, Western Union had found me. I made the necessary arrangements, telegraphed my intentions to Caesare and Marty and on Monday flew to Milan (this time I had a passport) to see Marty.

Caesare, accompanied by David, met me. I could see from their faces that there was a problem. Marty was dead. She died the day that Caesare 'mis-directed' the telegram. Not only was Marty dead Caesare had arranged for her cremation and had already, interred Marty's ashes in the local cemetery: the cement was barely dry. I do not recall any discussion of a funeral ceremony. Caesare was not the next of kin or Marty's executor and was certainly not legally qualified to make these decisions, but, after all, it was Italy. The circumstances surrounding Marty's death were not clear then and still are not. Valery, earlier in the year had visited Marty, while on a European holiday to as she said, "clear her head". She had reported that Marty did not look well but there was no mention of any specific illness or crisis. (Valery had also told me that Caesare and David had recently shown up, after eleven years absence. Since I had not heard from Marty following Valery's visit I assumed that all was well or at the very least not urgent.) I asked Caesare for Marty's death certificate. He demurred and it took some serious urging for Caesare to accompany me to the appropriate authorities. According to the paperwork, as it was explained to me by a fractious bureaucrat, Marty had died from a stomach/intestinal 'problem', possibly cancer. Had she been to a doctor? Not as far as I could ascertain. But then Marty wasn't that keen on doctors so that may not have been unusual. Had Marty been poisoned, possibly from her well which would have been subject to contamination from the neighbouring farm? Did she have, in fact, some form of undiagnosed cancer? There was no record of cancer in the family nor had Marty, for many years, been a smoker. Why was her death so sudden? The events seemed a bit dodgy then and still do. Under the circumstances, however, there was no way to find out. It was a sad and inconclusive end to a sibling relationship of strong and, often, mixed feelings. At least my last visit with Marty had been upbeat. Marty was only days short of her 59th birthday.

Caesare and Marty had not married. Because of that Marty was concerned that David might, in Italian law, be disinherited. Marty had received, on several occasions, my assurances that I would see that David received whatever was his due as if she and Caesare had been married. To this end I brought David back to the States. He stayed with me for a number of weeks, first in New York and later in New Lebanon. During the visit Marty's assets were appropriately and legally transferred to him. As David was still a minor (just) Caesare came over to actually take the funds in hand. When the transfers were complete, including a 'payment' to me, Caesare and David returned to Italy. I never heard from either of them again [188]. Perhaps I should have done more but what and could I have?

* * * * *

By 1990 Springland had ceased trading and the office at 17 Battery Place was shut. Russell Estates was complete and profitable though those profits would be consumed during the closing down period. At South Pond Farm there were only a few units left to build and the owners' association bought out the development rights from the First Agricultural Bank who had taken the property as security for the construction funding. This brought the project to a conclusion: a good move. Windfield Farms was taken over by the Troy Savings Bank, its funding source. The embryonic Princeton projects of Willow Creek and Blackwell Farm apparently never got further than model houses and were taken over by the Nassau Savings Bank. Our development involvement in Jiminy Peak ended voluntarily so as not to jeopardies the project. Brian, however, kept us on as a builder, essentially that meant Leonard Cowan and myself. In fact, I continued to provide architectural services for the Mountainside project as well as several other buildings at Jiminy Peak for another fourteen years. For the better part of a year I helped Dick in shutting down Springland.[189]. It was a costly and trying business. One of my tasks was to see that the furnishings of the model houses were appropriately sold. Among the furnishings was a painting I had purchased (for the South Pond Farm model) for six hundred dollars at a Caropresso[190] auction. It was a large canvas, a bucolic scene with a cow and cowherd. As it was in poor condition we had it restored for another six hundred and some hefty grumbles from Dick. It did look good in the model. During the de-accession phase I took a closer look at it and saw "Norge" painted faintly on the frame. The signature was also faint but it looked something like "Petersen" or "Peterson". Arnhild, Paul Buckhurst's Norwegian wife had a look and wrote to her sister in Oslo. Her sister came back, "… could the signature be that of Eilif Peterssen?" We looked at it again and collectively decided, "yes, it could". More Oslo conversations suggested it could be valuable but it the painting had to be properly examined: in Norway. With Dick's quite reluctant support I soon was on my way to Oslo with the rolled-up Peterssen. It was a nice trip. I met Arnhild's family and saw most of Oslo and its environs. Best of all I was able to call Dick and tell him that we had two options: we could auction it, with a guide price of $50,000 at a Norwegian Art sale scheduled in two months or, we could sell it tomorrow to the Nasjonalmuseet (National Gallery). The museum wanted the painting, as it was a long-lost[191] Peterssen for which they had been looking. However, the maximum they could pay was $35,000. Taking into consideration the "bird-in-hand" theory and a bit of "it's the right thing to do", Dick and I agreed on the Museum sale. I went around the next day with the painting, collected the check and headed home. Dick was modestly pleased. It was only a small contribution to Springland's financial problems that, as the principal shareholder, Dick had the most to shoulder.

The good news, for Springland's clients is that thirty years on the Projects built by Springland remain attractive and the 'resales' are financially satisfactory, or in the case of Russell Estates excellent. Russell Estates was a good project substantiating the axiom of "location, location, location". On the downside Springland's demise was depressing and financially difficult. Springland's end combined with the on-going Valery saga thus ended what had once started as "the best of times" but ended as "…a winter of despair", though that may be a bit too strong.

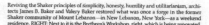

Springland Christmas party at the Forge - 1985?
Left to right: Artie Spanarkle, Charlotte Frieze, (our landscape architect), Dick and his wife

The Forge with repaired exterior - c. 1991
(*Architectural Digest*)

An 'A' house at Russell Estates
(one of the first of sixty houses)

With Marty Stachowski at Russell Estates

310

Representing the Trustee at a Darrow
Graduation in the eighties when I met State
Senator Bruno

South Pond Farm - a typical condominium unit

The first house at 'Windfield', the project
with Senator Bruno

One of the first 'Springland' buildings at Jiminy Peak

'A room with a view' - looking out of the flat at 63rd street . First Church of Christ's Scientists

Breakfast in the 'Dining Area' from which you could see the Church cupola

Reconstructing the 'lean-to' at the Forge - 'Health and Safety' look away now

Trina, Alden, Morgan, Valery and Jamie at the Forge - 1985?

15

INTERLUDE

Tech Panel System and William McDonough
New York – London – Tel Aviv
1990 - 1994

"It's déjà vu all over again"
Yogi Berra

By 1990 I was effectively unemployed; again. I use the word 'effectively' though actually I was very busy with work on Jiminy Peak, City College, arbitration, Darrow and the Village. There was very little income; certainly no regular paycheck. The Mount Lebanon Shaker Village was absorbing almost thirty hours a week. Bob Schwartz, a helpful Albany acquaintance, thought I should try to raise sufficient funds so that I could run the Village full time as an employee. It was an interesting idea but not realistic. Firstly, it was unlikely that we could raise that level of operating funds and secondly, my work at Jiminy, though somewhat irregular, was a reasonable earner for now and in fact the work was more than I could handle alone. Despite being 'unemployed' I had, as usual, too much on my plate.

About this time, at some now-forgotten event, I ran into Bill McDonough. Bill, also a Yale architectural graduate some twenty years younger than I, had worked at Davis Brody during my time there in the joint venture with Llewellyn Davies. Bill had worked on the Sabinal Project and we had become professionally friendly. Bill now had his own practice in an office on 23rd street off Park Avenue South. He told me he had some extra space if I needed it: I did. Working from the Forge and 63rd street was messy. I took Bill up on his offer and was then able to bring along a few ex-Springland architects, not as employees but free-lance work colleagues. We went to work on Jiminy. The work was still a hand-to-mouth operation, mostly my hand to my colleagues' mouths. We were also, in effect, building contractors as Leonard Cowan, at my suggestion and Brian's concurrence, moved from South Pond Farm to Jiminy when the building at South Pond ceased. Though Leonard was, technically, independent, in that he made his own estimates and took the construction risks, we worked 'hand-in-glove': we were all but fiscal 'partners'. Brian understood the close relationship and accepted it. We kept everything quite transparent. As it turned out the relationship would work so well that it lasted until Leonard's untimely death: twelve years on.

In 1990s the recession also affected the sales at Jiminy Peak but we (Leonard and I) muddled on. We were of course not the only ones 'in economic duress' our sub-contractors were too. One of these was a Swedish-American prefabricator of timber frames, whose plant was in Bennington, Vermont. The company had been supplying South Pond Farm and later Mountainside with large timber-framed panels and trusses manufactured to our designs. Mike Pinsker, a rather colourful, outspoken, large and energetic businessman, in his late forties managed the company for its Swedish owners. Before that, according to Mike, he had been in New York's 'rag trade' and was a Vietnam veteran, an infantry captain. I never saw any corroborating evidence to support the latter statement and he never spoke of any military experiences. It could have been as he said and this might explain, in part, his later sometimes bizarre and near violent behaviour that was not initially apparent: perhaps it was PTSD.

Anyway, one day when Mike was making a panel delivery to the Jiminy site he asked me, out of earshot, what I was going to do if, or more likely when, the building at Jiminy stopped altogether. His plant's owners were already talking about shutting down and Mike allowed that he didn't know what he would do but he had an idea and wanted to sound me out.

Israel at this time was in the throes of the mass immigration of Jews leaving Russia. In the 1990s nearly 1.6 million Jews emigrated from Russia: many of them headed to Israel. As a result there was a serious housing shortage and a consequent need for quicker building solutions than Israel's traditional concrete and block systems. Mike was Jewish and he 'confided' in me, "I have connections in Israel. Wouldn't our housing skills and prefabrication technology be great there?" We could indeed frame a large Jiminy condominium in about a week. I had no idea, but I also had no idea what I was going to do if Jiminy really stopped, so I answered, with no conviction and little enthusiasm, "I guess so, why not?"

We met shortly thereafter, one-on-one to discuss, in more depth, his ideas and shortly after that we met with Mike's friend and local Vermont lawyer Jeremy Dworkin at his offices in Londonderry. Dworkin, also Jewish, having been leaned on rather heavily by Mike, appeared open to supporting an enterprise that would help Israel and, if successful, reward him as well. The discussions moved on quickly and only a few weeks later we had formed a company, Tech Panel Systems (TPS). The name was Mike's suggestion. Mike was President, obviously, it was his idea. I was Executive Vice President, a typical arrangement for a two-person company. Actually it was a three-person company. A colleague of Mike's, Paul Fitzgerald was the third member. Paul, himself, provided some initial funding but Mike thought his family might provide much more. Paul was friendly, thoughtful and independently minded, he wasn't Mike's toady. Though Paul was a good addition he was only available part time and he never really played a significant role.

We agreed that the first step was an exploratory visit to Israel. Mike and I agreed to contribute our time and Jeremy and Paul provided the out-of-pocket cash. We left armed with some modest 'system' documentation and pictures of projects, but mostly we were armed with Mike's chutzpah.

In Tel Aviv we met, as planned, with Mike's contact, Mickey Weinstock, a very open minded, former Zimbabwean. I never found out how Mike knew Mickey, as their relationship did not seem 'close'. Mickey may have been simply a friend of a friend. Mickey had run his family's timber import/export business in Harare until the business was expropriated by the government (i.e. Mugabe). He now ran his own import/export firm, 'Tirosch Weinstock'. Mickey was helpful, practical, knowledgeable and guileless, a genuine good guy. He was also a liberal-minded Israeli. Once Mickey understood what we were about and what we could offer the Israeli housing market he came up with a list of potential clients and started arranging introductory meetings to anyone he thought might help. It was a 'shotgun' approach. It seemed there was no end to the number of organizations or individuals that were interested in getting a piece of what everyone thought was a housing bonanza. Some were qualified builders but others were, as the Scots say, 'chancers'. For example one such group with whom we met turned out to be two seriously cranky individuals who made (or just sold) cheap refrigerators!

A typical meeting commenced with our host of the moment offering us a cookie and some seltzer water (seldom coffee). This was followed by Mike's opening pleasantries that usually consisted of Mike explaining that he was Jewish, no surprise there, and that he thought all Arabs wore dishtowels on their heads. He would make any other anti-Arab comment that might come to his mind if he thought it might ingratiate us with the host. His remarks often fell into a cringe-making category. As the only goyim at the meetings I kept 'schtum' unless called on for some technical 'expertise'. After about ten minutes of nothing important we were asked the invariable question, "what's your system?" "Prefabricated wood panels" we confidently answered. That would usually, but not always, put full stop to further conversation. It transpired that Israelis didn't build with wood or anything with a cellulose structure except perhaps for temporary structures; they were wedded to concrete. We thought 'temporary housing' a real possibility but no request for temporary housing emerged during our talks. Why we didn't know about the 'wood problem' beforehand I cannot say. In any event we had a rejoinder, "…if you don't like wood we can build it in steel." We were 'winging it', of course, but we had to say something other than, "when's the next plane to New York?"

We also learned that any 'system' had to be approved by the Technion, Israel's leading technical university in Haifa. Mickey quickly made the necessary arrangements and took us up to Haifa. It was an interesting trip replete with

Mickey's Israeli history lessons and visits to some interesting sites. In Haifa we met with professor Dr. Rachael Becker who had the responsibility for evaluating building systems used in Israel. Dr. Becker, an engineer by training, was extremely knowledgeable, direct and fair though not very enthusiastic about building systems in general. Her mantra was, "any error in design is a systemic error that could be catastrophic." She carefully explained to us her performance-based criteria. The criteria were understandably tough and comprehensive. They included demonstrating structural suitability to earthquake, durability, acoustic quality; fire-safety (the system had to be incombustible), longevity, thermal effectiveness and in fact anything else Dr. Becker thought might be appropriate to our proposed system. It was a long list, to some extent it seemed designed to discourage 'systems' and we thought at the time, ours in particular, though there was no evidence that we were singled out. Despite the tough requirements we were optimistic that we could meet them, and of course, we had no options.

In the short time remaining before we were to return to New York Mickey had arranged one more potential client meeting in Tel Aviv. This was with Gideon Friedman an engineer who headed up the building division of the well-established Kibbutz, Haartzi. Gideon was a pragmatic engineer and thoughtful businessman. Short on pleasantries he went straight to the point of any discussion he was the epitome of pragmatic. He listened intently to our, well Mike's mostly, presentation. It turned out Gideon liked the idea of our prefabricated big-panel, steel 'system', such as it (theoretically) was. In principle we would deliver the structural steel frame and related components, e.g. windows, doors, exterior wall system stairs etc. to the kibbutz and provide expertise in the construction process (i.e. Leonard). The Kibbutz would do everything else. It was just what we wanted. At the end of two long meetings Gideon told us, "If you get Technion approval, we are interested. Subject, of course, to our agreeing to a final price we will build fourteen buildings consisting of twenty-four units apiece with your system, more if it turns out well". The order would be worth about four million pounds, gross, to us. We didn't understand why Gideon picked fourteen buildings but we didn't argue. Gideon, at our request, gave us, with perhaps with a little nudge from Mickey, a letter of intent. It had a number of caveats, system approval, some limiting dates and economic parameters but it was a great letter, even though in truth it was only an agreement to agree. But it justified, and then some, our trip. "Wow!" we thought. It seemed a remarkable end to an unlikely beginning. The fact that we hadn't a clue how we would deliver the system didn't worry us, though it would, soon enough. We thought we had hit the proverbial 'home run'. Mike and I thanked Mickey and returned to New York, broke, but optimistic.

Once back we calmed down and realistically evaluated our position. On the positive side we had as good a letter of intent as was reasonably possible, we could arguably call it an 'order', and we did. After that we were pretty thin on the good news. First, we didn't really have a 'system' we were just confident that we could come up with one and that we could get it through the Technion. Second, we had no idea who would manufacture the system-to-be and thirdly (and critically), we were without any operating funds. I still had some work at Jiminy and income from teaching and arbitration. However, Mike's factory had now shut down and he was out of work: completely.

After several long meetings with Leonard we agreed that designing the system and getting it approval was only a matter of time and hard work. As to manufacturing we believed that we would find someone when the time came. In any event Leonard, true to his everlasting optimism, said he could manufacture the system if necessary: a rolled-eye moment but probably true.

We agreed that I would undertake the preparation of the Technion documentation and that this would take place in London. Why London or more broadly the UK? First it was 3500 miles closer to Israel and the likely materials that would be used in the system could more easily be sourced there. It was not that they couldn't be sourced in the US. Tishman the real estate developer and constructor, for example, was also developing a system for Israel, a modification of one of their systems that was entirely sourced in the US. However, Tishman had deep pockets and could effectively subsidize their work and they had substantial Israeli connections. We couldn't really compete head to head with them – we had to be different. A UK production source would, at least potentially, provide the difference. Also, at the time, our understanding was that the UK was not active in the Israeli housing market and therefore that fact might possibly provide us with a unique marketing opportunity for an appropriate UK manufacturer. My UK connections were intact, particularly those through Chris Colbourne, of Bahrain days. Chris was now MD of Tibbalds Munro, architects and planners, in London.

For TPS to carry on we needed proper funding. Money was the big make or break issue and we didn't have any. Mike, Jeremy and I met to discuss our options. Jeremy went after local banks and Mike and I followed suggestions from various sources, meeting with anyone we thought could possibly help us. The list was long, the interest high, the results low. Nonetheless, we did manage to raise enough funds from friends, friends of friends[192] and friends of Israel to meet our immediate out of pocket expenses, i.e. getting me to London to start the Technion documentation. Mike and I continued to contribute our time and we worked to put the Haartzi deal together: quickly. It was a touchy business and one that, perhaps understandably, didn't bring out the 'best' in Mike; he had two daughters and a wife to support. Mike could sometimes get rather 'demanding' in his approach to potential colleagues and investors.

The financial break, after some difficult months of penury, came through Bill McDonough. Bill had taken an interest in the TPS venture even though it really didn't fit his core environmental agenda. As a result Mike had targeted him as a financial participant and Mike's conversations with Bill sometimes verged on the ugly, certainly the impolite. Bill, himself, however, could be quite aloof and I don't think the conversations bothered him. Bill nevertheless kept up his interest and finally, for reasons unknown, Bill agreed to introduce Mike and me to two of his acquaintances he thought might be interested in TPS. They were the Arnow brothers, heirs to a New York real estate dynasty. Both were in their early forties. Josh, the youngest was a Westchester County developer and David the oldest, a psychologist by training and an author. He was the managing principal in the

Arnow Family Fund. The fund supported educational and community facilities and organizations, mostly in Israel.

Bill, good to his word, arranged a meeting at which Mike and I, accompanied by Bill, made a presentation to Josh, David and their father, Robert, in the Arnow's rather sumptuous offices on 42nd street overlooking Bryant Park. Mike was well behaved and the presentation was short and simple. We explained how we were trying to bring, as a profitable business, good, economical housing to Israel through the auspices of TPS. We provided the details of our progress to date, the Haartzi 'order' and our financial requirements. It was a good meeting.

A few days later David called to tell us that they would invest $250,000 in TPS and the Haartzi project. The funds would be provided over a designated drawdown period and they would take an appropriate ownership position of approximately 50%. In addition the Arnows required that we would not construct or otherwise support housing on any disputed West Bank territory. The proposition was more than we could have possibly hoped for. As I recall, Mike was not quite as sanguine as I. The Arnow's investment meant that Mike's (and my own too) ownership position in TPS was now less than 20% (each). My own thought was that it was either this or nothing: no problem.

We could now finish pursuing the project with some alacrity and confidence. In London, initially, I worked out of a small serviced office in Richmond, rented on a monthly basis. I soon established working contacts with major suppliers including, among them, Rockwool, British Steel and British Gypsum. These contacts might have seemed unlikely but we had two factors going for us; one, we were new and different, (the 'different' included a subtle and positive 'American' factor) and two, the UK was in a building recession. The idea of possible material orders was attractive. British Steel recommended a structural engineering firm, Cairns Smith, whose offices were in Kew Gardens. We paid Cairns Smith a nominal fee but the significant support from the suppliers, including testing and documentation was given gratis. We also met, through a friend, Ian Watson, MD of OKO Trade a trading branch of the Finnish Bank, OKO[193] whose offices were also in Richmond. Ian, an engineer by profession, was an impressive no-nonsense manager and entrepreneur with an understated sense of humour. Ian became interested in the Israeli opportunity both from a personal point of view, he became a shareholder, and as a potential OKO Trade project. Ian's involvement gave the project a 'gravitas' it might not otherwise have had. Ian led our UK efforts to raise additional funds from both venture capital and industry sources; He became involved in any Tech Panel activity in which he could be useful. He travelled to Israel with us and helped us with the financial and contractual transactions. He was a tremendous asset to the fledgling company. Ian and his delightful wife Jackie became, and remain, close friends.

Finding a manufacturer was not as easy as we thought. With an introduction through Ian we initially worked with a manufacturer of modular buildings from Hull, R B ADDA. The relationship was friendly and we were initially optimistic. Mike came over to meet with the owners, Malcolm Cunningham the MD and John Gilfoyle the technical manager. We worked with them for a number of months until, for various reasons, mostly, so they said, their perceived financial risk of an Israeli transaction, they lost interest. ADDA ceased trading three years later so there may have been other reasons for their withdrawal. We needed another manufacturer.

It wasn't long before one of our British Gypsum friends introduced us to Steel Framing Systems (SFS), a related company. SFS was run by an enthusiastic, pleasant-enough, salesman, Bob Colver. SFS wasn't actually a manufacturer but rather a 'middleman' selling specialized light gauge sections used, mostly, for non-structural interior framing for British Gypsum plasterboard products. The source of the sections was a long-established 'steel basher', Ayrshire Metal Products (AMP) located in Irvine, an Ayrshire town, a forty-minute drive south of Glasgow.

AMP was a public company though one family controlled it. Ayrshire's primary business was making cold-rolled steel truck and bus frames for British Leyland, Volvo and other manufacturers. AMP of course also provided the steel sections for SFS and, for that matter, anyone else who wanted them. On a day-to-day basis, Ayrshire was managed by Hugh Lobban, a rather 'dour' (possibly because of his difficult relationship with AMP's principal owner but maybe just because he is a Scot) but a very friendly Scot from nearby Kilmarnock. Hugh had a quiet sense of humour and was a good listener. It seemed that TPS was usually in the presence of individuals with a sense of humour: under what were sometimes difficult circumstances this was helpful.

We arranged a meeting with Hugh at Ayrshire's plant. Mike came over and he, Ian and I made our way to Irvine (flight to Glasgow plus rented car). Hugh's office was workmanlike; it could have been a set from some grim and grainy 1930s B movie. Ayrshire expended no money on 'front', although Hugh did drive a big BMW whose boot always contained Hugh's golf clubs. Although, at first, Hugh appeared sceptical, our proposal was sort of 'far out' from his point of view, he was looking for new business and he listened.

By the time we met with Hugh we had progressed the system's design so that it was nearly acceptable to the Technion and, importantly, it was comprehensible to Hugh and his technical team. The outcome of the first meeting was positive. In due course Hugh agreed that he could manufacture the system for the Haartzi project. His agreement was subject, of course, to pricing and financing terms. But Hugh saw, too, that the system might have a UK market, Haartzi wasn't the only possibility. In fact as we continued to develop the system and worked with the various supporting manufacturers we were introduced to potential projects ranging from student housing to prison accommodation. It was clear that in addition to Haartzi there were plenty of opportunities for the 'system' in the UK.

By the Spring of 1992 the TPS design was all but approved by the Technion. Chris Colbourne 'invited', (I think that is an appropriate term, I may have asked) TPS (i.e. me) to move into the Tibbalds Munro offices on Earl Street, near Liverpool Street Station giving us a 'presence' that the little one room office in Richmond could not.

The manufacturing of the system by Ayrshire was getting in hand. We met with Hugh and his colleagues frequently, mostly in Ayrshire, and worked out the manufacturing details. We brought Leonard over to London and Irvine on several occasions to add his experience to the manufacturing process. His recommendations often provided pragmatic solutions to Ayrshire's manufacturing concerns. Ayrshire and TPS were soon talking about a joint venture operation. In addition, Jim Robinson of British Steel invited us to their corporate facility in Wales to explore an alternative long-term relationship. We were properly funded – and – Mike and I were salaried. TPS prospects were 'looking good'!

* * * * *

The Tech Panel work required me to be abroad for several weeks at a time. It was no longer possible to be involved on a day-to-day basis with the requirements of running the Village. I consequently resigned in August of 1991 turning the chair over to Arno Niemand. The board generously marked the occasion with a gift of a Tim Rieman candle stand, a complimentary board resolution and poem.[194] The almost ten years as chair had been a roller coaster ride but, I believe, a productive one. I remained a board member but now only attended meetings when possible. The EQBA grant application was progressing and all indications were that we would get it. This was a wake-up call to some on the Darrow Board. There was a now a political move to establish a second institution, the Mount Lebanon 'Foundation' that would become the owner of the property in the event the grant came into being. This was a political compromise to Hans Solmssen the Darrow Board chair. He and I were made co-chairs of the new structure, the Mount Lebanon Foundation (or something like that. Up to now Hans had been happy to be out of the loop, (I do not recall that he ever came to a Village meeting), so long as the Village was repairing buildings, showing visitors around and running a store. But, if there was going to be serious money and ownership issues that was another matter. We soon concluded that the co-chair scenario wouldn't work, Hans and I were not often on the same wavelength. Consequently, we sought out an individual to take over the Foundation. We came up with Gene Faul a specialist towel and bathrobe manufacturer from Sheffield, Massachusetts who was also a Shaker furniture enthusiast. He took over with a vengeance and tried, unsuccessfully, to scupper the work of the Village. Why? - no idea. In any event he was unable to raise funds and his tenure was short-lived as was that of the Foundation. The Village itself survived to live another day and it became the de facto owner of the site when the EQBA grant was awarded. The $1,000,000 grant was the largest given (at least up to that point). That was the good news. The bad news was that the grant nearly came undone as the Village and/or the Foundation (take your pick), was unable to raise the matching $1,000,000. To solve this problem, and it was a problem, the State permitted Darrow to 'lend' the Village/Foundation $1,000,000 thus creating the requisite match. After all the work it would have been 'awkward' to undo the award. (I think one would call it a 'smoke and mirrors' loan) The loan had a three-year term (as I recall). Though it would turn out that the 'loan' would create significant difficulties in the future, the immediate result meant that Darrow could pay off its long-term debt with the $1,000,000 from the grant. With this relief, and the help of the Board and others such as John Joline, Darrow survived the, 'terminal', crisis. Perhaps as a result, after three short-term heads, Darrow was able, in 1994, to attract a brilliant head, Larry Van Meter. Over the next seven years, Larry with his inspired academic leadership and management skills would put Darrow 'back on the map'.

Personal matters continued pretty much as before. Valery and I were still talking and meeting for lunches or dinners and even seeing Fredda Bruckner together. I met with Wilkie once or twice. By this time, though I had come round to having children, Valery was either not sure I meant it or as Fredda originally claimed, the 'split' was not all about children. The uncertainty of the relationship with Valery meant that I was unable to emotionally 'commit' to anyone else that I met. And, I did meet and have what could be called 'might work' relationships with several really attractive, intelligent and kind ladies. I probably could have had longer-term relationships had it not been for the on-going bond with Valery. My constant, sometimes lengthy, trips across the Atlantic didn't help either. As a result I continued to justify Wilkie's 'serial monogamist' moniker. Perhaps I should have worn some warning label, 'danger, this man may be unreliable'. The bond with Valery lasted up until one day in 1994 in Madison Square Park when Valery informed me that she was going to marry Hal Einhorn, a financially successful architect-developer. It had been nearly ten years since Valery and I 'separated', or whatever one may call it, it had not been 'the best of times': for anyone.

My frequent travels to London and Israel also meant that I saw less of the children than I would have liked. When it worked out, we did get together very happily, mostly at the Forge. There were at least four major family events; Jamie graduated from Yale Law School in 1989 and went to work at the State Department in what he referred to as the "drugs and thugs" department. I visited him in his office once, a very depressing place to work, but it was an important first step in his career. After a late start in the romance department Jamie met Lori Neal. They were married in Washington in 1992. Catriona (Trina) married Tom Parker in Edgartown, on the Vineyard in the same year. Molly made sure that my participation in the weddings, including Morgan's in 1988 in West Tisbury, was nominal. I attended but did not participate in any recognizable capacity. I was in London in 1991 when Maggie (Brelis) my first grandchild was born. Alden continued to visit from California when he could and when I was 'around'.

The TPS position in 1992 was positive, in fact 1992 would turn out to be, probably, the high point in the TPS tale. We did get Technion approval. It wasn't actual 'approval' more the Italian 'nulla osta', the "we have no objections" position. In any event Haartzi was satisfied. With Ian's help we came back from Israel on our post Technion approval trip with a legitimate and properly priced order. We now had to get the financing in place. Haartzi would of course pay for the materials but what, Ayrshire wanted to know were the guarantees that they would pay on delivery and who would be taking the exchange risk. This was a chicken and egg dilemma. Before Technion approval and a bona fide priced order no one would spend effort to sort out the financing details, primarily the export credit cover. Now they did and the results were negative. Ayrshire would not commit to an order unless they could get commercial insurance cover for payment and they either couldn't or it was too expensive. It transpired that we had a bona fide order that couldn't be financed. Ian did what he could to find alternative financing solutions and so did Ayrshire. This took time during which I looked for any alternative projects: there were many. Each, however, seemed to have its own peculiar problems. The impending negative denouement was driving Mike crazy. If, as it began to appear, TPS was not going to achieve its Israeli objective (or any other) it would mean that TPS would, in fact, 'fail'. Apart from anything else, for example retrieving the Arnow's investment, both Mike and I would be out of work. Mike began to 'demand' that either Ayrshire should fund us or that the Arnows should provide additional cash. Neither of those 'demands' was going to happen. Scottish Ayrshire didn't easily part with cash (if at all) and the Arnow's investment was all about Israel. Mike became difficult to the point where prior to a 'critical' meeting with Ayrshire, Ian had to separate Mike and me before one of us took a swing at the other. Mike was much bigger than I and it would have been one-sided: I appreciated Ian's intervention. Mike's behaviour finally resulted in his being removed as President and even as a director. I was asked to take over to manage what continuing interest that TPS might have. Mike offered to resolve any management issues on 42nd street pavement but the directors unanimously declined his offer. TPS, meaning essentially me, carried on trying to find alternative sources of work.

However, by mid 1993 I was, for all practical purposes, finished with TPS. Though the UK market was generally, encouraging potential UK clients needed a 'leap of faith' to commit to the TPS system. We spent hours, days and sometimes weeks pursuing one or another likely prospect. There was a lot of interest and numerous proposals were made for student housing, hotels, motels and more. In the end we just couldn't close a transaction. The appetite in 1992/3 for system building in the UK (and the US) just wasn't there. A bit like Macarthur's old soldiers, TPS simply 'faded' away.

As TPS came to its slow, painful, stop I had 'time on my hands'. As this coincided with the growth of Bill McDonough's practice there opened up an opportunity for me to work for him, in fact, to be his firm's managing director, Bill's suggestion. Bill's architectural practice was focused on 'sustainable', environmental design. Having leased space from him I was familiar with his work and staff. Bill needed someone to manage his office and his projects particularly those in which he was less interested. He wanted to spend his time[195] on project design and on his broadening environmental agenda. Because of my ongoing commitments I would work for Bill as a consultant and be paid on an hourly basis. This suited both of us. I could meet my obligations to Darrow/MLSV, Jiminy, teaching, and arbitration without worrying about how that would affect Bill's work. Bill was only obligated to pay me for time actually spent on his behalf. Bill's offer was one that couldn't be refused and I didn't.

Working for Bill was interesting: probably an understatement. As previously noted, Bill was a 1976 graduate of the Yale Architectural School. But he was more than an architect. He wrote, lectured, thought and probably dreamed about the environment. He was certainly, at the time, one of the most noteworthy, certainly press-worthy of environmental architects, both in reality and perception. Bill had broad contacts in the professional press and he was very good at his PR[196]. While Bill could appear super friendly and generous he was not a person I ever thought of as a friend, more as a colleague. We rarely, if ever, met outside the office unless it was to pursue a business interest.

Bill's clients were interesting, they all had environmental agendas and generally there was a good fit between the services that Bill could offer and the clients' requirements. Bill's clients were also diverse. In 1993, they included, among others, the Roedale Press, Herman Miller, The Body Shop, the Noyes Foundation, the Heinz Foundation, work for the city of Chattanooga, the Lakota Tribe, Calvassion (in France), the restoration an early Mies (maybe not Mies?) building in Berlin, and an apartment for Susan Sarandon and Tim Robbins.

To service these clients Bill had assembled a small staff of young, bright, environmentally dedicated individuals. They were, though, perhaps, somewhat inexperienced and often a little naïve, especially when it came to project economics.

Bill's staff was also too short in number to meet the challenge of completing projects within competing timeframes. We had to nearly double the number of employees to satisfy his clients: it wasn't easy. As a consequence management requirements increased and I became more involved in Bill's practice than either of us had expected. I was often working more than fifty, or even sixty hours a week. Even then, I could barely keep up with Bill's 'work load', or Bill's management eccentricities. I had been hired to help Bill but now I needed help myself. Bill was lukewarm on the subject but we nevertheless started looking for a marketing/administrative person to help support that end of the business. The most interesting CV came from Michele Wipfler who at the time was working in Washington. I had reason to go to Washington for the AIA and also to see Jamie so I arranged an interview with Michele. Michele appeared to have all the skills we needed. I returned to New York and recommended that Bill hire her. Bill was reticent but after some waffling he agreed. Michele was terrific, thoughtful, smart and enthusiastic, she was also rather good looking. I confess I was rather attracted to her. It turned out, however, that Michele had only one person in her sights and that, of course, was Bill. It was probably less than a year and a half later that Bill and Michele were married in the Cathedral of St. John the Divine in New York. Although Bill never acknowledged it Michele was probably my most significant contribution to Bill's person or his practice during a brief tenure as Managing Director.

Bill's practice went from strength to strength even though there were management shortcomings. Some caused by Bill's "I've got an even better design" philosophy. Bill's last minute design changes, even though, admittedly, they might be good, could frustrate a client. Roedale Press, as an example, asked Bill to stop his work and turn the large Roedale office project over to the local joint venture architect. I took over the direct management of some projects and tried to minimize last minute design changes. One of the projects was the office renovation for Gilder, Gagnon Howe. I worked closely with one of the most practical and intelligent of Bill's staff, Matt Frank a graduate of Tulane. Matt and I worked together easily and both of us got on well with the client Virginia Gilder, Richard Gilder's, the owner's ex (or ex-in -process) wife. Together we made a rather efficient, profitable team and Bill left us, mainly, alone. But this project was the exception. On most other projects Bill could not help himself from disrupting the orderly progress of a project by his unscheduled interventions. I spent hours trying to keep the projects on schedule and my consulting bills mounted up. Flying back one day from a meeting in Vermont with the Ben and Jerry's ice cream firm, Bill cornered me. He was very angry. It transpired that our bookkeeper had pointed out to Bill that my compensation might exceed his at the end of the year. Bill was irate but so was I. The confrontation was a bit ugly. I was only billing for the time spent on his work at the agreed sum. The fact that it was a lot of time reflected on the workload and to an extent, in my opinion, on some of Bill's own management inefficiencies. However, it was his office and his financial risks and I could, somewhat begrudgingly, understand his anger. We solved the crisis by my agreeing to a cap and I adjusted my time. I think Michele helped smooth matters over: a bit. As it would turn out this problem was short lived. In early 1994 Bill was offered the position of Dean of the University of Virginia Architectural School in Charlottesville and he accepted it.

By the summer Bill had shut the New York office and moved to Charlottesville. A few of the staff went with him but most found other positions in New York. All but two of Bill's projects were taken to Virginia. The end of Bill's New York practice was eased financially (from my point of view) as it was mutually agreed that two projects, the Noyes Foundation and Gilder offices, would be given over and finished by Matt, David Briggs, another intelligent friendly architect, and myself with minimal involvement from Bill.

Despite the problems, I learned a lot from Bill during the short time with him and I am grateful for this. I also learned from TPS and not just from the technical side. It had been an interesting, educational, if somewhat painful and expensive interlude.

Berlin - 1994 - Discussing renovation opportunities, informally, for an historic (Mies?) building in Alexanderplatz: Bill on left the other three are German architects with whom we were associated

A cheerful Ian Watson, in Tel Aviv: for the Haartzi project - 1993

Mickey Weinstock reviewing our Haartzi proposal at one of the usual lunch meetings in a restaurant on the coast, south of Tel Aviv - the white wine was excellent - 1994

With Hugh Lobban in Irvine, Ayrshire

16

THE FORGE COMPANY

New York - London
1994 - 2001

"I see in industrialization the central problem of building in our time. If we succeed in carrying out this industrialization, the social, economic, technical, and also artistic problems will be readily solved."
Ludwig Mies Van Der Rohe

"Death leaves a heartache no one can heal, love leaves a memory no one can steal."
Irish headstone

"Design is not just what it looks like and feels like. Design is how it works."
Steve Jobs

Bill's agreement with his clients, Virginia Gilder and Steve Viederman,[197] had left Matt Frank and David Briggs and me to finish the Gilder and Noyes Foundation offices. We were self-employed. I wasn't going to Charlottesville, for sure, neither was Matt or David. Actually, this was an opportunity that suited all of us: well, perhaps not Bill, he could be a bit possessive about 'his' clients. I would work on Gilder with Matt and on Noyes with David. Matt and David would do most of the work. Although I wasn't really necessary I did add a modicum of gravitas. I got on well with both Virginia and Steve and as well with Matt and David: good relationships all around. The work would keep the three of us reasonably, though not fully, employed for a few months. Matt and I had discussions following Bill's decision to take up his deanship offer. We sort of agreed to have a go together, nothing formal to begin with, maybe pick up where

TPS had left off, look for other work, whatever. David wanted to do his own thing. It was a good transitional situation – but to what?

Just before Bill moved we had the last Gilder job meeting in Bill's office. After the meeting, while waiting with Virginia for the elevator, Virginia turned to me and asked, "What are you going to do after Bill moves to Charlottesville?" While the question might have been Virginia's normal courtesy or curiosity, I sensed there was genuine interest behind the question. I mumbled something about working with Matt but not having any firm or detailed plans - though I did mention my interest in low-cost housing. As the elevator arrived Virginia suggested a meeting to discuss my embryonic ideas. Would I give her a call to arrange it? "Yes", was my (obvious) response.

In fact I had been thinking about how to capitalize on my long-term interest and experience in prefabrication[198], what in the UK is called "off-site construction". Prefabrication had first interested me at Yale. Later, the IDC 'paper' houses, the AT&T theatre project, the Shafer house, Bard College dormitories, Ahwaz worker's housing, Bahrain's self-help housing, Russell Estates, South Pond Farm, Jiminy Peak and TPS were confirmations of my continuing interest, if not obsession with prefabrication[199]. These projects all incorporated prototype systems, each quite different, each specifically tailored to the requirements of their circumstances.

Although in private practice with Peter and in Springland's work our clients were, for the most part 'high end' my real interest lay, not only in prefabrication but also in low cost housing. For example the projects we had worked on in the Caribbean, the New York State's Urban Development Corporation at Spring Valley, the Ahwaz housing and my work in Bahrain were all low cost housing. It was also the low-cost housing project at Yale that had brought me to Peter's attention when he was a visiting critic. This project and, likely[200], the Griswold connection led to his employing, mentoring and subsequently inviting me to be his partner. His mentorship had contributed to what could be considered my early architectural 'success'[195].

Virginia, Matt and I met as planned. I had prepared a short business plan for Virginia and she had sight of it prior to our meeting. The plan supported the concept of a company dedicated to innovating and constructing prefabricated low-cost housing. The meeting provided an opportunity for probing the plan and answering questions. Virginia didn't waste a lot of time and proposed, almost at once, that she would provide backing for the proposal. There were no stipulations as to where the work would happen, though perhaps not Israel! We agreed to call the entity The Forge Company, after all, apart from any personal considerations; the North Family Forge was a prefabricated building and in subtle ways the Forge epitomized my design 'philosophy' (though "philosophy" may be a bit ponderous). Our system would use light-gauge steel, LGS in short (no surprise there). As Delboy, of Only Fools and Horses, would often say, "…you know it makes sense".

Virginia's specific proposal would wait for a subsequent meeting. Virginia had to ponder her potential investment against our proposed needs, her financial tax consequences and ownership position. I was, to put it mildly, speechless. Having spent the better part of two years trying to raise funds for TPS, Virginia's unsolicited offer seemed miraculous. I didn't know Virginia that well but had I liked her from our first meeting. Virginia was smart, open to 'better' ideas, fair and genuinely friendly. I knew that Virginia was a donor to Republican causes and that she was separated from her husband Dick Gilder (by co-incidence a close friend of Arno Niemand) but that was about all. At the time I didn't know that she was independently wealthy, a philanthropist and an investor in start-up projects[201]. Virginia and I got on well professionally and I always looked forward to our friendly, thoughtful, project meetings. In my opinion, Matt and I had done a good job on the Gilder office and Virginia appeared pleased with our work. (Bill had been a rather distant contributor to the Gilder project; he did come up with a few interesting environmental components but the project was perhaps too 'run of the mill' for his full, enthusiastic, attention.)

With Virginia's backing for the new entity Matt and I were going to need an office. Brad Perkins, yet again, came to the rescue. Brad was now the principal partner of Perkins Eastman Architects and had offices at 437 Fifth Avenue, at 41st street, a convenient location (only a block from father's 40th street office of the 1920s). Brad let us have a couple of desks for a nominal sum and we moved in immediately. With a little help from a lawyer friend of Matt's The Forge Company was formed and in business.

In due course Virginia proposed that she own 50% of The Forge Company with Matt and I sharing the balance. Virginia agreed to invest $500,000 for her share, a generous and significant sum. Understandably, that was a top, 'don't come back for more' investment. Virginia made it clear, perhaps to make us comfortable, that while a return would be appreciated, if we were not successful, Virginia would be able to write off the sum with a minimum of impact to her finances. I don't know exactly what Matt though about all of this but I thought that we had had attained something of an architectural Nirvana.

The Forge Company was funded, it had an apt name and two architects but that was it. Forge had no specific system, no projects, not even an identifiable market but the reality did not lessen our optimism or dampen our enthusiasm. My previous start up experiences were mostly the reverse, projects in hand but short on money. We went to work. Matt and I undertook to develop details of a system based, initially, on past experience, including TPS but without the Israeli mandates[202]. Matt was an immediate help, unlike myself he understood the graphic component of computers and was computer-proficient. Thanks to Virginia we had the latest and best equipment and software from Apple. We immediately employed Leonard as an advisor. Leonard, while not big on environmental quality or the design side of construction, was (as noted) knowledgeable about manufacturing (or prefabrication) as he was about the practicalities of efficient construction. The combination of knowledge and technical knowhow represented by the three of us was probably, if I may say so, exceptional. Developing a market for our system was my responsibility. To this end, on the 28th of September 1994, I left for the UK to reconnect with my UK contacts and introduce them to The Forge Company and its emerging 'light-gauge steel, manufactured, environmentally sound, adaptable building system for low-cost housing'. The description was a mouthful, but that was, exactly, what we were determined to innovate.

During 1994/95 I made at least 10 round trips to the UK each one taking at least a fortnight leaving me little time to pursue any of my 'extracurricular' activities. I kept attending Darrow trustee meetings, minimized my ´Village´ involvement and gave up teaching and arbitration.

As for the ´Village´ Arno retired from the board when he and Brenda sold their New Lebanon house and moved to Boulder, Colorado. Arno was replaced by a joint chairmanship of board members John Adams and David Pearce. The board was, perhaps, 'uncomfortable' if either one of them was solely in charge. Both co-chairs were intelligent but they were opposites in their views on almost everything except their condescension towards Darrow. Adams and Pearce inherited the management of the EQBA transaction on behalf of the Village and New York State. This was not to be an amenable development.

An unusual situation had developed: the landlord, the Village, now owner of the buildings and land, owed its tenant, Darrow, a million dollars with the debt increasing yearly from accrued interest. I think everyone now agreed that the ability of the Village to raise funds to pay the debt was somewhere between nil and no. In addition, it became evident that there was to be no immediate alternative settlement given the various complications and, in my opinion, the intransigence, of the Village board (particularly its co-chairs) towards Darrow. Essentially, most of the board thought Darrow should 'forgive' the debt though there was 'fat chance' of that.

Almost ten years would go by before a resolution could be achieved. By that time I had all but retired from the Village board and did not participate in the resolution that was achieved in 2004. It was Darrow's trustee and former chairman, Trip Samson, who with the help of 'Wint' Aldrich[203] from the State would tease out a solution. In the end Darrow recovered the ownership of the buildings and land it required for its purposes to satisfy the debt. The Village retained the remaining buildings, essentially the whole of the North Family. There were other details, a number relating to the Second Meeting House (Darrow's Library) and the leasing of three buildings in the North Family, but the revised ownership was the principal resolution. Twenty years had passed since the first flicker of an idea to save the Mount Lebanon site was postulated. In the end the site that was genuinely 'at risk' was saved. Darrow had the buildings it needed and was relieved of its albatross of debt and unused/unneeded (by Darrow) buildings were in the public domain.

On the home front Alden graduated from the University of California at Santa Cruz and moved to Boulder: I am not sure why (I'll ask him). Jamie moved from the State Department to the post of Deputy Legal Advisor to the National Security Council and later, under Clinton, to be the NSC's Legal Advisor. In March 1995 Morgan gave birth to Ellie, my second grandchild. Trina was now teaching at a secondary school, Chatham Hall, in Virginia. As usual I saw the children either at the Forge or by visiting them when I could: unfortunately that wasn't often.

On the companion front, (if that is an appropriate word), now that Valery had made her decision, I was ready for a 'real' relationship. It wasn't long before I was introduced to Serena Rhinelander. Our first meeting was in the Polo Bar of the Hotel Westbury at 69th street and Madison Avenue. On the face of it there was little common ground between us. Despite that, after an hour or so, we found that we were getting on well - it is possible that our friend Stolichnaya may have helped. Drinks led to dinner and dinner led to late night telephone calls after each of us had arrived at our respective homes. We had connected; there was chemistry. Serena, a retired Harper's Bazaar model was stunning, that was appealing enough, but it turned out Serena was generous, kind, interesting and interested though, sometimes, it must be said, difficult. She belonged to the historic 18th century German-American Rhinelander family but Serena also had a French background and even had a shared interest with her sister in a house in Villefranche overlooking Cap Ferrat. Though I was clearly in over my head I was an enthusiastic participant in the relationship. We didn't move in together but we met regularly for dinner either eating out or, frequently, in Serena's attractive Park Avenue apartment, by coincidence at 93rd street. We often went to the Forge on weekends driving up from

New York in the 'Wombat', Serena's nickname for my white Peugeot 505 estate. It was Serena who also came up with my grandchildren's moniker by calling me "Granbear". The weekends were spent bumbling about the Forge sometimes with Serena patiently encouraging my early attempts at painting. We sometimes entertained visitors. Serena's sister lived nearby and her daughter Sheena was a student at Miss Hall's in Pittsfield[204]. we visited with both. It was an emotional, upbeat relationship – it certainly started that way.

My first Forge (the business) trip to the UK was more positive than I could have reasonably expected. Ayrshire, that is Lobban, was happy to see me. Before long we were discussing some sort of joint venture, even to the point of preparing a 'heads of agreement'. After Ayrshire I visited with several housing associations with which I had modest contacts. Those visits, however, were somewhat problematic. The association's managers were generally enthusiastic but all kept saying "… let us know when you do your first project, we will talk to you then." It was clear that breaking into the UK market with a new, untried system was not going to be easy. My last stop was at the Rockwool plant and headquarters in Bridgend, Wales. There I caught up with Mike Bourne and Steve Mulligan our helpful Rockwool contacts during the TPS saga. They introduced me to Mitch Gee, who would be Mike's replacement as Mike was moving on to a new job. Together they agreed that Rockwool would be prepared to help Forge develop a UK-oriented system assuming, of course, that appropriate Rockwool materials would be used throughout the system, this was a no-brainer. Rockwool was particularly interested in promoting their proprietary 'breathable' wall system.

At the end of a long day of discussions Steve asked me what progress we had made marketing the Forge system to housing associations. I told him that the meetings were all positive except that each association we talked to was waiting for another association to take the first step. In other words we really hadn't made much progress. Steve asked if we had talked to Gwalia the principal Welsh housing association located in Swansea: I hadn't. He suggested we call Gwalia's development director Phil Roberts whom he knew and with whom he had discussed the use of Rockwool products. I made the call: then and there. The conversation was short and went something like this:

> Me: "This is Jim Baker of the Forge Company. Steve Mulligan suggested I call as we have a housing system and he thinks you ought to see it."
> Phil: "Have you built any units yet?"
> Me, to myself: "ok, here we go again" but to Phil, I said the truth: "No"
> Phil: "Great, can you meet with me here in Swansea tomorrow, say 10 o'clock?"
> Me, surprised: "Absolutely, I look forward to it."

I am not exaggerating, that was the crux of the conversation. We met as planned. As Reader's Digest might have put it, Phil was a most 'memorable character'. Tall, with thinning red hair, a moustache just short of a handlebar and intense sparkling eyes Phil could have been taken for a rock star. He was friendly, intense, energetic, enthusiastic and outspoken; perhaps he had a few other attributes but these suffice. It was said that everyone in Wales knew Phil on sight.

The meeting went well. Phil liked what we were proposing, he was quite familiar with timber frame but we were the first to propose steel as an alternative. He accepted our premise that light gauge steel was equally environmentally friendly. By the time we finished lunch, (it was a long meeting), Phil had agreed, in principle, that he would use our system as soon as he could find a suitable project. We could not have imagined a better opportunity. When told about the meeting the Rockwool team was ecstatic: they were going to have their first wall system in place and in Wales, what could be better! Hugh also expressed enthusiasm but in his rather modest, not to say dour, Ayrshire manner, it was good enough. To finish off the trip there were more meetings with would-be suppliers of all kinds and more would-be clients. Gwalia, however, was the high water mark. I returned to New York with the good news.

Back in the New York Matt had finished work on the Gilder office and as well he and Leonard had made progress in detailing and documenting the Forge 'system'. We were off to a good start.

Matt, Virginia and I met to discuss the Gwalia meetings and the alternative possibilities of Forge building 'low cost' housing in the US and/or the UK. We concluded, perhaps a little reluctantly, that it would be too difficult to build in the US. There were three factors. The first was the manufacturing plant. Even with Virginia's investment we had insufficient capital to develop an appropriate manufacturing facility and there was no US supply chain comparable to Ayrshire. Secondly, Rockwool had become a critical component of the Forge system and Rockwool was not marketed in the US (a complex story, some other time). Even if we were able to get around the manufacturing issues there was the problem of the US market, perhaps an even more critical problem than the supply chain. The US approach to low cost housing was inconsistent, regional and very political. There would be a push such as the government driven one in the late sixties, lots of low cost housing starts and then: nothing. We understood, early on, that system (prefabricated) building, no matter how good could not succeed without, a consistent, steady market. Our own South Pond Farm, Jiminy Peak and Russell Estate projects had demonstrated that. In the US when there were low-income housing projects they tended to be too large for our start-up company, or too small for prefabrication. In the UK, by comparison, there was always a 'Social Housing'[205] market, essentially largely led by almost seventeen hundred not-for-profit housing providers. Of these probably about two hundred were potential clients with vested interest in new-build. Collectively, in the nineteen nineties, they constructed thirty to forty thousand units each year. The UK market was geographically cohesive and any potential project in the UK could be served from the Ayrshire plant. The UK market made sense: we would go for the UK market. I think Virginia was only modestly enthusiastic, Virginia, probably, would have liked a US base better but she accepted the logic of the UK choice.

For the next weeks we worked on what we thought would be an appropriate design concept for Wales. Matt also worked to finish the Gilder offices and in between we entered a competition for a Habitat for Humanity house. We didn't win but did receive a special mention. I also kept in touch with Phil Roberts, we didn't want him to forget us. In fact, it wasn't long before Phil called to say he thought he had an appropriate project, could we meet?

Within the week Matt and I were in Swansea to meet Phil. He had identified a small site in Garnant, a valley hamlet some twelve miles north of Swansea. The project would consist of eight units in four buildings, big enough Phil thought for a first project but small enough to be forgotten if the project didn't work out. We would be joint architects with a Swansea architect, Michael Batcup. The fees were meagre but it was the start we needed.

Phil liked our drawings but we soon learned that they were irrelevant as the overriding Welsh housing agency, Ty Cymru, had something called the 'Pattern Book'. The plans and details contained in the book were mandatory for funding. On the one hand the pattern book ensured that no grievous planning/design error would be made but on the other hand they also ensured architectural mediocrity. We got on well with Michael Batcup and quite quickly devised an architectural scheme that was approved by Gwalia and Ty Cymru and, as well, satisfied the rigors of the `pattern book`. But that was only the beginning. We now had to develop the details for the eight little eighty-square meter buildings.

The detailing was time consuming, sometimes frustrating and certainly costly. Everything was new, different and required justification, Phil was detail-minded and, justifiably, wanted to be comfortable with a new system. Without the technical help and support of our 'supply chain' notably Rockwool, British Gypsum, British Steel, Ayrshire and a number of others we would not have succeeded. Apart from being the manufacturer Ayrshire provided financial assurances that the system would be delivered and erected. Without this financial 'comfort' the project could not have proceeded. Rockwool built a mock-up of the new wall system at their plant to demonstrate that steel studs on 600mm centres would work, tested glues and their pull off resistances, calculated thermal resistances and also provided their own financial guarantees that the wall system, never used before, would perform as described. Rockwool was very supportive even taking me to their headquarters in Copenhagen to meet with and be entertained by their chief executive and head technicians. Visits to pertinent local low-cost housing projects were also included. The substrate, the material attached to the steel and to which in turn the Rockwool lamella was attached was an issue. We eventually settled on an environmentally friendly Norwegian material called Bitvent but not before I had also visited the Bitvent plant in Norway learning more than I could possibly have needed to know about Bitvent as well as Norway's timber industry. Phil asked what would happen if the steel frame was struck by lightning. The answer, "it's a Faraday cage,"[206] required research by British steel. Thermal breaks[207] were designed out of the system, windows, doors and other wall penetrations needed detailing, the plumbing and heating systems needed to be integrated into the steel frame and of course the prefabricated structure had to be detailed and engineered. Each house required about twenty panels and each panel contained about twenty parts each one of which had to be engineered and drawn. Since we were using the British Gypsum SFS system, the same as TPS we used their, good, pleasant but somewhat conservative structural engineer, Chris Legg of John Savage Associates. Without Virginia's investment in the Forge Company none of this would have happened. I suppose that even with the fees paid to us our costs that could be attributed to the Gwalia project approached $100,000. Our costs included, in addition to engineering, travel and subsistence the setup of a small office in the heart of Swansea. An added cost included new computers. The very night we opened the little one room office, "a person or persons unknown", according to the Swansea police report, entered the office through a skylight and stole our computers and anything else of value (or not), apparently not an unusual occurrence in Swansea. Fortunately Matt had remotely backed-up most of his work. With everything included the design process took more than nine months of intense work by everyone, and included multiple trips to the UK. When we had completed the drawings Matt and I returned to the US to tidy up our US work that now included new work at Jiminy Peak. Meanwhile Ayrshire began manufacturing the required 160 or so steel-panels for the Garnant project.

Shortly after returning to the States, while working away in our Fifth Avenue office, I took a call from Hugh Lobban. I expected it to be either an information update or question. Instead he rather sheepishly informed me that Bob Colver had flatly refused to permit the SFS (Steel Framing Systems) steel studs to be used on 600mm centres insisting on 300mm centres, thus doubling the amount of steel in the buildings. I think Hugh heard my asterisked response without my having to use the phone. Although this arbitrary intervention made a mockery of all the Rockwool testing and structural engineering there was a benefit, or as my mother often used to say, "it's an ill wind that blows no good". The Gwalia project was the not only the first but emphatically the last one in which Colver, SFS or British Gypsum or their engineers were involved. After the Garnant project we rolled steel sections to our own or Ayrshire's design and used Lafarge as our plasterboard supplier and innovator. Chris Walker, Lafarge's chief UK technician and sales manager was our main contact and he provided absolutely terrific help. In time, Lafarge conducted acoustic and fire tests on our behalf and help to ensure that the Forge system and projects met or exceeded UK building regulations. Chris Colbourne recommended and introduced us to our new structural engineer Mike Eatherley of the Michael Barclay Partnership. Mike was an absolutely first rate engineer and he and his team would provide all the engineering services for subsequent Forge projects in the UK. Mike was charming, sophisticated, a good artist and good company. Mike and his partner (later wife) Diana became good friends.

Notwithstanding the debacle on the steel framing, the Gwalia project was a great success. The twenty (or so) panels required for one house could be carried on one articulated lorry. A lorry would arrive at eight am having started the day before, 460 miles away, in Ayrshire. If all had gone according to plan[208] the panels would have been stacked in the right sequence. Their erection was accomplished by an excellent three-man crew from Robert Aitkin's steel fabrication shop in Cardiff. By four pm, more or less, the entire structural frame was in place. The fact that Atkin monumentally overcharged for his work, (his fees were almost as much as Ayrshire's manufacturing costs), was historically unimportant as we afterwards trained and used our own erection crews. We had a grand opening attended by almost everyone involved. Colver was not invited.

The project was well received by the architectural and housing press. "Tomorrow's Housing Today", "Growing Green in Garnant", "Wonder Wall" were the titles of three of the several articles written about the project. It wasn't brilliant architecture, the pattern book, ensured that, but it was, technically, a good first project and it provided not only the technical basis for our future work but an essential marketing tool to use when going back to those housing associations who had told me, "come back when you have completed a project."

I visited the Garnant project after about five years. The owners to whom we talked were happy. More recently I looked at the project on Google Earth. The houses still seem neat and tidy, a good sign, so I trust the owners are even now enjoying their homes.

With all the travel it was, understandably, not easy keeping up with Serena. A prostate cancer scare and attendant complications didn't help nor did the difference in our body clocks. Serena was a serious night owl and late sleeper. I needed to be at work early, partly to leave as much time as possible to communicate with the UK and partially just to get the work done. These ingredients were not a good mix. We discussed the issues as best we could but I think we were not too good at that. There were never any fights nor even anything one could call a misunderstanding; perhaps we were not playing with a full deck. After an intense two years or so in a long conversation after a convivial dinner in Serena's apartment we called time on our relationship. It was a sad and emotional parting.

Almost a year later, while I was puttering about the Forge doing this and that, (there was always something to do at the Forge either inside or out), the phone rang. It was Brenda. Brenda; "Jim, I have a friend visiting from London and I thought she might like to see the Forge. Could we come over?"

Me; "Of course".

I liked showing off the Forge and was ready for a break even if I might not have deserved one. Within the hour Brenda arrived with her friend of long standing, Rosemary Burgis. Brenda introduced us and then claimed to have a brief errand at the school she would return in twenty or thirty minutes leaving me to show Rosemary around on my own. Rosemary seemed to be interested and enthusiastic on the tour. I found Rosemary very attractive and an easy conversationalist. It was an affable visit. Brenda was true to her word and reappeared to pick up Rosemary, all too quickly. Rosemary thanked me for the tour and casually remarked that if I wanted to have a game of tennis in London she would be happy to sponsor me at her club, (I surmised that Brenda had told Rosemary that I played! Valery and I had spent hours playing on the Niemand's court.) I agreed and Rosemary gave me her number and with that detail in hand Rosemary and Brenda left.

It would be several weeks before I was back in London pursuing the next project with Gwalia and getting on with promoting the Forge Company. I did bring my tennis racquet and I called Rosemary. We played on the grass courts at Hurlingham, the very swish club in SW6. We had a good time and the tennis was quite even. Rosemary was a good, steady player while I was rather erratic – our game styles evened us out. We got on well and quite soon we were, in the colloquial phrase, "an item".

At the time I was staying with my architect friend, Colin Haywood, and his partner Jo Haynes (a marketing/pr specialist) at their flat in Riverview Gardens, Barnes. Rosemary was renting a room from her friend and long-standing tennis partner, Mwfany Roberts in her flat on Fernshaw Road, SW10. It made for difficult meetings but we managed, mostly by taking frequent weekends at various venues. On one exceptionally rainy one in Paris, while slogging our way back from a concert to our hotel, I decided, despite the rain (though it made the night time rather damply romantic), that it was the right moment for a pertinent question. So on the Pont du Carrousel I asked Rosemary if she would marry me, or at least I thought I did. My proposal had, if I recall correctly, something to do with badgers[209], probably pretty confusing. It wasn't a bended knee moment and perhaps because of that, and the badgers, Rosemary didn't say much in response. I couldn't even really make out any answer. I wondered what was going on but decided to let the matter rest for the moment. Our hotel, aptly named L'Hotel (Oscar Wilde's last home), was only a few minutes away and we set off, in soggy though cheerful puzzlement. On arrival I suggested a nightcap and ordered, appropriately I thought, Champagne. When it came Rosemary turned and asked, with what I would remember as modest hesitation, "Was that a proposal?" "Yes" and "Yes" were the answers.

We were married at the Forge on June 13th, 1997. New Lebanon's Justice of the Peace, a blacksmith by trade, conducted the ceremony. With him and the anvil in the living room the service mimicked Gretna Green traditions of the Marriage Anvil[210]. Following this secular event we proceeded to the Darrow Chapel where Sheldon Flory, Darrow's retired Episcopal priest and a good friend, conducted a traditional Episcopal marriage blessing. Following this service the fifty or so guests walked back to the Forge accompanied by bagpipe airs and marches played by an appropriately attired local, (though displaced) Scottish piper. A convivial lunch catered by the Darrow kitchen was served on the Forge's deck. The weather was perfect; all four children were there, a rare, if not almost unique, occurrence. It was a splendid and well-attended celebration of family and friends (including a number of Darrow faculty). The pictures tell the story.

Rosemary and I returned to London shortly thereafter and rented a small but quite cheery one bedroom flat in Elm Park Gardens, off Fulham Road. Rosemary went back to her job at Eaglemoss, mostly doing photo shoots for Gary Rhodes and other chefs and I went back to Wales.

Phil stuck to his word that if the Garnant project went well he would give us another. He soon set us up with (perhaps his favourite architect), Andrew Ogorzalek. Andrew, as his name suggests, was Polish by origin. He was cheerful, imaginative and enthusiastic, a very likable individual. Our project was a nine unit, four-story building to be constructed just behind Gwalia's headquarters and overlooked by Gwalia's chief executive's office: a bold move typical of Phil.

Andrew's design incorporated a curved roof giving us some technical difficulties but also an opportunity to demonstrate the design flexibility of our system. Leonard came over to lead the erection crew provided by Ayrshire and even I spent several days helping Leonard assemble the frame. The project was a success and earned several awards.

Working on the project, the trips back and forth from London, Scotland and points in between soon identified some inherent weaknesses in the Forge Company. The first was quite obvious; we were very 'thin on the ground', the second and third were the same. The original Gwalia project at Garnant was considered; I think by all, as a one-off, possibly even an experimental project. Consequently, a lot of latitude was given to administrative and management matters (or the lack of them) such as insurance, guarantees, erection staff, etc. From now on, however, we needed to answer tough questions of corporate financial credibility and staff availability. The question was one of corporate sustainability. Forge, in the UK was a one-man band. I was the CEO, chief financial officer, marketing director, designer, draftsman and even a field construction hand - it was a tough sell. Our initial UK offices, apart from our temporary offices in Swansea, were, as had been TPS's, in Tibbalds' large, well-staffed and managed offices on Earl Street behind Broadgate. Tibbalds' offices provided enough 'smoke and mirrors' so that we could invite prospective clients or supply chain participants there for meetings. However, we had not been there long before Chris and the late Maurice de Rohan sold the firm to one of its employees, George Gardner. Although George and I were, on the surface, friendly, (our desks were across from one another) and we bantered, George had absolutely no interest in the Forge Company's work, he was a brick and block aficionado. He had no interest in subletting space to Forge in his 'new' firm. We had to move on and out.

Chris Gaylord, an American architect working for Tibbalds and Colin Haywood, not being enthusiastic fans of George, had already set up an informal practice together in a little office at 2 Morwell Street just off Tottenham Court Road and they invited me to rent part of their office. As I had hired Jo Haynes, on a part-time basis, to help with marketing, this was all quite convenient; I took up their offer.

Back in the US Matt was in almost the same position as I, except he had Leonard's input. Leonard, by his choice, remained an independent' contractor but was almost full time with Forge. While the Welsh projects were underway we were commissioned by Jiminy Peak to design and construct the first phase of what was to be a large time-share hotel complex. This was taking up all of Matt and Leonard's time and would for at least eighteen months. The project also required Leonard to set up Forge's own mini steel frame manufacturing facility in a spare shed on Jiminy's grounds. Though this was good news and fine by Matt, it was clear that if Forge were going to succeed in the UK that Matt would have to join me there. Matt and this included his wife Alison, was not prepared for that. Work at Jiminy would keep him beneficially employed in the US for the immediate future. For the UK I needed to think about running the Forge without Matt's able, enthusiastic help.

In the immediate term Ayrshire helped on the financial side. Hugh stuck his neck out and agreed to provide, as he had for Gwalia, by the way of carefully worded guarantees, that Ayrshire would stand behind a Forge project, essentially taking financial responsibility for the design and construction of the frame. With a little persuasion Hugh even agreed to pay a monthly marketing fee to Forge, also very helpful. Ayrshire's commitment was sufficient enough for the West of Scotland Housing Association to commission Forge to construct a 30 unit project in Ayr just 12 miles from Ayrshire's plant. Despite these early successes the longer term still appeared difficult. However, several external events would help us along.

The first of these 'events' were invitations to speak at housing and building conferences, there were lots of them, all over the UK. I lectured in Wales, Scotland, England and even in Northern Ireland. The Garnant project had put us on the map, so to speak. We were new and different. Also it turned out that I was a pretty good speaker. The speaking events were well attended and many future contacts were made. The second was related. Rockwool sponsored me to promote the wall system innovated at Garnant. That was a no-brainer, more talks, more contacts. The third was the change in the UK government. The 1997 election brought the Labour party into power and with it a burst of construction activity, particularly in the social housing sector. Committees and quangos were formed to promote innovation in housing and off-site construction techniques. We were invited to participate in a number of these: more contacts.

The contacts made at the speaking events more often than not meant follow up meetings with those who were interested in what the Forge system could offer. One event led to another: I was very busy. In addition to the Gwalia and West of Scotland projects we were discussing manufacturing free standing offices for Hanover Housing, housing for the elderly, a penthouse structure in London for a private client, a project in Greenwich, the beginnings of a project for Ealing Family Housing Association. Jo's part-time work was good but often meant more work for me; I needed technical help and consequently better accommodation.

I discussed this with Mike Eatherly and he, in turn talked to his partners. They agreed that we could rent a spare desk or two in their well-positioned office on the Strand. I accepted promptly. In due course he and his partners let us renovate their canteen on the upper floor of their office. That was after the partners discovered, one day, that I could raise my voice to an attention getting level. I was talking to a really underhanded contractor who was doing his best to steal the Hanover project from Forge. He failed and I was moved a bigger office in the partnership's canteen, upstairs.

By 1998, after we moved to the canteen level, the Forge Company consisted of myself, a great part-time secretary, Gemma Williams[211], Jeff Harris, who previously had been our client at Hanover Housing, Mike Hardiman[212] an American architect (and Darrow graduate, 1975) who was looking for some part time work and a young architect, Alan Budden. We were doing quite well, making a little money and getting more enquiries or might-be orders. The enquiries were often a 'problem'. Each required work that included accurate pricing and this meant working through the project in some detail. Depending of the size and complexity of the project it could be a costly exercise. We probably closed one in six enquiries, the rest were 'loss leaders'. While we were no longer understaffed we still had a major shortcoming. We could design and manage a sophisticated supply chain but we did not have any real construction capability unless one could promote Leonard to a contractor but that was going a bit too far. The Hanover offices were a perfect example. Without a facility to prefabricate we would have to abort the work. We would be saved by a fortuitous circumstance.

Typically, after one of my lectures, some half-dozen or so attendees would gather round to ask questions. On one occasion a tall, well-dressed, late fortyish, well-spoken individual with a comfortable smile stood out. He introduced himself as Martin Smith the Technical Director of Llewellyn Construction. Llewellyn was a hundred-year-old family-owned construction firm located in Eastbourne but with plant and offices in London, Milton Keynes and Brighton. Llewellyn, he told me, had been, until a few years ago, a specialist in prefabricated timber-frame construction for housing but Llewellyn´s plant near Brighton was now outdated and had ceased operation. Llewellyn either needed to rehabilitate the plant or adopt an alternative system, timber or, Martin postulated, "… steel?" Could the Forge system be what they were looking for and could he meet me to have a further discussion? Of course he could: rather exciting. I thought, "would Llewellyn be our missing link?"

Martin met me in Michael Barclay`s conference room about a week later. I made another presentation and Mike Eatherley discussed the engineering side of the Forge system. The meeting went very well. It was clear that we had a convert in Martin. We liked each other from the 'off' and that helped. The immediate problem was that Martin was a director in name only. The main directors were second and third generation family members. Martin would have to 'sell' the Forge system to five family directors and their financial director, Gerald Geer, who, though not of the Llewellyn family, was a real director. The sell didn't happen overnight; in fact it took nearly a year. I saw a lot of Martin and Gerald and I met the Llewellyns, particularly, Tim and Judy Llewellyn the third generation co-chairs. We exchanged financials, marketing projections, engineering data, visited Ayrshire and talked with or met our key supply chain companies. In the end Llewellyn and Forge agreed to form a joint venture company, on a 50/50 basis, to be called Forge Llewellyn. I had kept Virginia up to speed and she was supportive of the proposal agreeing that it was a necessary ingredient for success. We signed up in London in October of 1999 with Virginia in attendance. By that time we were already collaborating on a number of projects including the Hanover offices.

The arrangement with Llewellyn was indeed the missing link. We now could actually build anything that could be constructed using prefabricated light gauge steel. What, in fact, could be constructed? The answer to that question to a large extent would be our extended mission. We continued to generate projects but so did Llewellyn and Forge-Llewellyn became very busy, very quickly. By 2000 we had moved into yet larger offices in the Leathermarket, in Southwark, a short walk from the London Bridge Station. We could soon justify some twenty employees on our own staff and those did not include another ten or so engineers working full time on our projects at Michael Barclay`s or Llewellyn`s[213]. I ran the operation as chief executive, met with Martin once a week and with Gerald about once a month. All in all, the joint venture partnership worked very well. We started making some money and with Llewellyn`s financial muscle our cash flow problems were solved. We started getting larger projects including the largest steel-frame project in Europe, a 300-unit housing project for Sentinel Housing in Basingstoke. The architects were HTA but we (Forge and Llewellyn) provided the prefabrication technology and construction. The Project received several awards including the Richard Feilden Award for Affordable Housing. Perhaps the most interesting project was Beaufort House for the Peabody Trust. I had made several presentations to Peabody and kept in touch with Dickon Robinson, Peabody's sophisticated, forward thinking development director. When we were asked by the architect, Feilden Clegg Bradley[214] to make a proposal to be the system builder for Peabody's sixty unit building, Beaufort House, on Lille Road he was encouraging. Our six million pound proposal to build the six-story building out of prefabricated steel panels, incorporating three dimensional prefabricated bathroom pods, was ground breaking, a first of its kind. Our proposal was successful. When finished Beaufort House would be widely published and would win numerous awards including the 2004 "Best example of Affordable Housing" award from the Housing Corporation. [215] Of course Beaufort House was a co-operative development: the architects, Mike Eatherley and his engineering team, Llewellyn's Rod Peck all contributed at the top of their form. But Forge's contribution was significant to the success. It took us a while to get there but we did: Beaufort House exemplified the objectives of the Forge Company, it also exemplified the truism, already noted, that a good project is the product of a good client, good architect and good contractor(s).

Back in the US, or more specifically, the Berkshires, we had completed the first phase of the Jiminy Hotel and had constructed a number of our Mountainside houses using the Forge steel frame system. Unfortunately, soon after the completion of the hotel's first phase, Brian sold the development rights on to a time-share guru. We met with him in the thought that we might carry on with what we had started but we were miles apart in all matters: personal and financial. Brian's sale was sensible for Jiminy Peak but it was effectively the end of our US venture; the odd Mountainside house was not sufficient to support a US office and/or mini fabrication plant. As a result Matt, not wanting to move abroad, resigned and went on to a good job with a Long Island development company. Anyone who had worked with Matt while he was with the Forge Company was sorry to see him leave and I particularly missed him. He was a great `partner` in the venture.

Even after closing down the little steel plant at Jiminy we continued to design and Leonard continued to build our Mountainside houses as well as Jiminy's new ski lift but the work reverted to timber frame. One of the last of the Forge steel frame structures (actually it was a composite structure) in the US was the Samson Environmental Centre that I had designed for Darrow. The design was worked out with Larry and the wastewater technologists known colloquially as "The Living Machine". The 'Centre' was also one of Leonard's last building projects. Leonard was a chain-smoker for his entire life and in addition, his life hadn't been an easy one. Cancer caught up with him and it was not long after the diagnosis that he died.

His son David carried on some building for us (Jiminy Peak) after his death but David was a bit problematical. We all missed Leonard: he was a 'one-off', proper, 'American type' and, importantly, he was a good, loyal, friend for some thirty years.

Rosemary's mother, Adela Love, died in 1999. Adela, though I do not believe I ever called her by her first name, was a small, modest woman who could be as firm as she was gentle ("the apple doesn't fall far from the tree" – in this case, perhaps, vice-versa). I couldn't say I knew her well but I think she liked, or perhaps just accepted me, I was after all Rosemary's third husband, not to overlook the fact that Rosemary was my fourth wife.[216] Rosemary's father had died some years before and her mother had stayed on in the little family house, 'Larkfield', on the main road just outside the village of Collyweston, near Stamford.

Upon her mother's death Rosemary inherited this unexceptional little house - actually a bungalow. After some debate, mostly financially based, on London versus Collyweston, we decided we would renovate 'Larkfield' and move from London. 'Larkfield' was Rosemary's home and she was loath to abandon it, certainly not in the first instance. If the commute to London was too much we agreed that we could always rethink. With two salaries and thanks to the joint venture with Llewellyn, we were relatively well off. The cost of renovation was manageable. In the end we turned Rosemary's little bungalow into a somewhat presumptive, but still small, two-story, three-bedroom house with a garage and studio. It was good.

Rosemary and I went to the States several times each year. We celebrated the millennium at the Forge. The trips usually combined visiting the children, attending Darrow Board meetings, meeting with Virginia and conducting architectural consultations at Jiminy and Darrow. At Jiminy the Mountainside houses continued and there was also a commission for a timber frame building for a general store. Thanks to a gift from the Seips, Darrow committed to building an arts centre and the Board asked me to be its architect. I worked with Larry on concepts including looking at the possibility of moving and renovating the Macdonald's Second

Family chair factory. By the spring Board meeting in 2000 we had agreed on the concept and the site just west of the Dairy Barn, where the 'green shack' still stood.

The committees of the Board usually started their meetings on Fridays, sometime after lunch, breaking up in time for a cheerful dinner that included wives and 'significant others'. The latter category was one that, for the preceding twelve or so years, had been, for the most part, my exclusive prerogative. As there was little for Rosemary to do at the Forge while I attended committee meetings on Friday, Rosemary decided that she would go off with Brenda to the Canyon Ranch in Lenox for a little pampering. I thought it a good idea.

When we met up again Rosemary told me that her visit to Canyon Ranch had been upsetting. During a massage the masseuse told Rosemary that he had felt a lump in her back - not where any lump should be. He had stopped the massage and advised Rosemary to seek medical advice as soon as she got home. Though I was unable to discern the masseur's "lump" we were both concerned.

We returned to London on a Sunday night flight. On Monday afternoon we were able to meet, in London, with Rosemary's physician John Cowen. He confirmed the masseuse's observations and arranged for x-rays and a scan to be taken immediately. By late Friday afternoon Rosemary and I were waiting in the Lister Hospital to meet Christopher Woodhouse the consultant surgeon to whom we had been referred by Cowen. Woodhouse laid out the x-rays for us: he didn't mince his words. There was no need for a biopsy, it was clear that Rosemary had kidney cancer and it had metastasized to create a mass in her back, exactly what the masseuse had felt. It was not good news: we were stunned to silence. Woodhouse explained that there were no easy options. He would schedule an operation to remove the kidney and secondary mass, as soon as possible. We drove back to 'Larkfield' and tried to be upbeat but we hardly knew what to say to each other.

Woodhouse operated on Rosemary at the Lister Hospital within the week. In spite of the complexity and extent of the operation Rosemary recovered rapidly. In about a month or so Rosemary was even going into Eaglemoss, at least part time. But Rosemary's treatment was only beginning. Not more than six weeks later

Rosemary was admitted to the Royal Mardsen for a follow up course of chemotherapy under the kind care of the oncologist Martin Gore[217], a specialist in kidney cancers. The course was rugged but Rosemary managed it without complaint. Rosemary, remarkably, recovered quickly and Gore was 'cautiously' optimistic for a full recovery. By August Rosemary was not only back at work but we were able to take a pleasant holiday in Normandy mostly in and around Honfleur but also to Giverny. To an extent we followed in grandfather Twachtman's footsteps.

Despite Martin Gore's optimism, he is quoted as saying to the Tatler magazine sometime after these events, "… I guess you could say that my main hobby is optimism." I was haunted by John Cowen's remarks to me following Rosemary's operation. Cowen was not a 'Gorian' optimist. Sitting behind his old desk in his old fashioned office, he looked straight at me and said, simply, "It's a rum business". His opinion was quite clear, Rosemary's cancer was terminal, it was found too late. It would not be a drawn out affair. I never revealed Cowen's comments to Rosemary – or anyone; there was no point. I opted for Gore's optimism: so did Rosemary.

In September (2000) we had learned that President Clinton had appointed Jamie to be a Judge of the US Court of Appeals for the Armed Forces. Jamie was a logical choice for this judicial posting and was unanimously confirmed by the Senate. His investiture would take place on Friday the first of December. By that time Rosemary was well enough to accompany me to Washington for a ceremony that was quite moving, in part because of the distinguished guests who spoke on Jamie's behalf. Jamie, as noted, had previously served as Special Assistant to the President and Legal Advisor to the National Security Council. As a result he was in frequent contact with senior members of Clinton's cabinet among them, Sandy Berger the National Security Advisor, Attorney General Janet Reno and Beth Nolan Counsel to the President. These three would speak on Jamie's behalf as would Michael Reisman, Jamie's Yale law professor and co-author of their book *Regulating Covert Action*. I played the proud father, though some thought John

Flender was Jamie's father, a slight irritation. Molly was there, of course, and we chatted amicably about Jamie: all quite civil.

After the investiture and an unrelated inaugural ceremony at the AIA on Saturday night we made our way to the Forge for a few days to discuss the design of the Arts Centre with Larry, catch up with Brian at Jiminy and attend to the Forge's 'needs' before we returned to the UK.

We now settled into the renovated 'Larkfield'. Starting on Monday the 8th [218] of January I would commute from there to London via either Peterborough or Kettering. We arranged to have a local acquaintance from the Church, Christina, come in during the day to help around the house but mostly to be a companion for Rosemary. The commute wasn't great but I could work on the train, preparing for the day's activities or whatever. But no amount of planning could prepare me for the news that greeted me on arriving at the Leathermarket that Monday morning.

My first call came from Gerald Geer bearing the news that our Llewellyn compatriot and friend Martin Smith had died of a heart attack following his final run of the day on his Christmas Alpine ski holiday. As Rosemary wrote in her dairy, that day, it was "shocking news". Martin had been our loyal supporter, we were his 'find' and he couldn't do too much to help us. He was always optimistic and enthusiastic. I suspect he may have driven the Llewellyns and Gerald to distraction in his dedicated support of Forge. Martin's unique diplomatic qualifications that helped us convince 'Doubting Thomases' among Llewellyn´s conservative middle managers to build with steel were irreplaceable. He would be sorely missed. Most importantly he was a good personal friend, Rosemary really liked him: that says a lot for Martin.

His funeral was held at the crematorium in Tunbridge Wells, his hometown. It was well attended by family and friends and perhaps fifty of Llewellyn's management staff. The ceremony was not the elegant affair it should have been. There is something tacky about the several crematorium ceremonies I have attended with the moving coffin and plush curtains, though it was certainly not as fraught as Mother´s cremation.

Gerald's choice for Martin´s replacement was John Chinnock a good, pleasant and workmanlike staff member. John tried hard to support our 'cause' but he was a bit perfunctory and not that interested in light gauge steel prefabrication. He was not Martin but he was dutiful. We got on.

During 2001 I continued to commute, almost on a daily basis, and worked mostly at the Leathermarket. Sometimes, however, when Rosemary was particularly unwell, I worked from 'home'. During 2001 'home', because of treatments, occasionally became London during the week. Initially this was in a service flat on Cadogan Square, later, during a particularly long bout of chemotherapy we rented a flat on Redesdale Street in Chelsea from one of Rosemary's friends. Both locations were only about thirty minutes' drive from the Leathermarket and I could visit Rosemary at almost any time during the day. Rosemary had a good coterie of friends from Eaglemoss, Hurlingham and the English Speaking Union to visit her in between my visits and for the most part they did. Trina came over for a special visit, as did Jamie. When Jamie came he and I took a long weekend and visited Normandy, most of the D Day beaches and the Bayeux tapestry. Rosemary´s family was, in my opinion, less supportive. To the best of my recollection, they never visited her in London and only sporadically in Collyweston. Most of Collyweston's help or 'moral support' came through the members of the little Church of St Andrew. David Simmonds the non-stipendiary vicar was, himself, attentive, though I think sometimes, that Rosemary thought his attention was too good. Rosemary wasn't terribly enthusiastic about having the congregation pray for her and asked David to omit her name from the Sunday prayers. We muddled on, keeping busy, Rosemary went back to work part time and Forge Llewellyn's projects continued to accumulate.

Trips to the US on behalf of Darrow of Jiminy Peak continued and when possible these included Rosemary. On one trip in the Spring of 2001 we gave up the flat in New York and sold off the furniture as best we could. Since Rosemary was in charge that meant we sold off almost everything, Rosemary was quite determined and thorough.

The Darrow's spring board meeting would be Larry's last as he had accepted the headship at Mooreston Friends: the Board was sorry to see him go but it was 'an offer he couldn't refuse'. Nancy Wolf, previously a math teacher at Darrow had been selected as the next head. I would be working with Nancy to oversee the construction of what was now called the Joline Arts Centre.

Despite periodic chemotherapy treatments, the early months of 2001 were pretty good. Rosemary had clean results from checkups and she felt well: in fact well enough to visit her longtime friend June Ansorge in Florida. Rosemary and I were even playing tennis. Rosemary's checkup in June came as a blow to this brief idyll. Her scan showed small growths in her thoracic cavity necessitating an almost immediate operation. This took place at the Royal Brompton in the second week of June. July was not a good month. Most of the time Rosemary was in pain and very tired. We stayed in London for most of the month only returning to Collyweston on the 25th. August was better, Rosemary's health was improving and we were getting out and about: everything was brighter. Tuesday afternoon the 17th of August put an end to that.

Rosemary was at home in Collyweston while I was at the Leathermarket. In midafternoon my phone rang. It was Rosemary but her voice was so garbled that I could barely make out what she was telling me. It was with some difficulty that I understood that Rosemary had been on the phone to her friend Ann Chilton, (one of Rosemary's English-Speaking Union friends[219]), when Rosemary had what she described to me as a "minor-stroke" losing her ability to talk clearly. Ann had called the ambulance service and Rosemary was now waiting for it to arrive. She would be taken to Peterboro hospital: I would meet her there. I left the office and headed for the train at King's Cross.

By the time I got to the hospital some two hours later Rosemary had been admitted. I found Rosemary in a very gloomy ward. Rosemary was, understandably, depressed. By this time most of Rosemary's speaking ability was now quite clear and firm. Rosemary also made it very clear that she wanted out of there. It took some phone calls to the Marsden but we succeeded and some hours later were back home at Collyweston. The next day I drove Rosemary to the Marsden for tests. The results were immediate and alarming. They revealed that Rosemary had a number of brain lesions, assumed, under the circumstances, to be malignant. Immediate radiation treatment was recommended and accepted. Rosemary was also told that she could no longer drive and this deeply affected Rosemary. It meant that she was dependent on others, mostly me, to get around. It was a statement of some finality that Rosemary was really ill.

In between bouts of radiotherapy we behaved as normally as we could. I took time off from work. We split our days between London and Collyweston. In London we went mainly to Hurlingham and out to dinner. In Collyweston we had neighbours over and also went out to our favourite places. The Niemands came to visit at the end of August, a treat for Rosemary. On the 4th of September Rosemary made this entry in her diary, "look good, feel good". Despite the upbeat entry it was clear to me that all was not going well. Rosemary's speech was now getting more difficult to understand, her writing was shaky and she was having some difficulty walking. These limitations might have stopped many people but Rosemary continued on as if she only had a minor cold. Nevertheless we made an appointment to see Gore on Friday the 7th of September, for a checkup.

By Friday Rosemary's speech was nearly unintelligible. While Gore was examining Rosemary his colleague Dr. Julia Riley head of palliative care at Marsden, took me into a consulting room. She explained to me how ill Rosemary was. Her conversation ended by her telling me, "If you have anything to say to Rosemary, do it now, don't put it off." Her words were chilling, the meaning clear. I broke down.

We drove back to Larkfield almost in silence. On Saturday we puttered around the house in the morning and had a nice lunch at the White Hart in Lyddington. On Sunday our outing took us the New Bield a rather eccentric unfinished Elizabethan structure and had tea at one of our favourite haunts. Monday we stayed home and Christine came over to help around the house. We didn't talk much it was too difficult. We communicated mostly with looks. I was now doing the cooking but still with help from Rosemary. At the end of dinner Monday night Rosemary struggling to speak, looked at me and said, "I couldn't have managed without you." I helped Rosemary get up from the table and we embraced - I could barely hold back my tears.

Rosemary indicated she was tired and wanted to go to bed. I helped her get sorted in the downstairs bedroom to which we had moved. Rosemary fell asleep almost immediately. I tidied up the kitchen, watched some news and joined her.

At about two in the morning I woke as Rosemary tossed about in bed in the throes of a seizure. I had never seen anything like it. Rosemary was unconscious and there was absolutely no communication. In accordance with the emergency plan that had been set up with our local doctor, John Mitchell, I called him and then Charmian Ling[220]. Both of them responded immediately. Within fifteen minutes they were at Larkfield as was the ambulance that Mitchell had called. Rosemary remained unconscious; in fact Rosemary was in a coma. The paramedics stood by while Mitchell, Charmian and I discussed the options. Mitchell took control of the conversation saying that there was no point in moving Rosemary, she could be looked after as well, if not better, in her own home, (rather than the dreaded Peterboro Hospital) with round the clock care brought in. He would arrange it. He let the ambulance go, made sure Rosemary was comfortable and left, promising that he would be in touch in just a few hours. Charmian left shortly after telling me that she too would be back in a few hours.

By eight am, Monday, the first of the round-the clock nurses arrived. Mitchell returned shortly thereafter and set up the routines to be followed. I did some necessary shopping, sat by Rosemary, sat in the study, watched the BBC news, sat by Rosemary, talked to the nurse on duty, talked to Charmian when she came back, sat by Rosemary; I did my best to keep busy, there was little or no sleep. Early Tuesday afternoon I was on a break, in the study, more or less watching some BBC program, when the program was interrupted with the News from New York: harrowing pictures filed the screen. In Collyweston it was just after one forty-five, it was five hours earlier in New York: it was the 11th of September.

The next days remain blurred there is not much that I remember. Nurses came and went. Rosemary's (more or less estranged) brother visited. Charmian came frequently. Mitchell checked in regularly. Members of St Andrews came by. Mike Eatherley and Diana visited. It was all quite busy, quite unreal, and sad. In between visits, I sat with Rosemary and talked to her as best I could. I ran the occasional errand. I dozed on the couch in the study, watched the news and began to plan for the end that came, quietly, almost an anti-climax, late Saturday evening. The following days were busy planning Rosemary's funeral, notifying our friends and relatives and dealing with the necessary legal formalities.

Rosemary's funeral took place on the following Friday, September 21st. in the church of St Andrew, It was simple, elegant and well attended. David Simmons officiated. Rosemary was interred in Collyweston's cemetery. Neither the children nor Rosemary's close American friends could attend because of the travel restrictions and difficulties following 9/11. Jamie, however, spoke for all in his written eulogy that was read, haltingly, by our Collyweston friend Mike Steele.

> Jamie wrote:
> "Remembered by her American Family …
> I remember Rosemary."

I remember Rosemary's keen sense of order, to which I was first introduced on her wedding day. We were put to work ironing napkins, sheets, table clothes, and anything else to which an iron might affix. My father and I soon found an urgent task requiring our presence outside of the house. I did not know at the time that ironing was one of Rosemary's joys and that she would have a room dedicated to ironing at Collyweston. Nor did I know at the time that Rosemary and Pop would come to call each other "Badger," after a most tidy and meticulous animal.

Rosemary's keen sense of order was just the waterline of a strong and even keel. She was courteous. She was fair. And, as we all know so well she was courageous. Behind a gentle, almost frail countenance was a legion of determination and steel, which bound to life in loyalty and love for my father. She was his right and left arm; his stonewall.

I remember that Rosemary was a good and caring grandmother. She loved young Jamie, with a love that was manifest and obvious not just to us, but to a one-year old. She was also capable of communicating this love from near and afar, asking real questions on the telephone, eager for the next word spoken. Stuffed animals and books were treasures saved in bureau drawers, not airport afterthoughts. Jamie will always have the fortune of knowing grandmother Rosemary; Rosemary lives on in Jamie.

I remember how quickly and easily Rosemary bonded with Lori. Rosemary was always sensitive and caring about others, even when she had every right to focus her attention at home. Rosemary and Lori seemed to appreciate and understand so much about each other without having to ask or tell. Apparently, they shared a common empathy that had something to do with their husbands.

And, we as a family remember many moments of friendship together. Tea outside Canterbury: Shopping in London and Old Town: A visit to Clouds Hill: Walks and kittens at the Forge: Thanksgiving dinner: Scrambled eggs and bacon just off the plane at Collyweston: Collyweston, which felt immediately like home, even before it was renovated.

Rosemary didn't try to be anything she wasn't, only herself, and in the process she became so much more, a friend and a member of our family.

Most of all, I think of father and Rosemary together. We are happy for love found last - a Forge wedding day. I remember how many times I called Collyweston - at any hour of the day -- and was told, "We are just sitting down to dinner in the garden for Father's favourite." Rosemary loved to please Pop with an elegant setting and food to match. And, he loved to show-off for Rosemary, perhaps with a paintbrush or a gratuitous display of knowledge.

I remember watching my father test Rosemary's sense of order, sometimes intentionally. Other times by chance. Invariably, a smile would come to her eyes. And, sometimes to the corner of her mouth, before she complained with mock dismay, "Oh, I have so much to teach father. What am I going to do with him?" They were always fun to be with in good times and well times. Their friendship was graceful, respectful, and daily.

And, they were always there for each other in difficult times … Soul mates from a timeless marriage. I remember Pop describing for me a country drive. This was near the end – just a few weeks ago - when Rosemary found it difficult to communicate; indeed, she likely would have found it impossible to communicate to you or me. They drove through the country and over the hills where they had so often driven together. He did not know their destination, but he knew that Rosemary wanted desperately to get there. Instinctively, he turned, and he turned, down less travelled roads, until they found a little inn in a quiet village. Rosemary smiled; her destination found. They ate together and went home happy and full… Full of friendship… Full of a marriage well done… And, full of the love they will always share and we will always remember with happiness. So,

> Gentle Lady, Graceful Lady,
> Sailing into the Mist.
> Take our hands in kindness
> And forever hold our love."[221]

A Pewter Spoon

The marriage ceremony at the Forge: Justice of Peace Weaver Presiding

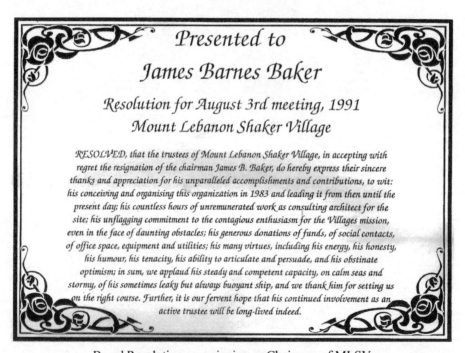

Presented to

James Barnes Baker

Resolution for August 3rd meeting, 1991
Mount Lebanon Shaker Village

RESOLVED, that the trustees of Mount Lebanon Shaker Village, in accepting with regret the resignation of the chairman James B. Baker, do hereby express their sincere thanks and appreciation for his unparalleled accomplishments and contributions, to wit: his conceiving and organising this organization in 1983 and leading it from then until the present day; his countless hours of unremunerated work as consulting architect for the site; his unflagging commitment to the contagious enthusiasm for the Villages mission, even in the face of daunting obstacles; his generous donations of funds, of social contacts, of office space, equipment and utilities; his many virtues, including his energy, his honesty, his humour, his tenacity, his ability to articulate and persuade, and his obstinate optimism; in sum, we applaud his steady and competent capacity, on calm seas and stormy, of his sometimes leaky but always buoyant ship, and we thank him for setting us on the right course. Further, it is our fervent hope that his continued involvement as an active trustee will be long-lived indeed.

Board Resolution on resigning as Chairman of MLSV

364

Virginia Gilder (now Manheimer) with Matt Frank
and Phil Roberts - Swansea, Wales 1996

Commemorating the opening of Garnant:
Rosemary Matt and Phil

Second Gwalia: Swansea - The skeleton erected by
Leonard, the Ayrshire team and me: (a little)

The finished structure - 9 flats

Darrow: The Samson Environmental Centre

'Larkfield', Collyweston: before renovations - 1997

The Studio at 'Larkfield' after renovation - 2000

A Hanover office being installed - 2000

Leonard and Jeff Harris discussing something 'big' in our offices at Michael Barclay Associates

Alden, Leonard and his wife Rohda in Ayrshire – Alden worked on Ayr and Leonard was a consultant on the project - 2001

The Project at Ayr for West of Scotland

17

ENDGAME

London 2001 – 2005

"The end is in the beginning and yet you go on." ...
Samuel Beckett

Memories of the days immediately following the funeral are foggy. I was busy, there was a lot to do, people to see, letters to write and, of course, work. I commuted to London from Collyweston most days. In the evening I made pasta for supper and, mindlessly, watched television. I slept, as best I could, on the comfortable couch in the study: it was awhile before I could manage our bedroom. I met with Claire Dunnell a NHS bereavement counsellor a number of times: that was helpful. In fact the NHS experience, on the whole, had been competent, caring and often more.

The office was busy. Beaufort House was nearing construction, Basingstoke was under construction and its next phases were on the boards. The Joline Arts Centre was scheduled to be finished around June. A growing number of other projects and possible projects were in the pipeline. Forge Llewellyn had a lot of work and remarkably, everything was under control. In fact, looking back, the fall/winter/spring of 2001/2002 might be considered the 'high watermark' for Forge Llewellyn.

Because of the catastrophic events of 9/11 Rosemary's American friends and the children, as noted, had been unable to attend her funeral. It seemed altogether appropriate, therefore, to arrange a service for Rosemary in the States. I set a date in early October for a memorial service in the Darrow Chapel. The service, a mirror image of Collyweston's, was also elegant, moving and well attended. Jamie gave his eulogy in person. Following the service we held a luncheon reception at the Forge: it was the omega of the marriage.

By December I was back to sleeping upstairs. Personal life was not exactly 'normal' but it was manageable. Christmas was coming, under the circumstances not a good time to be alone. Understanding this Anne and John Fraser suggested that I join them on their Christmas break (it coincided with the traditional two week construction industry holiday) in France, in their Jura farmhouse. I accepted with enthusiasm it would be good to 'get away'.

However, before the Christmas holiday an event was to significantly alter my future personal life. The event was an exhibition of Macartney-Snape illustrations at the Sloane Club[222]. Well, the 'event' was not the artwork, it was Jill Jackson who for a fortuitous moment was looking at the same illustration as I. We fell into a conversation that ended up with me saying, "Would you like to meet for a drink or something?" I got Jill's number and promised to call and I did. As it is said, 'the rest is history'.

I went to France with the Frasers, enjoyed the snowy visit and returned to take up with Jill where we had left off. It was not long before I was splitting my time between Collyweston and Greenwich, Jill's home, (Greenwich, funny that), and Mayfield. Mayfield, because Jill's daughter had been a student at St Leonards-Mayfield school (now just Mayfield) and that had been the catalyst for Jill to buy a lovely Georgian house in the middle of that iconic English village. In 2002 Jill was still in the process of renovating the house. I would pitch in where I could but it was Jill's project from the go.

* * * * *

Meanwhile work was coming in 'over the transom'. We were appointed to be the system builders on Lingham Court, a 70ish unit project for Metropolitan Housing Trust. Additional work included projects for BAA[223] and a number of housing start-ups for Llewellyn. Forge Llewellyn was ticking over quite well; we could imagine soon reaching 1000 housing units in the pipeline. We were even profitable, at least on paper. I thought to myself, "… something must be wrong", "it's never been this good". And, yes, soon enough 'something' was 'wrong'.

One afternoon during one of our well attended, (and sometimes boring) typically about 20 individuals, frequent Beaufort House partnering meetings held at the architect's office, (it seemed we were always at meetings), a receptionist broke into the meeting; "Mr. Baker, you have a telephone call." Any meeting interruption was highly unusual, "who would interrupt a meeting?", I wondered, not a little embarrassed and alarmed, as well. I got up, exited the meeting, and took the call: it was Hugh Lobban.

Typical Hugh, he got right to the point: "Jim, I just thought you ought to know right away, I've just been fired." His voice flat and expressionless, he might have been saying "I've just sneezed" for all the emotion Hugh transmitted.

I was 'gob smacked' and didn't know what to say. Hugh had always stood up to Ayrshire's owners and I knew the owners were sceptical of Hugh's interest in Forge, Forge Llewellyn and construction. Did we cause the fracture? Hugh wouldn't say. He did say that his number two, Steve Adams, the financial director, would be taking over and I was not to worry. Not to worry, was Hugh kidding? Forge Llewellyn depended on a close relationship with its steel supplier Ayrshire: would that remain? I went back to the meeting 'poker-faced' and said: nothing.

After the meeting I told Rod Peck, Llewellyn's, supportive, amiable and talented professional project manager, about the call. He was non-pulsed. Rod understood our 'problem' but also understandably wanted assurances that we could fulfil our obligations. I set about to find some assurances and called Steve. Steve told me the Beaufort project was safe. Beaufort had been priced correctly, as far as he was concerned, and Ayrshire was "ready to roll". That was the good news. The bad news was that Steve could not give me much comfort about our other projects. "Help!" I murmured to myself. For the moment we were ok but in due course: what?

We held discussions with Gerald Geer, other Llewellyn players and started, quietly, to identify potential alternative suppliers while keeping in close touch with Ayrshire and Steve Adams.

* * * * *

In late June 2002, Jill and I travelled to Darrow to celebrate the opening of the Joline Arts Centre. It had been more than three years since the first meetings had taken place with Larry Van Meter. We had gone through a few iterations before Larry and I settled on the final concept. I still have the little cardboard concept model of made in 2001 in my Collyweston studio. The Joline Arts Centre was enthusiastically received by Darrow and, (I think), by its principal donors, the Seips. Nancy, without my knowledge, had raised funds on my behalf so that one of the studios was named for me. Altogether the opening was a moving event. Darrow's description of the Joline Arts Centre is succinct:

> "The Centre … serves as a vital resource for the local art community and nationally recognized art education programs. From its courtyard to its skylights, the building provides the resources that support the needs of students, teachers, and guest artists. The Joline Arts Centre is a work of art itself"

* * * * *

In July, back in the UK, we were making headway on finding alternate steel suppliers, Steve Adams was being helpful and Ayrshire was still working with us. Despite the Ayrshire 'problem' we were quite optimistic. On Tuesday the 30th of July I received a call from Gerald he said he needed to meet with me at our typical meeting place, the Hilton Hotel at Gatwick, "... could we do it tomorrow afternoon?" Gatwick was our chosen meeting place as it was about an hour's drive from Llewellyn's Eastbourne office and an hour or so by underground and train from the Leathermarket, fair enough. By 2002 meetings with Gerald had become irregular and on an 'as needed' basis. They usually had to do with budgets and just overall catch up. Gerald liked face-to-face and I liked Gerald, he was pleasant, cheerful and supportive. I looked forward to our meeting.

As I crossed the hotel's lobby I could see Gerald sitting at one of the coffee table set-ups: he did not look amused, was I late? I didn't think so. He ordered coffee and made a few passing remarks, "… how was the trip? … etc." The coffee came, silence, we drank a little, Gerald looked at me, I was getting a little wary, what was up?

"Jim, I'm sorry to tell you, Llewellyns has been sold." That was what was up.

Gerald appeared genuinely apologetic for having to tell me about the sale, after the fact. Gerald told me that he had been sworn to absolute secrecy by the Llewellyns just in case some leak might have spoiled the sale. The bottom line was that Forge had a new, unknown, partner and it was too late to do anything about it. It was my turn to not look amused: I wasn't. Forge's new partner, Gerald told me, was ROK, a construction firm from Exeter headed by one Garvis Snook. "What did Snook know about Forge?" I asked. The disturbing answer was: nothing. Forge-Llewellyn as an entity had not factored in the transaction: at all. Gerald said that Garvis would be calling me and I would have to work out my relationship with ROK on my own.

I had the impression that Gerald was not 'crazy' about the sale. Among any other considerations he would be out of a job, one that I believe he enjoyed. My guess was that the Llewellyns, after some hundred years, and in the third generation in the construction business, had 'had enough'. I learned that the price was sixteen or so million, probably close to the value of Llewellyn's fixed assets in real estate. ROK of course got Llewellyn's order book, (a good part of which was developed by Forge-Llewellyn), and a highly professional management staff. Except for our experience and developed supply chain relationships it appeared that Forge was back to its beginning. I returned to London, depressed.

Would ROK respect our work? Would we be able to continue our progress as before? These were only some of my thoughts. Forge-Llewellyn was, arguably, the leading design-builder using light gauge steel. But it wasn't just the light gauge steel that made Forge-Llewellyn singular and a leader: we had a demonstrably competitive cost, environmentally efficient, manufactured building system. We didn't achieve this by ourselves and perhaps this was our unusual achievement. The system was the collective result of Forge but also Llewellyn, Ayrshire, Rockwool, Lafarge and the Michael Barclay Partnership. Led by their partner Mike Eatherley, the Michael Barclay expertise in developing engineering programs for LGS was critical to the advancement of the system. Anyone could build a LGS two story residential structure. By 2002, however, we were pioneering six story LGS buildings (Beaufort House and Lingham Court) and beginning work (with Wates) to design a twenty-story tower. Thanks to Lafarge and Rockwool we had been able to fire-test our system and develop robust details to provide strong acoustic performance as well. On the construction side, Llewellyn's shop in Milton Keynes had been set up for the fabrication of modular components. We were significant players in BRE (the Building Research Establishment)[224] publications on off-site construction. In addition we participated in industry led research and development for wall systems, and of course LGS systems in collaboration with the Steel Construction Institute. The cost of most of the R & D was borne by our supportive supply chain. That is not to say the Forge and Llewellyn also made proportional fiscal contribution: though in the case of Forge, mostly in kind. The Forge Llewellyn systems were, sometimes, not the least costly on the market but they were, arguably, the best value for money in affordable housing. And Gerald said ROK and Llewellyn didn't even discuss Forge: that was not only depressing but downright discouraging.

My first meeting with Garvis did not augur well. He was polite, perhaps even pleasant but he was clearly not interested in design-led construction let alone innovation. The latter implied 'risk' and as he explained, "in my opinion markets didn't like risk." It was clear that Garvis wasn't a builder he seemed closer in mentality to a stockbroker: his stock of course. It was only days after he bought Llewellyn that a prominent sign appeared on each of the reception desks of the several former Llewellyn offices showing the morning's value of ROK stock.

In the second meeting Garvis stepped down from being maybe a 'nice guy' and announced, simply, that he would divest himself of Forge and that he might assist as a first option, in a management buy-out. Negotiations started immediately. I needed help and sought out Ian Watson. Ian joined Forge as a non-executive director to help with the transition; whatever that might be. Meanwhile Ayrshire in spite of Hugh's absence was still supplying Forge with LGS frames. Unfortunately, about the same time as ROK was divesting us Ayrshire's owners announced that they were shutting down the Irvine plant (our steel source): completely. We were now, as the song goes, "…right back where we started from", actually, even a little further back.

Except: we had an 'order book' of about 750 units, depending, exactly, on how one counts. Our preliminary work, on at least 500 of these had commenced before Llewellyn sold out to ROK. Of course, there was a 'slight' problem with our 'orders': we had no steel supplier, no financial management structure (Financial management, e.g. payroll, cash flow support, etc., had been handled, in large part, by Llewellyn's office in Eastbourne), fiscal (cash) support or the ability to provide required guarantees!

However, at the same time, there was some good, though modest, news. Ayrshire's demise resulted in making their acting managing director, Steve Adams, redundant. Steve knew LGS, he was a financial manager (a trained accountant) and he knew our staff. We made him an offer he didn't refuse and he came on board. Forge had 'problems' to be sure, but we had a really good team, possibly our best. Ian, Steve and I set out to negotiate the separation from ROK, find a supplier and, if possible, a partner to replace Llewellyn.

Michael Martin, an LGS colleague[225], introduced us to one possibility. The potential supplier/partner was Fusion, a successful[226] Irish LGS specialist and developer of low cost, market rate housing using their own LGS and plastic-based exterior insulation system. Fusion was managed and owned by John Fleming. We had a number of what we thought were encouraging meetings with Fusion until we surmised that their main interest was in seeing if they could get our order book by 'hook or crook'. We did not 'sing from the same hymn sheet'. Our interest in LGS was to use it as a means to provide the best, environmentally sound affordable housing. Most 'steel-bashers' were only interested in selling steel at the best possible price: a position with which one could certainly understand. Ayrshire, that is to say Hugh Lobban, however, and perhaps uniquely for a steel-basher, appreciated the Forge concept of 'best value'.

In any event Fusion, i.e. John Fleming, didn't get our 'order book' but we did negotiate a mutually agreeable supply arrangement. Fusion manufactured panels to our design and specification and sold them to us for incorporation into our projects. It worked: for a while. We continued to look for other options, as we were a little uncomfortable with the smooth, possibly too clever; John Fleming and his sycophantic side kick Robert Clark.

Hugh Lobban, (yes we were still in touch and, in fact, we stay in touch even today) recommended Hadley Steel. Hadley was a well-established, typically conservative, steel basher from Birmingham, not too different from Ayrshire except there was no Hugh Lobban. Nevertheless we had a number of encouraging meetings with them that lead to a draft joint venture agreement. The potential 'deal' came apart when Hadley insisted on equal funding for the joint venture: we did not have the suggested five hundred thousand pounds. Hadley, I think, was: (a), skeptical of the value of our 'order book' and (b) afraid of getting, potentially, involved in construction: disappointing. Hadley's current web site incorporates much of what we talked about suggesting that a joint venture might have worked. Several other steel supply possibilities were explored but the explorations came to nothing for various similar, but now unimportant, reasons.

* * * * *

By early 2004, following the sale of Larkfield Jill and I were living together in Jill's flat in Mcartney House, (Greenwich). Jill was running Chloe on a daily basis (including Sundays) and I was commuting into Forge's office in the Leathermarket on the DLR. Jill's house in Mayfield was nearly completed and we occasionally camped out there to oversee the details of its completion. Jill was very specific in her instructions to the workmen but I helped out where I could. Jill's mother, now nearing her hundredth birthday, was living with us as was Jill's lovely, Megan, a retriever/spaniel, cross. Megan and I got on well and I helped out with her "walkies".

On the evening of the first of April 2004, on returning from an early evening "walkie" I sat down in the kitchen feeling a little 'off', slightly nauseous. I told Jill. Jill must have picked up on my tone of voice or something because she asked, "should I get my coat and take you to A&E?" I was beginning to feel really strange. "No", I replied, "call an ambulance". Within fifteen minutes two green-uniformed paramedics were assessing me as I lay, uncomfortably, on our bed. Within minutes, after a short examination, the medics were carrying me down the stairs to their ambulance: the blue light went on and we headed to Lewisham Hospital. Jill followed in her Range Rover. I do not remember much of next hours. I was on a gurney in the A & E, there was a lot of not very clear talk, injections and wires being placed here and there. By the time I was relatively clear-headed I was in a ward with more wires attached and a watching intern hovering over me. More conversations between doctors (I presume they were doctors) led to my being reinstalled, in the 'wee' hours, into another ambulance to take me to King's College Hospital on Denmark Hill. Jill was notified and made her way there in time for my surgeon to give her a cup of coffee before inserting a stent into one of my arteries. I stayed at Kings for a few days then transferred back to Lewisham for a few more, then back to Macartney House. I was able to return to work, at least part time, in a few weeks. To my relief the office had apparently run well during my absence and I picked up, more or less, where I had left off.

Despite the heart attack and the other obvious difficulties we were still quite optimistic about the future for what was in 2004 now known as 'The Forge Company (UK) Limited' wholly owned by the US Forge Company. We had the projects, we could get steel, we knew we could fabricate the steel if we had too, and we had hired an able construction manager to oversee steel erection. The situation was difficult, admittedly, but with our knowledgeable 'team' and remaining supply chain, Lafarge, Rockwool, and the Michael Barclay partnership it was manageable: until.

Until one day in July when Rod Peck and Neal Hunt (an ex Llewellyn manager, ostensibly now an arm's length ROK client) came into the office, wearing long, dour faces. They announced that ROK would be cancelling our orders for two of the projects on which we had been working for over a year. And, they added, by the way, ROK had no intention of paying for our work to date: work to the value of nearly £250,000. Of all the events affecting us this was a terminal, unsustainable event.

One has to understand a little of the typical procurement process for social housing that existed at the time. Projects did not receive government funding until they were 'packaged', i.e. site purchased, project completely designed, priced and contracts signed or committed. Consultants and contractors were expected to self-fund their work up to that point. Only when a 'project' was closed and 'packaged' to the government's satisfaction, would the project be funded and the 'pre-contract' work paid. The process was based on 'good faith', on everyone's part. Up to our experience with ROK, this procurement process, while a bit of an economic strain, had worked.

There were now only two options for Forge: a Deus ex Machina (aka investment angel) or shut down. Ian and I scrambled for the first. Ian came up with a few possibilities. I came up with none and none of Ian's were realistic. After a morning meeting at Crossways attended by Ian, Mike Steele (an entrepreneur friend of Ian's), Jill and in telephone consultation with our helpful account Sam Parsons, as officers, directors and advisors we concluded that we had to shut down:

voluntary liquidation. While at that moment, we were fiscally sound (just), we all knew that our resources were insufficient to continue operating without taking unacceptable risks. We gathered the staff and told them of our decision: most understood. We appointed a receiver. One could go into a 'what happened next' mode but it would be irrelevant: Forge was 'history'.

Lille Road (Beaufort) under construction

Lille Road (front) - completed

The Leathermarket - Location of Forge Llewellyn - (just two studios) 2002-2005

Mike Eatherley in his offices in the Strand

The Joline Arts Centre - Darrow - 2003

EPILOGUE
(POSTFACE)

Mayfield – Torbay – Sao Bras de Alportel
2005 – 2018

I'm very pleased to be here. Let's face it, ... I'm very pleased to be
anywhere.

George Burns

What did Sergio (remember Sergio?) say after listening to my condensed professional life story? Did he say "interesting", "different", I cannot remember exactly. In any event he was polite. We left the buzzing wedding party shortly after the story telling was over and returned to our 1720 house lodgings.

On Sunday, following a post wedding breakfast in Chilmark, we spent the day visiting with Jamie, Alden and Trina and saw Trina and Alden off to Boston on the evening ferry. We, ourselves, left early Monday morning and headed to Manchester, Vermont to visit with Nancy Wolf. We skipped a possible stop at Darrow. I no longer felt any 'real' welcome there and I was not enthusiastic about the upcoming landscape and work proposals for the site. After the usual pleasant visit with Nancy we ended our trip in Cambridge with Morgan and Matt We returned to the UK with Norwegian Airlines: excellent.

* * * * *

The demise of The Forge Company was depressing. Obviously, my work as CEO now irrelevant though there were a lot of loose ends to tie up. At the same time as we were putting Forge to sleep Jill decided to sell, Chloe. Jill found a buyer almost immediately (actually, the buyer found Jill). After years of very busy lives both Jill and I were now without our daily work rituals. I had been elected President of the UK Chapter of the AIA and that took up a little (emphasis on 'a little') of the slack as did my election to the Worshipful Company of Chartered Architects. Jill's time was absorbed by looking after her mother, now, a frail but totally compos ninety-eight, and by her final 'go' to finish her long-term renovation work on Crossways. Though there were no daily work rituals we were not without 'things to do' including 'faffing' about in antique stores.

It was not long after Crossways was 'finished' that we (or it could have been just Jill) decided that now we had no reason to live in London. It was time to sell the Macartney house flat. About that same time a business friend of Jill's, Brian Wren and his wife Diane, invited us to visit at their house in Monchique in the Portuguese Algarve. The Wrens, while happy to entertain us, really wanted Jill to buy their house. Fortunately Jill did not. However, we were 'taken' by Portugal and before we knew what had happened Jill had bought the delightful, Monte do Cerrito in Sao Bras de Alportel, in central Algarve, twenty kilometres north of Faro and a good two hours' drive from Monchique. We didn't see much of the Wrens after that.

Monte had been designed and built in stages, starting in 1994. At its core was a large, columned music room for one of the original owners, a professional singer. In order to comply with the Camera's regulations, of the time, a small kitchen, bedroom and toilet was appended to the music room. Subsequently, a second floor, study, pool, garages and courtyards were added making the property architecturally eccentric, but charming. An architect acquaintance of ours said of Monte, "It is like walking through the back of a wardrobe": it is. Jill and I had fallen in love with the house in thirty seconds. Actually, Monte needed updating, a lot of updating. Planning the renovations, seventeen drawings worth, and executing the work took eighteen months. This was fine as we could not use the property while still looking after Jill's Mother.

Jill's Mother died in 2007, shortly after reaching her hundredth birthday. Her death more or less coincided with the completion of Monte's renovations. We started to spend time in Monte, perhaps as much as four of five months a year thereafter, mostly spring and fall. (summers are too hot and winters too wet.) One of the benefits of Monte is its studio. Jill paints too but quite differently to my quasi-impressionist style. I enjoy the pursuit and process as much as the end result. Jill has a rare talent and is able to copy anything: precisely. Jill works in the kitchen in a small neat area. I spread out a bit. Jill would argue, "a lot". We and our friends and family who have visited have enjoyed (and, in fact, continue to enjoy) Monte. It is Jamie's "favourite house". It is, however, now on the market: we may miss it but not the 'getting there'.

Monte was not the only house venture undertaken after our 'retirements'. Victoria, indirectly, inspired a second house venture, though she didn't mean to. Having qualified as a barrister and joined chambers in Lewes, Vic decided that representing or prosecuting petty crooks was not her thing. She forwent that option and joined the civil service taking up a legal position in the Home Office. At the time there was talk of her Home Office section being transferred to Bristol. That was enough of an impetus for Jill and I to think about the 'West Country'. The 'theory' was that Jill would sell Crossways and we would remove ourselves somewhere west to be in the general area of Bristol. It turned out we were premature. Vic did not move but we did. After looking at almost a hundred houses in Cornwall, Somerset, Gloucestershire, Dorset and Devon we settled on Sanford Orleigh, a rather grand early (1837) Victorian Mansion in Newton Abbott, Devon. The building had been remodelled into five large freehold units, ours was the largest of them. It was another case of walking into a property and mutually agreeing, "this is it!". The property, all six thousand square feet of it, consisted of a large 'hall', formal living room, large kitchen, large conservatory, four bedrooms, three and a half baths, huge basement and a two car garage, a bit more than we needed. We moved there in the fall of 2008. Jill had a buyer for Crossways but the closing on that transaction was sliding, we now had three houses in total, eleven bedrooms, and fourteen sofas worth: definitely a house too many. But, there wasn't much we could do about it as the sale of Crossways was pending.

Our initial reaction on moving in to Sanford Orleigh was positive. We had four neighbours including the prospective Conservative candidate, Anne-Marie Morris, as our abutting neighbour. We got on well with Anne-Marie and her cheerful but somewhat 'bolshie' partner Roger. We worked for her, with enthusiasm, during the 2010 campaign: she won.

What wasn't so great was the painting of Sandford Orleigh. Our timing of the purchase coincided with the first painting, since its renovation, of the exterior of the whole building. As part of the purchase agreements everyone signed a 'covenant' consisting of common agreements regarding the management of the property. Among those agreements was one stipulating that all owners would contribute equally to the cost of paint the entire structure every seven (or so) years. The painting, managed by one of the owners was going well when we arrived. However, before our unit was painted the painting 'cash pot' was empty. The result meant, at least according to the 'covenant' that we would all have to 'chip in' additional funds to complete the work. Guess what, two of the unit owners refused, justifying their refusal on the basis that our unit, which was the last to be painted, was much "the biggest". More disagreements over 'this and that' followed. The ensuing 'hoorah' (an understatement) goes on to this day: ten years and thousands of pounds in legal expenses later. Meanwhile the sale of Crossways fell through, a "good and bad news" event: we would sell Sanford Orleigh. We got out, more or less whole, after five years. As nice as the place was, architecturally, it was no place to live: peaceably. We told ourselves never again to buy into a jointly managed property: however, we did like Devon.

Moving on, we then bought a flat (Jill bought two additional ones for rental investment) in Sidcup thinking we would go into London if it were 'more convenient'. It was and we didn't. Our London forays usually started and ended at the Portrait Gallery followed by our looking at each other and agreeing to a quick return to Sidcup or even Crossways. We found London had become too crowded and, I guess, after the number of years during which we, collectively, had enjoyed the city, it was enough. After two years of Sidcup we bailed out. It was a good idea, didn't work. Jill did keep one of her rental flats: a good investment.

After selling Sidcup and with the decision to sell Monte we decided on a replacement for Monte, in advance of its sale. We went back to Devon we do like Devon. We looked at, maybe, twenty houses and flats from north to south Devon. Bid on some, aborted on others and ended up buying a flat in a 'retirement village' in Torquay: Torquay, where we had started ten years previously. We enjoy visiting there and we have made some good friends, there you go: we were too early again, we are back to three houses! Anyway the plot is we will use the flat a lot more when Monte is sold, that's plan A: there is no plan B!

* * * * *

Meanwhile back in the US there has been plenty of activity. Trina, is now an associate professor and chair of the animation department at Lesley. Trina and Curvin have moved: only a few miles but it is a big event. Jamie, as noted earlier, is Director of the Institute for National Security and Counter Terrorism in Syracuse. He, Lori, Jamie and Grant are acclimating to the move. Jamie is off to Georgia University in August and Grant continues on his exciting basketball trajectory. Morgan and Matt made the big move: to Hawaii where Matt took up a position with Hawaiian Airlines. It did not work out and after a year they have returned to Cambridge. Maggie and Jay are still in LA. Ellie is doing well in her nascent acting career. Alden, alone, has stayed put enjoying his work in the emergency department of University of Utah Hospital. Alden, Heidi, Noe and Rowen enjoy their frequent trips up and around the mountains, near and far. Victoria and Richard have moved from Hove buying a house about six miles from Crossways. We have the benefit of seeing the lively Molly and Eleanor.

It has been an exciting and interesting career: a fair number of good times as well as a fair number of not so good times. Perhaps Dickens' words from *A Tale of Two Cities* are appropriate to recall:

> *"It was the best of times, it was the worst of times, it was the age of wisdom, it was the age of foolishness, it was the epoch of belief, it was the epoch of incredulity, it was the season of light, it was the season of darkness, it was the spring of hope, it was the winter of despair."*

Now Jill and I have a different but still exciting and interesting life, some of it vicarious, to be sure: it is now, in fact, "… a season of light".

The Darrow Board with faculty, staff and supporters 2005/6?

Nancy Wolf in middle with Larry Van Meter on her right.

Probably one of my last events before retiring from the active Board

Crossways', Jill's Mayfield house - early summer

My painting of the entrance to 'Monte do Cerrito'

Relaxing in 'Monte's' courtyard with Mike Eatherley

The pool at 'Monte'

Enjoying Portugal - and more

ACKNOWLEGMENTS

And thanks: First of all, I thank my partner, Jill, for putting up (for years) with the boring bit of my writing this story. But, more importantly, Jill provided me with justified criticism and helpful comments. Richard from the iStore in Tunbridge Wells patiently helped with 'Word': a necessity. I also have been encouraged by volunteer readers including, Veronica Brown, Karin Crooks, Brenda Niemand and my family. My thanks to them for their editing and comments. Also, thanks to Helen Stockton and Quill & Apple Publishing who took *A Pewter Spoon* under care and were instrumental in getting it 'over the line'.

James Baker
Crossways
March 2022

ENDNOTES

[1]   18 February 1933: Named after my Great-Great Grandfather Maj. Gen James Barnes (1801-1869) as well as for my Great Uncle James Barnes Baker (1862-1918) the New York architect (a premonition?). The suggestion was Great Aunt Christine's. Mother told me that father would have named me William Edgar but for the event that having no issue at the time father had given his younger brother Alan permission to use the name for his son born in 1923. Sadly William died in 1931. Out of respect father chose not to name me after him. Alan's family continued to use the name in later generations.

[2]   My father, William Edgar Baker Jr., was born in Palestine, Texas, in 1885. Palestine seems like an odd place relative to Greenwich but Grandfather Baker (William Edgar Baker - 1856-1921) as a young man, worked, for several different railroads, probably through 'Uncle Stewart's connections. (John Stewart Kennedy (1830-1909) owned or was a major shareholder in a number of emerging railroads. See <u>The Man Who Found The Money</u>, Engelbourg 1996) In 1885 Palestine was a thriving railroad centre. Grandfather Baker in due course became a leading electrical engineer involved with the electrification of railways, primarily, in Chicago, New York and London in the 1890s and early 1900s. The Chicago 'L', or at least part of it, reputedly the first electrified railway in the US, was his (electrical) design. I gave the large silver cup commemorating its opening in 1899 to Jamie as well as the ship's wheel allegedly used to operate the first electrified 'L' train. Apparently the handle to operate the motor was misplaced on opening day and the only substitute to be found to fit the motorcar's operating stud was this ship's wheel obtained from a boat moored on Lake Michigan. The wheel was subsequently used on father's boats.

[3]   Father married mother, Violet Twachtman, (1895-1964) the youngest daughter of the impressionist painter John Henry Twachtman, on 6 December 1928. This was father's second marriage. The first, in 1914, to Marion Lindley was apparently annulled because there was no issue. However, based on bits and pieces of family lore and material found on the Internet, this explanation, given to me, 'officially', years ago, by mother, appears to be simplistic. I suspect the divorce was more complicated!

[4]   Martha (Twachtman) Baker: aka Marty was born on 29 November 1929. I do not know whether the 'Twachtman' was a recorded name or not. Marty used the name when she felt like it. Marty was named for her grandmother Martha Scudder Twachtman. Grandmother Twachtman's father John M. Scudder, was a distinguished physician in Cincinatti. The Scudder Family originated in Kent. Thomas Scudder, the founder of the Scudder Family in America came to America in 1633.

[5]   The house, in 2017, when I last saw it, only from the road, although altered and expanded, seemed to retain some of its original architectural character, at least as I remembered it.

[6]   Godfrey Twachtman, nicknamed 'Jackie', was Twachtman's youngest son (1897-1983) and closest in age to mother. Mother appreciated Jackie's wisecracks and his, sometimes, sardonic sense of humor. Next to Jackie, mother probably saw Aunt Marjorie (mother's older sister) and her children, Elizabeth and Peggy most – at least during the Greenwich years. Marty and I participated as flower girl and pageboy in Peggy's 1938 wedding to Emery Katzenbach.

[7]   Why the French army? There is no primary reference to support any reasonable answer. We know, from letters he wrote to his friend Godfrey Rockefeller, that he also served in the French Army in WWI. One letter is all about how he was trying to find his brother Alden. Perhaps he was just following his older brother ?

8   I think father was stirred by this speech despite the fact that, as noted, he had little positive to say about Roosevelt – his dislike (perhaps too strong a word) could be attributed to one thing only, taxes. The mother and father were Wilkie supporters in the 1940 election and continued to follow Wilkie, especially after the publication of his book <u>One World</u>. I still have a Wilkie button.

9   Uncle William was Great Grandfather's (Henry Martyn Baker) oldest brother (1819-1846). His portrait, allegedly painted by Waldo & Jewett c. 1844, hangs at Crossways in Mayfield, E. Sussex. William died prematurely following an operation to remove a tumor in his face, possibly cancer.

10   Eugenia Griffin Baker born in Chicago (1893 -1979) was the third child of William Edgar Baker.

11   Harriet Griffin Baker (1862–1941) was born in Maine, the daughter of Captain George K. Griffin. He was a "pioneer and woodsman, a Yankee sailor, skipper, shipbuilder and owner, a California miner and plainsman, a Klondiker, general traveller and sportsman." *The Springfild Homestead Feb 6,1904*. He died in Holyoke, his home after 1872. His son Eugene was a Brig. General (a West Pointer he served in the Spanish American War) and later Vice President of General Electric.

12   Grandfather Baker died in 1921. Following his death Grandmother Baker lived in Rome from 1922 to 1938 in a sumptuous penthouse apartment near the Spanish Steps. In 1938 she returned to New York to live at 45 E 62nd Street. She did spend some time in the US during her Roman period as the 1936 picture taken at the Greenwich Field Club attests. Co-incidentally, ten years after her death, mother would buy one of the two penthouse apartments at 45 East 62nd Street!

13   Before marrying my father, mother earned a living painting murals for up-market architects and other clients in and around New York City. A 'family' mural (c. 1938) painted for father's studio now hangs in 'Crossways' in Mayfield, East Sussex.

14   Uncle Jackie memorialized this in a three-minute film he made on Easter, 1936. In addition to Marty and myself the film shows Mother, Father, Aunt Marjorie and the Cairn terrier, Zephyr.

15   One incidence of toy breakage stands out. On this occasion, Marty had, once again, broke one of my planes - this time with mother as a witness. Mother <u>insisted</u>, as retribution and perhaps because she though it might stop Marty, that I consequently break one of Marty's favourite toys, a small glass Parrot in a cage. Though I did I am still dubious about Mother's 'solution' as a choice of 'educational punishment'.

16   Twenty years later, mother gave the Dutch marquetry cabinet to the Brooklyn Museum – I suspect she thought this would avoid an inheritance hoorah between Marty and myself, as we both liked it. In any event neither of us had homes that would accommodate the piece. I do not know the provenance of the cabinet.

17   I recall visiting three; one was off Lake Avenue, a guesthouse for William Rockefeller the other two were on North Porchuck Road. One of these was for cousin Nancy Belcher (wife of Benjamin Moore Belcher of paint fame). I do not know who owned the third house.

18   'Blueprints' were copies of tracings made with a cyanotype process the background of which were deep blue and the lines white. Their use was phased out in the early 1940s.

19   Prior to Princeton father attended the Hill School. He was in the Princeton Class of 1909. I am not able to reconcile this class with father's age, 24, at the time of his graduation.

20   McKim Mead and White, the New York architectural firm, rose to prominence in the late 19th century. As a matter of coincidence White was a friend of grandfather Twachtman. Uncle Quentin (Twachtman's second son, 1892-1954) worked for the firm around 1920 and White's granddaughter Anne was married to Harry Buttrick, a colleague of mine in the 1960s. A layout of McKim's office drawn by father c. 1911 remained in my possession until 2013 when I gave it to Columbia University for their McKim archive.

21   Judging from photographs, silver cups and the fact that he belonged to Squadron A in New York, father was apparently a good rider. He was with Squadron A in 1916 when it was called up to patrol the border with Mexico. Despite this fact, I was told by mother that father was not fond of horses – actually detested them! Father did not serve in WWI.

22   Col. John Alden Twachtman, ('Uncle Alden') Grandfather's eldest son was born in 1883 and died in 1975.

23   The rumble seat was an upholstered exterior seat that opened up from the rear deck of the car, a breezy and fun ride for us but hardly a safe one!

24   The workbench provided an area where my father constructed the hull model for what he hoped would be his next boat to be called, as I recall, Seven Bells. The model was constructed in laminated layers of carefully shaped soft white pine. In the process father taught me how to use a drawknife, plane and lots of sandpaper. This hull model has survived some 70 years and is still in the family.

25   Waukeela is still going but Wonalancet apparently closed in 1960.

Chapter 2 – Round Hill Road

26   The house at Porchuck Road received publicity in both House & Garden and Architectural Record (November 1932)

27   Martha Scudder Twachtman: (1861 – 1935): Grandmother was an artist in her own right but gave up a potential professional career in order to raise her family of seven children. As noted, her father, John Milton Scudder, was a well-known Cincinnati physician.

28   A good description of the house is found in John Henry Twachtman An American Impressionist by Lisa N. Peters, High Museum of Art, 1999. Another is in Susan Larkin's article, On Home Ground: John Twachtman and the Familiar Landscape, *American Art Journal,* Vol. 29, No.1/2. (1998), pp52-85

29   This connection later led to my occasionally being invited as a child to play with two of William's grandchildren Christina and Georgia Rockefeller. Letters suggest that Georgia's father, Godfrey, had been a close friend of Uncle Jackie when they were neighbours at the time of WWI. In the 1950s, while at Princeton, I sometimes escorted Georgia or Cristina to New York debutante parties.

30   Karin Crooks has read most of the Elsie Rockefeller's dairies. From these emerges a picture of Mother's social life before her marriage to father.

31   Uncle Jackie (another note!) was in and about Greenwich until sometime early in 1939 when he went to France joining the French Army as an artillery officer. He had previously served in the French Army in WWI (a fact I only learned about from Karin Crooks in 2013). After the fall of France in 1940, Jackie escaped capture and made his way to Lisbon. There he met his wife to be, Miriam, to us Aunt Mim. Mim was related, (I believe) by her first marriage, to the papal Chigi and Barberini families. Mim had, herself,

escaped the clutches of Mussolini. The US Government, as now, took a dim view of its citizens fighting for a foreign government so Mim and Jackie made their way back to the US through Canada but only after some political intervention. In due course Uncle Jackie and Mim married and settled in Independence, Missouri. at 620 North Delaware Avenue, almost opposite their friend President Truman. Mim became a senior member of the American Red Cross in the Mid West and Jackie optimistically pursued several business ventures, none of which were terribly successful. Uncle Jackie died in 1983.

32   So-called by Grandfather: it is the subject of many of Grandfather's paintings. See Larkin, ibid p56.

33   Eric Christian died aged one and a half in 1891. Elsie (named for Elsie Rockefeller?) died of scarlet fever in 1894, aged nine. Grandfather did a pastel of Marjorie and Elsie that is still in the family.

34   I know little of Aunt Louise (nee Trimble). My recollection is that mother and father regarded Aunt Louise as difficult though she was friendly enough to me. More recently, however, I have discovered Aunt Louise's sense of humor and poetry through her writings; unfortunately a little late, she died in 1951. Uncle Alden did not remarry but apparently was rarely without female companionship in the ensuing years.

35   Uncle Alden told me that his orderly gave the (captured) rifle to him during a dodgy bit of fighting. The Mauser was regarded as a better weapon than the Springfield rifle, the standard US issue. On some visits Uncle Alden took time to entertain me with some of his WWI experiences – my memories of this seem to have been reduced to mud, noise, horses and artillery pieces. In later years a number of pictures and records have been found which add a reality to his stories.

36   The citation read: "The President of the United States of America, authorized by Act of Congress, July 9, 1918, takes pleasure in presenting the Army Distinguished Service Medal to Colonel (Field Artillery) John Alden Twachtman, United States Army, for exceptionally meritorious and distinguished services to the Government of the United States, in a duty of great responsibility during World War I. As Battalion and later Regimental Commander, 103d Field Artillery, 26th Division, in the Aisne-Marne, St.- Mihiel, and Meuse-Argonne offensives, Colonel Twachtman was conspicuous for his courage, marked ability, and leadership qualities. At all times he displayed superior tactical judgment and knowledge of artillery, and by his devotion to duty, great resourcefulness, and high military attainments he rendered the maximum support to the Infantry to which he was attached, thereby contributing in a large measure to their success."

37   Uncle Alden's military career apparently started (somewhere in the background was polo) in the Providence 'Marine' Corps of Artillery (aka the 103rd FA) before 1915. The unit became part of the Rhode Island National Guard and later of the 26th 'Yankee Division'. In any event the unit was called into national service in 1917 to be part of Pershing's 'expedition' against Pancho Villa. Uncle Alden at the time was a captain and battery commander. In 1917 the division was recalled from that assignment and mobilized for action in France. Uncle Alden was promoted to major just before the unit sailed. He was later promoted to lt. colonel and in late 1918 before the Armistice, he was promoted to full colonel and regimental commander of the 103rd FA Regiment. He was the last commander of that unit in WWI. He saw action on the Marne, at Chateau Thierry, and at the St Mihiel and Meuse-Argonne battles. Uncle Alden always wore the little ribbon associated with the medal. He led Greenwich's 4th of July parades, dressed in his distinguished WWI uniform for more than ten years. I saw him in his uniform only once and that was at Uncle Quentin's house after a wedding, perhaps cousin Charlotte's? His red, wooden mailbox on Round Hill Road always sported, in elegant hand-painted calligraphy, "Col. J. Alden Twachtman."

38   Ira Spanierman is the founder of the Spanierman Gallery in New York and the publisher of several books on Twachtman as well as mounting a number of Twachtman exhibitions. He is also the publisher of the (still) forthcoming Catalogue Raisoné of Grandfather's work.

39   In the thirties there were few architectural commissions. These large house commissions were mostly completed in the twenties.

40   In addition to Uncle Alden the other uncles were; Alan Baker (father's youngest brother), (Dr.) Carl Knapp (married to Aunt Phoebe (father's sister), Quentin and Jackie Twachtman. Actually I liked them all and had good relationships with them. However, I saw much more of Uncle Alden and he took a special interest in me. My father had paid for David (and perhaps Eric) to go to sailing classes in the twenties and, perhaps, there was some reciprocity at work.

Chapter 3 – Casey and Siesta Keys

41   "Airline" referred to the shortest distance between two points; the railroad never owned a plane.

42   Casey Key was remote and we needed to have a car. In the 1930s renting a car was still a novelty.

43   "On Monday they would leave town and drive along a highway near a town. Then they would place Burma Shave signs (without having to pay for the placement) along all the highways leading to the town. Each set of signs contained five placements, one for each line and then the last one that actually said "Use Burma-Shave." Then they would proceed to the next town and do the same thing. Late on Thursday and into Friday they would back track and call upon the local drug store(s) and ask, "No doubt you have had calls for Burma-Shave." They would take orders and leave the merchandise along with reorder forms. That's how they got started in the thirties and they did it for years." Source the Internet – a typical set of signs of the period follows:

"SHE EYED
HIS BEARD
AND SAID NO DICE
THE WEDDING'S OFF
I'LL COOK THE RICE
BURMA SHAVE"

44   The railroad ceased operating in 1967.

45   The school is now the highly rated Out-of-Door Academy.

Chapter 4 – Deer Park

46   Source: Karin Crooks – Karin Crooks of Greenwich has spent several years   researching the Twachtman family history. It was she that discovered this particular ancestral fact. Where her research supports other historical facts I have simply footnoted her as the source.

47   I am not sure how long mother stayed at Silver Hill; however, it was nearly five years before mother would buy another house. When she did, in 1948, it was a penthouse apartment at 45 East 62nd Street, by coincidence, as noted, Grandmother Baker's former address. Grandmother Baker apparently bought her apartment at 45 East 62nd street upon her return from Rome c. 1938 though, as noted, she did visit during her Roman sojourn. Mother must have known this at the time but, oddly, omitted telling us.

48   "The Bush-Holley House is a National Historic Landmark and historic house museum at 39 Strickland Road in the Cos Cob section of Greenwich, Connecticut. It was constructed circa 1730 and in the late nineteenth century was a boarding house and the centre of the Cos Cob Art Colony, Connecticut's first art colony. From 1890 to 1920, the house was a gathering place for artists, writers and editors, and scores of art students came to study with leading American Impressionists including: John Henry Twachtman, J. Alden Weir, Theodore Robinson, and Childe Hassam. It is currently operated as a historic site by the Historical Society of the Town of Greenwich, and is open for tours." – Wikipedia entry

49   Aunt Eugenia was born in Chicago in 1893. She was a graduate of Rosemary Hall and went on from there to Bryn Mawr – hence why Marty went on from Rosemary to Bryn Mawr. She taught at Rosemary for 17 years before becoming Headmistress in 1938 serving until 1953. She was married to Henry Herbert Jessup (1919) a businessman. Aunt Eugenia and he were divorced in 1935. Aunt Eugenia's brother-in-law was the eminent Jurist Philip Jessup. Aunt Eugenia had two sons, Henry, the oldest, graduated from Yale in 1940, and his brother John two years later. John was a naval officer during the war and later returned to Yale to get his law degree.

50   Although meat was rationed we managed to get lamb chops or ground beef from time to time.

51   Rosemary Hall, with its 16 buildings and 18 acres was designated as a National Historic Site in 1998.

52   Her cookbooks include, among others, June Platt's <u>Plain and Fancy,</u> <u>New England Cookbook</u>, and <u>Dessert Cookbook.</u>

53   Though mother was diffident about her painting she was actually a very skillful artist.

54   Carl served with the Eighth Air Force: as a B17 tail-gunner. We were told that he was decorated for valour for having saved the life of his bombardier in an unusual manner: Carl never confirmed nor denied this.

PART TWO - EDUCATION

Chapter 5 - Darrow

55   Clothing requirements were quite simple: Blazer, grey and blue flannel suits, white shirts, half with detachable collars, some work clothes, black and brown shoes, socks, underwear, and some winter clothing.

56   Mr. Heyniger 'purchased' the school c. 1938. It was founded as the 'The Lebanon School' for Boys but it is my understanding that Heyniger did not think that a marketable name. He adopted the name Darrow from the farmer who owned the land before the Shakers and who himself became a Shaker. I have heard that Heyniger may have thought the name, Darrow, recollected the English school, Harrow.

57   Mount Lebanon was established in 1783 and became the lead ministry of the Shaker movement in America in 1787. At its peak, in the 1840's there were around 600 Shakers living in eight, so-called 'families' on some 4,000 acres of farmland. There were approximately 120 buildings of all kinds.

58   A site plan dated "6/5/30", without attribution, titled "NEW LEBANON SCHOOL, INC." shows the locations of 37 structures. I recollect, in 1944, that of these, 21 Shaker structures remained. Excluded in the original count of 37 was the garage behind Wickersham, removed in 1967, and the mill located above the Wash House. Of

the 21 buildings remaining in 1944, two were sold, two lost to fire and two demolished, leaving 15 remaining of the original 37.

59   The Shakers believed that the second coming of Christ had occurred in the form of their leader and founder Ann Lee. The sect practiced celibacy and gained supporters and members through conversion. This worked well up until the period of the Civil War. Their name derived from their ritualistic, spiritual dances in which they 'shook' out their sins. In England they were known as 'Shaking Quakers'.

60   Whether she held this 'conversion' against me or the school I do not know. Mother visited Darrow only once during my six years there. She came to take me to Deerfield for a visit with Boris, in the fall of 1947 and I suspect to explore whether I could transfer to that more prestigious school. As Deerfield's headmaster Frank Boyden was a friend of Mr. Heyniger's and a trustee of Darrow I think the exploration was a non-starter.

61   The dining room was furnished with grey marble-topped Shaker tables. Seating was by low-back wooden chairs, sort of a cross between a stool and a chair. Each table was overseen by a master. Students were assigned to tables on a weekly basis and also served as waiters by rotation. Food was served 'family-style'. Mr Heyniger had a head table, English style, and it was a dubious privilege to be assigned to his table: no adolescent foolery there. Emma, the no-nonsense, loyal black dietician oversaw the kitchen staff including the affable chef Joe. The food was, by my recollection, straight-forward and 'healthy'. Emma would continue as the school's dietician for many years.

62   The sisters left in 1947.

63   "Neither snow nor rain nor heat nor gloom of night shall stay these couriers from the swift completion of their appointed tasks"

64   Walter Barnum was the owner of the yacht Brilliant that in 1933 crossed the Atlantic, west to east, in 15 days 1 hr and 23 minutes, a record at the time. Brilliant is still sailed at the Mystic Seaport.

65   On reflection, I may have 'won' that year's bird spotting contest.

Chapter 6 - Princeton

66   In 2019 about $70,000. all in.

67   Most English cars came with a set of tools and the Riley was no exception. It was expected that a Riley owner would take care of the car's basic maintenance including of course fixing flat tires.

68   Drinkwater's was for years the principal mover/storage company in Greenwich. Most anything of perceived value was stored here following the sale of the Porchuck Road house.

69   In our freshman year Harry married his long-time girlfriend and withdrew from Princeeton. He joined Dupont and was involved in the initial years of commercial television.

70   Boris had contracted meningitis and was not considered medically fit to enter Princeton.

71   About 250 classmates joined the Navy ROTC and another 400 plus the Army's artillery unit, out of a class of seven hundred and something.

72   Charlie went to Princeton Graduate School and subsequently became the Secretary of Washington's Fine Arts Commission. I stayed in touch with Charlie after Princeton. I last saw him in Washington just before he retired in 2004 after 42 years of service. He died while crossing a street in Washington in 2008 after being hit by a car.

73   'Peter' was a nickname for John Knott Maxwell. His father owned the Knott hotel chain that in 1954 owned and operated the Westbury Hotels in New York and London. Peter and I spent a happy week or two in the UK in 1954 travelling about in his 4.5 litre, open Bently. 'Pete' died in 1995.

74   Paul's wedding took place at his home 1n Uniontown, Pennsylvania. He lived with his wife in Princeton in his junior and senior years. Some of us thought it was perhaps to legitimise his XK120! He ultimately became a writer and poet. We corresponded occasionally but our paths did not cross after 1958. Paul died from MS in 1989.

75   Princeton Eating Clubs are private clubs where junior and seniors eat and participate in social events. Members are selected through a process called 'bicker' when members of the sophomore class are vetted by club committees. There are eleven clubs and a number of alternatives. I was a member of Charter Club along with many of my close friends.

76   Hugh served in the Army after Princeton Graduate School and then joined Jo Mielziner, the leading New York set designer. (I recall that David Twachtman also worked for Mielziner for a short time after WWII.) Later Hugh started a very successful architectural firm that eventually became, Hardy, Holzman, Pfeiffer. I served as best man at his wedding and worked with him on several projects in the 60s. Hugh died in early 2017 following a fall getting out of a taxi in New York.

77   I believe it was the St Louis-San Francisco Railway.

Chapter 7 - Army

78   Later "Chiz" become a well-known film producer and actor. He was President (1954) of the Triangle Club.

79   Dimitri was at the time associated with the American Academy in Rome.

80   I am not sure what, exactly, Mim's relationship was with these two families. I suspected it was more than just friendship. Was Mim titled? Had she been married before? That would have been likely, but to whom? In typical Twachtman manner the matter was never discussed. Whatever the facts, the relationships were certainly close.

81   750 miles doesn't seem much in 2017 but in the pre-interstate days of the 50s it was probably more than a 20 hour drive (without counting stops).

82   The 'Gyroscope' plan entailed the moving of complete units rather than individuals –allegedly an economy.

83   MATS – Military Air Transport Service

Chapter 8 – Yale

84 I am not sure any of these 'ditties' still exist. It is possible that Molly's brother, Whitney, might have them.

85 Prior to the Bass boat Whit had a catboat: see The Guardians by Geoffrey Kabaservice

86 Phyllis Lambert, nee Bronfman, was responsible for her father Samuel Bronfman hiring Mies to design the iconic Seagram Building in New York. Phyllis became a distinguished and highly renowned Canadian architect.

PART 3 – WORK

Chapter 9 – Apprenticeship

87 From *The Junkman*:

88 As in Alsace-Lorraine, not the dog!

89 Heyniger did have professional help, from one or more professional friends, for the Chapel, general planning, Wickersham and Whittaker houses.

90 See Jerry Grant's book on the Second Meeting House:

91 See Architectural Forum, c. 1963?

92 A catalog was published by the The American Federation of Arts.

93 Probably around $125 per square foot, today.

94 I understand that was demolished sometime after 2010.

95 References to Life, Time Magazine and New York Times (to be provided).

96 The airport was originally called Idelwild but, in 1964, had been renamed John F. Kennedy (JFK) following his death.

Chapter 10 - Baker & Blake Part 1

97 I have visited the cemetery twice. The first time in 1983 and the second time in 2005. I found mother's niche in 1983 but could not in 2005. In fact in 2005 the cemetery officials said I was "mistaken" there was no Violet Baker in the cemetery.

98 The Times, 1 February 2010, on Andy Murray after his defeat by Roger Federer

99 This was the first, and last, I heard about this.

100   Despite the extensive renovations, the Glens decided to leave Michigan and move east. Together we roamed the countryside just outside Philadelphia. Eventually finding a farmhouse on a striking site in Birchrunville. The first structure was a guesthouse, useful while we designed the second, a main residence. The Glens some fifteen years later sold Birchrunville and moved to Princeton where, by chance, they bought a condominium backing on to Russell Estates.

101   Bill was Governor of Michigan from 1969 until 1983, Michigan's longest serving Governor. He is a moderate Republican and even voted for Hilary Clinton in 2016.

102   Peter was Bud's son by his first wife.

103   Craig, though known as an architect was never a <u>licensed</u> architect.

104   Apparently the missionaries used Biblical names in rotation to provide Christian names to the children passing through their hands.

105   Some time after the last Shakers left the North Family property in 1947, the Shaker trustees sold the property to a Christian sect. The sect ran a school there during the fifties but the school and/or the sect became bankrupt. In the early sixties the property was put up for auction.

106   I am not sure of this date.

107   See, <u>Mount Lebanon Shaker Collection</u>: Published by Mount Lebanon Shaker Village Library of Congress No. NK838.N34F5 – 1987

108   John Joline, Dave Thompson, Darby, Nick, and later board members Bill Hudnut, Herb Hudnut, Pete Conrad and myself were all Princeton graduates.

109   I am not sure what the contact was, it may have been Peter, though he had no specific relationship with the college or for that matter ceramics. It may well have been a 'cold call' by Randall to Architectural Forum to identify potential candidates for the work.

110   Dr. Wikie's Obituary, below, tells more than I knew about him when I knew him.

WILKIE--George Hamilton, 75, died on April 14, 2007, of cancer after a short illness. Husband of the late Suzannah Ryan Wilkie, he is survived by his children, Angus Wilkie of New York, NY, Austin Wilkie of New York, NY, and Serena Wilkie Gifford of Cambridge, MA, and by his grandchildren, Suzannah Gifford and Abbott Gifford. Born in Tamsui, Formosa, he was a graduate of Williams College, Harvard Medical School and New York Psychoanalytic Institute. He practiced psychoanalysis privately in Manhattan for over 40 years, while also serving as Associate Professor of Psychiatry on the faculty at Columbia College of Physicians and Surgeons. In summer months, he was president of Lac a Gravel trout fishing club in Charlevoix, Quebec, and organist at Murray Bay Protestant Church. Work and family were his music; his concise judgments and succinct wit in all endeavors will be long-remembered. …

111   Alex died in 2016 this is his obituary notice:

"Alexander Grinnell, Yale-educated architect and champion of affordable housing …, An active member of New York's Century Association, an antiques collector, and an experienced sailor, Mr. Grinnell died on August 8.(2016) Born into a prominent New York family, Mr. Grinnell achieved his Masters in Architecture from Yale in 1960, and went on to a long career as an innovator in the field of affordable housing, first in his own practice, then with Jim Baker, and later with a long tenure at Steven Winter and Associates. Mr.

Grinnell enjoyed taking loved ones out on his sailboat Sooloo on Cape Cod's Waquoit Bay, participating in the New York Century Association, collecting antiques, and birdwatching on Long Island with wife Kirsten Childs. Mr. Grinnell is survived by his first wife Kate Grinnell, second wife Holly Bodman, children Eliza Grinnell and David Grinnell, and grandchildren Phoebe Grinnell and Lyra Fernandez. …"

112   In 1960 Blake and Neski was hired to work on the official US exhibition in Moscow. I was Peter's 'grunt' on the project. Peter worked closely with a state department official, the client, who was a bit of a live wire – (his name fails me). In any event it was while Peter and his client was visiting Moscow that this phrase was coined.

Chapter 11 – Baker & Blake 2

113   Modern design obviously is an evolving concept. The use of the term here is relative to the 1960's only.

114   The use of the word 'designer' includes licensed as well as unlicensed architects and architects-in-training– a role as much as a title.

115   From Google "Goodreads": With over 60 million copies of his books sold, Richard Bach remains one of the world's most beloved authors. A former USAF fighter pilot, Air Force captain and latter-day barnstorming pilot, Bach continues to be an avid aviator-author, exploring and chronicling the joys and freedom of flying, reporting his findings to readers.

116   This was a fairly 'modern' design and, at least, one step too far for the then President. I think he wanted a nice 'Georgian' manse, we didn't do them then but I could now.

117   I believe there is a 19th century theory that an octagonal room focused energy and was beneficial to its inhabitants – in any event Margaret believed it.

118   At the time Bard had a policy that faculty could build a single-family house, at their own expense, on Bard land designated for the purpose. Bard retained right of approval over the design.

119   Lumber was used in two-foot modules to minimise cutting and the overall house was dimensioned to accommodate 4 x 8 sheeting material. Used flooring and other second-had materials (parts of an dismantled green house for example) were used where appropriate.

120   SUCF, the (NY) State University Construction Fund was, on the whole, a remarkable public client. As an organization it had class and style and was responsible for many excellent campuses and buildings. Most of the managers with whom we worked were excellent. There were, however, a few managers of lesser talent and even a few classic construction 'bullies'.

121   The buildings need to be revisited – I haven't seen them for twenty years, at least.

122   Chauncey was a widower/divorcee (I need to confirm) and following this event, converted to Catholicism. One result of his conversion was the construction of a small chapel within the house. The artist Annigoni had decorated the chapel, rather sumptuously, with murals. The exquisite house and grounds are now open to the public.

123   I believe Elsie Rockefeller (Nee Stillman) was Chauncy's Aunt.

124   Arne and his wife divorced some years later and he married Diana Ross. He later gave up the shipping business and returned to his love, mountaineering. He ascended Everest amongst other peaks. He died in a fall in 2004.

125   Also known as the Aeolian Islands consisting of: Lipari, Salina, Volcano, Panerea, Stromboli, Filicudi and Alicudi.

126   ASTM: American Society for Testing Materials

127   AllanTalbot , author of *Power Along the Hudson*, 1972.

128   The description of IDC stated that it was, …"an environmentally oriented development company (designed) to promote … development … in the USA, Europe, Africa, the Middle East, Asia and Latin America" – In retrospect, I don't know what we could have been thinking! However, possibly prophetically, in due course, it transpired that I would work in each of these geographic areas, though not as IDC.

129   "Michele Michahelles (b. Italy, 1936) is an Italian and Swiss architect, best known for his work in Paris with MBA, the Marcel Breuer and Associates practice.

    "Michahelles was born in Florence into a prestigious artistic family that included the American sculptor Hiram Powers, painter Ruggero Michahelles, the Futurist designer and visionary Ernesto Michahelles (better known by his pseudonym "Thayaht"), as well as the portrait painter Assia Busiri-Vici. Trained as an agronomist, he left Italy to pursue architecture at the Harvard Graduate School of Design. His father, Dr. Marco Michahelles, was the leading wheat geneticist in Italy and other Countries. … Michele Michahelles works now in Italy, where he was involved in the touristic development project of … Filicudi …, and is now active in projects of restoration of country estates and the development of tourist compounds." - Wikipedia

130   Most of the Filicudians had left during the extensive late 19th, early 20th century emigration of southern Italians to better economic climates. By the 1970s the actual ownership of property on Filicudi was obscure. The only possible solution was to acquire abandoned properties through governmental acquisition.

131   His name needs to be confirmed, Roberto Romano is a place marker.

132   Llewellyn-Davies Associates (LDA) was the New York Office. In London the practice was called Llewellyn-Davies, Weeks, Forester-Walker and Bor. Other offices had differing names reflecting other ownership interests. I use LDA for the sake of simplicity.

133   I am not sure about Sidney (though definitely Australia) and there may haven been others.

134   In addition I was in discussions with Jim Polshek , a well known architect and then dean of Columbia University Architecture School. We actually got so far as printing stationary for, 'Polshek-Baker and had a project to do work for AG Becker, which David Mitchell had recently joined as a partner. This Polshek-Baker partnership had the possibilities of being a good, conventional, practice, in principle much the same as Baker and Blake. However, when the LDA offer was tabled I opted for it despite its unknowns; I had had enough of the known vicissitudes of conventional practice. I made contrite apologies to Jim. He, I think, was understanding, he acted that way though perhaps he was a little put out as he did need a number two. The Becker work was successfully completed by Jim (mostly) and myself.

Chapter 12 – Llewellyn Davies

135   I learned later that Otto died intestate in 1994. At the time of his death (and before) the building tenants were on rent strike and in litigation with Teitler. Some of the litigation was so complex that it became a cause celebre in New York with politicians involved on both sides. In fact a search of the internet suggests that the building was a seat of litigation from the start. Otto was more than a little 'tricky'.

136   Ronald Tree had been a Conservative Member of Parliament and was a friend of Churchill. A colourful figure he was also the promoter and developer of Sandy Lane in Barbados, where Mother stayed after she left New York. I found him a courteous and friendly person, not quite so imperious as Marietta. He died shortly after this lunch, though I do not think because of it.

137   The National Directors of the AIA are based on regional areas according to architectural population. New York, for example had two Directors, while Montana, Wyoming, North Dakota and South Dakota might have had one in 1975. There were about 35 directors (plus officers) in 1975.

138   With four Board meetings, committee meetings, travel and work in between meetings, being an AIA Director took up at least five working weeks a year. For officers and certain directors it was much more.

139   From the congressional district around Indianapolis: He served only one term. Later, Bill said, " ...my constituents preferred to have me at home." He later became a high profile three-term Mayor of Indianapolis with a national reputation. Bill died in late 2016.

140   "AIA Fellowships are recognized as the AIA's highest membership honor for exceptional work and contributions to architecture and society. The prestige of FAIA after your name is unparalleled and the judging is rigorous. Architects who have made significant contributions to the profession and society and who exemplify architectural excellence can become a member of the AIA College of Fellows. Only 3 per cent of the AIA members have this distinction." (AIA description)

My citation read: "An architect with a wide range of abilities, James Baker has played a major role in the emergence of the City College School of Architecture as a school of acknowledged excellence."

141   Roy was a friend of Boris from days before IDC. Roy, a UK citizen turned Jamaican, helped us from time to time on the IDC project. Roy's primary interest in life was golf. After the political troubles in Jamaica, Roy emigrated to Florida. I would meet up and work with him there some years later.

142   Much of Llewellyn-Davies' work was in hospitals, and they were, at the time, considered one of the leading hospital architects. Llewellyn-Davies himself, had been the head o the Nuffield Trust: this helped.

143   The work was completed and turned over to AUB. I do not know what, if anything, became of the recommendations contained in the report.

144   NIOC, National Iranian Oil Company.

145   The 'baristis' are shelters make of any reclaimed materials, sticks, scavenged wood, corrugated metal etc. which cold be used to provide a shelter. They are sort of a 'birdsnest' approach to housing.

146   United States Information Service

147   The project was a joint venture between LDA and Davis Brody. I became their joint Project Manager.

148   Noni is married and spends her time on South Africa and the South of France, still pursuing her career.

149 In the twenties, when still married to Marion, father, for various reasons, came to the conclusion that there would be no issue. He decided, therefore, to leave, in trust, a portion of his estate to his nieces and nephews with the remainder to Marion. In time there was some kind of a hoorah, I do not know the details, though some are hinted at on one or two websites. In any event Marion and father were divorced. Subsequently (I don't know how subsequent to the divorce) father remarried mother and thereafter came Marty and, three years later, me. Consequently father wanted to change his will therefore revoking the trust. This was not an easy matter; there was, I understand, up to that time no precedent for changing a trust. The legal fees charged to change the trust and, in fact, to set a new precedent were Dickensian and reduced the trust to a token of its original worth.

150 Colin Archer, a 19th century Scottish émigré to Norway became the leading designer of seaworthy Norwegian pilot boats, hefty, seaworthy double-ended sailboats. His designs are copied, even now.

151 Joe moved to California practiced architecture for a while then retrained as an attorney. He runs a specialized architecture practice and I understand is very successful. We kept in touch for some time.

152 A reference to Morris Lapidus an American Architect famed for his rather theatrically kitsch Miami hotels.

153 Yogi Berra, catcher fo6 the New York Yankees from 1949 to 1963.

154 On later reflection this may have been a decision by the Cuban authorities to discourage any escape in the boat.

155 This chapter covers a period of a particularly active and busy time. My notes, for example, fill some 20 journals and diaries, covering a broad variety of work related activities. What is written here is the broad and general substance of the period. Some activities and events have been left out, or shortened, as being, in my opinion, not particularly relevant, too complicated or boring. I have also, mostly for continuity and clarity, presented projects or events in their entirety rather than over multiple year periods.

Chapter 13 – Eaton and Park Tower

156 Cy's son

157 Maurice John de Rohan AO OBE (13 May 1936 – 5 October 2006)[1] was an Australian engineer, former Agent General for South Australia,[2] and nominee for Governor of South Australia.

158 Managing an architectural practice did require cash flow planning, an understanding of balance sheets, profit and loss statements and the like. However in a practice turning over around $500,000. a year, these were fairly fundamental and generally prepared by our accountant. The Cayo Sabinal project required forward financial planning for capital costs in excess of $250,000,000. and operating costs in excess of $50,000,000.pa: the words extensive and complex come to mind.

159 I would be 'President' of a new company Park Tower. Almost everyone working in Eastern Europe needed to have an 'appropriate' title – a matter of 'protocol'. Initially there was only one employee, me, but in due course the company would consist of about twenty professionals of various skills. The compensation was good, a significant improvement over LDA. One could consider it a 'good deal'.

160 The use of the word 'arrange' was used to collectively cover the several sources of funds required to execute a project. First, there was the cost of identifying and developing the concept for the project. These costs

were usually covered by Eaton or, alternatively, by specific, Western, joint venture partners brought in by Eaton. Then there were costs associated with the procurement of construction components purchased from the 'West'. Export credit financing from the country providing the goods usually covered these. Fees for professional costs, architecture, engineering and project management, could, usually, be built into the construction costs. Finally, if additional hard currency was required this might be provided through relatively normal banking resources, (or not so relatively normal). Cy was quite imaginative in this area. An underlying quid pro quo was that the 'local', i.e. the Soviet Bloc partner in the transaction, needed to provide a 'sovereign' debt guarantee for any funds borrowed. These and related guarantees, were often sticking points. All of this was quite complex and required many meetings, presentations, long negotiations and the preparation of extensive documentation. Complexity was added to each project by differences in languages, ethics, customs and sometimes ignorance of each side's necessary requirements. As a result the cost involved before a transaction could be signed, properly financed, sealed and delivered, were substantial as were the potential rewards. Eaton's business, simply put was based on a high-risk high reward strategy. So far it had apparently worked.

[161]   From the book, "A Simples Life" by Aleksandr Orlov the meerkat, Ebury Press London

[162]   "Tall, strongly built, ruddy faced and bearded, Ramon Castro looked uncannily like his younger brother, Fidel. … A *Washington Post* journalist once wrote. " He's the Billy Carter of Cuba. A bottle of rum, a pretty woman, a guitar, a tractor that works – and he's happy." *New York Times* February 27th, 2016.

[163]   Karsten appeared to have a relatively 'captive' source of seemingly limitless funds through an associated firm, Castor Holdings run by a German colleague, Wolfgang Stoltenzberg. The actual relationship was not made clear to any of us. I think Cy met Stoltenberg a few times and I vaguely recall meeting him once.

Much later I learned through happenstance that the whole Castor Holdings, Stoltzenberg, Von Wersebe relationship was dodgy and fraudulent to the tune of 1.5 billion Canadian dollars. Stoltzenberg is wanted by Canadian authorities and is apparently in hiding in Germany. The story is available on the internet. Von Wersebe seems to be still in business in Canada.

[164]   Park Tower was conceived as a development vehicle, to play an entrepreneurial role in the creation of projects. It was not intended to be an owner of a project. If Park Tower 'packaged' a project it would either look to its partners (Cy and Karsten) to provide the necessary ownership capital or to third parties.

[165]   Brad's father was the founder of Perkins and Will. I had the pleasure of working with him in Beirut for a few days when we were doing sketches of the AUB site. He was a very good concept sketcher and a pleasant companion.

[166]   In 1978, before the advent of Karsten, the Park Tower staff consisted (besides myself) of Terry Fimano my splendid secretary, Michael Kiesser (previously of the Southampton Princess), and Frank Codella. Neither Michael, who lived in Bermuda, or Frank (who lived in New Jersey) came to the office, unless there was a special reason. Since I had 'inherited these two individuals, their loyalty, not surprisingly, ran directly to Cy who had hired them. Despite Cy telling both to report to me they were unenthusiastic and I did not have a good working relationship with either of them, nor did either contribute much besides help with matters of protocol, meeting and greeting potential partners and clients. They were good at that.

[167]   It was not until 2011, through the work of Karin Crooks, that I learned that the Twachtman family came from Erichshagen and that Great Grandfather, Frederick Christian had served in the Royal Great Britannic-Hanoverian 4th Battalion of the Line.

168 Peter employed an associate, Rick Rice, whose father ran a leading architectural firm in Raleigh. It was through this connection that Peter knew that the City of Raleigh was looking for a developer to construct a downtown hotel to work in connection with Raleigh's new downtown convention centre.

169 The name 'Clarendon' was borrowed from Claire Cox's historical ancestral home, near Salisbury.

170 Digby, an English architect, was an almost typical English eccentric, at least he played the part. He was nearly always wearing Bermuda length shorts, long stockings and seen carring his pet Staffordshire Bull Terrier under his arm. He had done work for Michel Roux's restaurants in London and had a good relation with them. So good in fact that Roux entertained me at his own expense when I, at Digby's insistence, visited Roux's restaurant, La Gavorche in London in 1977.

171 Brad had introduced Feresteh Bekhrad, an architect, to me when he and I were together in Tehran (I am not sure how Brad knew her). Her father was vice president of Tehran University. She (and to a lesser extent) her friend Behroz Nournia became friends and I often saw them socially while working in Iran. She immigrated to the US in 1978, just before the fall of the Shah. With not too many work options at her disposal and despite some language and cultural differences I offered her and Behrooz positions in Park Tower, initially on a trial basis. The principals were not too enthusiastic but, nevertheless, went along with me. It would, in the longer run, turn out to be a good choice for at least one of the partners, Karsten.

172 Having three ex-Princess hotel staff was not a coincidence. Prior to my becoming part of Eaton's 'team' Cy had used D.K. Ludwig's Princess Hotels as a partner in several would-be East-European projects. I believe the Dubrovnik project (several years before my time) was looked at with Princess Hotels proposed as the operator. Thus Cy got to know some of the individuals and one thing led to another, as they say.

173 I do not know why Cy had selected Beckett for the Moscow project (that was before my time). It probably was a reasonable choice. Because of the debacle of the Moscow site containing secret underground KGB cables the hotel construction was abandoned. It was my understanding that Becket was not paid what he thought he was due and was hounding, i.e. suing Cy. Thus Cy hired Beckett for the 'Great Wall Hotel' in Beijing; possibly another instance of the second prize being two nights in Philadelphia?

174 A postscript; Karsten continued to operate York Hanover in the US for a number of years. Eventually, however, he and his financial partner Stoltzenburg were caught out in one or more unsavoury deals and were indicted, tried and convicted of investment fraud; the Internet suggests that Karsten served time but that Stoltzenberg as of 2008 was still on the run!

175 Sometimes spelled Jin Jaing

176 The agreement – to be added

Chapter 14 - Springland

177 The Nassau Club in Princeton is the hundred and twenty five year old eating/residential club catering to graduates of Princeton and other universities.

178 Jerry Ford is a Princeton classmate and a well-established, competent, local architect. Frank Eliseo had been the NYS Mental Hygiene Fund's representative when Baker & Blake designed the Binghamton Rehabilitation Centre. Roe was a Princeton graduate When it appeared that the Eaton saga was going to end badly I had several long conversations with them with a view of joining their firm. I didn't, but we stayed in contact.

179   Steven worked for Baker & Blake briefly in its early days.

180   The school closed in 2017.

181   Joe Bruno was at the time the sate senator whose district included Darrow. Two of his sons attended Darrow. A sensitive issue was that any State/Federal funds provided for the buildings could not be seen to directly benefit Darrow. Given the historic importance of the site the public versus private use issue was a close-called interpretation.

182   Bill had a hankering for old construction equipment. The large field behind his house was littered with ancient cranes, trucks and earth moving machinery. Much of it actually operated including the ancient rusty crane he used to affix the steel buttresses supporting the fragile south wall of the barn. They are still there!

183   The Village had raised funds to stabilize the Great Stone Barn, the Carriage Shed, Wash House, Granary and a small agricultural building. I had renovated the Forge and Springland had renovated and restored a portion of the North Family's Brethren's Workshop. As noted elsewhere, Charles Flint had produced a very credible document on Darrow's collection of Shaker artifacts. The site was open to visitors during the summer months. At the peak we had a thru-put of over 3,000 visitors. In all, these were significant achievements for a very new organization.

184   The Board in fact voted (not unanimously) to close the school shortly before the proposed transaction would take place. However, a group of trustees, former trustees, a former Head, the late John Joline, and others raised sufficient funds to keep Darrow open. (See Chapter 15)

185   Kim was part of the Miller family in Pittsfield. In 1985 the Millers owned the Berkshire Eagle the well-known local newspaper and his Aunt, Amy Bess Miller was the long-standing Board Chair of Hancock Shaker Village.

186   Since Carl was originally a Steers employee Dick considered him 'his' employee rather than Springland's.

187   As noted Marty had no electricity let alone a phone. Marty and I communicated by letter: occasionally. If I were making a trip to see Marty I would telegraph her with the necessary information.

188   From time to time I tried to find Cesare but without success. Finally in 2013 with the help of Trina's friend (now husband) Curvin on the computer we located David in Tuscany where he apparently owns a farm machinery business. I sent him an e-mail, hoping to get a chance to meet up with him at some point. In his response he told me to "have a nice life" and not to bother him. I haven't.

189   I did, however, receive some compensation, in kind, through the acquisition of furniture and furnishings from the model houses.

190   Carapresso was a local auctioneer in Lee, Massachusetts. We purchased a number of items for Springland and the Forge in his auctions. Some of these items were later sold to the Wolfs in 2005.

Chapter 15 - Interlude

191   Probably painted in the 1890s it had been sold to a British collector. It is unclear how it made its way to Lee, Massachusetts where it had languished in a smoke-filled study, for decades.

192   omitted.

193   Catherine Gould, for example, a friend of Valery's, invested and remained a friend and help throughout the TPS saga.

194   OKO Bank was renamed Pohjola Bank in 2008.

195   The objective of most 'young' architects is to own and run their own practices thus permitting them to design and/or control design. In fact this often means that most of the principal's time is spent on management, administration and, perhaps especially, marketing.

196   It was Bill who introduced me to an editor from the Architectural Digest that resulted in the magazine publishing, in its March 1992 issue, an article on the Forge written by the noted author Brendan Gill.

197   Though I do not know it for a fact, I believe that both Virginia and Steve, more or less, insisted that their respective projects be handled from New York, not from Charlottesville.

Chapter 16 – The Forge Company

198   'Prefabrication' in reference to building has, as noted before, a negative connotation, suggesting inferior quality. While in some cases this may be true, in principle it is not true. Properly done the quality of a prefabricated structure can far exceed site-built structures.

199   There were a number of other prefabrication projects, mostly un-built. The ones mentioned were the built ones, with the exception of the TPS/Israeli exercise.

200   There is no direct evidence to support this supposition but it remains a reasonable surmise. Peter respected Griswold and his obituary of AWG in Architectural Forum supports this.

201   Virginia (now Manheimer) is a philanthropist supporting a broad variety of projects, primarily conservative in nature.

202   The TPS system was tailored specifically to the requirements of the Technion and Israeli building regulations. As Israel prohibited any wood materials we were obliged to use concrete or 'cementitious' materials throughout the system. While fine for Israel the TPS system was not necessarily an appealing option for other locations, certainly not the UK or US. The Israeli system was also no exemplar for its environmental qualifications; they were secondary to cost and practicality.

203   In the small world department 'Wint' was Rosiland Aldrich's, (Alden's godmother), brother.

204   Bill Doswell, an interim Darrow Headmaster now taught science at Miss Hall's a curious coincidence. I saw him there a number of times.

205   "Social Housing is a term mostly associated with the UK. Public housing is a form of housing tenure in which the property is owned by a government authority, which may be central or local. Social housing is an umbrella term referring to rental housing that may be owned and managed by the state, by non-profit organizations, or by a combination of the two, usually with the aim of providing affordable housing. Social housing can also be seen as a potential remedy to housing inequality. Although the common goal of public

housing is to provide affordable housing, the details, terminology, definitions of poverty and other criteria for allocation vary within different contexts." Source Wikipedia

This is a good, useful definition for the purposes of this chapter.

206 "A Faraday cage operates because an external static electrical field causes the electric charges within the cage's conducting material to be distributed such that they cancel the field's effect in the cage's interior. This phenomenon is used, for example, to protect electronic equipment from lightning strikes and electrostatic discharges." – Wikipedia

207 Thermal breaks are points in a building´s envelope where lhe outside temperature is transfered through metal (or other material) directly into the interior thus forming a point of likely condensation.

208 The 450-mile trip did not always result in an on-time arrival. A late start, weather, road closures, traffic or police could delay the arrival with potential costly consequences. Happily, Ayrshire's deliveries were mostly on time.

209 Badgers you ask? Sometime not long after we were married I read an article about a badger sett located near a golf course. The badgers specialized in collecting golf balls and had some 100 neatly stored in their sett. The article went on to describe the domestic characteristics of badgers though they didn´t iron. I thought their domesticity was characteristic of Rosemary´s housekeeping. I started calling Rosemary, Badger and the name stuck.

210 "Gretna's two blacksmiths' shops and countless inns and smallholding became the backdrops for tens of thousands of weddings. Today there are several wedding venues in and around Gretna Green, from former churches to purpose-built chapels. The services at all the venues are always performed over an iconic blacksmith's anvil. Gretna Green endures as one of the world's most popular wedding venues and thousands of couples from around the world come to be married 'over the anvil' in Gretna Green." Wikipedia

211 Gemma was a student at Greenwich temping for an agency that was run, in sheer coincidence, by an acquaintance. We hired her for an hour but Gemma stayed part time for nearly four years. Her specialty at school was HR. She is now a professional author and senior consultant with a 140,000 person international consulting company. Gemma was a great addition to the Forge Company.

212 I met Mike Hardiman through the London branch of the AIA. I had known of Mike as he was one of only two or three Darrow graduates who had become architects. I believe he was in the class of 1975.

213 Forge(F) and Forge Llewellyn (FL) Projects 1994 to 2003 (JB/RB) nc- not constructed, P – Proposal Developed – This is a partial list.

F	Garnant Houses (8); Gwalia Housing
F	Time Share Hotel (40 suites); Jiminy Peak
F	Swansea Flats (9); Gwalia Housing
F/FL	Prefabricated Offces (20); Hanover Housing
F	Houses in Ayr (30); West of Scotland HA
F	Vincent Square Penthouse Flats (2); Private Client

F	Reading Housing (25); Ealing Family HA
JB/RB	Collyweston House; Personal
F	Peabody Prefabricated House; Peabody HA (nc)
F	Darrow Environmental Centre; Darrow School
F	Shop, Jiminy Peak; Jiminy Peak
F	Ski Lift; Jiminy Peak
F	Mountainside (14), Jiminy Peak
FL	Lille Road, Beaufort House (London) (60); Peabody HA
FL	Dagenham, (London) Flats (15); Circle 33 HA
FL	Savoy Hotel (London) (40); Savoy Hotel (nc)
FL	Annesley Avenue Flats (15); Local HA
F	Arts Centre; Darrow School
FL	Basingstoke (150); First phase, Sentinel HA
FL	Basingstoke Phase II & III (150)
FL	Lingham Court (64)
FL	West Kent – Eco House Prototype
FL	Cambourne – Circle 33 HA (20)
FL	Vartry Road – (5)
FL	Rowhill – (?)
FL	Reading II – (85)
FL	Network Housing – (?) P
FL	Ladbrook Grove – (20)
FL	BAA – Various (mostly nc)
FL	Wates (100) P

214   Omitted

215   The Housing Corporation was the non-departmental public body that funded new affordable housing and regulated housing associations in England. It was abolished in 2008 with its responsibilities being split between the Homes and Communities Agency and the Tenant Services Authority.

216   Rosemary's first marriage was to Richard Klein who died in New York in the seventies. Rosemary's second marriage was to W. S. Burgis: that marriage ended in divorce.

---

217   Martin in due course became the Medical Director of the Royal Marsden.

218   The UK construction industry shuts down for two weeks every Christmastime.

219   Rosemary was not a member of the ESU but attended many of their lectures and events as a guest of one or another of her friends. Naturally I accompanied Rosemary ESU events.

220   The Lings were good friends, part of the St Andrews crowd. We often socialised with them. Philip, Charmian's husband was estate manager for Burley House in Stamford.

221   These four lines are on Rosemary's headstone in Collyweston. The headstone design, itself, is based on that of grandfather Twachtman in Glouster.

222   The Sloane Club, just off Sloane Square, was a corresponding club to both Squadron A and the Yale Club in New York. I occasionally stayed there or visited for events.

223   Forge-Llewellyn was a designated prefabrication specialist for BAA. We were called on periodically to provide studies such as: prefabricated airport shops, prefabricated housing for airport electronics, and 'air-side' facilities of various kinds. These turned out to be mostly studies, in fact I can only remember one or two that were constructed. The income was good though.

224   The "Building Research Establishment (BRE) is a leading centre of building science owned by the charitable organisation the BRE Trust. It is a former UK government national laboratory that was privatised in 1997. With a mission to drive positive change across the built environment for the benefit of people and the planet, BRE provides research, advice, training, testing, certification and standards for both public and private sector organisations around the world. BRE has its headquarters in Watford, with regional sites in Glasgow, Swansea, America, India, the Middle East and China.", (Source Google

225   In the 1990s the Steel Construction Institute (SCI), a highly respected trade body for the UK steel industry did their best to promote LGS along with more traditional uses of hot-rolled steel. One could say LGS was a hot topic. The SCI sponsored forums and working groups. Both Ayrshire and Forge were members of these groups along with a number of other LGS firms. It was in one of these working groups that I met Michael. We had become 'professional' friends.

226   Fusion was sold in 2010 when Fleming was declared bankrupt owing some one billion pounds. Since then both Fleming and Fusion have re-emerged as successful developers and manufacturers, respectively. (Source Google)